THE von Hoffmann Bros.'
BIG DAMN BOOK OF
SHEER MANLINESS

BY TODD von HOFFMANN
with BRANT von HOFFMANN, COLBY ALLERTON & SOME OTHER WISEGUYS

GENERAL PUBLISHING GROUP, INC.

Manly Publisher: W. Quay Hays

Manly Editor: Colby Allerton

Manly Art Director: Kurt Wahlner

Production Director: Trudihope Schlomowitz

Pre-Press Manager: Bill Castillo

Production Artist: Gaston Moraga

Production Assistants: Tom Archibeque, David Chadderdon, Gus Dawson, Russel Lockwood, Roy Penn, Scott Saltaman

Copy Editor: Mark Lamana

Many thanks to the long list of friends, family, sports and manufacturers who lent their expertise, wisdom and sense of grandiose silliness to this mighty tome. The Herculean efforts of young Colby and Kurt, my new brethren, will long be remembered in song at our campfires. Heartfelt prostrations to Mac, Steve the Water Moccasin and Mike Hamilburg. And special thanks to the vigorous and lusty GPG production crew, and in particular to Quay the Bold for making all of this damn fun and foolishness possible. Here's to ya, you beauties.   —TvH

For information:
General Publishing Group, Inc.
2701 Ocean Park Boulevard
Santa Monica, CA 90405

Library of Congress Cataloging-in-Publication Data

Von Hoffmann, Todd.
    [Big damn book of sheer manliness]
    The von Hoffmann bros.' big damn book of sheer manliness.
        p.   cm.
    Authors: Todd von Hoffmann and Brant von Hoffmann.
    Includes bibliographical references and index.
    ISBN 1-57544-050-4
    1. Men—Humor. 2. Masculinity—Humor. I. Von Hoffmann, Brant.
II. Title. III. Title: Big damn book of sheer manliness.
IV. Title: Sheer manliness. V. Title: Von Hoffmann brothers' big damn book of sheer manliness.
818' .5407—DC21
                                                            97-4485
                                                            CIP

Printed in the USA by RR Donnelley & Sons Company
10 9 8 7 6 5 4 3 2 1

General Publishing Group
Los Angeles

TABLE OF CONTENTS

ALLIGATOR
80/16-11/2
BEST QUALITY SUPERCHARGED
FLASHLIGHT CRACKERS

YAN LEE KEE HONG
MADE IN CHINA

DO NOT HOLD IN HAND AFTER LIGHTING

Dedicated to our grandfathers—two of the greatest guys we never got to know; And to our dad—one we're sure as hell glad we do.

To Man: he is mad; he cannot make a worm, and yet he will be making gods by the dozens.

—Montaigne

THE STAR-SPANGLED BANNER

By Francis Scott Key

O say, can you see, by the dawn's early light,
What so proudly we hailed at the twilight's
last gleaming?
Whose broad stripes and bright stars,
through the perilous fight,
O'er the ramparts we watched, were so
gallantly streaming!
And the rockets' red glare, the bombs
bursting in air,
Gave proof through the night that our flag
was still there.
O say, does that star-spangled banner yet
wave
O'er the land of the free and the home of
the brave?

On the shore dimly seen through the mists
of the deep,
Where the foe's haughty host in dread
silence reposes,
What is that which the breeze, o'er the
towering steep,
As it fitfully blows, half conceals, half
discloses?
Now it catches the gleam of the morning's
first beam,
In full glory reflected, now shines on the
stream:
'Tis the star-spangled banner: O, long may it
wave
O'er the land of the free and the home of
the brave!

And where is that band who so vauntingly
swore
That the havoc of war and the battle's
confusion
A home and a country should leave us
no more?
Their blood has washed out their foul
footsteps' pollution.
No refuge could save the hireling and slave
From the terror of flight or the gloom
of the grave:
And the star-spangled banner in triumph
doth wave
O'er the land of the free and the home
of the brave!

O thus be it ever when free-men shall stand
Between their lov'd home and the war's
desolation;
Blest with vict'ry and peace, may the
heav'n-rescued land
Praise the Pow'r that hath made and
preserv'd us a nation!
Then conquer we must, for our cause it is
just,
And this be our motto: "In God is our
trust."
And the star-spangled banner in triumph
shall wave
O'er the land of the free and the home of
the brave!

PLAY
BALL

WHAT GUYS KNOW

"A Bombastic Manifesto"

WE HOLD THESE TRUTHS TO BE SELF-EVIDENT . . .

What Guys Know About Life—Life is too short. Start counting your blessings right now, because every dawn on this greatest of all possible worlds is a gift. Life is particularly too short for dogs. If there was ever a clear error made by God, evolution or whatever you choose to call the great determinant, it was the life span of dogs. There's just no logical reason for dogs living as short as they do. The promise of genetic engineering could rectify this problem in a few years—let's get on it. Man's best friend? In a heartbeat.

What Guys Know About Lives—Lives are apportioned one to a customer—no dress rehearsals, no return engagements. Own up, play ball and bring hell down on those who don't. You are what you do, and you get one shot to do it. Just ask, "What would the Duke do?" Or ask a kid's opinion, and let that bus driver go ahead of you, for chrissake, don't you know how tough that job is?

What Guys Know About God—There is a God, absolutely no question about it. Beer, breasts and bass are proof enough, but besides that. . . We've come a long way in understanding evolution, chemistry and the formation of celestial bodies, but the big bang theory, right or wrong, just doesn't cut the mustard when it comes to explaining the existence of existence. You just don't get something from nothing. Arguing over who or what God is, who's chosen, who's in, who's out or whatever can make for interesting discussion but amounts to so much bullshit. Arguing to the point of throwing spears or bombs at the other guy, aside from being pure dumb vanity, is to miss the point entirely. Cut out that crap and go buy a copy of *The Quiet Man*.

What Guys Know About Little Green Men—We are not alone. Any objective review of the facts leads to this conclusion. Regardless of the debate over the evidence of life on Mars, the bottom line remains that initially scientists were surprised not to find any. If life occurred (or almost occurred) on two of the planets in this little solar system, then it's a long shot that life has not emerged somewhere else among the limitless solar systems of space. Bottom line? Get over yourself, you arrogant prick.

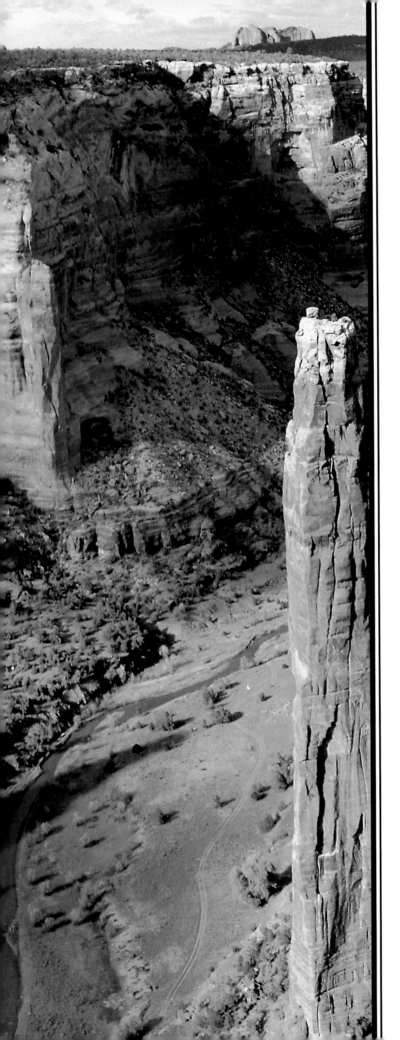

What Guys Know About Mars

Men are not from Mars. Women might be from Venus or wherever but, except for maybe some places like France, men are from Earth. Men love Earth—we want to go out into it right now. We want to walk it and hunt it and fish it and turn over rocks and logs. We want to climb all over it and hope we get scared by it. We want to cruise over it in machines and go as fast as we can. We want to fight it and bite it and kick the shit out of it. (We want to kick the shit out of something, I can tell ya.) We started out as hairy apes, and we're not fools enough to think we've come too far since then. That beast is with us all the time—he's the guy jiggling our leg under the table while we sit around under these fluorescent lights. Guys love rocks, ponds, woods, caves, deserts and critters, the sea and oxygen and all the great Earth stuff. We want to pick it up and figure it out and try to make great stuff of our own. We love fire and smoke and noise and blowing stuff up and raising hell. We want to challenge Earth and fear and death and see how we do. We want to laugh at the whole business and laugh at ourselves.

What Guys Know About Women

A man needs a woman, but a man does not need a woman who needs a man like a fish needs a bicycle. Also, women aren't as crazy about this Earth stuff. The facts are plain at any big newsstand rack—countless titles, increasingly narrowcast to the pursuits and passions of men—these in turn augmented by thousands of newsletters, events and clubs. In contrast stands the inch-thick woman's magazine, filled with fashion, perfume and makeup ads. These are interests completely alien to the men of Earth. The covers of these magazines invariably feature some incredible model with her breasts falling out. If these are women's magazines, then who are these breasts for? We can't figure it, but it seems pretty clear that this whole beauty business is geared toward impressing other women, not attracting men. Whatever it is, it doesn't seem to have much to do with Earth. It is illustrative of one of the principle communication problems between the sexes. Earth men feel that they are pursuing the natural course for living on Earth and have trouble holding in equal regard those who do not. The wife, therefore, who begrudges the Earth man his occasional fishing trip is not only being an unnecessarily selfish nuisance, but is also interfering with the natural order. In contrast, the wife who understands and encourages the Earth man's necessary forays is a gal and a goddess—highly wondrous but increasingly rare, thanks to the meddling of today's PC liberal clueless killjoys and other wayward muck-ups.

What Guys Know About Giving Birth—Men have absolutely no resentment about the fact that women, not men give birth to and breast-feed babies, so any theories about our behavior running contrary to that are bullshit. A man may never be happier than when his kid falls asleep on his chest, but as far as the manufacturing process goes, while we are in awe of women for possessing this greatest of gifts, we're also happy as hell with our end of it.

What Guys Know About Fighting—A man will encounter from time to time a brother who isn't just asking, but begging, indeed, crying out to have his ass kicked, and it is your honor-bound duty to accommodate him and at any given moment that brother might be you or me.

What Guys Know About Driving—Say someone is stopped at a light in front of you in the left lane. If, after the light changes, they roll their car into the intersection and then, and only then, signal a left turn, then that someone deserves a heat seeker up the tailpipe.

What Guys Know About Politics—Men know there is a reason why cynicism and disgust underlie all political discourse. Any discussion of the problems of the nation or planet amount to doodley-squat if it's not about the big P—population. To bring another life onto the planet is unquestionably the most important decision faced by man or woman during their existence. Those who do so without consideration, resources or responsibility are beneath contempt and invite the revocation of their procreative parts. All the good work by conservationists, recyclers, scientists and humanitarians for the betterment of mankind is summarily snuffed by the yearly population bomb. The U.S. democracy may be the greatest government achievement in history, but as it evolved, the electorate devolved. We don't deserve a free society until we earn it. Until then, we support a benevolent dictatorship and a minimum income requirement to give birth. Face it, if Visa denies you a credit card based on your application, the chances are pretty damn good they're doing you a favor.

What Guys Know About Family—A man who doesn't spend time with his family can never truly be a man. (Two points if you know who said that and when.)

What Guys Know About Fear—The Black Dog is waiting, but whining never solved anything except to separate the men from the boys.

DRY FLIES
Adams

BASEBALL

THE GREAT AMERICAN PASTIME

Even though most sports historians agree that baseball evolved from such popular ball-and-bat games as town ball and rounders, its actual origin is steeped in controversy. For a time, England maintained that baseball was nothing more than an aberration of their own game of cricket, organized formally in the 18th century. However, when American players apparently introduced the colorful habits of spitting and crotch-grabbing into the proceedings, the English pretty much pulled their claim.

In 1905, seven prominent men were appointed to the Mills Commission to determine once and for all where and how the game of baseball was invented. They were Col. A.G. Mills of New York, the fourth president of the National League; Hon. Morgan G. Bulkeley, U.S. Senator from Connecticut, who served as the National League's first president in 1876; Hon. Arthur P. Gorman, a former player and ex-president of the National Baseball Club of Washington; Nicholas E. Young, a longtime player who was the first secretary and later fifth president of the National League; Alfred J. Reach of Philadelphia and George Wright of Boston, two of the most famous players of their day; and the president of the Amateur Athletic Union, James E. Sullivan of New York. After a three-year study during which they were deluged with information, the commission received from Abner Graves, a mining engineer from Denver, Colorado, testimony that figured prominently in the final report.

SUPERFINE QUALITY SELECTED
FLASHLIGHT FIRECRACKERS
HOME RUN
BRAND
20 REPORTS
DO NOT HOLD
IN HAND
AFTER LIGHTING
MADE IN CHINA
中國廣州利豐廠造
DISTRIBUTED BY
W. L. STEWART CO.

Graves claimed that he was present when Abner Doubleday, a young West Point cadet, made changes to the then-popular game of round ball, which involved 20 to 50 boys in a field, attempting to catch a ball hit by a "tosser" using a four-inch flat bat. Doubleday's refinements included marking out a diamond-shaped area in the dirt, limiting the number of players and adding bases (hence the name baseball); Doubleday also introduced the concept of a pitcher and catcher to the game. On December 30, 1907, the commission officially announced that "the first scheme for playing baseball, according to the best evidence obtainable to date, was devised by Abner Doubleday in 1839 at Cooperstown, N.Y." Baseball was invented in Cooperstown. The Baseball Hall of Fame is in Cooperstown. Coincidence? Who's to say.

Few would argue against the claim that your most colorful athletes are baseball players. First of all, it's widely agreed that you don't have to be particularly athletic or in any sort of physical shape to be a good baseball player. One look at the pear-shaped physique of first baseman John Kruk, and one would have to agree that the only sport he looks suited for is a good ol' fashioned pie-eating contest. Second, baseball is rarely referred to as a sport. Instead, it's usually referred to as a game. Games are usually played by kids. And one thing is for certain: regardless of their age, baseball players are (definitely) nothing more than big kids in a state of perpetual adolescence.

The only difference between a major leaguer and the average five-year-old is that the major leaguer's temper tantrums tend to be a bit more severe. For example: a bunch of eight-year-olds are playing a pick-up game at the local sandlot. It's the third inning and the pitcher is already losing 57 to nothing. The player on first adds insult to injury by stealing second. Under these circumstances, the pitcher will most likely burst into tears, take his ball and go home. In a major league game, under the same circumstances, when the base-stealer makes his next plate appearance, the pitcher will most likely illustrate his displeasure by firing a 95-mile-an-hour fastball directly at his head. (This is fondly referred to as "chin music.") When interviewed later, the pitcher will offer some excuse for his actions like, "Hey, he shouldn't have rubbed my nose in it. He had it coming." The offending player's widow would probably offer a word of disagreement. What a game.

Black Gnat

FOOTBALL

"The Duke," so called after the boyhood nickname of New York Giants owner Wellington Mara, was retired as the official NFL football in 1969. (Right) "Winning isn't everything, it's the only thing." Attributed to Vince Lombardi, the guy who actually said it was the other Duke (John Wayne), in Trouble Along The Way *(1953). What Lombardi said was, "Winning isn't everything, but wanting to win is."*

No sport in history epitomizes American male machismo more than the game of football. Now, I'm not talking about the kick-the-ball-only-with-your-feet-cuz-if-it-touches-your-hand-it's-our-ball-played-the-world-over-also-known-as-soccer kind of football. No, I'm talking about the Orange Crush-Steel Curtain-Four Horsemen-New York Sack Exchange-Fearsome Foursome-Monsters of the Midway-Purple People Eaters-tackle-the-quarterback-tear-off-his-leg-and-beat-him-over-the-head-with-it kind of football.

I'm talking about the kind of football whose fans are so devoted that they can't wait for Monday so they can grab the sports page to read all about the games they watched the previous day.

Now, where did this game originate? Well, once again it seems that football is another example of clever Americans stealing an English game, changing the rules and making it fun.

From soccer was born rugby on a fateful day in the 1820s, when a student named William Webb Ellis at the Rugby School in England stunned his teammates by picking up the ball in the middle of a game and running with it. One can understand why rugby developed a close resemblance to pure unadulterated "smear the queer."

In 1871, a sport that combined kicking and carrying the ball was developed in the United States. Soon after, the Intercollegiate Football Association was formed, and teams consisting of 11 players were approved. The field was reduced from 163 to 110 yards and a system of downs was established. Teams had to gain at least five yards on three downs or surrender possession of the ball. (This, of course, was later changed to 10 yards on four downs.) Also, the kick-off was made from midfield, and a scrimmage line was devised.

In the early days, blocking using the wedge formation meant moving the ball by brute force with brutal tactics. Needless to say, this kind of maneuver led to extreme injuries and, in some cases, death. In fact, football's reputation as a game of unbridled violence drew this admonition from President Theodore Roosevelt in 1905: "Clean up your game or I'll see that it's abolished!"

Around 1908, the forward pass was introduced, and that pretty much gave us the game we know today. A short while later, pretty girls in short skirts and pom-poms, called cheerleaders, were added and the rest is history. . . Look it up!

Henryville Caddis

BASKETBALL ORIGIN

Would you believe that basketball began as an exercise to keep people in shape between the football and baseball seasons? And it was started in a YMCA, by a Presbyterian minister? And it was almost called boxball? Well, it's true. Most hoop fans have heard of Dr. James Naismith, but many don't know the curious details surrounding his act of invention.

In December, 1891, Naismith was working as a physical education instructor at the Springfield, Massachusetts, YMCA. He discovered that gymnastics and calisthenics (as most men know) were proving too boring—and much too lame—to keep men in shape. So he asked a staff member to find him two large boxes. Why? Because he had devised a game using a soccer ball, to be thrown into a box hung from the balcony at either end of the gymnasium, with all sorts of scrambling to result in between. The staff member, however, could only find a couple of peach

baskets, and they were used instead. So it almost was "boxball." (Kids who've read this may already be punching the bottoms out of some of your good cardboard boxes, but just make sure they tape them up in the garage or outside. They may be smarter than Naismith though, because in 1891 after each score some person on a ladder had to scurry up to retrieve the ball from inside the basket—they'd kept the bottoms on!) In 1895, iron baskets with netting were used, but some contraption with a cord had to be added, which, when pulled, would lift the net to pop the ball out of the top. It wasn't until 1912 that open-bottom baskets were introduced. (Which must have put a number of poor ball-fetchers out of business.)

Originally there were nine men per team, but at times the game was played with as many as 50 players on the court. In 1897, after fans complained of losing sight of the ball amidst all the mayhem (and certainly some whiny "franchise" players complained they weren't getting their share of shots per game), the number of players was reduced to five per team, resulting in the game's premium on speed and athleticism. Another crucial quality—height—was already a necessity because of that high balcony Naismith hung his baskets on.

OK. . . baskets, five tall athletic players, but why the backboards? Because rowdy fans, like Green Bay Packer supporters, would hang out in the balcony and commit all kinds of heinous acts, even poking shots away with broomsticks and umbrellas and the like. So it was to discourage fan interference that backboards came into being around baskets. And you thought today's stomping and balloon-waving was a nuisance to free-throw shooters!

It's funny that this simple game is now so huge, certainly as big as sports get in the U.S., and growing in the rest of the world (note the

Olympics' Dream Team's phenomenal popularity). But basketball is about watching and *playing*, and if you and some buddies haven't recently run three-on-three against some young punks, or basked on a sunny afternoon in a driveway game of H-O-R-S-E with some cold beer flowing, what are you waiting for?!

Lawson Brown Paradrake ™

BOXING

JUST WHAT THE HELL ARE THE MARQUESS OF QUEENSBURY RULES?

When Sean Thornton (the Duke) and Red Will Danaher (Victor McLaglen) proceed with beatin' the crap out of each other in The Quiet Man, Michaeleen Oge Flynn (Barry Fitzgerald) pronounces, "Gentlemen if you please, the Marquess of Queensberry rules will be observed at all times." Sure, we figure they're probably the proper pugilistic procedures, but just what are they, anyway? If Danaher knew, he sure didn't let on—his next blow is a boot to the Duke's face. Back in 1867, Englishman Henry Sholto Douglas, the eighth (or ninth depending on who you talk to) Marquess of Queensberry, sponsored a formal boxing code based on his experience with the sweet science at Oxford. He wrote this up with a member of the British Amateur Athletic Club, John Graham Chambers. Obviously the gents felt that elbows, biting, head butts and boots to the face and groin just weren't "cricket." Of course, the present-day Ultimate Fighting Championships have seen to it to correct their meddling.

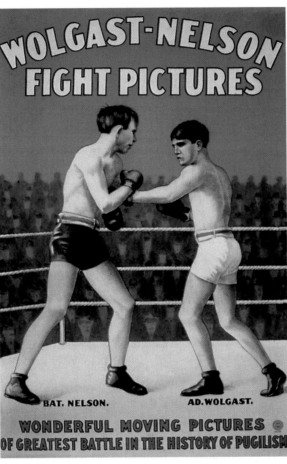

WOLGAST-NELSON FIGHT PICTURES

BAT. NELSON.   AD. WOLGAST.

WONDERFUL MOVING PICTURES OF GREATEST BATTLE IN THE HISTORY OF PUGILISM

The Marquess of Queensbury Rules

1. To be a fair stand-up boxing match in a 24-foot ring, or as near that size as practicable [*yep, that's a real word*].

2. No wrestling or hugging allowed [*kissing, goosing and ass grabbing are also presumably out . . . and absolutely no tongues*].

3. The rounds to be of three minute's duration, and one minute's time between rounds.

4. If either man falls through weakness or otherwise, he must get up unassisted, 10 seconds to be allowed him to do so, the other man meanwhile to return to his corner, and when the fallen man is on his legs the round is to be resumed and continued until the three minutes have expired. If one man fails to come to the scratch in the 10 seconds allowed, it will be in the power of the referee to give his award in favour of the other man.

5. A man hanging on the ropes in a helpless state, with his toes off the ground, shall be considered down.

6. No seconds or any other person to be allowed in the ring during the rounds.

7. Should the contest be stopped by any unavoidable interference, the referee to name the time and place as soon as possible for finishing the contest so that the match must be won and lost, unless the backers of both men agree to draw the stakes.

8. The gloves to be fair-sized boxing gloves of the best quality and new [*same shall also be devoid of brass knuckles, coin rolls, rocks and horseshoes*].

9. Should a glove burst, or come off, it must be replaced to the referee's satisfaction.

10. A man on one knee is considered down and, if struck, is entitled to the stakes.

11. No shoes or boots with springs allowed [*I believe this was the Warner Bros. Amendment*].

12. The contest in all other respects to be governed by revised rules of the London Prize Ring.

These are good to know next time a little difference of opinion (say Stabler vs. Elway or Hershey's vs. Bosco) takes you to the alley behind the pub. Have your Second explain them to the opposition while you case the joint for pallets and garbage cans.

Royal Wulff

THE GREAT GAME

The popularity of golf is one of the simplest things in the world to understand when you consider the basic elements, which, particularly for a guy, are just irresistible. Golf is steeped in tradition, played in weather perfect for even Aztec sun gods, gets a fella out of the house for a while, works as a sanctuary for social (or solitary) pleasures, and lends itself readily to characters, cocktails, cursing and clubhouses. The Great Game also provides an excuse for outrageous bets, loud clothing and riding around in golf carts. Ahhhhh—golf.

Golf also has, at its heart, a poetic sense of grandiose silliness. If you've actually gone to the range some, you've probably felt that strong satisfaction of having willed a very unlikely event into existence: that in just seconds, a little white part of you drops lightly from hundreds of yards away to within the shadow of the pin. For more on that, reread *Golf in the Kingdom* by Michael Murphy (or try Herbert Warren Wind, Tom Boswell or P.G. Wodehouse). For more justification to play, consider that if there are 24 hours per day, many of them taken up with an artificial existence of freeways, fluorescent lights and bills to pay, what's four hours spent trekking through pastoral foothills, having fun with some old or new friends, hoping that over the next hill is something great and knowing that, if there isn't, there's still a bartender at the 19th? Excuse us, we're off to play a round. . . .

Everybody knows that golf originated in the rolling gorse and hollows of Scotland, around 1440. By 1457, so many Scots were playing that the government *outlawed* the game. But golf endured until a great event occurred: Himself—James IV, king of Scotland—took up the game in the early 1550s, which validated it. By the time Mary, Queen of Scots, maybe the first par-eyed female duffer, became attracted to the game, golf was well on its way to full-bore mania. It did take hundreds of years for an organized golfing society to emerge: the Honorable Company of Edinburgh Golfers, founded in 1744. Ten years later, the hallowed Royal and Ancient Golf Club of St. Andrews came into being. Many courses had between five and 18 holes, but the archetypal course at St. Andrews had 18, which became the standard.

The first tournament considered to be an official championship was played in 1860 on Scotland's Prestwick course, a contest that in 1861 became known as the British Open. Here, the likes of Willie Park, Old Tom Morris and Tom Morris Jr. emerged as stars of the day.

During the 1870s, golf hopped over to England, Ireland, Canada and, eventually, the United States. One of the first U.S. courses, if not *the* first U.S. course was St. Andrews of Yonkers, New York. At that time, "the man" of the day was among such great British players as John H. Taylor, James Braid and Harry Vardon, the latter winning his first *U.S.* Open in 1900. That same year, about 1,000 golf courses were scattered across the U.S.

Vardon was defeated in the 1913 U.S. Open by American amateur Francis Ouimet, which even Bill Murray might admit was the original Cinderella story (please garble appropriately). Walter Hagen emerged with the 1914 U.S. Open crown, paving the way for a stampede of great American players: Bobby Jones Jr., Gene Sarazen, Lawson Little, Nelson, Hogan, Snead, Zaharias, Palmer, Nicklaus, Watson, Floyd, Stewart, Couples, Tiger Woods. It doesn't hurt that since 1927, the international Ryder Cup, contested every two years by the best of the American and British pro players, has been won in favor of the Americans 23-6-2. (Another example of clever Yankees horking a British game and putting it through its paces.)

The only problem remaining is the popularity of the sport, which has resulted in the offense of taking sometimes *six hours* to complete an 18-hole round. If the reader is an offending duffer, please take fewer practice swings and less time lining up putts. In all honesty, if you're a healthy guy sweating out 3-foot putts on your way to a 103, you really ought to have your ass on the driving range taking lessons, not hacking up the course, you wanna-be. Nick Faldo's mom payed for some lessons for him when he was 14, and he practiced hard for three months, hitting balls into a long-jump pit before he was taken to a course. He shot a 78 that day, the first time he was ever on a course.

Royal Humpy

Horse racing, aka the sport of kings," is probably called that because you need the treasury of a small, unpronounceable European principality in order to breed, maintain and race the participants; and success is still far from a certainty. English kings have been the traditional sponsors of the sport. Charles II, in fact, built the first American track on Long Island in 1664. But for every Affirmed that's run, there are a thousand Infirmeds. . . or an Alydar. This horse has the dubious distinction of losing all three Triple Crown races to Affirmed by a total of less than two lengths, making him the Buffalo Bills of horse racing.

Most people are at the track for the action, and that means money. Wagering. Betting. Personally, I don't know a trifecta from a defecta but I do know an exacta—it means just what it sounds like (more below). Unfortunately, I found out the hard way what it means to "box" it. That's when you cover the two horses for both possible one/two finishes. Nothing like betting the one and three horse, and having them finish three then one—makes your beer taste bitter real fast. It's also unnerving to play an exacta and have your ponies come in first and third. That doesn't pay squat either.

Some horse players have real fun at the track people watching. This is best done in two principal areas: the clubhouse (Turf Club, or the like), and the grandstand (preferably around the betting windows). The former is like watching the Roman patrician class, and the latter is. . . well. . . to borrow a line from Jay Leno. . . like going to an open casting call for a Fellini film.

You may think at times you're a character in a Damon Runyon story and, if you hang around the $2 window for a while, count on hearing a few Runyonesque yarns. My favorite is the one about the two thimbleheads who went to Bay Meadows, and between there and the closed-circuit telecast at Santa Anita, managed to pick 11 out of 14 winners. They also lost 150 bucks each.

Seems they played all exactas. . . neither one "put it on the nose," to "win" bet. . . and they repeatedly had the win and show horses. Eavesdroppers seated near them were making a ton by just betting one horse to win. Cleaned out but wiser, our heroes went home. Needless to say, "demon beer" was the true villain in this episode. (The names of the thimbleheads will be withheld to spare your author further embarrassment.)

Make no mistake, horse racing's a grand sport and its animals are some of the most beautiful critters on the planet. Whether you're watching Thoroughbred, quarterhorse or harness racing, when they head down the stretch, your pulse rate quickens. It's one of the few sporting events TV fails to enhance.

Psst, Bud, Some Tips & Track Talk. . .

Go with a Pal—The most amazing things happen every day at the track. All the better, or just plain hilarious, when shared with someone who can remind you of such happenings years later.

Be Prepared (Homework was Never this Fun)—Go to a newsstand and pick up *The Turf Guide* or your local racing form the night before. Compare notes and let the warm folly of this behavior flow over you.

Get There Early—Comportment at the track demands studied composure, wild exhilaration, maudlin affection and agonized cries of despair, but each in their own time. First, and first to go, is studied composure. Allow time to find good seats, review the official program, locate the tote board, windows and bathrooms, and appease the pony gods.

Appease the Pony Gods—The energy at the track makes you rabbity even in the parking lot—by the time you emerge into the light of the grandstand, it's practically ferocious. Slow down, boy. You need a Bloody Mary. Try to buy the first round and leave a big tip. Then retire to your seat for a few minutes, say as many complimentary things about your surroundings as possible and try to stop giggling like an idiot.

Placing Your Bet—The first rule of betting (and this is a lifesaving tip) regards basic courtesy: THERE IS POSITIVELY, ABSOLUTELY NO FIDDLING AROUND PERMITTED AT

THE WINDOW. Keep in mind the shutout scene in *The Sting*. If you have any questions, collar a green-jacketed gent or some other likely sport before getting in line (and make sure it's the correct line).

The bet taker requires only four bits of information. They are delivered in the following order:

The number of the race.

The amount of your wager.

The type of your bet.

The number (not the name) of the horse.

For Example: "In the second race, $2, to win, on No. 6. Thanks." (Then make sure the info is correct on your ticket.)

Paint-by-the-numbers-art by Colby Allerton.

STANDARD WAGERS

WIN — A bet that your horse will finish first.

PLACE — A bet that your horse will finish either first or second.

SHOW — A bet that your horse will finish first, second or third.

MULTIPLE WAGERS
(Rules for the New York Racing Association)

DAILY DOUBLE — A bet to win for both the first and second races. This bet is also available for the final two races of the day.

EXACTA — A bet on the horses you pick to finish-first and second in a single race, in that exact order. Exacta wagering is accepted for all races.

BOXED EXACTA — Two exactas, which you can do at any time. Let's say one bet is for horses No. 3 and No. 6, in that exact order. "Boxing" means you're also placing a bet on the reverse outcome, or No. 6 and No. 3, in that exact order.

QUINELLA — Similar to an exacta, except the horses may finish first and second in a single race, in either order. Available for races two and four.

TRIPLE — A bet on the horses you pick to finish first, second and third in a single race, in that exact order.

PICK THREE — A bet on the first-place finishers in races two, three and four, or races six, seven and eight. These bets enter a pool that goes to whoever selects all three winners or comes the closest.

PICK SIX — A bet on the first-place finishers in races three through eight. Winners take in 75 percent of the day's pool. If no one picks them all, 25 percent of the Pick Six pool goes to whoever comes closest. Remaining moneys are rolled over to the next day's pool.

HOCKEY

A great athlete once said, "Only bullfighting and the waterhole are left as vestigial evidence of what bloody savages men used to be."

Beautiful—though, obviously, he's left out hockey. Here's a sport (along with maybe football and boxing) that's retained a pretty pure dose of blood lust. How many games allow 250-pound men to chase after little objects with sticks (OK, that could describe a lot of sports), but then let one guy beat the crap out of another guy 'cause of his displeasure with something that guy did or said, resulting in those two guys slugging it out until one drops to a knee or is too exhausted to continue, penalizing those two players for a "major" rule infraction, only to allow them back on the ice in a couple of minutes to do it all over again! They should use this kind of logic to rid us of small claims court, dammit! Tommy Bolt, the great sport who uttered that opening quote, would have agreed. Bolt, remember, was renowned for his fiery temper and fearsome stick-hurling on the field of play—and he was a golfer!

Blue lines, two-line passes, high-sticking, boarding, spearing, slashing—there are lots of rules, but basically it's the appreciation of great athletes skating around and making some athletic moves in and around brutalizing the heck out of one another that makes the game so appealing. A great cross-check, which sends an opposing player through the glass and into some lady's plate of nachos, is a real crowd-pleaser, and could quite possibly result in a standing ovation from the crowd. What a game. A favorite Canadian/Northern U.S. Friday night can be marked by a few good friends, a case of Molsen Golden and a nice selection of newly compiled hockey fight tapes. Really.

It's been established that the game started in Canada, but from there, debate rages. One popular scenario has a game played on Christmas Day, 1855, in Kingston, Ontario, between members of the Royal Canadian Rifles. Which is great, but other historians maintain that the sticks used in this game were *on loan* from the Halifax Garrison, evidence that hockey originated in Halifax, Nova Scotia. The first organized hockey league *did* appear in Kingston in 1885, and the Stanley Cup—the enduring NHL championship trophy, which has seen so much champagne and so many joyful, toothless kisses over the years—was first presented to a league champion eight years later.

Hockey skipped over the border into the U.S. at several points, courtesy of wild-eyed Canucks personally transporting it. In 1893, it's reported to have appeared simultaneously in New Haven, Connecticut, and Baltimore, Maryland. Take your pick—from there, it spread to other major cities, to be played on real and artificial ice, growing into the storied game it is today.

The puck is a black vulcanized piece of rubber, 3 inches in diameter, 1-inch thick and weighing about 6 ounces. The goal posts are 4 feet high and 6 feet wide. A standard rink is 200 feet long and 85 feet wide. Before 1914, officials *placed* the puck between opposing players' sticks during face-offs, resulting in countless broken knuckles. Helmets were rare through the 1970s, and players played with broken noses and grillwork resembling the picket fences lining Route 66. Helmets are still optional, but the player has to sign a release form. Few, if any, choose to go without 'em today.

Great historic players include Jean Beliveau, Gordie Howe, Maurice "Rocket" Richard, Eddie "Old Time Hockey" Shore and some of these new millionaires like Lemieux and Gretzky.

Any individual study begins and ends with the movie *Slap Shot*, starring Paul Newman.

Braided Butt Damsel

THE WORLD'S STRONGEST MAN

It doesn't get a heckuva lot more manly than this. These are the most powerful guys in the world—by and large, ex-Olympian and world-champion power lifters and weight lifters, plus a couple of all-purpose tough guys, Polynesian warriors, the guy with the biggest biceps in the world, etc. The bottom line is they're all absolute behemoths. . . and they *sound* like it too. Even before you see him, a guy named *Gerrit Badenhorst* is picked first or second in any game of pickup football.

They're also contenders in the World's Strongest Man international competition, a variety of events big on entertainment: fire engine dragging, telephone pole hurling, small car carrying, jousting, etc. Watching some of the strongest men in the world employ astonishingly heavy, everyday objects to push their bodies to—and past—their limits is an incredible experience. While the premium is on power, mobility and agility definitely come into play.

The finals are televised every year on local sports stations (check ESPN or ESPN2), and produced by London-based TWI. Starting in the U.S. in 1977, all finals after 1982 have been held in such spots as the Bahamas, Spain, the Canary Islands and Iceland (many finalists are Scandinavian).

About two dozen contestants compete in qualifying rounds, then eight finalists vie for the big title. Count on rooting for a favorite—it's inevitable. Currently, Magnus ver Magnussen (from Iceland, 6'2", 286 lbs.; first in '91 and again from '94-'96), Riku Kiri (from Finland, 6'4", 312 lbs.; second in '96, third in '94) and Gerrit Badenhorst (from South Africa, 6'2", 308 lbs.; third in '96, second in '95) are the bulls to watch.

One of the great events is the "concrete-slab-chucked-over-the-head-backwards" event. One gargantuan at a time stands with his back to a height-adjustable wall. He'll grab a 200-or-so pound chunk of concrete from between his legs and hurl it over his head about 12 feet in the air, hopefully over the wall. (To get an idea, just try throwing a 20-pound muscle ball *anywhere*.) As contestants fail, the height of the wall is increased, eventually leaving a winner. But there's great entertainment in the misses. Sometimes, after teetering on top of the wall for a second, the concrete slab will come hurtling back down at the behemoth, who has to scramble away just before he or some part of his body is crushed! Just the noise the weight makes when it hits and seeing the ground shake is scary. This is seriously cool stuff.

Clark's Cicada™

The great ham-fisted Irishman remains one of the most loved character actors of all time. Huge in every respect, he is known to us as the consummate sergeant from John Ford's cavalry trilogy, busting out of his uniform, barking orders, grinning like a devil at new recruits, as quick with a laugh as a tear, brawling, hard drinking, loving all that is Irish. With his characteristic slow burn of pained exasperation, he'd run one of his enormous paws over his big boxer's mug or give his little cough, eyes fluttering innocently, just prior to punching some sap through a wall. The guy is just terrific in everything.

One of the greatest joys in our research came when we discovered that Victor McLaglen, about whom we found no articles in the periodical index, believe it or not, had actually written an autobiography! Then, it was tragedy to realize that it had been written in 1934—five years before he made *Gunga Din*—and not a word about his Ford films, Ward Bond (himself) or the Duke. Not even an anecdote about making *Wee Willie Winkie* with Shirley Temple—a great bloody shame to be sure, laddie. Still, it tells an incredible early story of the big man, and is definitely worth searching for (*Express to Hollywood* from Jarrolds Publishers of London).

VICTOR McLAGLEN

McLaglen was an established star in America by 1934. He had already appeared in about 50 films—many of them silent and in the UK. They're not films that most folks remember today or that you're likely to see on TNT. He made his first film with Ford, *The Fighting Heart*, in 1925 but only mentions it and star George O'Brien in passing. His success came in 1926 with the silent film role of Capt. Flagg in *What Price Glory?*—an odd brawling combination of comedy and drama set during World War I and directed by Raoul Walsh. Four years later, Walsh "discovered" the Duke loading furniture as a prop man and cast him in *The Big Trail*. Walsh really knew how to pick the big fellas. Capt. Flagg and his pal Sgt. Quirt (Edmund Lowe) were so popular that McLaglen and Lowe played the characters in a series of film adventures. If you love McLaglen, and you damn well should, by God, try to run down a copy of *What Price Glory?*

McLaglen lived a life as big and burly as himself. Here's a guy who answered the call of the hairy nomad with a vengeance. Our lad was born in Tunbridge Wells, near London, on December 11, 1886—that's right, he was an Englishman, ya squint! But Victor's mother was of Irish descent and his father, Scottish. There were eight brothers, all big scrappers, and a little sister. He worshiped his brother Fred, the oldest, and when Fred left home for the army and the Boer War, Victor followed. He was 14 but passed for 19, and joined the London Life Guards. Boxing won him several service titles and a tour of exhibitions—it was his love and the profession McLaglen felt best suited his future and his frame.

After leaving the army, Big Vic sought the boxing game but his father intervened and found him a stable office position. Victor readily took to his business career. The challenge and excitement of the solicitor's office was a completely new experience. He learned everthing he could and greeted each day with the dauntless enthusiasm of a new thoroughbred born to the race. He was on his way as a bright junior executive. Then, after a week, he was on a ship to Canada.

McLaglen tramped all over the north country, looking for adventure. He tried farming, fishing, gold and silver prospecting and served as a policeman and fitness trainer. The talent that always guaranteed a few dollars in his often empty pockets was boxing. The northern frontier mining towns and camps were short on entertainment, and always welcomed a bit o' rough and tumble. The basic promotion technique in those days was equivalent to John L. Sullivan pounding his fist on a bar and declaring, "I can lick any man in the world!" The usual game involved setting up a ring and challenging all comers. Victor first encountered such a show at the quaintly named Happy Land Park in the sporting quarter of Winnipeg. A big wrestler named Hume Duvel offered $25 to any man, jack or son who could last 15 minutes with him (in his autobiography, McLaglen actually declines to reveal the man's true name because, at the time of publication, Duvel was pursuing a successful career as a New York businessman—what a pal). Victor, who'd had some wrestling experience by that time, came away from the bout with $25 in his pocket.

The park soon offered him Duvel's job, which he accepted reluctantly. Wrestling, he felt, "could never work on my imagination like boxing. I always loved the flicker of the gloves, the tap of feet on the canvas, the snort of breath as the punches beat home. There is merely a clash of forces in the wrestling ring." McLaglen stayed with this game for some time, taking on up to eight challengers in one night and never giving up the gold. His final match at Happy Valley was a crazy big ballyhoo affair in which he had to drop an entire football team within one hour. The tactics were, he admits, pretty ugly, but he finished them off with four minutes to spare. The exhausting battle became part of the local mythology, a testament to raw power and brutality.

Stalcup Crane Fly™

Now that's a fight we would've walked a whole long way to see. McLaglen and Duvel became great pals and hit the carny circuit as a team offering the requisite 25 bucks to anyone who could last 15 minutes on the mat with Duvel or three rounds of boxing with McLaglen. Later they even put together a rough vaudeville routine, coating themselves with silver cream and recreating famous statues and fight scenes—just amazing stuff.

McLaglen could have been a contender to be sure, but events never aligned themselves properly to let that happen. His venues were crude but he was no ham 'n egger. One telling encounter you may have heard about was his fight with then reigning heavyweight champ Jack Johnson. Boxing rules were often a tangled mess, and stipulations for this exhibition bout at the Vancouver Athletic Club represented a perfect example. The rules called for a six-round, no decision match, which meant there would be no winner except by knock out. McLaglen went the distance without a single count but was clearly impressed with the champ. He describes the fight: "I do remember how I tried my very best to rattle him during the last two rounds, conscious of the fistic immortality that would be mine were I lucky enough to slip a 'sleeper.' But his grinning face (a characteristic that often rattled Johnson's opponents) darted in and out behind the thud of his gloves. . . . My best leads frequently pawed the air altogether, for that amazingly supple body of his weaved and pranced around me. . . . Johnson was undoubtedly the hardest man to hit whom I ever met. . . . He was certainly the greatest boxer I ever saw in action."

McLaglen's amazing wanderlust found him in India in service to a raja, lion hunting in Africa and shipwrecked in the South Seas

while pearl diving. As he put it: "A man had one life to live, and one world to live it in. The most he could hope to do with it was to sample that world and its sensations to the full, knowing that every new country and thrill he struck was another tweak to the beard of time." Boxing kept calling him back, and he decided to have a final shot at a career but World War I intervened and all eight of the McLaglen boys rallied round to the cause. Victor served as a captain against the Turks and Germans in Mesopotamia. His boxing reputation had preceded him homeward and he became a highly successful recruiting officer. It's easy to imagine how effective he was with his imposing, uniformed figure standing before a crowd, bellowing out the call like the barker he had been.

After the war, when a producer friend suggested that he take a stab at acting, McLaglen shrugged at the odd notion but, with no other immediate prospects, decided to have a go at it. His first appearance was in 1920. The camera liked him, and a steady contract put some some silver in his pockets, but his impression of the business and the people was typical—he found it all pretty damn silly. "Acting never appealed to me, and I was dabbling in it solely as a means of making money. I rather felt that the grease paint business was somewhat beneath a man who had once been a reasonably useful boxer."

He made a string of silents until 1924, when Hollywood called him for an aptly named production called *The Beloved Brute*. We have no idea if this film still exists, but it would be a gas to have a look at it. McLaglen's filmography is packed with sensational-sounding titles, but we may never have a chance to see them today. Tod Browning's *The Unholy Three* (1925) is still around and truly fascinating—don't miss it. Not enough can be said for today's film preservationists or against the shortsighted bastards who let their films rot into oblivion by the thousands.

THE *Informer*

WITH

VICTOR M^CLAGLEN
HEATHER ANGEL
PRESTON FOSTER
MARGOT GRAHAME
WALLACE FORD
UNA O'CONNOR

A JOHN FORD
PRODUCTION

RKO
Radio

FROM THE STORY BY LIAM O'FLAHERTY
ASSOCIATE PRODUCER CLIFF REID

Royal Green Humpy

Royal Red Humpy

WOMEN WHO KILL US

MAUREEN O'HARA—As Esmerelda, she brought Sir Cedric Hardwicke to the edge of madness in *The Hunchback of Notre Dame* (1939). Her skill with a sword was the only highlight in Errol Flynn's *Against All Flags*. And no one could go toe-to-toe with the Duke like this magnificent Irish amazon. John Ford knew it in a heartbeat. She committed early on, after *How Green Was My Valley*, to make his great love story, *The Quiet Man*, a reality. This fiery lassie remains the consummate Technicolor goddess.

GENE TIERNEY—"Captivating" is the word for Gene Tierney. When Hollywood needed the kind of brain-melting beauty that would send men to their knees and sell their souls, boats and fishing tackle for, Gene got the call—remember Don Ameche in *Heaven Can Wait* (1943) or Dana Andrews in *Laura*

Ella Raines (left); Marjorie Main (below); the Duke with Maureen O'Hara in his arms in She Wore a Yellow Ribbon *(right), and with her in mud from* McLintock!

(1944). Gene's debut was *The Return of Frank James* (1940) with Henry Fonda, followed by some other greats like *Son Of Fury* (1942), *Leave Her to Heaven* (1945), and *The Razor's Edge* (1946). She was never more desirable than as the spirited widow of Gull Cottage, romanced by two very different men in *The Ghost and Mrs. Muir* (1947).

RAQUEL WELCH— Raquel Welch as "Lust" in the 1967 Peter Cook/Dudley Moore cult classic, *Bedazzled*, filmed in Bonerama (well, at least her sequence).

EDNA MAY OLIVER—God had something special in mind when he put this great long-faced gal together. Character actress and comedienne, she was such an original screen presence that she naturally stole every scene (even from W.C. Fields in *David Copperfield*). Oliver was fearless as Mrs. McKlennan in *Drums Along the Mohawk*—proud, plainspoken and resigned to the foolish ways of men. Don't miss her

JEAN SIMMONS—She almost didn't get the role of Varinia in *Spartacus* because Kirk Douglas wanted to reserve British accents for the patrician Roman class—but, boy, are guys happy she did (including Kirk, finally). Sure, there was some obligatory cheesecake (her nude swimming scene begs a few instant replays), but she contributes empathy, sensuality and pure stoic dignity to the role, playing it to perfection. Definitely see her in *Young Bess* and *The Robe* from 1953. The ultimate Jean Simmons dual seduction double-feature home rental, however, has to be *Elmer Gantry* (1960) and *Guys and Dolls* (1955). Appearing on AMC recently to discuss her career, she was elegant, gracious, funny and still a knockout.

barroom catfight in *A Tale of Two Cities* (1935). The "Termite Terrace" gang at Warner Brothers loved Oliver. You can instantly tell a classic cartoon fan by the way he says, "Mi-i-iles Sta-a-ndish!"

MARJORIE MAIN—She once told an interviewer that Ma Kettle (whom she originated in 1947's *The Egg and I*, with Percy Kilbride as Pa) was her favorite character, saying, "I would rather make people laugh than anything else." Main's country characters were more than loud dirt-floor rubes— she imbued them with an unshakable faith and a complete lack of "citified" pretension. Her breasts may have hung somewhere near the belt line, but her heart was in the right place. She was also great in *Dead End* (1937), *Heaven Can Wait* (1943) and *Friendly Persuasion* (1956).

CLAUDIA CARDINALE—Momma mia! Has the screen ever seen anything as sexy as Claudia? Think of her pouting beauty in Fellini's *8¹/₂*. Think of her on that tigerskin rug being seduced by David Niven in *The Pink Panther*. Think of her as the stolen object of desire in *The Professionals*. OK, now think of her eyes and her mouth in some of those luscious, sunburnt Sergio Leone close-ups of her in *Once Upon a Time in the West* with Ennio Morricone's score playing in the background. (Now, uh. . . excuse me, back in a minute. . .)

ANN BLYTH—So damned adorable in *Mr. Peabody and the Mermaid* (1948) that a whole generation of guys just couldn't wait for their midlife crisis. As Lenore, the embodiment of William Powell's lost youth, she just rips your heart out. Lovely, innocent, naive, devoted, sings hauntingly but never speaks, goes naked, loves to make out, lives in the pool, loves to fish and is indeed half-fish—just shy of perfect.

SHIRLEY TEMPLE—Are we the only ones who wish Shirley and Victor McLaglen had made four and 20 sequels to *Wee Willie Winkie* with John Ford? If you're a new daddy looking to imbue

your little girl with images of character strength then stop right here. Forget that syrupy stuff—this is one tough and talented little gal—a helluva lot more Mark Twain than saccharine. Check out *Captain January* (1936), *The Little Colonel* (1935), *The Little Princess* (1939), *Little Miss Marker* (1934),

Poor Little Rich Girl (1936)— pretty much any of the "Little" series.

ELLA RAINES— Not a household name as actresses go, perhaps, but if she had made only *Tall in the Saddle* (1944), that would have been more than enough. The Duke helped develop this story of an honest but deadly, gal-fearin' stranger in a corrupt town. A love triangle forces the Duke to choose between a Polly Purebread-type and a wild dark-haired beauty who tries to kill him twice (Raines). He does not disappoint. Ella is quite a dazzler. Don't feel bad if you come away from this film with visions of her straddling your back, wielding a whip—it's quite natural.

From left to right: Shirley Temple; Edna May Oliver; Raquel Welch and Dudley Moore in Bedazzled; *Claudia Cardinale close-up, and below with her director, Sergio Leone, on the set of* Once Upon a Time in the West; *Ann Blyth; Michelle Carey; Jane Russell.*

Lawson's Henry's Fork Hopper™

Shel-Bob's Gravelbar Onions

Great on burgers, dogs or just on the side. Start with a cast-iron skillet over an open fire. Ring or chop enough onions to fill the skillet. Melt 1/2 stick of butter in the skillet, and dump in the onions. Shake in some Worcestershire, Tabasco and lemon pepper. Keep stirring, and add 1/3 can of Bud as you go. Browned and ready in 10-15 minutes!

Eat a Snake

Skin rattlesnake, and cut into 3-inch pieces. Roll in mixture of flour, corn meal, milk and egg. Salt and pepper. Deep fry in hot oil. Serve hot.

Campfire Corn

Get as many ears as will fit around your coals. Pull the husks back—don't rip them off. Remove the silk as best you can. If there's room in your cooler, soak the ears in the ice water for about half an hour.

Meanwhile, melt up some butter in a pan. Dry off the corn, coat with butter and sprinkle with

Kaufmann Bronze Seducer™

salt (or lime, or. . .). Now replace the husks and wrap each ear in foil.

Place foil-wrapped ears right on the coals (or touching the perimeter if you're cooking something else over the center fire). Rotate occasionally so they don't burn. They'll be ready to eat in about 30-40 minutes.

Macon's Politically Incorrect Salt Steak

This recipe involves more than a modicum of showmanship, and is guaranteed to command the attention of your dinner guests. For maximum effect, have them scrub up and get involved with the preparation.

But first, a word about your dinner guests. If your friends are the type who stew over the sodium content of their Diet Cokes, who cringe at the fat content in a Caesar salad, who fret knowing that their Bordeaux contains sulfites, who wouldn't dream of using real butter on a baked potato, who use ground turkey when making a batch of chili. . . if this describes your peer group, then the first order of business is to go out and cultivate a more lively set of friends!

When you succeed in befriending that gang who savors a good single malt before dinner, accompanied by a generous portion of cheese, followed by a sumptuous repast dripping with rich sauces and a variety of wines, all topped off with a good cigar and a snifter of cognac. . . now you're ready to pull out the salt steak! (Contrary to popular belief, your new friends may have a greater life expectancy because they spend much less time worrying about chicken shit.)

Ingredients:

1 large sirloin steak, 1-1/2 to 2 inches thick (porterhouse is also nice!); the larger the piece of meat, the better, as it decreases the salty outside to tasty inside ratio

6 sheets of newspaper, no color print (we prefer the *Wall Street Journal*)

1 large bowl of rock salt

1 jar whole pepper corns

2 jars Lawry's lemon pepper

1 bottle Worcestershire sauce

1 jar of Grey Poupon mustard

1 roll of masking tape

1 giant bucket of water

10-pound bag of Kingsford charcoal

Start by laying your fire. The biggest risk is not using enough charcoal (more on this later). Your charcoal bed should be at least 6 inches thick (leave the grill off after you light the fire).

After you've got the fire started (and you've replenished your favorite beverage), mix the spices (rock salt, pepper corns and lemon pepper) together in a big bowl. Lay the six sheets of newspaper open, and plunk that hunk of beef down in the middle of it. Open the jar of mustard, and slather one side of the meat with a 1/4-inch-thick layer of it **(1)** (your friend's eyebrows should raise perceptibly at this point).

Next, grab several handfuls of the spice mixture, and plaster it into the mustard. You should have enough spice on there so that you don't get any mustard on your hands. Then dump enough Worcestershire on there to color the whole thing brown. **(2)** Carefully turn the steak over, and repeat on the opposite side.

When you're finished making a mess of this beautiful

piece of meat, wrap it up in the paper, and secure with masking tape **(3)** (try to cover as little area as possible with the tape—think of the ribbon on a Xmas present). When the bundle's secured, immerse the whole thing in your bucket of water **(4)**—your guests should be howling by now!

Replenish your drink, and tell a few dirty jokes while you wait for the fire to reach its peak. Let the bundle soak.

When the fire has reached its zenith—and your Weber is about to melt—pull the soggy package from the bucket, squeeze out the excess water, and throw it directly on the coals. (Pray that the fire does not go out!)

Depending upon the size-of-fire to size-of-bundle ratio, allow about 10 minutes on each side. The paper should dry out, and be on the verge of catching fire.

When the bundle is looking good and charred, **(5)** rescue it from the fire, and (using your now-empty bucket) remove the paper and scrape all the mustard and spices off the meat. The steak at this point has been partially steam cooked, and will have a sickly white appearance.

Put the grill back on your kettle, and brown the steak for 3-5 minutes per side. When it looks like an edible piece of beef again, **(6)** slice into 1/4-inch-thick strips and serve. If you've done it right, the steam from the newspaper has traveled through the spice layer and impregnated the meat with flavor while retaining the juices—a marvelous little example of applied physics.

Be careful not to overcook it though—there's a fine line between a perfectly seasoned piece of meat and a salt lick. Good luck!

Will Rogers called it the "bowl of blessedness." And, as far as folks can figure, it's another true American product—not from Mexico, as a lot of people might believe. (Though chances are, the chili peppers and beef on the hoof that went *into* that first bowl were rounded up south of the Rio Grande.) Imagine some grizzled old cattle drive cook (picture Walter Brennan in *Red River*) slinging together a spicy stew that became the first chuck-wagon chili.

CHILI

However chili came about, there's no question about its enduring popularity—chili is one of *the* perfect foods. Since there's no set way to make the stuff, if a

guy can cook up only one thing, it's probably a bowl of red. This is great for guys who like to experiment and then covet their secret recipe (meaning pretty much any guy). Now, the debate continues as to whether to include beans or preserve the purity of honest-to-God Texas chili (no beans, not never), but the author's sentiments don't fall one way or the other. Considering the huge amount of prairie berries that folks in the West regularly put away, it's hard to imagine that original chili recipes didn't include 'em, but since chili is the official food of Texas, they can define real chili any damn way they please.

TODDY BOY'S COLON CLEANER CHILI—

California has just started getting a wider distribution of Wick Fowler's 2-Alarm Chili Kits from Austin, Texas. Now, California's been pretty much the exclusive domain of that other great chili packet—and the current best seller in the country—Carroll Shelby's Original Texas Brand Chili Mix. They're both equally great (in the humble opinion of the authors), representing the standard for folks who don't start from scratch—the first rule in any competition.

Toddy Boy's Colon Cleaner Chili

READ ALL INSTRUCTIONS FIRST

NOTE:
This recipe is safe for company and kids. Add diced hot chilis for the Hellfire version.

Start with a good old wooden spoon, a box of Saltine Premium Crackers and two packages of either Wick Fowler's 2-Alarm Chili Kit or Carroll Shelby's Chili Mix. Brown the following in a large skillet:

2 lbs. ground turkey (yes, turkey! No fat to drain off and it tastes great. Gordon Fowler even likes it. Of course the great thing about chili is that you can add whatever meat you like—stew beef, rattlesnake, whatever)

2 lbs. hot Italian turkey sausage

Shred ground turkey and chop sausage into fingertip-size chunks. Be sure to remove the sickening and disgusting sausage skins before cooking. While meat is simmering, dump the following into a large chili pot on low heat:

Two 28 oz. cans of chopped peeled tomatoes with basil (don't get tomato

sauce by mistake—it just ain't the same)

1 bottle beer—a decent Mexican is preferred, but that GD horsepiss Rico swills will do in a pinch

Two 15 oz. cans of Ranch Style jalapeño pinto beans—whole (may substitute red kidney beans, but drain off first and rinse)

One 15 oz. can of black beans—whole

Drain off fat, if any, put in the turkey and stir it around. Now add from chili package:

The works but only one half of a salt packet. Stir in real well after each chili mix packet.

Dice and add:　　1 red pepper
　　　　　　　　1 green pepper
　　　　　　　　2 yellow peppers

Stir into pot with another bottle of beer and cover. You can't overcook this stuff. Keep covered on lowest heat and stir occasionally all afternoon (a bare minimum of two hours).

Leave cover off for a while or add a pulverized fistful of tortilla chips or saltines if you want it to thicken (spoon should stand up in the middle). Serve in bowls or large plates covered with Premium Saltine Crackers. Spoons are not used to consume this chili (hence, little salt is added). Stock the fridge and bathroom with plenty of cold beer and new magazines, respectively, and remember my family in your prayers.

X Parachute Caddis

THE GREAT CHILI COOK-OFF—OCTOBER 1, 1967

Wick Fowler and Carroll Shelby helped put together the first World's Championship Chili Cook-off on Shelby's ranch in Terlingua (meaning "three tongues"), Texas. It was 1967—the Duke was making *The War Wagon* and *El Dorado* and had probably figured by then that the whole damn country and it's crazy hippie kids had gone right to hell.

Like the origin of chili, the origin of the first cook-off is part of Texas lore and the subject of friendly dispute. The Shelby camp gives credit to publicity man Tom Tierney, whom they say organized the event with the support of Dallas newspapers in a scheme to help Shelby and his partner unload the Terlingua property. Shelby had asked Tierney, "What do we do to get rid of that 150,000 acres of rocks?" The cook-off, bringing folks out to look the property over, was his answer.

The Fowler camp remembers it more like a duel in the sun. Humorist H. Allen Smith laid down the challenge, they say, in a *Holiday* magazine article entitled "Nobody Knows More About Chili Than I Do." It declared that Shelby's recipe (with beans) was the one and only, and that so-called Texas chili wasn't worth a hill of 'em, beans that is. Fightin' words fer sure. (This one makes for a cooler story already, don'cha think?) Well sir, Wick wasn't going to stand for none of that. He grabbed his 2-Alarm recipe, his pot and his wooden spoon and went to face down the dirty dog. Smith and Fowler got to Shelby's place and faced off at high noon on the porch of the derelict Chisos Oasis Saloon. Eyeing each other down, they commenced to choppin' an' cookin' an' stirrin' up bowls of bubblin' hellfire for the three judges and 200-odd (very odd, actually) beer-totin' desperadoes (spectators, that is). The three tongues (Terlingua, get it?) of the judges went to work as the blazing Texas sun and the eyes of those still standing burned into them. The first vote went to Fowler and the next to Smith. A hush fell over the crowd—folks later claimed the place got so quiet you could hear a horny toad fart. The pressure was on the third judge. He sampled one after the other, then, shaking his head sadly, and perhaps wisely, informed the gathering that he would have to abstain—his taste buds had done burned out. A tie was declared, a rematch was planned and a legend was born.

The cook-off made great news copy and has since become an institution, well actually, two institutions. The original sponsor, the Chili Appreciation Society International, still puts on the Terlingua event, now called the Wick Fowler-Frank X. Tolbert Memorial Chili Cook-off. Tolbert, an original organizer, was a columnist for the *Dallas Morning News*. This cook-off is held each year on the first weekend of November.

In 1975, Carroll Shelby, his buddy C.V. Wood Jr. (famous for buying the London Bridge and bringing it to Lake Havasu in Arizona), and some other CASI members formed the International Chili Society, moving the World's Championship Chili Cook-off to Tropico Gold Mine in California. Reasons for the split vary, but basically ICS wanted to bring a little more organization, serious judging and "the business of show" to the table, while CASI was more interested in keeping things loose and just having fun. No argument, however, about the proceeds—the cook-offs, along with hundreds of local sanctioned events across the country, help raise millions each year for charity.

THE CHILI GODS: WICK FOWLER AND CARROLL SHELBY

WICK FOWLER—As a war correspondent for the *Dallas Morning News*, Wick had a front seat at some of the most historic events of World War II. He was on the front line of the Italy campaign with the 36th Texas Division, received a Purple Heart for a wound at Anzio and covered the Battle of the Bulge and Patton's drive into Germany. Later he went to the Pacific theater and was on board the USS *Missouri* for the Japanese surrender. He was of one the first three newsman allowed into Hiroshima to witness the devastation of the atomic blast.

This talented Texan wore many hats. Prior to the war, he was in the merchant marine and worked as a Texas highway patrolman and as a detective. Later he worked as a sailboat designer, and as an aide to the governor of Texas and to a U.S. senator. He then resumed his correspondent role to report on the war in Vietnam. He brought along plenty of his new chili packets and dispensed them freely among the troops, earning him the nickname Chili Cong.

Wick put together his first chili packages as gifts for friends back in 1964. They got to be so popular that retailers were soon putting in orders, and Wick found himself with a business: the Caliente Chili Co. One story tells how Wick managed production assisted by a team of Mexican women, who, seated at a long table, filled cellophane packets with the spices, then sealed them with a clothes iron. Naturally, as business grew, he hired more workers—and bought another iron.

Wick Fowler's extraordinary life of adventure was cut short by Lou Gehrig's disease in 1972, but Caliente Chili continued to grow and prosper under the management of his son Gordon and daughter Ann. The company, which in 1991 became a subsidiary of Luzianne-Blue Plate Foods, enjoys ever-widening distribution (witness my local grocer) and the unbound enthusiasm of the current 2-Alarm standard bearer, Tom Nall. As divisional sales manager, Nall has jumped into the saddle to ensure that the Wick Fowler legend lives on.

CARROLL HALL SHELBY—

Racing, chili and fund-raising have made Carroll Shelby famous and beloved in the U.S., but the staggeringly muscular Shelby AC Cobra made him a world legend. At its introduction in 1962, a lengthened British AC Ace roadster married to a Ford 260-cid V-8 engine jolted the car culture. Shelby had approached then Ford Motor Co. VP Lee Iacocca with the idea of a dream vehicle that would blow the doors off a Corvette. He needed $25,000 to create this brute. Iacocca sized up the proposal from the confident young man in the black cowboy hat and boots and said, "Give this guy $25,000 before he bites somebody." After modifying the body in 1965 to help accommodate a Ford 427, Shelby had the most ferocious street sports car on the planet. Off the floor, she could do 0–100–0 mph in 14 seconds. She's a beast of beauty.

The authors recall being taken into Manhattan each year for the Coliseum car shows. They saw all the great concept cars, "Big Daddy" Roth one-offs and the new Wankel rotary engine. That's where they first saw the Cobra.

But not really knowing who Carroll Shelby was, the authors' first introduction to his legend was from Bill Cosby. Cosby's comedy album 200 MPH includes a brilliant 22.5-minute routine about Cosby's lust for,

and giddy receipt of, a hand-crafted Shelby street machine capable of (guess). Cosby's monologue hits on the unspoken question that squirms around in a guy's brain when faced with anything that big, fast, sexy and powerful: can I handle her? Back then, looking at those amazing curves on that Cobra, that was the real issue: could anyone other than Steve McQueen do justice to this baby? Cosby, fried after his first spin, ends up shakily handing the keys over with instructions to give the car to George Wallace.

By the time Shelby hosted the first World's Championship Chili Cook-off in '67, he was at work on another pet project with Ford: turning stock Mustangs into rockets. His GT series conversions ran from 1965 to 1970 with 1968 being a stand-out year. That's when he introduced the ultra-hot Shelby GT-500KR. The "KR" stood for "King of the Road," referring to some modifications that delivered lip-curling acceleration. The limited edition fastback coupes and ragtops featured the Ford Cobra Jet 428, with oversize heads and intake manifold and a Holley 735-cfm carburetor— these ponies were a lot to handle but could really gallop. The emblem was a now-familiar coiled cobra in anodized gold.

Often, like Wick Fowler, bugged for his chili recipe, Shelby handed out tons of the stuff, about $35,000 worth according to his accountant. Wick's success inspired him to go into business himself, but, as Shelby puts it, "I never sold it in Texas as long as Wick Fowler was alive, because I kinda had taken his idea." Shelby's mix took off, to be purchased years later in a lucrative deal with Kraft.

Today, in the true spirit of 90s conglomeratization, the two classic chili packages that brought bowls of red to greenhorns across the country share the same parent company. William B. Reilly, Inc., a massive food distributor, now sees to it that the traditions of these two legendary Texans carries on into a fiscally secure future. Raise a cold one.

Royal Coachman Bucktail

Beef

· RETAIL CUTS ·
WHERE THEY COME FROM
HOW TO COOK THEM

ROUND
SIRLOIN
SHORT LOIN
RIB
CHUCK
FLANK
SHORT PLATE
BRISKET
FORE SHANK

ROUND

Round Steak
Braise, Panfry

Top Round Roast
Roast

Top Round Steak
Broil, Panbroil, Panfry

Boneless Rump Roast
Roast, Braise

Bottom Round Roast
Braise, Roast

Tip Roast, Cap Off
Roast, Braise

Eye Round Roast
Braise, Roast

Tip Steak
Broil, Panbroil, Panfry

SIRLOIN

Sirloin Steak, Flat Bone
Broil, Panbroil, Panfry

Sirloin Steak, Round Bone
Broil, Panbroil, Panfry

Top Sirloin Steak
Broil, Panbroil, Panfry

FORE SHANK & BRISKET

Shank Cross Cut
Braise, Cook in Liquid

Brisket, Whole
Braise, Cook in Liquid

Corned Brisket, Point Half
Braise, Cook in Liquid

Brisket, Flat Half
Braise

CHUCK

Chuck Eye Roast
Braise, Roast

Boneless Top Blade Steak
Braise, Panfry

Arm Pot Roast
Braise

Boneless Shoulder Pot Roast
Braise

Cross Rib Pot Roast
Braise

Mock Tender
Braise

Under Blade Pot Roast
Braise, Roast

Blade Roast
Braise

Short Ribs
Braise, Cook in Liquid

7-Bone Pot Roast
Braise

Flanken-Style Ribs
Braise, Cook in Liquid

THIS CHART APPROVED BY
NATIONAL LIVE STOCK & MEAT BOARD

SHORT LOIN

T-Bone Steak
Broil, Panbroil, Panfry

Boneless Top Loin Steak
Broil, Panbroil, Panfry

Porterhouse Steak
Broil, Panbroil, Panfry

Tenderloin Roast
Roast, Broil

Tenderloin Steak
Broil, Panbroil, Panfry

RIB

Rib Roast, Large End
Roast

Rib Roast, Small End
Roast

Rib Steak, Small End
Broil, Panbroil, Panfry

Rib Eye Roast
Roast

Rib Eye Steak
Broil, Panbroil, Panfry

Back Ribs
Braise, Cook in Liquid, Roast

FLANK & SHORT PLATE

Flank Steak
Broil, Braise, Panfry

Flank Steak Rolls
Braise, Broil, Panbroil, Panfry

Skirt Steak
Braise, Broil, Panbroil, Panfry

OTHER CUTS

Ground Beef
Broil, Panfry, Panbroil, Roast (Bake)

Cubed Steak
Panfry, Braise

Beef for Stew
Braise, Cook in Liquid

Cubes for Kabobs
Broil, Braise

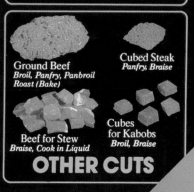

Royal Coachman

George Stephen of Illinois is the man behind the mighty Weber. Backyard brick barbecues were all the rage at the beginning of the '50s, but experience has taught a lesson to suburban chefs—the big grills were impressive to look at, but a pain in the ass to work on. The fire was difficult to control, wind was a problem, and they became critter condos when neglected.

George wanted some way to elevate the fire and cover the food. He tried to improve the design

THE WEBER

of his own brick grill without success. Inspiration came to him at the office. He had a job with the Weber Brothers Metal Works and took a keen interest in the marine buoys they manufactured for Chicago Harbor. Two metal halves were joined to create a watertight, hollow sphere. With a tripod stand, this was just the shape he needed, by Jiminy, and by July 1952, he was selling George's Barbecue Kettle.

He formed a barbecue division of Weber Brothers in 1955 and the next year sent out his first catalogue. The year 1957 brought the marketing windfall of the century—the Russkies sent a Weber-shaped satellite into orbit. George's grill had a nickname, "sputnik."

The superior quality of the new kettle was unquestioned, but the price, back then about five times that of other backyard cooking devices, established it as a symbol of the kilty crowd. Today, Weber is the No. 1 barbecue supplier in the world, and George's invention is a comparative bargain. In the process it has become deeply ingrained in American culture. While toasting marshmallows with a pal, I remember discusing the merits of the "controlled burn" approach. His reply: "You can always tell someone who's grown up around a Weber."

There probably ought to be a "great moments in Weber cooking" section here, like the infamous WD-40 moments shared in this book, but readers ought to be busy making those moments for themselves, now shouldn't they??

The One-Match Fluid-Free BBQ Fire

Lighter fluid might have been fun to play around with when we were kids, but it really has no business at a BBQ. (If you can tell when the guy two doors down is pouring it on, why would you want anything that stinky anywhere near your own food?) Maybe people are dependent on the stuff, or maybe they like squirting it into the fire for effect. But for a better tasting, less dangerous experience in outdoor cooking, the following simple steps will help kick the can—for good.

Put on an apron (guys should always BBQ with an apron—dressing the part keeps a cook focused and less likely to burn something—chef hats might be pushing it unless you're working with a team), and get a pair of those bargain variety leather-palm work gloves. This is a BBQ outfit—keep it together. And remember: Don't use those gloves for oil changes or taking out the trash.

Remove the upper and lower grills and make sure that any vents on the bottom of the kettle are left open.

Tightly twist up newspaper logs, two full sheets at a time, and place them slightly apart in the bottom of the kettle. Fill just the space under the lower grill (four or five sheets will probably do it). Replace the lower grill on top of the paper logs.

Now pour in fresh charcoal briquets and pile them up in the center.

Reaching below the grill, strike a stick match and light four corners of the newspaper. This can be kind of a smoky stage as the paper burns—but not for long. Smoke will follow you around a BBQ kettle. (This used to be shrugged off as a myth, but it seems to me that some research institute spent a few million and discovered that smoke actually will billow into your face no matter where you stand in relationship to the kettle.)

Next replace the upper grill, let it warm up and then take a stab at cleaning it. A seasoned grill will remain black, of course, but make a good show of it and be sure the guests are watching.

Now go get a beer.

In about 10 minutes the briquets should be red enough so that you can spread them out. In another 10 minutes, or maybe less, they'll be ashed over—and ready to go.

Kaufmann's Hatching Midge™

KINGSFORD ORIGINAL CHARCOAL BRIQUETS

Is there a single living soul in these United States who has not cooked with—or eaten a meal grilled on—Kingsford Charcoal Briquets? With the possible exception of maybe a couple of French tourists, we think not. The name Kingsford has become synonymous with the great American afternoon BBQ, but it may surprise the reader to discover the original name behind this classic product: Ford, as in Henry Ford. The folks at Kingsford consider Henry Ford to be the baron of the backyard BBQ. Why?

The Ford dynasty was built on ingenuity, great products that a modest income could handle and a bold embrace of automation. But it was also built on prudence. Mr. Ford was not a man to tolerate waste—he didn't waste time and he didn't waste materials.

At the turn of the century, production of the Model T was cranking right along and car ownership ceased to be the exclusive domain of the rich. North of Motor City, Ford operated a sawmill that punched out the wooden framing. What should catch Ford's eye but the huge piles of discarded scrap—surely there must be some use for all that material.

He came up with the idea of chipping the lumber waste and compressing the bits, scorching these into char, grinding them into a powder and compressing them into the now familiar pillow-shaped briquets. The bags were labeled Ford Charcoal and marketed through his automobile agencies. The name was later changed to Kingsford, still the No. 1 seller in the country.

- Kingsford offers the following BBQ tips in their literature:

- Apply vegetable oil or nonstick cooking spray to the grill to prevent food from sticking and pulling apart.

- Don't start grilling too soon—the coals should be at least 70 percent ashed over to sufficiently burn off any solvent.

- Soak wooden shish kebab skewers in water for 20 minutes to keep them from burning.

- Let the grid warm over the fire to ease cleaning. A stiff wire grill brush or crumpled ball of foil works best.

- Use tongs or spatulas. Forks allow juices to escape and dry out the meat.

- Add sauces toward the end of cooking to avoid burning.

Parachute Caddis

> "Here's to the Bull who roams the Wood, He does the cows and heifers good. Were it not for his long, long rod, What would we do for beef, by God?"
>
> — **Mark Twain**
>
> *Toast used at a gathering of randy fishermen cronies calling themselves The Mammoth Cods*

Worcestershire Sauce

OK, everyone's probably heard the tale that this famous product got its name when some old-timer down South tried it for the first time and asked, "Whas' dis here sauce?" Well, that's not exactly how it happened.

Lea & Perrins' Worcestershire, that versatile miracle tonic, has been around for more than 150 years. The 19th century English gentlemen responsible, John Wheeley Lea and William Perrins, were druggists and partners in Worcester's chemist shop, and were visited one day by a Lord Sandys, who had just returned from a stint as governor of Bengal. Now, the beauty of foreign service for Englishmen was that no matter where they were stationed, the food was bound to be better than at home. Lord Sandys relished the cuisine of India and, in particular, an exotic flavorful sauce made from the tamarind bean local to those parts. Could the chemists whip up a batch if he furnished a recipe? Lea and Perrins prepared the ingredients as instructed, and perhaps to satisfy their curiosity, set some aside to try for themselves. Well, they couldn't stand the dark stuff. The bottles were left forgotten in a cellar until one fateful day when, like good scientists, they decided to try it once more before pitching it into the trash forever. Blimey, it was bloody wonderful! Aging had matured the sauce, revealing the make-or-break step in the process.

Family and friends found it to be some serious sauce too, and urged Lea and Perrins to offer it for sale. Sweeping through Europe, it became the secret ingredient in countless dishes. (Lord Sandys, meanwhile, was a trifle miffed, and made it clear that his family name could not be used to promote the product.) It didn't matter much. *Worcestershire* sauce was literally sailing out the door. The clever chemists made sure that cases left port with every ocean liner, as ship stewards who agreed to offer the product to passengers also left port with a few extra quid. That's right, they greased the blighters!

A Manhattan businessman, John Duncan, had great success importing Worcestershire sauce in the 1830s, and arranged for stateside production. One hundred years and countless millions of little paper-wrapped bottles later, Duncan & Sons became Lea & Perrins Inc. The company entered into the Wall Street Shuffle during the go-go '80s and is now part of a French consortium called DANONE. (Why, gettin' their hands on this world-famous sauce had likely been a secret French plan for generations!)

McIlhenny Co. Tabasco Pepper Sauce

That familiar little red 2-ounce bottle of Tabasco pepper sauce has been a welcome sight in America's restaurants, cafes and diners for more than 125 years. Chefs and short-order cooks always have a bottle handy, and no bartender worth a lick would ever be without the Tabasco/Worcestershire combo—about as common in homes across the U.S. as salt. Tabasco sauce is one of those products that brings to mind that old television ad for Golden Blossom Honey: "Just look in your cupboard—it's in there somewhere." You've got some, right?

The inventor of Tabasco sauce was Edmund McIlhenny, a fifth-generation American of Scotch-Irish descent. He was an excellent marksman, competitive yachtsman, prize-winning horse breeder and worked as a Louisiana banking agent before the Civil War. He often visited local sugar plantations in the course of lending and collecting.

McIlhenny's in-laws, Daniel Dudley Avery and his wife, Sarah, owned their own island off the Louisiana Gulf Coast. There they ran a 2,300-acre sugarcane plantation literally atop a mountain of solid salt. In 1863, Union troops invaded the island and totally destroyed the plantation. McIlhenney and his wife assisted in the laborious process of reconstruction, and it was during this time that Tabasco was born.

McIlhenny tended the plantation's vegetable garden, nurturing a special variety of red capsicum pepper given him a few years before by a friend returning from Mexico. McIlhenny had planted them before the war and, surprisingly, they survived the devastation. He delighted in their piquant (that's right—*piquant!*) flavor, which added excitement to the monotony of foodstuffs available in the Reconstruction South.

Experimenting with pepper sauce, McIlhenny eventually hit upon a formula that involved crushing the ripest reddest peppers, mixing a half-coffee-cup of local salt with each gallon, and aging the concoction in crockery jars for 30 days. Then he added "the best French wine vinegar" and aged the mixture for another 30 days, hand-stirring at regular intervals to blend the flavors. After straining, the sauce was transferred to small cologne-type bottles with narrow necks, which were then corked and dipped in green sealing wax. A sprinkler device was attached to the neck of the bottle, and the definitive dash to perfect a Bloody Mary or a dozen raw oysters was soon to be introduced to the world. The McIlhenny family had invented a *great* product to sustain the family into the future: the American dream.

Lawry's Lemon Pepper: Seasoning of the Gods

Here's a true story: I went over to a buddy's house with a bag of fresh bagels (I don't even toast 'em when they're this fresh), some lox, Philadelphia Brand cream cheese and a real honest-to-goodness beefsteak tomato, and started whipping up some serious snack food. I presented my buddy with this beautiful stack on a still-steaming onion bagel and asked him where they kept the lemon pepper. You know what he said to me? "Oh, lemon pepper? I'm not sure if we have any." True story. That's like saying you're not sure if you packed any cold ones for your fishing trip. Don't ever, ever, ever be out of lemon pepper. This stuff is truly the all-purpose seasoning of the gods. Whether it's salt steak, Perch, simple roast chicken or the last additive to a Bloody Mary before you fine tune with Tabasco, you must have it and you must know when you're about to run out of it so you can get more. Fortunately, Home Club and other purveyors of megapackaging carry monster-size shakers of the stuff. Go get one... go get two and sleep better.

Snyder's of Hanover Sourdough Bavarian Pretzels

Another item a guy just never wants to be out of. Because a cold beer doesn't taste any better than when it hits a mouthful of Snyder's. Many folks—including us von Hoffmans—used to carry or ship these babies to the West Coast from New Jersey (along with Wise Potato Chips). Then this wonderful outfit called Trader Joe's started carryin' 'em and saved us the trouble. Now, rightfully, they're everywhere—the No. 1 seller in America.

The postwar period saw the introduction of these babies by the Pennsylvania-Dutch Snyder family. They started a family bakery in 1924, producing angel food cakes and egg noodles. Two Snyder sons joined the company and started chipping potatoes to sell as snacks. The pretzels came along in 1947.

How do they do it? Go and see for yourself—Snyder's welcomes the public to tour the facility. Imagine chowing down on 'em the minute they come out of the oven—better bring a road pack. And if you spy two gals named Lucy and Ethel working the line, I don't want to hear about it. (Please note the complete absence herein of puns on the word *twisted*. I thank you.)

Extremely Important Pretzel Tip: If the 'zels are not resealed immediately after opening, you're dead. These go stale almost as fast as Saltines, and the packaging is equally useless for reclosure. A large Ziploc fits the Snyder's bag perfectly. Just drop the whole bag in, zip up the Ziploc and stick the bag back in the box—nothing to it. We're happy to do our bit toward putting to an end forever the needless pain and suffering brought on by a blah stale Bavarian.

Claussen's Dill Pickles

A big honkin' homemade Dagwood just isn't finished until a dill docks up next to it. You'll be hard-pressed to find anything better in your local market than Claussen. Not as sour as the old-time deli pickle if that's your standard (although Claussen makes those too), but a damn fine dependable domestic dill. An absolute killer with cold cuts and beer.

Cucumbers become pickles when soaked over time in vinegar brine, a practice that seems to be about 4,000 years old. You may hate cucumbers but love pickles—not unusual since the transformation is something like that between Jekyll and Hyde.

Leave it to no less a personage than Thomas Jefferson to deftly combine pickles and fishing. He once said, "On a hot day in Virginia, I know of nothing more comforting than a fine spiced pickle, brought up troutlike from the sparkling depths of that aromatic jar below the stairs in Aunt Sally's cellar." Testify, Tom.

MYTHIC HAUNTS

Philippe, the Original

Established by Philippe Mathieu in 1908, it's one of the oldest and best loved restaurants in Los Angeles. On any given day, the long counter is packed with French dip lovers waiting to bite into the original. Don't worry about having to wait—they're used to moving a small army through the place and speeding the orders right along with a smile.

The restaurant claims the distinction of having created the French dipped sandwich—by accident, it turns out. Mathieu got a little help from the law back on that fateful day in 1918. The French roll for a policeman's lunch order accidentally fell into a roasting pan filled with hot beef juice. The cop told Philippe not to worry— he would take the sandwich "as is." Well, that officer was back like a shot the next day with some of his pals, asking for one of those "dipped sandwiches."

Freeway construction back in 1951 bumped Philippe's restaurant to its present Alameda Street location. It feels like it hasn't changed a bit since. Ask for hard-boiled eggs and try their home-made lemonade, potato salad, cole slaw and hot mustard. Also, if you've never tried pig's feet, here's your chance—they serve about 300 pounds of the little fellas per week. A final tip: Don't ask for ketchup—it has never been served at Philippe.

Rocky Mountain Oysters

Never tried this infamous prairie delicacy? Well, here's where to go, pard: On I-17, between Phoenix and Flagstaff, Arizona, you'll find the home of the Hogs 'n' Heat BBQ & Nut Fry. Every last Saturday of the month, the Rock Springs Cafe, an honest-to-goodness ol'-time saloon and stagecoach stop, serves up an All-U-Can-Eat Testicle Festival.

Less adventurous hombres are encouraged to swing on in regardless. The beer's ice cold, and the regular chow is fantastic. Rock Springs' World Famous Penny's Pies are alone worth the drive from anywhere. Be sure to check out the trading posts and say hello to Jerry, who operates the mining equipment and curio shop. He's a wealth of knowledge about gold prospecting, and he sells claims in the area.

A one-horse town? Let's put it this way: As you exit the cafe, a sign declares: You Are Now Leaving Rock Springs. Likewise catching your eye, as you ponder the items you've just swilled—for reasons not entirely clear to you—are signs making such observations as: A Wise Monkey Never Monkeys With Another Monkey's Monkey. [???!]

Blue Dun

Another Philly original (probably). The apocryphal hoary hoagie origin story tells of the Italian ship builders on Hog Island who came to be know as "hoggies." Lunch was invariably a wet mess o' coldcuts and cheese on a fresh roll. Man and sandwich became one. Sub, Dagwood, Grinder (heated), Hero—you can tell where a guy's from by what he calls one of these big luscious stinkies.

The Philadelphia Cheese Steak

Down on 9th Street in South Philly is where you'll find Pat's King Of Steaks, the original home of this American classic. Pat Olivieri and his brother Harry started with a hot dog stand about 1930—the start of the Great Depression. Business was so good they couldn't get away from the place. For lunch they'd have a cabbie friend pick up some steaks, which they grilled up their own way. The cabbie was getting tired of hot dogs too—he wanted one of those special steaks for himself. The brothers were like, "Hey, this is our dinner," but the guy insisted. *Ba-da-bing, ba-da-boom*: a new item was on the menu.

Frank Olivieri, Pat's son, owns the place now and runs it with the help of his son, Frank Jr. Frank was born across the street (in a building he now owns) and started working at the store when he was 11—peeling corn and making change using one of those coin belts. "When people come to Philly," he says, "they visit Pat's, the Liberty Bell, and Betsy Ross's house—in that order. Don't ask for a menu—don't have one." But customers are keenly aware of the legacy. "They come to grab all the hot peppers they can and sometimes rip off a salt shaker so they can say they got it from Pat's."

Philly-Speak tip: Ask for a "chee wi" or "peppah chee wi" (pepper cheese steak with onions), and don't order your cheese fries at the wrong window.

The Noble Hot Dog

Every guy knows that there's only one place to get the world's greatest dog—at your local ballpark. Period.

Royal Red Humpy

COLEMAN CAMPING GEAR

For almost 100 years the Coleman name has been associated with the Great Outdoors. Dragging out your cookstove or lantern starts the blood going—these things mean you're getting ready to go howl at the moon. Campers, explorers, miners and fishermen have long depended on Coleman gear with their lives.

The Coleman Lamp—William C. Coleman was a Kansas schoolteacher who knew a good thing when he saw it. One evening around the turn of the century he was walking through a small town in Alabama. Passing a drugstore, he was amazed at the light given off from a lamp in the window. Called the Efficient Lamp, it was made by the Irby-Gilliland Company of Memphis, and operated with that now familiar (but still mysterious) cloth wick. The wick, or "mantle," invented by Karl Auer Von Welsbach in 1885, is the heart of the operation but don't expect any details here— the damn thing is a puzzler.

Electrical light was spreading across the country, but Coleman knew he had a winner to fill in many gaps. He bought the rights, made some improvements, and by 1905 was manufacturing his own Coleman Arc Lamps in Wichita, Kansas.

The Coleman Stove—Next time you're out in the woods enjoying a hot meal off your camp stove, remember to rub your beard and give thanks. The story goes that around 1910 a local barber who owned one of W.C.'s lamps asked if the burner could be adapted to heat a pan of water for shaving. The rest, as they say. . . Check out your grandfather's gear or keep an eye out at garage sales and you might find a Coleman Model No. 1. This collector's item from 1923 is the earliest Coleman two burner.

The Coleman Cooler—Somewhere along the line some genius got the idea to make an ice chest with a ruler built into it. The folks at Igloo and Coleman aren't sure who did it first, but that's how they both make 'em. In the old days, Fish and Game distributed "legal limit" stick-on rulers for your boat so you could measure your catch. Some guys stuck them on their coolers, and that's how it started.

The Coleman Fish-N-Tackle Cooler has taken one little feature and extrapolated magnificently. The ultimate ice chest, it features a tackle tray, drink holder, cutting board and a top hatch that lets you grab a brew and keep in the cold. The hatch also lets the cooler serve as a handy live well. The introduction of this baby at fishing shows sent grown men to their knees.

Light Cahill

The Swiss army knife regularly travels into space as part of the standard equipment of the space shuttle crew. It's in the Museum of Modern Art in a permanent design exhibit. It has a reputation for design and technical excellence recognized throughout the world. And plenty of guys love to carry this cool-lookin' gadget around, open stuff up and cut with it, tighten people's doorknob screws with it, pop battery panels open with it and show it to people who need help opening wine bottles but forgot a corkscrew and are too dumb to have a Swiss army knife of their own.

Anyone who regularly carries a pocket knife knows that naked feeling when you don't have one. It's simply a matter of completeness. Have you ever left the house, patted your thigh a few blocks from home only to discover that your knife was missing, then blasted back home to get it? Then you *know*. For regular knife carriers, it's not a matter of self-defense or the feeling that you might suddenly be called upon to butcher some game or open a can of beans. . . you just know it's there.

Manufacturer Victorinox knows all about guys and tools. (They've even recently changed the mother company's name to Swiss Army Brands, Inc., so we don't have to remember that Victrola-nox thing word.) A guy's usually busy and active, building stuff and fixing VCRs and trucks and things. Swiss Army knows that if a resourceful guy doesn't have the

SWISS ARMY KNIVES

Talk about functional: it's said that you could build a house with one of these, or somebody built a house with one, or something like that. Available in specialized variations, they are mighty useful: the "Swisschamp" (above) and "Deluxe Climber" (opposite page).

Black Flying Ant

right tool handy, he'll go ahead and court disaster using the old substitution method—instead of wasting time driving and spending money to get the right tool. Swiss Army knows why a flat head screwdriver can look like somebody used it as a chisel, and they know why there can be dings in a Skilsaw that look like somebody used it as a hammer. Their knowledge is particularly acute when it comes to using a knife as a screwdriver—a situation that unfolds like this: 1–You don't have a screwdriver handy. 2–You use your good single-blade pocket knife instead. 3–You hear that sickening snap, and 4–voila! Now you *do* have a screwdriver.

The combination of tools in the Swiss army knife provides an elegant solution to this problem. The great design offers, on a flagship model, five "official" kinds of screwdrivers, pliers with wire cutter, large blade, small blade, metal saw with metal file, wood saw, wood chisel, can opener, scissors, magnifying glass, fish scaler with hook disgorger, reamer with sewing eye, toothpick, tweezers, straight pin and corkscrew and a couple of other things. With the Multiplicative Rule, that's gotta be thousands (millions?) of uses. In 1891, a guy named Karl Elsener, a German-speaking Swiss with a background in crafting razors and surgical equipment, headed a group that developed a pocketknife for the Swiss army. Later that year, a wooden-handled model contained a blade, a

screwdriver, a can opener and a punch. The soldier's knife. Technical innovations, such as utensils on the back of the knife that use the same springs as those used by the front blades without increasing the handle width, have continued, and the public now has a model of truly remarkable engineering.

Testimonials are widespread. And the more adventuresome your lifestyle, the more uses the knife provides. It's been to the poles, across the deserts, over the seas and into the jungles. If you've ever been camping, you know one of the little suckers is totally indispensable. It's one of the few things that lets a guy get away with actually using a bloated word like indispensable. At times, the Swiss army knife has meant the difference between life and death. Adventurer Sir Ranulph Fiennes, during an assault by terrorists in Oman in 1968, lived to report that he unjammed the magazine of his rifle using a Swiss army knife. On a British expedition up Mount Everest in 1975, Doug Scott used a Swiss army knife to clear the ice-clogged oxygen system of his fellow climber Dougal Haston, thus allowing him to reach the summit.

Chain one of these puppies to your keychain, and she'll never stray. Luckily they're affordable, because as far as things a man has to take to the proverbial desert island, they're tied for second with your dog, behind yer lady. What a beauty.

BUCK KNIVES

An outdoorsman has at least a handful —and probably a bunch—of knives. A number of them are probably Buck knives, or imitators of Buck knives. Right now, your outdoorsman's likely got a reliable all-around Buck on him; another in his glove compartment; a new one in his wife's glove compartment; one or two in his tackle box; an old beat-up one in his toolbox and an even older, more beat-up one in the bottom of a sock drawer with his grandfather's fingerprints worn into the wooden handle. Regular guys might have only one or two, but they cherish them nonetheless. The Buck knife carries memories of when we first learned to fish. And it also carries tradition 'cause the first new knife you bestow upon junior is likely to be a Buck, tough and substantial.

The Buck knife story is an all-American one. Hoyt Buck was an apprentice blacksmith in Leavenworth, Kansas, about the turn of the century. He was experimenting with different steels and tempering techniques to improve grub hoes, i.e., agricultural tools. Using castoff rasps, he hit upon a special tempering technique with high-carbon steel, which forged a durable blade that wasn't brittle. Over time, the quality of these grub hoes led to requests for knives made of the same material, and the first edge-holding Buck knives were produced.

Hoyt bounced into the insurance business, lumberjacking and raising a family, and wound up during World War II as a millwright in Mountain Home, Idaho. He began making knives in his basement to donate to the nearby Army air base, where they became a prized possession. And so the fame of "Buck's knives" spread with the men in the armed forces.

After moving to San Diego, Hoyt and his son, Al, started selling knives via local stores and mail order, and gradually professional sportsmen began writing in for purchases and offer suggestions. It's funny how quality can evolve into a legend. With an array of models sporting varying adornments and blade shapes, the Buck tradition is carried on by grandson/president Chuck and great-grandson/VP Charles (C.J.), who craft and personally field-test these beautiful, highly useful pieces of equipment, loved and collected worldwide.

Kaufmann Olive Hare's Ear™

BOWIE KNIVES

There are conflicting reports on the origin of the Bowie knife, the favorite weapon and tool of frontiersmen of the American West. This is great, because it offers terrific opportunities to spin elaborate yarns about one horse thief or another. One *relatively* substantiated report appears below.

This tale speaks of Rezin P. Bowie (1793-1841), who, after slamming a *pre*-Bowie knife into a wild heifer, severely sliced up three of his fingers. He directed a Louisiana blacksmith, Jesse Cliffe, to make a knife that would not slip in the hand. The resulting implement had a pronounced guard between the blade and the handle, more curve than normal near the tip of the blade, and was better balanced for throwing. The knife was a success, particularly in hunting, and demand for it rose. After Bowie's brother James used it effectively in 1827, in a fight on a sandbar in the Natchez stretch of the west Mississippi, it's reputation was solid. Even British manufacturers knocked out large quantities to sell on the American frontier. The blade could vary from nine to 18 inches in length, with handle varieties including wood and bone.

Another tale waxes about a fateful night on a Mississippi riverboat in 1832 near storied Natchez, again regarding a James Bowie. This account introduces James simply as the inventor of the Bowie knife, and later a hero at the Alamo. He was among the spectators at an onboard poker match, a game he immediately saw was rigged. Watched a poor young fella lose a bundle of money that wasn't his, James did, and helped keep him from jumping overboard when the kid tapped out. James returned to the table and got into a game with the three gamblers. Soon the table was piled high with the less-common presidents. James noticed that a card flicked almost imperceptibly out from one of the gambler's sleeves. Just about simultaneously, James ripped an enormous knife from his shirt with one hand and grabbed the guy's arm with the other. "Show your hand!" he cried. "If it contains more than five cards I shall kill you!" The stiff flinched, but James' grasp did not. He twisted the man's wrist and down dropped six cards: four aces, a queen and a jack.

"I shall take the pot," announced James, "with a legitimate poker hand: four kings and a 10." Some $70,000 would allow James to give the $50,000 back that the sucker kid had lost, and still keep $20,000.

"Just who the devil are you, anyway?" questioned the gambler.

"I am James Bowie."

According to an old account of the incident: "The voice was like velvet. But it cut like steel into the hearts of the chief gambler's confederates and deterred them from any purpose or impulse they might have had to interfere. They, with the crowd, shrank back from the table, smitten with terror by the name. Bowie softly swept the banknotes into his hat and lightly clapped it on his head."

(Above) The Duke model Buck knife. Alas, she's named so because she's part of the royalty line Buck offers, like the Prince model, Duke model, etc. It is sweet to imagine she's named after the real Duke though, so go ahead and imagine she is if you own one. . .

Yellow Humpy

CORRY'S SLUG & SNAIL DEATH

If there's any sweet opportunity this book affords it is to sing the praises of Corry's Slug & Snail Death. Now here's a product that speaks directly to a man. Got a problem with garden pests? Well, what better solution than Corry's Slug & Snail Death? The sheer audacity of the product name is remarkable. It carries a pure, no-nonsense, unabashed, unmatched guarantee: This stuff doesn't discourage, annoy or repel—*it's death.* Indispensable for any gardener or landowner.

If that weren't enough, just look at the box art— giant mutant marauding snails seemingly caught in the instant before nuclear annihilation. While a huge red fireball from an atomic blast looms behind, the lead snail has this wonderfully confused look. From the position of his (apparent) lower lip one can tell just what he's saying, his last words being, "What th'. . . . ?!"

How many people would you figure have one of those familiar blue and yellow cans kicking around somewhere? Try 80 percent of American households. . . *yowza!* Now you might think to yourself, OK, sure, I've got a can, everybody's got a can, so how much of a product can you sell if everyone already has it? After all, a little squirt goes a long way and I've been using the one in my garage for I don't know how long and it's gotta be months since I lost that little red applicator straw. So how much can they sell? Try over a million cans each week!

WD-40 was created for the aerospace industry in 1953 by the Rocket Chemical Company of San Diego, California. Norm Larson and some local investors had started the company in order to develop a line of rust-resisting and rust-removing products. The defense contractor Convair asked Larson and his team for a protective rust inhibitor to coat the skins of their missiles. After 40 attempts, they succeeded in designing the water displacement formulation they were after, hence the name WD-40. It just happens to be one of those situations (like with the cereal Product 19) where the product names itself in the lab and is so catchy that it bypasses the advertising and marketing boys altogether.

After a few years of great feedback, particularly from WD-40's use on NASA's Atlas missile, Larson began to believe that an aerosol version might be a hit with the public. He was probably inspired by company employees who were sneaking the stuff home to use on their cars and door locks. By 1960, Rocket Chemical was selling WD-40 from the trunks of salesmens' cars, and the company swelled to seven employees. WD-40 was a hit and Rocket decided to run with it. They phased out their other products and, in 1969, became simply WD-40 Company, Inc. In 1993 they

When I contacted Ken Matson, the son of founder E.M. Matson, he figured, pretty rightly, that I was nuts. Trying to keep him from hanging up on me was like playing a bass on a three-weight. But he eventually agreed to take a look at the book's outline. Then, hesitantly, I dropped the question I was sure would confirm any doubts about my sanity: I was a real fan of his product's box art—would he consider licensing it for a shirt? "Hell, you want a shirt? I'll send you a shirt," he replied. Rapture, unbound respect and gratitude, Ken, you beauty.

broke $100 million in sales—just in time for their 40th anniversary—and today sell worldwide, in close to 150 countries.

Yes, but how is it as a dessert topping?

Part of the lore of WD-40 is the increasingly bizarre uses people. . . OK, guys. . . keep finding for it. Following are a few examples:

AMA Meets AAA—There have

been a number of claims about the medicinal qualities of WD-40 (none endorsed or encouraged by the company, of course). The most common is as a treatment for arthritis. Folks swear that a little spray job on the knees and elbows loosens them right up. The product has been recommended in medical journals, but only as a cure for appendages stuck in tub faucets and bottles. A case report from the Stanford School of Medicine told how WD-40 won out in extraction properties over soapy water, oil, ice and petroleum jelly.

WD-40 Saves Bird's Life!—A

woman in California with a mouse problem kept a bunch of those rodent-catching sticky trays around the place (*yech*) but caught her parakeet instead. The vet had a ready can of WD-40 and performed a successful goo-offemy.

WD-40 Cures Sex Problems!—

Here's another extraction problem. A man (another California resident, naturally) reported a unique case of *Felix interruptis*. A neighbor's cat snuck into his yard and was quickly and firmly locked in an intimate embrace with his own cat. Much as he tried, he couldn't pull them apart and the cats certainly weren't offering him any assistance. A carefully aimed shot of WD-40 did just the trick. (Word is this resourceful gentleman still has most of the flesh on his arms and face.)

A Georgia resident told the following tale from his college days: "One of my fellow residents (whom I shall call Fred) was enamored of a certain young lady, who returned his affections enthusiastically, repeatedly, and often—but always late at night. The dorm residents were soon complaining of the loud and incessant caterwauling of Fred's bedspring. I was consulted, a plan conceived, and the deed done. Yes indeed, we sneaked into Fred's room, removed the mattress, and thoroughly doused the bedspring with WD-40. Not another sound was heard, and the bloom of youth and vigor soon returned to the cheeks of us all—all that is but Fred, who continued sleepless but without complaint."

WD-40 Catches Fish!—Any fish-

erman will tell you that WD-40 is a must when it comes to caring for your tackle. Saltwater gear in particular needs a freshwater rinse and a few shots of WD-40 in the reel and along the rod. There are a lot of guys, probably the same ones who use spark plugs for weights, who spray the stuff on their bait too. Catfish are said to love it on a nightcrawler.

WD-40 Saves a Big Dumb Naked Guy!—A burglary suspect was

trapped while (allegedly, sure, right, whatever) trying to break into a Denver cafe. He removed his clothes to try to skinny down a 14-inch vent pipe but got stuck with his hands on the roof and his toes dangling over a dishwasher. He had been there about five hours by the time employees discovered him in the morning. Police were unable to pull out the 6-foot-2, 175-pound suspect. Firefighters arriving on the scene doused him with WD-40 and were finally able to yank him out. The suspect naturally skipped the thank-yous and called for a lawyer.

It's been said that man's first discovery was fire, and it follows that an invention to easily make it would become tremendously valuable. So how excited would a caveman have been if he'd been given a Zippo lighter with a pinup girl carved in it? Pretty darn grunting excited, to be sure.

The noble George G. Blaisdell made the first practical windproof lighter back in 1932. It was square-cornered and formed from rectangular brass tubing. Top and bottom pieces were soldered to the hollowed tubing to form the lid and bottom of the case. The hinge was soldered on the outside and chrome-plated. The prototype was pretty impressive, simple and reliable. Since 1932, Zippo has manufactured more than 250 million windproof lighters.

Over time, decorative lines, customer logos, new materials (even 14 karat gold), the

demand on the battlefield. . . [it] is the most coveted thing in the army." These older models, and virtually all others, have become serious collector's items. Working so flawlessly and handsomely in your palm, these beauties have become symbols of American excellence.

ZIPPO LIGHTERS

presidential seal, Civil War motifs, D-Day commemorative designs and yes, even pinup girls, have been added to personalize this handy gem. What owner isn't proud to swing the lid open and light a pretty lady's cigarette with one?

Interestingly, due to shortages of brass and chrome during World War II, cases were made of a porous steel and painted with a black crackle finish. Zippo's entire production was distributed to army exchanges and naval ships' stores, and noted war correspondent Ernie Pyle reported, "The Zippo lighter is in great

Zippo Windproof Lighter
ANATOMY

EYELET
CAM SPRING
CAM
CAM RIVET
PLATE
INSIDE CASE
RAYON BALLS
FELT PAD
FLINT
SPRING TIP
FLINT SPRING
SCREW
BRASS LID
HINGES
HINGE PIN
BRASS BOTTOM CASE

WICK
FLINT WHEEL
FLINT WHEEL RIVET
TUBE INSERT
TUBE

Although the Zippo windproof lighter has a very simple working mechanism, its construction is quite intricate.

It consists of 22 parts and requires 108 manufacturing operations.

STREAMERS
Egg Sucking Leech

Whitlock's Near Nuff Crayfish™

NAME YOUR BOAT, PLANE,

Amberjack (Mr. Peabody's gaff rig skiff) & Lenore (Mr. Peabody's mermaid)

Araner (John Ford's 110 ft. ketch named for the Aran Islands off Galway)

Argosy (John Ford's production company)

Asta (Scottie in *The Thin Man*)

Betsy (Col. Davy Crockett's long rifle)

Bob (John Wesley Hardin's horse, which he rode to death over 100 miles in order to see his wife. Said Hardin, "I got home about four A.M. but forever ruined a good horse worth $50 or so. The sight of my wife recompensed me for the loss of old Bob.")

Buck (Gable's St. Bernard in *Call Of The Wild*)

Ceres, Pallas, Juno, Vesta (The first four asteroids)

Clyde (Clint's orangutan pal in *Any Which Way You Can*)

Cochise (the Duke's horse in *El Dorado*)

Copperfin (Sub in *Destination Tokyo*)

Cul de Sac (the bronc Yakima Canutt rode to win his first rodeo championship of the world)

Dollar (the Duke's horse)

Fala (FDR's black Scottie dog)

Fido (no less than Abraham Lincoln is credited for first naming his dog Fido, which ever since has vied with Rover, George Washington's dog's name, as the most popular moniker for our cold-nosed buddies.)

Gidyap (freakish sway back horse featured in *The Little Rascals* shorts, among others)

HMS Lydia (Capt. Hornblower's ship)

Lady (Gary Cooper's horse that won't be passed in *Friendly Persuasion*)

Little Jewel (Ed "Big Daddy" Roth's first named ride—a 1930 Ford Model A two-door sedan with overhead V-8 Olds engine & tranny)

Lulubelle (tank in *Sahara*)

Mandan (trapper boat in *The Big Sky*)

Mary Ann (B-17 in *Air Force*)

Pal (actor who often played *Lassie*)

Pard (the "deadman's dog" from *High Sierra*—a good name to avoid)

Phoenix (from *Flight of the Phoenix,* of course)

Picadilly Lily (Gregory Peck's B-17 in *Twelve O'Clock High*)

Sammy (the Duke's horse in *Lady Takes A Chance*)

Santana (Bogie's beautiful yawl, which he named after the boat in *Key Largo*)

Scirocco, Zaca (Errol Flynn's sailboats)

Soledad (Harry Carey Jr.'s horse)

Straddler (Bill Pickett's bulldogging horse)

Sunny (Harry Carey's Jr.'s horse)

The Matilda (early tank)

Tom, Dick or Harry (tunnel names for real-life Great Escape in 1943)

Traveller (Gen. Lee's horse)

We're Here (fishing schooner in *Captains Courageous*)

Werewolf One (the Great Santini's jet)

Wild Goose II (the Duke's converted mine sweeper)

Wonderboy (the bat in *The Natural*)

DOG OR HORSE APPENDIX

Matuka

John Ford's masterpiece,
Stagecoach, *was based on the short story "Stage to Lordsburg,"
by Ernest Haycox. It is reproduced here from* Colliers *magazine,
where it first appeared April 10, 1937.*

STAGE TO LORDSBURG

by Ernest Haycox

This was one of those years in the Territory when Apache smoke signals spiraled up from the stony mountain summits, and many a ranch house lay as a square of blackened ashes on the ground and the departure of a stage from Tonto was the beginning of an adventure that had no certain happy ending. . . .

The stage and its six horses waited in front of Weilner's store on the north side of Tonto's square. Happy Stuart was on the box, the ribbons between his fingers and one foot teetering on the brake; and John Strang rode shotgun guard, and an escort of 10 cavalrymen waited behind the coach, half asleep in their saddles.

At 4:30 in the morning this high air was quite cold, though the sun had begun to flush the sky eastward. A small crowd stood in the square, presenting their final messages to the passengers now entering the coach. There was a girl going down to marry an infantry officer, a whiskey drummer from Kansas City, an Englishman all length and bony corners and bearing with him an enormous sporting rifle, a gambler, a solid-shouldered cattleman on his way to New Mexico and a slim blond man upon whom both Happy Stuart and the shotgun guard placed a narrow-eyed interest.

This seemed all until the blond man drew back from the coach door; and then a girl known commonly throughout the Territory as Henriette came quietly from the crowd. She was small and quiet, with a touch of paleness in her cheeks, and her dark eyes lifted at the blond man's unexpected courtesy, showing him a faint surprise. There was this small moment of delay and then the girl caught up her dress and stepped into the coach.

Men in the crowd were smiling, but the blond one turned, his motion like the swift cut of a knife, and his sharp attention covered that group until the smiling quit. He was tall, lean-flanked, and definitely stamped by the guns slung low on his hips. But it wasn't the guns alone; something in his face, so watchful and so smooth, showed his trade. Afterward he got into the coach and slammed the door.

Happy Stuart kicked off the brakes and yelled: "Hi!" Tonto's people were calling out their last farewells and the six horses broke into a trot and the stage lunged on its fore-and-aft springs and rolled from town with dust dripping off its wheels like water, the cavalrymen trotting briskly behind. So they tipped down the long grade, bound on a journey no stage had attempted during the last 45 days.

Out below in the desert's distance stood the relay stations they hoped to reach and pass. Between lay a country swept empty by the quick raids of Geronimo's men.

The Englishman, the gambler and the blond man sat jammed together in the forward seat, riding backward to the course of the stage. The drummer and the cattleman occupied the uncomfortable middle bench; the two women shared

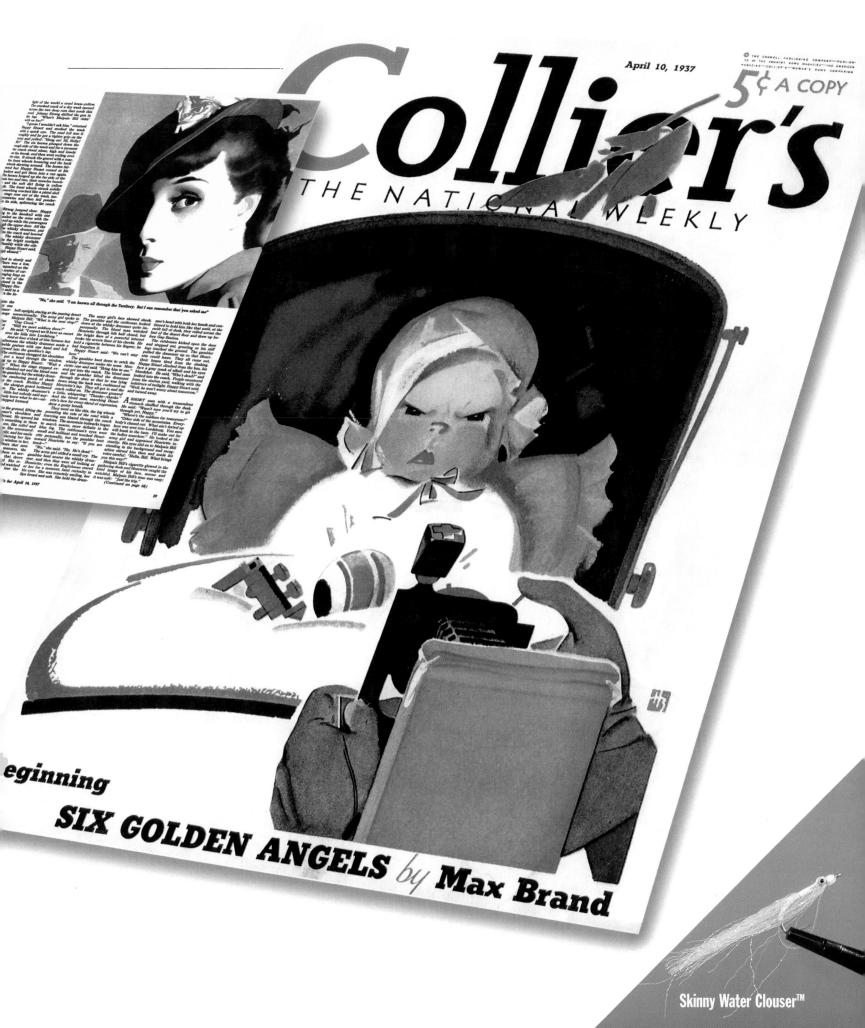

the rear seat. The cattleman faced Henriette, his knees almost touching her. He had one arm hooked over the door's window sill to steady himself. A huge gold nugget slid gently back and forth along the watch chain slung across his wide chest, and a chunk of black hair lay below his hat. His eyes considered Henriette, reading some-

thing in the girl that caused him to show her a deliberate smile. Henriette dropped her glance to the gloved tips of her fingers, cheeks unstirred.

They were all strangers packed closely together, with nothing in common save a destination. Yet the cattleman's smile and the boldness of his eyes were something as audible as speech, noted by everyone except the Englishman, who sat bolt upright in his corner, covered by a stony indifference. The army girl, tall and calmly pretty, threw a quick side glance at Henriette and afterward looked away with a touch of color. The gambler saw this interchange of glances and showed the cattleman an irritated attention. The whisky drummer's eyes narrowed a little and some inward cynicism made a faint change on his lips. He removed his hat to show a bald head already beginning to sweat; his cigar smoke turned the coach cloudy and ashes kept dripping on his vest.

The blond man had observed Henriette's glance drop from the cattleman, and something bright disturbed his observant eyes; he tipped his hat well over his face and watched her—not boldly, but as though he were puzzled. Once her glance lifted and touched him. But he had been on guard against that, and was quick to look away.

The army girl coughed gently behind her hand, whereupon the gambler tapped the whiskey drummer on the shoulder. "Get rid of that." The drummer appeared startled. He grumbled, "Beg pardon," and tossed the cigar through the window.

All this while the coach went tearing down the ceaseless turns of the mountain road, its heavy wheels slamming through the road ruts, whining at the turns, rocking interminably on its fore-and-aft springs. Occasionally the strident yell of Happy Stuart washed back: "Hi, Nellie! Hi, yi!" The whiskey drummer braced himself against the door and closed his eyes.

Three hours from Tonto the road, making a last round sweep, let them down into the flat desert. Here the stage stopped and the men got out to stretch. The gambler spoke to the army girl, gently: "Perhaps you would find my seat more comfortable." The army girl said, "Thank you," and changed over. The cavalry sergeant rode up to the stage, speaking to Happy Stuart. "We'll be goin' back now—and good luck to ye."

The men piled in, the gambler taking the place beside Henriette. The blond man drew his long legs together to give the army girl more room, and watched Henriette's face. A hard sun beat fully on the coach and dust began to whip up like a fire smoke. Without escort they rolled across a flat earth broken only by cacti standing against a dazzling sunlight. In the far distance, behind a blue heat haze, lay the faint suggestion of mountains.

The cattleman reached up and tugged at the ends of his mustache and smiled again at Henriette. The army girl spoke to the blond man: "How far is it to the noon station?" The blond man said courteously: "Twenty miles." The gambler watched the army girl, something somber on his thin face, as though the run of her voice reminded him of things long forgotten.

The miles fell behind and the smell of alkali dust got thicker. Henriette rested against the corner of the coach, her eyes dropped to the tips of her gloves. She made an enigmatic, disinterested shape there; she seemed past stirring, beyond laughter. She was young, yet she had a knowledge that placed the cattleman and the gambler and the drummer and the army girl in their exact places; and she knew why the gambler had offered the army girl his seat. The army girl was in one world and she was in another, as everyone in the coach understood. It had no effect on her, for this was a distinction she had learned long ago. Only the blond man broke through her indifference. His name was Malpais Bill, and she could see the wildness in the corners of his eyes and in the long crease of his lips; it was a stamp that would never come off. Yet something flowed out of him toward her that was different than the predatory curiosity of other men; something gallant, something gentle.

Up on the box Happy Stuart pointed to the hazy outline two miles away. "Injuns ain't burned that anyhow." The sun was directly overhead, turning the light of the world a cruel brass-yellow. The crooked crack of a dry wash opened across the two deep ruts that made this road. Johnny Strang shifted the gun in his lap. "What's Malpais Bill ridin' with us for?"

"I guess I wouldn't ask him," returned Happy Stuart and studied the wash with a quick eye. The road fell into it roughly and he got a tighter grip on the reins and yelled: "Hang on! Hi, Nelly! Hi!" The six horses plunged down the rough side of the wash and for a moment the coach stood alone, high and lonely on the break, and then went reeling over the rim. It struck the gravel, the front wheels bouncing and the back wheels skewing around. The horses faltered but Happy Stuart cursed at his leaders and got them into a run again. The horses lunged up the far side of the wash two and two, their muscles bunching and the soft dirt flying in yellow clouds. The front wheels struck solidly and something cracked like a pistol shot as the stage rose out of the wash, teetered crosswise and then fell ponderously on its side, splintering the coach panels.

Johnny Strang jumped clear. Happy Stuart hung to the handrail with one hand and hauled on the reins with the other, and stood up while the passengers crawled through the upper door. All the men, except the whiskey drummer, put their shoulders to the coach and heaved it upright again. The whiskey drummer stood strangely in the bright sunlight, shaking his head dumbly while the others climbed back in. Happy Stuart said: "All right, brother, git aboard."

The drummer climbed in slowly and the stage ran on. There was a low, gray 'dobe relay station squatted on the desert dead ahead with a scatter of corrals about it and a flag hanging limp on a crooked pole. Men came out of the 'dobe's dark interior and stood in the shade of the porch gallery. Happy Stuart rolled up and stopped. He said to a lanky man: "Hi, Mack. Where's the Injuns?"

The passengers were filing into the 'dobe's dining room. The lanky one drawled: "You'll see 'em before tomorrow night." Hostlers came up to change horses.

The little dining room was cool after the coach, cool and still. A fat Mexican woman ran in and out with the food platters. Happy Stuart said, "Ten minutes," and brushed the alkali dust from his mouth and fell to eating.

The long-jawed Mack said: "Catlin's ranch burned last night. Was a troop of cavalry around here yesterday. Came and went. You'll git to the Gap tonight, all right, but I don't know about the mountains beyond. A little trouble?"

"A little," said Happy briefly, and rose. This was the end of rest. The passengers followed, with the whiskey drummer straggling at the rear, reaching deeply for wind. The coach

rolled away again, Mack's voice pursuing them: "Hit a lick, Happy, if you see any dust rollin' out of the east."

Heat had condensed in the coach and the little wind fanned up by the run of the horses was stifling to the lungs; the desert floor projected its white glitter endlessly away until lost in the smoky haze. The cattleman's knees bumped Henriette gently and he kept watching her, a celluloid toothpick drooped between his lips. Happy Stuart's voice ran back, profane and urgent, keeping the speed of the coach constant through the ruts. The whiskey drummer's eyes were round and strained and his mouth was open and all the color had gone out of his face. The gambler observed this without expression and without care; and once the cattleman, feeling the sag of the whiskey drummer's shoulder, shoved him away. The Englishman sat bolt upright, staring at the passing desert unemotionally. The army girl spoke to Malpais Bill: "What is the next stop?"

"Gap Creek."

"Will we meet soldiers there?"

He said: "I expect we'll have an escort over the hills into Lordsburg."

And at four o'clock of this furnace-hot afternoon the whiskey drummer made a feeble gesture with one hand and fell forward into the gambler's lap.

The cattleman shrugged his shoulders and put a head through the window, calling up to Happy Stuart: "Wait a minute." When the stage stopped, everybody climbed out and the blond man helped the gambler lay the whiskey drummer in the sweltering patch of shade created by the coach. Neither Happy Stuart nor the shotgun guard bothered to get down. The whiskey drummer's lips moved a little but nobody knew what to do—until Henriette stepped forward.

She dropped to the ground, lifting the whiskey drummer's shoulders and head against her breast. He opened his eyes and there was something in them that they could all see, like relief and ease, like gratefulness. She murmured, "You are all right," gently, and her smile was soft and pleasant, turning her lips maternal. There was this wisdom in her, this knowledge of the fears that men concealed behind their manners, the deep hungers that rode them so savagely, and the loneliness that drove them to women of her kind. She repeated, "You are all right," and watched this whiskey drummer's eyes lose the wildness of what he knew.

The army girl's face showed shock. The gambler and the cattleman looked down at the whiskey drummer quite impersonally. The blond man watched Henriette through lids half closed, but the bright flare of a power-

> **There was this wisdom in her, this knowledge of the fears that men concealed behind their manners, the deep hungers that rode them so savagely, and the loneliness that drove them to women of her kind.**

ful interest broke the severe lines of his cheeks. He held a cigarette between his fingers; he had forgotten it.

Happy Stuart said: "We can't stay here."

The gambler bent down to catch the whiskey drummer under the arms. Henriette rose and said, "Bring him to me," and got into the coach. The blond man and the gambler lifted the drummer through the door so that he was lying down along the back seat, cushioned on Henriette's lap. They all got in and the coach rolled on. The drummer groaned a little, whispering, "Thanks—thanks." And the blond man, searching Henriette's face for every shred of expression, drew a gusty breath.

They went on like this, the big wheels pounding the ruts of the road while a lowering sun blazed through the coach windows. The mountain bulwarks began to march nearer, more definite in the blue fog. The cattleman's eyes were small and brilliant and touched Henriette personally, but the gambler bent toward Henriette to say: "If you are tired—"

"No," she said. "No. He's dead."

The army girl stifled a small cry. The gambler bent nearer the whiskey drummer, and then they were all looking at Henriette; even the Englishman stared at her for a moment, faint curiosity in his eyes. She was remotely smiling, her lips broad and soft. She held the drummer's head with both her hands and continued to hold him like that until, at the swift fall of dusk, they rolled across the last of the desert floor and drew up before Gap Station.

The cattleman kicked open the door and stepped out, grunting as his stiff legs touched the ground. The gambler pulled the drummer up so that Henriette could leave. They all came out, their bones tired from the shaking. Happy Stuart climbed from the box, his face a gray mask of alkali and his eyes bloodshot. He said, "Who's dead?" and looked into the coach. People sauntered from the station yard, walking with the indolence of twilight. Happy Stuart said, "Well, he won't worry about tomorrow," and turned away.

A short man with a tremendous stomach shuffled through the dusk. He said: "Wasn't sure you'd try to git through yet, Happy."

"Where's the soldiers for tomorrow?"

"Other side of the mountains. Everybody's chased out. What ain't forted up here was sent into Lordsburg. You men will bunk in the barn. I'll make out for the ladies somehow." He looked at the army girl and appraised Henriette instantly. His eyes slid on to Malpais Bill standing in the background and

> **"Well, Lordsburg is a long ways off and the damn mountains are squirmin' with Apaches. You won't have any cavalry escort tomorrow. The troops are all in the field."**

recognition stirred him then and made his voice careful: "Hello, Bill. What brings you this way?"

Malpais Bill's cigarette glowed in the gathering dusk and Henriette caught the brief image of his face, serene and watchful. Malpais Bill's tone was easy; it was soft: "Just the trip."

They were moving on toward the frame house whose corners seemed to extend indefinitely into a series of attached sheds. Lights glimmered in the windows and men moved around the place, idly talking. The unhitched horses went away at a trot. The tall girl walked into the station's big room, to face a soldier in a disheveled uniform.

He said: "Miss Robertson? Lieutenant Hauser was to have met you here. He is at Lordsburg. He was wounded in a brush with the Apaches last night."

The tall army girl stood very still. She said: "Badly?"

"Well," said the soldier, "yes."

The fat man came in, drawing deeply for wind. "Too bad—too bad. Ladies, I'll show you the rooms, such as I got."

Henriette's dove-colored dress blended with the background shadows. She was watching the tall army girl's face whiten. But there was a strength in the army girl, a fortitude that made her think of the soldier. For she said quietly: "You must have had a bad trip."

"Nothing—nothing at all," said the soldier and left the room. The gambler was here, his thin face turning to the army girl with an odd expression, as though he were remembering painful things. Malpais Bill had halted in the doorway, studying the softness and humility of Henriette's cheeks. Afterward both women followed the fat host of Gap Station along a narrow hall to their quarters.

Malpais Bill wheeled out and stood indolently against the wall of this desert station, his glance quick and watchful in the way it touched all the men loitering along the yard, his ears weighing all the night-softened voices. Heat died from the earth and a definite chill rolled down the mountains hulking so high behind the house. The soldier was in his saddle, murmuring drowsily to Happy Stuart.

"Well, Lordsburg is a long ways off and the damn mountains are squirmin' with Apaches. You won't have any cavalry escort tomorrow. The troops are all in the field."

Malpais Bill listened to the hoof beats of the soldier's horse fade out, remembering the loneliness of a man in those dark mountain passes, and went back to the saloon at the end of the station. This was a low-ceilinged shed with a dirt floor and whitewashed walls that once had been part of a stable. Three men stood under a lantern in the middle of this little place, the light of the lantern palely shining in the rounds of their eyes as they watched him. At the far end of the bar the cattleman and the gambler drank in taciturn silence. Malpais Bill took his whiskey when the bottle came, and noted the barkeep's obscure glance. Gap's host put in his head and wheezed, "Second table," and the other men in here began to move out. The barkeep's words rubbed together, one tone above a whisper: "Better not ride into Lordsburg. Plummer and Shanley are there."

Malpais Bill's lips were stretched to the long edge of laughter and there was a shine like wildness in his eyes. He said, "Thanks, friend," and went into the dining room.

When he came back to the yard, night lay wild and deep across the desert and the moonlight was a frozen silver that touched but could not dissolve the world's incredible blackness. The girl Henriette walked along the Tonto road, swaying gently in the vague shadows. He went that way, the click of his heels on the hard earth bringing her around.

Her face was clear and strange and incurious in the night, as though she waited for something to come, and knew what it would be. But he said: "Apaches like to crawl down to a settlement and wait for strays."

She was indifferent, unafraid. Her voice was cool, and he could hear the faint loneliness in it, the fatalism that made her words so even: "There's a wind coming up, soft and good."

He took off his hat, long legs braced and his eyes quick and puzzled in their watchfulness. His blond hair glowed in the fugitive light.

She said in a deep breath: "Why do you do that?"

His lips were restless and the sing and rush of strong feelings was like a current of quick wind around him. It was that unruly. "You have folks in Lordsburg?"

She spoke in a direct, patient way as though explaining something he should have known without asking. "I have a house in Lordsburg."

"No," he said, "it wasn't what I asked."

"My folks are dead—I think. There was a massacre in the Superstition Mountains when I was very young."

He stood with his head bowed, his mind reaching back to fill in that gap of her life. There was a hardness and a rawness to this land and little sympathy for the weak. She had survived, and had paid for her survival, and she looked at him now in a silent way that offered no explanations or apologies for whatever had been, still a pretty girl, with the tragic patience of all the past years in her eyes, in the inexpressiveness of her lips.

He said: "Over in the Tonto Basin is a pretty land. Piece of a ranch of mine there yet—with a house half built."

"If that's your country why are you here?"

His lips laughed and the rashness in him glowed hot again and he seemed to grow taller in the moonlight. "A debt to collect."

"That's why you're going to Lordsburg? You will never get through collecting that kind of debt. Everybody in the Territory knows you. Once you were just a rancher. Then you tried to wipe out a grudge and then there was a bigger one to wipe out—and the debt kept growing and more men are wait-ing to kill you. Someday a man will. Run away from the debts."

His bright smile kept constant, which made her shoulders lift in resignation. "No," she murmured, "you won't run." He could see the sweetness of her lips and the way her eyes were sad for him; he could see in them the patience he had never learned.

He said, "We'd better go back," and turned her with his arm. They went across the yard in silence, hearing the under-tone of men's drawling talk roll out of the shadows, seeing the glow of men's pipes in the dark corners. Malpais Bill stopped and watched her go through the station door; she turned to look at him once more, her eyes all dark and her lips sober, and then passed down the narrow corridor to her own quar-ters. Beyond her window, in the yard, a man was murmuring to another man: "Plummer and Shanley are in Lordsburg. Malpais Bill knows it." Through the thin partition of the adjoining room she heard the army girl crying with a sup-pressed, uncontrollable regularity. Henriette stared at the dark wall, her shoulders and head bowed; and she afterward returned to the hall and knocked on the army girl's door, and went in.

Six fresh horses fiddled in front of the coach and the fat host of Gap Station came across the yard swinging a lantern against the dead, bitter black. All the passengers filed, sleep-dulled and cross, from the house. Johnny Strang slammed the express box in the boot and Happy Stuart said, "All right folks," gruffly.

The passengers climbed in. The cattleman came by and Malpais Bill drawled, "Take the corner spot, mister," and got in, closing the door. The Gap host grumbled: "If they don't jump you on the long grade you'll be all right. You're safe when you get to Al Shrieber's ranch." Happy's bronze voice shocked the black stillness and the coach lurched forward, its springs squealing.

They rode for an hour in this complete blackness, chilled and uncomfortable and half asleep, feeling the coach drag on a heavy-climbing grade. Gray dawn cracked through, fol-lowed by a sunless light rushing all across the flat desert now far below. The road looped from one barren shoulder to another and at sunup they had reached the first bench and were slamming full speed along a boulder-strewn flat. The cattleman sat in the forward corner, the left corner of his mouth swollen and crushed, and when Henriette saw that her glance slid to Malpais Bill's knuckles. The army girl had her eyes closed, her shoulders pressing against the Englishman, who remained bolt upright with the sporting gun between his knees. Beside Henriette the gambler seemed to sleep, and on the middle bench Malpais Bill watched the land go by with a thin vigilance.

At 10 they were rising again, with juniper and scrub pine showing on the slopes and the desert below them filling with the powdered haze of another hot day. By noon they reached the summit of the range and swung to follow

Muddler Minnow

hauled a .44 from a back pocket and laid it over his lap. He considered Henriette more carefully than before, his taciturnity breaking. He said: "How old are you?"

Her shoulders rose and fell, which was the only answer. But the gambler said, gently: "Young enough to be my daughter. It is a rotten world. When I call to you, lie down on the floor."

The Englishman had pulled the rifle from between his knees and laid it across the sill of the window on his side. The cattleman swept back the skirt of his coat to clear the holster of his gun.

The little flinty summit meadows grew narrower, with shoulders of gray rock closing in upon the road. The coach wheels slammed against the stony ruts and bounced high and fell again with a flat jar which the springs could not soften. Happy Stuart's howl ran steadily above this rattle and rush; fine dust turned all things gray.

Henriette sat with her eyes pinned to the gloved tips of her fingers, remembering the tall shape of Malpais Bill cut against the moonlight of Gap Station. He had smiled at her as a man might smile at any desirable woman, with the sweep and swing of laughter in his voice; and his eyes had been gentle. The gambler spoke very quietly and she didn't hear him until his fingers gripped her arm. He said again, not raising his voice: "Get down."

Henriette dropped to her knees, hearing gunfire blast through the rush and run of the coach. Happy Stuart ceased to yell and the army girl's eyes were round and dark, yet showing no fright. The walls of the canyon had tapered off. Looking upward through the window on the gambler's side, Henriette saw the weaving figure of an Apache warrior reel nakedly on a calico pony and rush by with a rifle raised and pointed in his bony elbows. The gambler took a cool aim; the stockman fired and aimed again. The Englishman's sporting rifle blasted heavy echoes through the coach, hurting her ears, and the smell of powder got rank and bitter. The blond man's boots scraped the coach top and round small holes began to dimple the paneling where the Apaches' bullets struck. An Indian came boldly abreast the coach and made a target that couldn't be missed. The cattleman dropped him with one shot. The coach hubs screamed as its wheels slewed around the sharp ruts and the whole heavy superstructure bounced high in the air. Then they were rushing down grade.

The gambler said, quietly, "You had better take this," handing Henriette his gun. He leaned against the door, with

its narrow rock-ribbed meadows. The gambler, long motionless, shifted his feet and caught the army girl's eyes.

"Shrieber's is directly ahead. We are past the worst of it."

The blond man looked around at the gambler, making no comment; and it was then that Henriette caught the smell of smoke in the windless air. Happy Stuart was cursing once more and the brake blocks began to squall. Looking through the angled vista of the window panel, Henriette saw a clay-and-rock chimney standing up like a gaunt skeleton against the day's light. The house that had been there was a black square on the ground, smoke still rising from pieces that had not been completely burned.

The stage stopped and all the men were instantly out. An iron stove squatted on the earth, with one section of pipe stuck upright to it. Fire licked lazily along the collapsed fragments of what had been a trunk. Beyond the location of the house, at the foot of a corral, lay two nude figures grotesquely bald, with deliberate knife slashes marking their bodies. Happy Stuart went over there and had his look, and came back.

"Shriebers. Well—"

Malpais Bill said: "This morning about daylight." He looked at the gambler, at the cattleman, at the Englishman, who showed no emotion. "Get back in the coach." He climbed to the coach's top, flattening himself full length there. Happy Stuart and Strang took their places again. The horses broke into a run.

The gambler said to the army girl, "You're pretty safe between those two fellows," and his small hands gripping the sill. Pallor loosened his cheeks. He said to the army girl, "Be sure to keep between those gentlemen," and looked at her in a way that was desperate and forlorn, and dropped his head to the window sill.

Henriette saw the bluff rise and close in like a yellow wall. They were rolling down the mountain without brake. Gunfire fell off and the crying of the Indians faded back. Coming up from her knees then she saw the desert's flat surface far below, with the angular pattern of Lordsburg vaguely on the far borders of the heat fog. There was no more firing and Happy Stuart's voice lifted again and the brakes were screaming on the wheels, and going off, and screaming. The Englishman stared out of the window sullenly; the army girl seemed in a deep, desperate dream; the cattleman's face was shining with a strange sweat. Henriette reached over to pull the gambler up, but he had an unnatural weight to him and slid into the far corner. She saw that he was dead.

At five o'clock that long afternoon the stage threaded Lordsburg's narrow streets of 'dobe and frame houses, came upon the center square and stopped before a crowd of people gathered in the smoky heat. The passengers crawled out stiffly. A Mexican boy ran up to see the dead gambler and began to yell his news in shrill Mexican. Malpais Bill climbed off the top, but Happy Stuart sat back on his seat and stared taciturnly at the crowd. Henriette noticed then that the shotgun messenger was gone.

A gray man in a sleazy white suit called up to Happy: "Well, you got through."

Happy Stuart said: "Yeah. We got through."

An officer stepped through the crowd, smiling at the army girl. He took her arm and said: "Miss Robertson, I believe. Lieutenant Hauser is quite all right. I will get your luggage—"

The army girl was crying then, definitely. They were all standing around, bone-weary and shaken. Malpais Bill remained by the wheel of the coach, his cheeks hard against the sunlight and his eyes riveted on a pair of men standing under the board awning of an adjoining store. Henriette observed the manner of their waiting and knew why they were here. The blond man's eyes, she noticed, were very blue, and flame burned brilliantly in them. The army girl turned to Henriette, tears still in her eyes. She murmured: "If there is anything I can ever do for you—"

But Henriette stepped back, shaking her head. This was Lordsburg and everybody knew her place—except the army girl. Henriette said formally, "Good-bye," noting how still and expectant the two men under the awning remained. She swung toward the blond man and said: "Would you carry my valise?"

Malpais Bill looked at her, laughter remote in his eyes, and reached into the luggage pile and got her battered valise. He was still smiling as he went beside her, through the crowd and past the two waiting men. But when they turned into an anonymous and dusty little side street of the town, where the houses all sat shoulder to shoulder without grace or dignity, he had turned sober. He said: "I am obliged to you. But I'll have to go back there."

They were in front of a house no different from its neighbors; they had stopped at its door. She could see his eyes travel this street and comprehend the kind of traffic it bore. But he was saying in that gentle tone: "I have watched you for two days."

He stopped, searching his mind to find the thing he wanted to say. It came out swiftly: "God made you a woman. The Tonto is a pretty country."

Her answer was quite barren of feeling. "No. I am known all through the Territory. But I can remember that you asked me."

He said: "No other reason?" She didn't answer, but something in her eyes pulled his face together. He took off his hat and it seemed to her he was looking through this hot day to that far-off country and seeing it fresh and desirable. He murmured: "A man can escape nothing. I have this chore to do. But I will be back."

He went along the narrow street, made a quick square turn at the end of it, and disappeared. Heat rolled like a heavy wave over Lordsburg's housetops and the smell of dust was very sharp. She lifted her valise—and dropped it. And stood like that, mute and grave before the door of her dismal house. She was remembering how tall he had been against the moonlight at Gap Station.

There were four swift shots beating furiously along the sultry quiet, and a shout, and afterward a longer and longer silence. She put one hand against the door to steady herself, and knew that those shots marked the end of a man and the end of a hope. He would never come back; and he would never stand over her in the moonlight with that gentle smile on his lips and with the swing of life in his casual tone. She was thinking all that, humbly and with the patience life had beaten into her. . . .

She was thinking all that when she heard the strike of boots on the street's packed earth; and turned to see him, high and square in the muddy sunlight, coming toward her with his smile.

> He murmured:
> "A man can escape
> nothing. I have
> this chore to do.
> But I will be back."

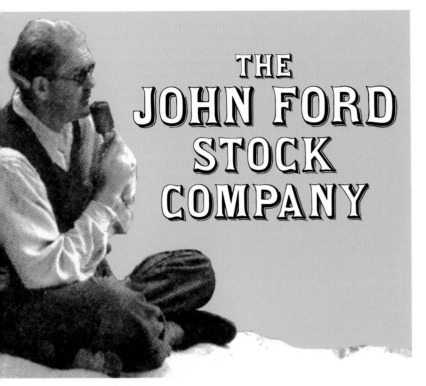

THE JOHN FORD STOCK COMPANY

mending him to Carl Laemmle, the head of Universal. (Laemmle is supposed to have said, "He yells good and loud—he'll make a good director.") The films Ford and Carey made together were the proving ground where Ford developed his style. Charles Russell and Will Rogers (his ranch was just down the road) were regulars at the Carey ranch in California.

JOHN WAYNE—Wayne claimed that while many people had directed his films, John Ford directed his life. He deemed "'Pappy' Ford the greatest storyteller he ever knew and *She Wore a Yellow Ribbon* his favorite film. It's easy to understand why westerns hold so much appeal: the "taming of the West" represents on a more immediate level the dreams, fears, challenges, romance, heartbreak—and breakneck ambition—that forged the first expansionist American colonies. Drawing on real and imagined exploits, the western adventure stories of guys like Owen Wister, Jack London, Zane Grey, Max Brand and Louis L'Amour created our very own red-blooded American fiction. The Duke was the latest and greatest incarnation of the American western star. Wayne's persona was built on a legacy of pioneer tough guy actors like Bronco Billy Anderson, William S. Hart and particularly Harry Carey, Sr., to whom he owed and often acknowledged his greatest debt. Ford told Duke to study everything about Carey—his walk and talk, how he rode a horse and where he put his hands.

JOHN FORD—AKA Pappy, Pop, The Old Man, Coach. Called "terrifying," "sadistic" and "cruel," he was known to introduce himself: "My name's John Ford. I make westerns." He made the best in the world. An incredible memory allowed him to keep even the minutest details of a film in his head. Ford often said that *Wagonmaster* was his favorite, but that might been another way to zing the Duke, who wasn't in it. He reveled in the role of manipulator and puppet master. If Ford got pissed off at a botched line or whatever, he would stop everything, drag his victim to the center of the crew, tell him to bend over, then kick him in the ass. He would bully and bark, but always from behind dark tinted glasses. The glasses covered eyes that were unmistakably kind, warm and sentimental. Ford knew they could destroy his credibility as a mean old bastard.

HARRY CAREY, SR.—Carey was born 1878 in New York City, in a rural section way uptown that later became Harlem. He earned the distinction of being expelled from New York University by stealing some bloomers from the madam of a local whorehouse

and running them up the flagpole. Coming West with D.W. Griffith's company, he helped start Ford's directing career by recom-

CHIEF JOHN BIG TREE—The Seneca tribesman, born in 1875, is shown here as Blue Back in *Drums Along The Mohawk* (1939). In 1912 he posed for the Indian head nickel, and in 1915 started his prolific acting career. Chief Big Tree became a Ford regular after appearing as the Cheyenne chief in *The Iron Horse* (1924). He performed as a stuntman with Yakima Canutt in *Stagecoach* and is probably best known as Pony That Walks in *She Wore A Yellow Ribbon* (1949). In that film he tells the Duke that they are "too old for war" and should instead "smoke pipe, shoot buffalo, get drunk together. . . Hallelujah!"

WARD BOND—Jack Ford on Bond: "Let's face it, Bond is a shit. But he's my favorite shit!" The Duke's football pal at the University of Southern California, Bond appeared in every Ford film in which the Duke starred. The 6' 4," 220-lb. Trojan tackle was one of the few—perhaps the only—guy on the set who didn't fear the often domineering director and would even piss him off just for sport. Ford loved it. The Nebraska-born, bellowing Bond left us way too early in

1960 at the age of 57, but went out at the top. He loved his starring role in television's "Wagon Train," a show that at the time was killing the competition. Interviewed shortly before his death, Bond said, "Heck, I'm ready to play Major Seth Adams the rest of my life."

HARRY CAREY, JR.—"Dobe" was so nicknamed by his father for his adobe brick colored hair. He was born on his famous dad's ranch, then electricity-free, under light provided by a Model T Ford truck. His was a childhood of horses, Navajo friends and famous visitors. "Uncle Jack" Ford told him on his first picture, "You're going to hate me when this movie is over, but you're going to give a great performance." The film was *3 Godfathers*, a remake of *Marked Men*, which Ford had made with Harry Carey, Sr., many years before. When the Duke complimented him on his work, Dobe asked if he'd ever hear as much from Ford. The Duke said, "No—he won't tell ya. He won't ever tell ya." Then the Wayne grin. "But ya' jes might work fer the old bastard again." In Dobe's first film with the Duke, his character got trampled to death by stampeding cattle—it was Howard Hawk's great sagebrush version of *Mutiny on the Bounty, Red River* (1948). Dobe played a terrific Sheriff in the recent *Tombstone*.

VICTOR McLAGLEN—Jack Ford cruelly manipulated a performance out of McLaglen for his role as the swaggering ape Gypo Nolan in *The Informer*. Ford would get McLaglen shit-faced on Irish whiskey in the evening, then rouse him in the morning with new lines. Humiliating him on the set was a regular occurrence. Years later, McLaglen

swapped Ford war stories with Dobe: "Vic: Mean to ya', was he? Dobe: Oh God, yes. Very mean. Vic: Yeah-yeah-yeah. I know, lad, I know. He's a sadist he is. A sadist." From all accounts, McLaglen was in real life very much like the cavalry sergeant he often played. After all, how could he not be? He has a typically great moment in *She Wore A Yellow Ribbon* when prepping the troops for a march. He stops to pet an obvious mongrel and says, "Nice dog. . . nice dog," then declares with a prideful sniff, "Irish Setter." It was one of those bits that Ford often thought up on the spot, but Carey has a hilarious story in his book, *The Company of Heroes*, about how the scene came together. Nothing beats the firsthand account from the guy who was there—get the book; it's priceless.

BEN JOHNSON—A true sure 'nuff Oklahoma ranch cowboy and world champion roper, Johnson was known to say, "I was a cowboy from the time my feet hit the ground." He came to Hollywood in 1939, when delivering some of his father's horses to Howard Hughes. The money from horse work, stunts and doubling for guys like Wayne and Jimmy Stewart kept him around, not any love of acting. Still, he

conveyed strength on the screen in his easygoin' shy way—he had the face of a man you could depend on. Ford saw it and brought it out of him. "That John Ford, I worked for him for six years. I mean, he was a mean old bastard, but if you listened to him, you could learn something. . . The last words Ford ever said to me was, 'Ben, don't forget to stay real.' I think that's pretty good advice anywhere."

JOHN CARRADINE—A veteran actor of countless films from great to gawdawful, Carradine had a hide that was uncommonly impervious to the wrath of Ford, as he shrugged off attacks with a smile. His stand-out Ford performances are in *Stagecoach* and *The Grapes of Wrath*. He's been great in so many films—check out *Son of Fury* with Tyrone Power and the always luscious Gene Tierney or *Captains Courageous*. One of Carradine's most hilarious roles came as the oily undertaker in the Duke's final film, *The Shootist*—with that classic gallows humor line of his: "The early worm gets the bird."

MILDRED NATWICK—Natwick was terrific as the Widow Tillane—a right-propertied woman for Squire Danaher ("And the best man in Innisfree, as if I didn't know it!"). She invariably offered solid support as the matriarch in films like *She Wore A Yellow Ribbon* and *3 Godfathers*.

BARRY FITZGERALD—Born William Joseph Shields in Dublin in 1888, he was past 40 before his acting career really got started. When he died (a Protestant!) in 1961, the beloved Fitzgerald got the kind of send-off reserved for heads of state. The man could pull off more scene stealing business by just lighting his pipe than most could throughout an entire picture. His incarnation of the whiskey-filled bookmaker/matchmaker Michaeleen Oge Flynn in *The Quiet Man* is a thing of beauty to be sure, laddie. His awe-struck reaction to the destroyed wedding bed is one of the most repeated lines in history: "Impetuous. . . Ho-omeric. . . " (This bit was actually banned in Ohio.)

Byford Zonker Purple Black™

FRANCIS FORD—Jack's brother was a silent screen star who gave his brother his start in the business.

KEN CURTIS—When Roy Rogers left his slot as lead singer with the Sons of the Pioneers, Curtis took over. Later, Curtis married Ford's daughter, Barbara. Ford loved music, and a son-in-law who could beautifully sing his favorites (like "I'll Take You Home Again, Kathleen" in *Rio Grande*) set just fine with the director. His goofy Charlie McCorry role in *The Searchers* led to his classic Festus character.

MAUREEN O'HARA—This fiery amazon was the only gal with the brass and stature to match the Duke. One story has it that some joker told Errol Flynn about a new Irish beauty on the lot who just loved to have her breasts touched. Flynn went up to her and tried it out—O'Hara decked him. Ford first directed her in the beautiful black-and-white film of *How Green Was My Valley*—whose Welsh coal mining village was constructed in Malibu. O'Hara later dazzled in the Technicolor location shots around Ireland for *The Quiet Man*.

HANK WORDEN—"You were born old!" is how the Duke describes Worden's character, Ole Mose Harper, in *The Searchers*. But when the crazy-sounding Worden stumbles shirtless and half-dead into the Duke's "rockin' chair," you can't help but notice the body on him—the guy looks like he could kick some serious butt.

ANDY DEVINE—When Devine was a kid in Flagstaff, he somehow fell when he had a stick in his mouth, damaging his vocal chords—it was an accident that helped launch a career. There are a number of distinctive voices that guys love, like Edward Everett Horton's (the narrator of "Fractured Fairy Tales") and Bill Ward's (Bullwinkle), but when it comes to just plain crazy originality that sounds like nothing on Earth, you're talking about the Titanic Triumvirate of Tongues, namely Eugene Pallette (the bull frog-ish businessman in *My Man Godfrey*), Sterling Holloway (the voice of Winnie the Pooh and the narrator of such Disney classics as *Susie, the Little Blue Coupe*) and Andy Devine. Devine sounds like he grew up eating glass and sand—it's beautiful. He was a jock at Santa Clara U. and, like the Duke,

went from football to acting (but not before working as a Venice Beach lifeguard!). As Buck the driver in *Stagecoach*, he brought a genuine talent with horses. Ford was griping at him one day, wondering out loud why he ever hired him. "Because Ward Bond can't drive six horses!" shot back Devine. His distinctive shape also won him the role of Santa Claus at Ford's Christmas gatherings. The great character star drove that stagecoach to the final depot back in '77.

JANE DARWELL—There's only one word that comes to mind when you think of Jane Darwell: "Ma." Darwell was Henry Fonda's mother in just about every film in which Fonda's character had one and, in the process, became the embodiment of all things "Ma"—loving, strong, worried, selfless, forgiving—"Ma." *The Grapes of Wrath* is her stand-out, but she was unforgettable in her final role as the Bird Woman in *Mary Poppins*—there was something heartbreaking in that smile.

VERA MILES—The beautiful Vera Miles is another star placed in the sky by Ford. Twice she played the daughter of "Swede" (Jack Qualen): in *The Searchers* and *The Man Who Shot Liberty Valance*. The story goes that Ward Bond had a monstrous turgid lust for Miles when they were making *The Searchers* and tried to tempt the fair lassie by strutting his mighty nakedness through the open door of his dressing of his room. It didn't play.

JEFFREY HUNTER—More than another pretty face, Hunter was a convincing addition to the Ford family. Watch him in *The Searchers*; he gets to rage, fight, love, play a resentful second banana and act the fool, and he's terrific. Of course, the Duke was so intense as Ethan Edwards that even the rocks and cactus never looked better. Hunter's also great in *Sergeant Rutledge*.

ENOS EDWARD "YAKIMA" CANUTT—Probably the greatest stuntman of all time. 'Yakima' was his rodeo nickname. With a cry of "Let me have him!" he won the *Police Gazette* belt for the All Aroun Cowboy Championship of the World four times. At the Duke's suggestion, Ford hired Canutt to coordinate the stunts for *Stagecoach*. A wise decision in that the gags he designed are considered to be some of the most spectacular ever shot. His fall and drag from the stagecoach, a bit he originated in Republic serials, caused theatre audiences to stand up and cheer. After the picture wrapped, John Ford said to him, "Any time I'm making an action picture and you're not working, you are with me."

Stunt coordinating and/or second unit credits include *Gone With the Wind*, *Gentleman Jim*, *Spartacus*, *Ben-Hur* (his son doubled for Heston in that heartstopping flip over the chariot). He is without question the standard by which all future greats will forever be compaired.

WOODY STRODE—Simply one of the most ridiculously perfect human physical specimens to ever walk the Earth. Woodrow Wilson Stode once actually posed for portraits commissioned by Leni Riefenstahl! What a life. He led U.C.L.A. to it's first undefeated football season in 1939 playing alongside Jackie Robinson (not much of a baseball player then) and his best friend Kenny Washington. The three of them (Washington was the first) broke the pro sports color barrier. Strode was instrumental in winning the Grey Cup for the Calgary Stampeeders in 1948 and became the first black wrestling star. Stunt work and muscleman parts led to his starring role in Ford's *Sergeant Rutledge* (Strode's favorite) and a close relationship with "Papa." Unforgettable in *Spartacus* and *The Professionals*. His final screen appearance was in *The Quick and the Dead* (1994) with Sharon Stone. He died, perhaps mercifully before its release. Look for his autobiography (now out-of-print), *Goal Dust*.

ARTHUR SHIELDS—If you need an Irish minister then here's your guy. Though not as animated as his feisty brother Barry Fitzgerald, his quiet support roles were often just as solid. Great in *The Long Voyage Home* but best loved as "Snuffy" the pugilistic parishless Protestant preist in *The Quiet Man*. Actually starred opposite Gloria Talbot (The pointiest breasts in the West) in the 1957 clunker *The Daughter of Dr. Jekyll*.

GEORGE O'BRIEN—Tom Mix, who made two Ford films in 1923, introduced O'Brien to the director. A year later, Ford starred the newcomer in his silent classic, *The Iron Horse*. The success of this film gave Ford his independence, O'Brien an exclusive contract, and Fox Studio a badly needed hit. With McLaglen in *The Fighting Heart*. "Pappy", in typical fashion, goaded the two powerful guys into a real slugfest for the cameras. Tramping through the South Seas with O'Brien, Ford jokingly wrote back to his wife, "I've never felt better and certainly never looked better in my life. Even O'Brien looks at me admiringly (however it will do him no good)." His last film, fittingly, was a Ford film, *Cheyenne Autumn*.

HENRY FONDA—Tied with the Duke as the most recognizable voice on film (also unforgettable, say "G-A-F"). Didn't always agree with Ford (*Mister Roberts*, for instance), but the

two shared great respect and affection. His best early work was with the director; disarming a lynch mob in *Young Mr. Lincoln*, recounting the horror of battle in *Drums Along The Mohawk*, as Wyatt Earp in *My Darling Clementine* and Tom Joad in *The Grapes Of Wrath*—an incredible series of performances. Fonda, Wayne, and Bond were in the 'Emerald Bay Yacht Club', Ford's anti snobbery collective ("Jews but no dues")—their booze cruise fishing trips aboard Pappy's 110' gaff-rigged ketch, the *Araner*, became legend.

Man Mixed With Character, John Wayne Defines The Guy: Fierce loyalty to his pals, a straight shooter, loved to work, did not suffer fools, a nose extremely sensitive to bullshit, skilled at the arts of riding, shooting, fishing, boating, drinking, cursing, fighting, smoking, card playing. Loved his family, his country, chess, Zane Grey novels, the desert, well done char-broiled steaks. Attractive and respected by both sexes for his unwavering resolve, his off-hand self-deprecating manner, huge features genuinely larger than life, accessibility, a rascal-like smile and an easy laugh.

Sure he was charming all to hell and a badass, but also respectful of authority. He was a patriot who hurt when something hurt the country, disgusted with and angered by injustice, hypocrisy, gutlessness, the liberal media and being indirect.

Anti-War Films

"A few movies may have taken it upon themselves to find fault with the American fighting man, but no one can dim the power to rally 'round when freedom is under attack, or the thrill you feel remembering great events in a time of courage." from *Oscar Presents the War Movies and John Wayne*

Buddies

When he wasn't making some of the world's greatest films, John Ford could usually be found hanging out with pals at The Hollywood Athletic Club or booze cruising on his 110' ketch *The Araner* (though his buddies did most of the drinking). Duke and Ward Bond were always in tow. Now John Wayne was pretty respectful around the old master, but Bond lived his life as the vainglorious center of the universe and could be a pretty obnoxious sonofabitch. Fact—the *Araner*'s captain made the following log entry during a run along the Baja peninsula: "Caught the first mate pissing in Bond's flask this morning—must remember to give him a raise."

Duke's Drink

Wayne loved Sauza Conmemorativo Tequila and had a unique way of serving it. *The Wild Goose* would occasionally encounter icebergs on northern runs and Duke would have the crew chop off a hunk, winch it on board and store it in a large freezer. He wet cocktails glasses with lemon juice, coated the rim with salt, added a few chips of 1000-year-old iceberg and poured on the Sauza.

Code

"I won't be wronged, I won't be insulted, I won't be laid a hand on. I don't do these things to other people, and I request the same from them." —J.B. Books, *The Shootist*

Wayne's own code included some sound advice from his father; Keep your word, never insult anyone unintentionally and don't go around looking for trouble, but if you do get in a fight, make sure you win it. *The Shootist* was Duke's last film. He had optioned a novel by Buddy Atkinson called *Beau James* but the project didn't even progress to screenplay.

Jokers

Practical jokes were pretty regular on the set and a favorite target was Ward Bond. Ford had many terms of endearment for the actor, cute pet names like "big ugly stupid gorilla." He just missed Bond's head with a whiskey bottle one day and, cursing his poor aim, swore off the drink. Big Wardell had one chink in his armor: he was a little self conscious about his rather prominent buttocks and Duke and Ford knew it, of course. Next time you're watching *Fort Apache* you may notice how many times Bond's ass is the star of the shot.

What's In A Name?

Kirk Douglas recalled working with Wayne on *The War Wagon* in his autobiography *The Ragman's Son*. For whatever reason Douglas refused to call the actor "Duke" (some typical actor ego thing probably) and insisted on calling him "John." If he only knew. . . . When Wayne was born on May 26, 1907 (a 13 pounder!), he was named Marion Robert Morrison but his mother took the name from him and gave it to his brother, born five years later. Wayne's name became Marion

Rubber Leg Wooley Bugger

Rubber Leg Woolly Bugger

The Duke's Refuge

Wayne bought *The Wild Goose,* a converted WWII mine sweeper with 3" thick wooden hull, in 1963. The yacht is available for charter from Hornblower Yachts in Newport Beach, California (714/631-2469).

Mitchell Morrison. He got the name Duke when he was about 10 years old and living in Glendale. The family Airedale was named Duke and some local firemen got to calling Wayne "little Duke." It was a welcome change from "Marion" which could be deadly in the playground, and the name stuck. Prior to making *The Big Trail* in 1930, director Raoul Walsh

Duke was aware of it's "Charlie Brown" qualities. He told an interviewer, "It's a name that goes well together and it's like one word John Wayne." But he never was known as or responded to "John." Said the Duke, "I've always been either Duke, Marion or John Wayne. . . if (people) say John, Christ, I don't look around. . . ."

and 20th Century Fox studio boss Winnie Sheehan gave the actor his new name. Walsh admired General Anthony Wayne. The "John" may have come from Ford. Wayne came to like it but had nothing to do with choosing it. Anyway,

Marlene Dietrich's unforgettable response the first time she saw Wayne, "Oh daddy, buy me that."

Censorship

Wayne was sickened by the increasing amount of sex and violence in films, as movies in his day had always been a medium for the whole family. Yet when the religious right sought his support for a new Hayes Code-type referendum on the entertainment industry, he rebuffed them. Wayne didn't like some

Rabbit Leech

of the things he saw but he defended their right to exist. The ultra-conservatives attacked him for this stand.

Therapy

"Couches are only good for one thing."

In 1948, a Hollywood columnist actually wrote, "Wayne has been at it for twenty years now and is still on top. What gives?"

God

Wayne objected to the traditional dogma and doctrine of organized religion, but the idea of God came naturally. He once said, "There must be some higher power or how does all this stuff work?"

Draft Dodgers

Predictably, the Duke felt that you had the right as a citizen to speak out against involvement in any war but that you were honor bound, again as a citizen, to answer the call when it came. This was the example set, for instance, by Charles Lindbergh at the outset of WWII. Duke was disgusted by Carter's immediate pardon of the Vietnam War rabbits, thinking that the act was a slap in the face to those who served.

Being A Man

"I want to play a real man in all my films and I define manhood simply: men should be tough, fair and courageous, never petty, never looking for a fight, but never backing down from one either."

Steve McQueen: "Sometimes kids ask me what a pro is. I just point to the Duke."

Lead Eye Woolly Bugger

Vera Miles: "They used to say of the Old West, 'Men were men and women were grateful.' Well, that's how he makes you feel as a woman."

Professional Competition

Wayne was a modest guy but had a healthy ego to be sure. When asked about awards in his 1971 *Playboy* interview he replied, ". . . I didn't really need an Oscar. I'm a box office champion with a record they're going to have to run to catch. And they won't." Maureen O'Hara recalled this exchange during *McLintock!*: "He didn't like the way I was doing a scene, and he said angrily, 'C'mon, Maureen, get going. This is your scene.' I said I was trying to go fifty-fifty. 'Fifty-fifty, hell,' he said. 'It's your scene. Take it.' Then he added under his breath, 'If you can.'"

O'Hara testified before the House after Barry Goldwater advanced the notion of striking a gold medal to honor the Duke. O'Hara suggested that the inscription read, "John Wayne, American."

The John Wayne Cancer Institute

The "Big C" for the Duke was a "real bitch." Talk about understatement. The disease also claimed his mother, brother, John Ford and many friends. The current odds state that one out of every three people will have to face this bastard too. You can honor the Duke and support one of the country's leading research facilities by contacting them in Santa Monica, CA at 310/449-5222.

Working With Other Directors

John Wayne after observing a vicious confrontation between director Henry Hathaway and Robert Duvall on the set of *True Grit*, "If Duvall had put a hand on the old man, I'd have sent him sprawling across the goddamn field!"

Wayne's disgust over excessive screen violence was well known. When his personal makeup man Dave Grayson was asked by director Mark Rydell to apply gorey makeup to the Duke in *The Cowboys* he replied, "Look, Mark, I can do it if Duke permits me to. But it'll take four makeup men."

"Why four makeup men?" Rydell asked.

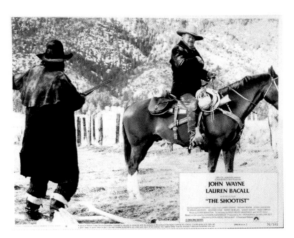
JOHN WAYNE LAUREN BACALL "THE SHOOTIST"

"Three are gonna have to hold him down."

Wayne showed up exceptionally snockered to makeup one day and after bruise and stage blood were liberally splashed on his face and shirt he turned to Grayson and said sarcastically, "For crissakes why don't you put a little MORE blood on me?"

"I can't," Grayson replied, "You drank it."

John Wayne said of director Don Siegel after one of many blow-ups during *The Shootist*, "That bastard couldn't get out of a trolley car with both doors open."

Juan Wayne?

In the early years, Wayne and John Payne were constantly getting each other's mail and being mistaken for one another. Once Payne flew to a movie bash in Mexico and after listening to the speeches he realized that they had Wayne in mind. Pretending to be Wayne he made a gracious acceptance speech praising Mexico and returned with a sterling silver statue with "John Wayne" engraved on it. Later he told Duke, "It's in my den and I'll be damned if I'm going to give it to you, I'm the one who had to sit and listen to those damned speeches about what a fine actor and great human being you are."

Critics

"When people say a John Wayne picture got bad reviews, I always wonder if they know it's a redundant sentence, (but) hell, I don't care. People like my pictures and that's all that counts."

Eula (Kathryn Hepburn) at the end of *Rooster Cogburn*, "I've got to say it Reuben. . . living with you has been an adventure any woman would relish for the rest of time. I look at you with your burnt out face, your fat belly, your shining eye and your bear-like paws and I have to say you're an honor to the whole male sex. And I'm happy to have you for a friend."

Of the *Rooster Cogburn* character, Wayne said, "He's a mean old bastard, and that's me! I played it faithfully." Of Hepburn he said, "Miss Hepburn. . . is a delight. There's only one thing—she's a little more conservative than I am. But then, who isn't?"

His Legacy

Wayne told a *Time* interviewer in 1969, "I would like to be remembered, well. . . the Mexicans have a phrase, 'Feo, fuerte y formal.' Which means: he was ugly, strong and had dignity."

Rabbit Leech

John Wayne a Racist? BullSHIT!

Appalling trends, people and speech are traditionally among the chief exports of Los Angeles. (Attention book reviewers!) But the anything goes atmosphere in this city, while repellent to most of the country, serves America well. Though the public dialogue may be no more than a shouting match, at least grievances are aired rather than simmering in polite society.

A perfect example is the recent controversy involving John Wayne and the Los Angeles County Fire Department. It began, or at least came to light, when a black battalion chief removed a photo of Wayne that had hung in the Carson fire station for 20 years. Maggie Hathaway, founder of the Beverly Hills/Hollywood branch of the NAACP, defended the battalion chief who felt that the image was antagonistic. She went on further to call Wayne "an avowed racist (who) seldom had anything to do with blacks."

The action of the battalion chief seems clearly inappropriate and probably had more to do with the kind of simple personnel conflicts that plague offices everywhere. However, Ms. Hathaway is unfortunately correct in that Wayne's image has in the past been wrongfully embraced by racist individuals, and also wrongfully targeted by others. But the Duke was not a racist, and there is nothing in this man's intensely scrutinized life nor from those who knew him to support such a claim. Indeed this conclusion is backed by the recent, serious biographical study of the actor/icon, *John Wayne, American* by history professors Randy Roberts and James S. Olson. In the course of this book's research, the author spoke with the authors of *John Wayne, American*, and asked directly, "Is there or was there any evidence to support the claim that John Wayne was a racist?" Olson replied with conviction, "Absolutely not."

The culprit is Wayne's notorious May, 1971 interview in *Playboy*. Wayne was openly disgusted with much of the 60's counterculture revolution and he was often baited by journalists who considered him an establishment dinosaur. His patriotism, chauvinism and unexpurgated plain speech made him a perfect subject for the magazine and Wayne welcomed the opportunity to vent about "perverted films," draft dodgers, hypocrisy and Commies.

When interviewer Richard Warren Lewis asked about activist Angela Davis, Wayne replied as follows: "With a lot of blacks, there's quite a bit of resentment along with their dissent, and possibly rightfully so. But we can't all of a sudden get down on our knees and turn everything over to the leadership of the blacks. I believe in white supremacy until the blacks are educated to a point of responsibility. I don't believe in giving authority and positions of leadership and judgment to irresponsible people."

YIPES! What outrageous insensitivity from a man you thought you admired, right? What a damn fool racist generalization from a former senior high school president, a man who claims to love this country and a guy who should bloody well know better, right? Wrong. This is nothing more than sloppy speech, easily misconstrued today, but which needs to be examined in the context of his life and times. Wayne wasn't talking about white supremacy as in vile hate mongering collectives. He would abhor being associated with such people. What he was referring to in his clumsy way was the *status quo*. Further, he wasn't saying that blacks, or anyone else for that matter, were incapable of taking leadership roles in this country. Just the opposite. He was railing against tokenism which *allowed* race to enter the evaluative process. Wayne busted his ass working up from crew jobs and slaved for years in low budget films. He believed passionately in a meritocracy and objected, certainly naively then, to needed programs like affirmative action. John Wayne's sin was one of his most endearing qualities—it was his deep faith and belief in the American people to put aside prejudices and, independent of government dictations, do the right thing. This should not make him a symbol of and for white people, it makes him a champion for all of America, black and white and everybody else too. The honorable standards by which he lived should be applied to all of us, and his legacy should not be corrupted by one easily misconstrued statement.

SPARTACUS
THE MANLIEST FILM OF ALL TIME

Woolly Bugger Rubber Leg

A Little History

Stanley Kubrick and a few sniffy film reviewers whined about historical inaccuracies in the screenplay of *Spartacus*, but such protests are a bit ridiculous. Dramatic license appears obligatory in nonfiction Hollywood-style. John Ford, for instance, got the story of the gunfight at the OK Corral direct from Wyatt Earp but had Victor Mature's "Doc" Holiday die in *My Darling Clementine* (we'll never understand that one). Today, of course, Oliver "Deep Thought" Stone has set about imposing his agenda on history like some character created by George Orwell.

A few details in *Spartacus* may be off but the essence of the character's story, at least as told by the Greek biographer

UNIVERSAL zeigt:

SPARTACUS

KIRK DOUGLAS · LAURENCE OLIVIER · JEAN SIMMONS · CHARLES LAUGHTON
PETER USTINOV · JOHN GAVIN und TONY CURTIS als Antonius

Regie: STANLEY KUBRICK · Musik: ALEX NORTH · Drehbuch: DALTON TRUMBO
nach dem Roman von HOWARD FAST · Produktion: EDWARD LEWIS · Produktionsleitung: KIRK DOUGLAS
Eine BRYNA-PRODUKTION · Technicolor · Technirama · Ein Universal-Film im Verleih der CIC

Plutarch (c. A.D. 46–120), is on the screen. The Thracian Spartacus was a nomadic tribesman who escaped from service in the Roman army. He attacked some towns with a small band of men but was soon recaptured and sold as a slave to the gladiator school of Lentulus Batiatus in Capua, south of Naples, Italy. Most of the school's other "students" were enslaved, brutalized Gauls or Thracians—in 73 B.C., close to 80 of them broke out by overwhelming the guards with knives and spits stolen from the cook's shop. Spartacus had a wife who either escaped with him or joined the outlaws at a later time. She is described provocatively as a "prophetess, and one of those possessed of the bacchanal frenzy," but her fate is unknown. Rome was alerted after the band began raiding estates from a base camp at Mt. Vesuvius. The Gladiatorial War had begun, and the effect on the empire was like that of a firestorm.

As they swept across southern Italy, the slave army grew to more than 90,000. In addition to his deadly fighting skills, Spartacus was an inspiring leader and a fearless battle strategist. Plutarch describes him as "a man not only of high spirit and valiant, but in understanding also, and in gentleness superior to his condition, and more of a Grecian than the people of his country usually are." (It's interesting how unabashed the Greeks were about their place in the world.)

southward. Marcus Licinius Crassus, appointed general of the Roman legions, succeeded in briefly cutting off Spartacus at Rhegium (the "boot toe" of Italy). An escape plan to Sicily involving Cilician pirates ended in betrayal and forced a costly battle against Crassus. The slaves always maintained a tactical advantage—Roman victories only came through sheer force of numbers. A report on the more than 12,000 slave dead marked their bravery: only two were found wounded in the back.

The armies of two Roman consuls were crushed as Spartacus drove north to the Alps—and freedom.

But his men wanted more. Their confidence and aggression forced an attack on Rome itself. The gods did not favor this hubris. Rome sent increasingly larger armies against them, and bloody engagements again raged

Spartacus led his final assault against Crassus in Lucania, not far from Capua, knowing that reinforcements from Rome had set the odds against his band. To rally them, he killed his horse, declaring that their victory would provide him with hundreds more to choose from. Despite their courage and resolve, they were overwhelmed.

Spartacus' last thought was to kill Crassus. He hacked through two centurions to reach the Roman general but, surrounded by the enemy, was "cut to pieces." The survivors of the slave army raced northward toward freedom but Crassus, anticipating this move, had recalled Pompey's army from Spain to cut off their escape. The two armies met at the foot of the Alps for a final lopsided battle, and Pompey, not Crassus, was honored with the triumph of ending the slave war along with his success in Spain. As a warning against future uprisings, 6,000 prisoners were crucified along the Appian Way leading to the gates of Rome.

The slave revolt was a heroic blow against tyranny that ultimately had a mortal effect on the empire. Fear of another such attack hastened Caesar's dictatorship and the end of the republic. The fall of Rome wouldn't come for almost another 400 years, but the war Spartacus led may have made it inevitable.

Spartacus—*A Bryna Production / A Universal-International Release (Clockwise from left) Spartacus rallies the slave army; Break-out at the gladiatorial school; Signaling the attack on Crassus; Thracian sword against the trident of Draba (Woody Strode); Tigranes (Herbert Lom) bears news of betrayal by the Cilician pirates.*

Kirk on Kubrick (left), who called the script "pretty dumb": "He'll make a fine director some day if he falls flat on his face just once. It might teach him how to compromise."

SPARTAFACTS and SPARTAQUOTES

Legendary stuntman Yakima Canutt was hired to set up some of the bloodier special effects, like arms getting hacked off. Asked to rig a beheading, he considered the shot too gruesome and was relieved when it was cut (one of the few bad things that can be said about the guy).

Peter Ustinov relayed a telling anecdote about the two years of filming. His daughter, born during the production, was asked by a playmate what her father did for a living. "*Spartacus*," she replied.

Woody Strode was concerned that his age, then 45, would hurt his chances at the audition. Having heard that Kirk Douglas was 32, he figured that Douglas wouldn't want a gladiator opponent so much older. So he shaved off 10 years and said that he was 35. Douglas, it turns out, had done the same thing—he was actually 42.

Howard Fast, a victim of the blacklist, had to publish his novel, *Spartacus*, himself. The script adaptation by fellow blacklist victim Dalton Trumbo, which Fast objected to, is a pretty amazing piece of transformation. The novel is no page turner.

Trumbo recalled in a 1961 interview in *Time* that Ring Lardner Jr. of the Hollywood 10 was joined at the penitentiary by Congressman J. Parnell Thomas (convicted of padding his office payroll). "Almost every jail in the country during that curious time found congressman and contemptee standing cheek to jowl in the chow line, all their old

malignities dissolved in common hunger for a few more of them there beans."

Trumbo refused to cooperate with the House Committee on Un-American Activities and was given a 10-month jail term. Douglas' determination to give him an open credit (his first in 15 years) effectively broke the Hollywood blacklist.

Alex North: "Most composers get a 10-week contract and are expected to deliver a score in three weeks, with seven weeks to make changes and orchestrate. Kirk gave me carte blanche. I was on *Spartacus* 13 months—a record, I think."

Robert Lawrence, who had edited *Spartacus* 30 years earlier, joined Jim Katz (producer of Paul Bartel's wild *Scenes From a Class Struggle in Beverly Hills*) and Robert A. Harris (restoration specialist on *Lawrence of Arabia*) in a virtual frame-by-frame restoration in 1991. Technical problems, including a ruined original negative and the Technirama process, made the job incredibly tough.

The restored *Spartacus* includes the classic "oysters and snails" scene, shot at Hearst's castle and censored by the Legion of Decency. Filming the homoerotic seduction of Antoninus (Tony Curtis) by Crassus (Sir Laurence Olivier) took incredible brass back in 1960. The restoration team found the footage, but the dialogue track was missing. Curtis returned, more than 30 years later, to dub his voice. Anthony Hopkins gave a flawless impersonation of Olivier, by then deceased. Alex North's odd scoring for the scene plays perfectly.

(Clockwise) Jean Simmons as Varinia; Sir Laurence Olivier as Marcus Licinius Crassus;
Tony Curtis as Antoninus; Peter Ustinov as Lentulus Batiatus

Douglas: "When I came on the set before shooting began and saw the row of dressing rooms marked 'Sir Laurence Olivier,' 'Peter Ustinov,' and 'Charles Laughton,' holy smoke, I thought! Is someone kidding? It's a dream come true. A dream, that's what it is. I don't dare look at it realistically."

Robert A. Harris claims: "[*Spartacus*] is a beautiful big sprawling epic [of the type that] can't be made anymore. Is it one of the two or three greatest films ever made? No. [But] it's a damn good film, and it's a film that needed to be restored." (How wrong and right can a guy be?)

Tom Pollock, MCA Motion Picture Group chairman, gave the go-ahead on the restoration, which probably cost the studio about $1 million. There should be a song written about this guy.

Douglas was more gracious about their differences, describing in his autobiography Kubrick's introduction to the crew: "I took Stanley into the middle of the arena. 'This is your new director'. They looked down at this 30-year-old youth, thought it was a joke. Then consternation—I had worked with Stanley (*Paths of Glory*), they hadn't. That made him 'my boy.' They didn't know that Stanley is nobody's boy."

Douglas told *American Film* magazine, "Kubrick did some wonderful things. Brilliant director. In my book I called him a shit, which I think he is, but he's a very, very talented guy."

Kubrick: "I don't mean to minimize the contributions of the others involved, but the director is the only one who can authentically impose his personality onto a picture, and the result is his responsibility—partly because he's the only one who's always there."

Douglas: "My concept of *Spartacus* was to make it as if it were a little picture; every character would become more dominant than the background. The trouble with those epics is [that] usually the characters become flat, they aren't three-dimensional."

Kubrick: "Let's say that I was more influenced by [Sergei] Eisenstein's *Alexander Nevsky* than by *Ben-Hur* or anything by Cecil B. De Mille."

In 1959, a *Newsweek* reporter caught up with Douglas in his dressing room, donning the ragged slave costume for the opening sequence. He reminded the actor of his insistence, after *The Vikings*, that he would never produce another picture. Douglas says, "It's true. I said it. *The Vikings* ran over $4 million and now I'm making a picture that will cost $6 million. It scares the hell out of me but it's fun." (The film, which required 100 major set pieces, more than 8,000 extras, and two years to complete, finally cost over $12 million)

Stanley Kubrick directed (and often cowrote) some of the greatest-ever films for guys, including *The Killing* (1956), *Paths of Glory* (1957), *Dr. Strangelove or: How I Learned to Stop Worrying and Love the Bomb* (1964), *2001: A Space Odyssey* (1968), *A Clockwork Orange* (1971), *Barry Lyndon* (1975), *The Shining* (1980) and *Full Metal Jacket* (1987).

Howard Fast: "I wrote this novel because I considered it an important story for the time in which we live. Not in the mechanical sense of historical parallels, but because there is hope and strength to be taken from such a story about the age-old fight for freedom—and because Spartacus lived not for one time of man, but for all times of man. I wrote it to give hope and courage to those who would read it, and in the process of writing it, I gained hope for myself."

Draba (played by Woody Strode) is hung upside down in the gladiator quarters after he is killed by Crassus. A plaster cast of Strode was created for the scene, but the dummy when finished never looked convincing. Strode had to do the scene himself. According to his son, Kalai, the replica of his father hung inside the entrance to Universal's prop room for years. It may still be there.

Spartacus 1960

Stars: Kirk Douglas, Laurence Olivier, Jean Simmons, Tony Curtis, Peter Ustinov, Charles Laughton, Herbert Lom, Woody Strode, John Gavin, Nina Foch, Charles McGraw, John Ireland; Director: Stanley Kubrick; Screenplay: Dalton Trumbo (based on the novel by Howard Fast)

The Quiet Man 1952

Stars: John Wayne, Maureen O'Hara, Victor McLaglen, Barry Fitzgerald, Arthur Shields, Ward Bond, Mildred Natwick; Director: John Ford; Screenplay: Frank Nugent (based on the short story by Maurice Walsh)

Apocalypse Now 1979

Stars: Martin Sheen, Marlon Brando, Robert Duvall, Frederic Forrest, Sam Bottoms, Scott Glenn, Albert Hall, Lawrence Fishburne, Harrison Ford, G.D. Spradlin, Dennis Hopper, Colleen Camp, Tom Mason; Director: Francis Ford Coppola; Screenplay: Francis Ford Coppola, John Milius (based on *Heart of Darkness* by Joseph Conrad); Music: Carmine Coppola

Coppola said that this film was not about Vietnam, it was Vietnam. Well, after completing a film like this, he can be forgiven that kind of shagged out, post-trauma, heat-of-the-moment pretentious crap. The whole wild story gets a commendably candid accounting in the fascinating documentary *Hearts of Darkness: A Filmmaker's Apocalypse* (1991). Martin Sheen threw himself so completely into this project that it almost killed him. It almost killed everybody. Choppers & Wagner, napalm, gunboats, drugs, Duvall, surfing, Mr. Grenade Launcher Man, Hendrix, *Playboy* Bunnies—don't blow a chance to see the film on the big screen with big sound. A slap in the brain pan.

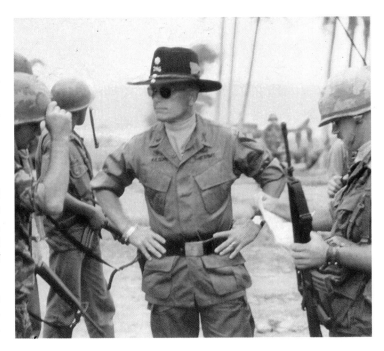

TOP 25 GREATEST GUY MOVIES OF ALL TIME

(In no particular order—order 'em yourself, or argue with friends about it)

PARAMOUNT PICTURES PRESENTA

il Padrino

the Godfather

The Godfather, Part I 1972

Stars: Al Pacino, Marlon Brando, Robert Duvall, James Caan, Diane Keaton, Talia Shire, Richard Castellano, John Cazale, Sterling Hayden, Al Lettieri, Abe Vigoda, Richard Conte, Alex Rocco Director: Francis Ford Coppola Screenplay: Mario Puzo and Coppola Music: Nino Rota

The Godfather, Part II 1974

Stars: Al Pacino, Robert De Niro, Robert Duvall, Diane Keaton, John Cazale, Talia Shire, Lee Strasberg, G.D. Spradlin, Bruno Kirby, Joe Spinell, Harry Dean Stanton, Roger Corman, Danny Aiello Director: Francis Ford Coppola Screenplay: Mario Puzo and Coppola Music: Nino Rota, Carmine Coppola

So seductive and influential that mob guys were mimicking screen characters that were based on them in the first place. Here's the recommended way to watch these films on video: Stock the fridge, invite over some other Corleone junkies, run *The Complete Epic, 1902-1958* chronologically combined 6-hour, 26-minute version, and repeat. There are worse ways to kill a day.

Braveheart 1995

Stars: Mel Gibson, Sophie Marceau, Patrick McGoohan, Catherine McCormack, Brendon Gleeson, James Cosmo, David O'Hara, Angus McFadyen; Director: Mel Gibson; Screenplay: Randall Wallace; Music: James Horner

Whoever expected to see a film like this again? Amazingly brutal, heartbreaking saga of 13th century Scottish patriot William Wallace and his struggle against English tyranny. Mel gets it all—funny as hell moon shots to beautifully strong roles for all the women. It's tough to admit but Gibson looks even better in a kilt than Victor McLaglen. Sure now, and it's also fun to try and crush old friends "like a wurem." Without question the manliest film since *Spartacus* and remarkably similar in dramatic and historic content. (If Mel and his second unit crew didn't study *Spartacus* by way of preparation, I'll eat last week's haggis.) With an obligatory tough times soundtrack—Horner's score has the restorative powers of the Golden Fleece. Vivid and horrifying battle sequences bury the needle on the Squirm-O-Meter.

Ben Hur 1959

Stars: Charlton Heston, Stephen Boyd, Jack Hawkins, Haya Harareet, Sam Jaffe, Cathy O'Donnell, Hugh Griffith, Martha Scott; Director:

Kaufmann Scud™

William Wyler; Screenplay: Karl Tunberg (based on the novel by General Lew Wallace); Music: Miklos Rosza

Third and greatest adaptation of General Wallace's immensely popular 1880 biblical novel (Wallace sentenced the commandant of Andersonville to death). Yakima Canutt's painfully realistic chariot collisions created rumors about deaths on the set (false). That's Yak's 21-year-old son Joe doubling for Heston in the forward flip, though Chuck could really drive those ponies. If the 15-minute race sequence, directed by Andrew Marton (*Men of the Fighting Lady*), doesn't get your heart thumping like a rabbit, then you're some kinda dope. Another magnificent score from Miklos Rosza. Note: If you buy Gore Vidal's horsehockey claim that Heston and Boyd's characters are gay (NOT that there's anything wrong with that), then you probably believe that Bogey and Claude Raines traipsed off to Free French Fire Island at the end of *Casablanca*.

The Bridge on the River Kwai 1957

Stars: William Holden, Alec Guinness, Jack Hawkins, Sessue Hayakawa, James Donald, Geoffrey Horne, Andre Morell, Ann Sears;

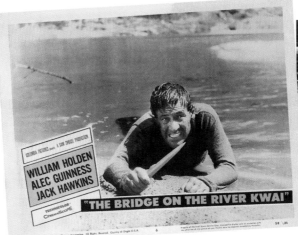

Director: David Lean; Screenplay: Michael Wilson, Carl Foreman (based on the novel by Pierre Boulle); Music: Malcolm Arnold

If a pal doesn't recognize a whistled version of the Colonel Bogey March, DON'T slug the poor ignorant sap, just remember what to get him for his next birthday. Holden's performance ties him with James

Garner (*The Americanization of Emily*) for the Disgusted American War Cynic/British Stupor Breaking Championship Cup. Holden lets Guinness have it right in his stiff upper lip. Ford and Howard Hawks were considered but this story demanded an English director. It got the best. Lean puts the audience right in the water with Shears (Holden) for that final agonizing scene, screaming, "Kill him! KILL HIM!" Holden later recalled how, thanks to Sri Lankan mahoots upstream, he had to dodge elephant dung "the size of cannon balls."

McLintock! 1963

Stars: John Wayne, Maureen O'Hara, Chill Wills, Edgar Buchanan; Director: Andrew V. McLaglen; Screenplay: James Edward Grant

The film that launched a thousand feminist careers. McLaglen's first big budgeter reunites the Two Titans in this outrageously over-the-top Barnum & Bailey brawl-a-rama. Everything here but the "KABLOWEE!" balloons from the 60s "Batman" show and a Carl Stalling soundtrack. Leo Gordon achieves immortality as the guy on the business end of the greatest roundhouse in history. Talk about good sports—the lovely Maureen, dragged through sheep dip in *The Quiet Man*, gets thrown in a trough and also tarred and feathered. Then of course there's the public spanking and mythic mud-wrestling scene (it took over a week to shoot). This one could make Tank Abbot wince. Hokey Smokes, Batjac!

The Road Warrior (Mad Max 2) 1982

Stars: Mel Gibson, Bruce Spence, Vernon Wells, Mike Preston, Virginia Hey, Emil Minty; Director: George Miller; Screenplay: George Miller

Two years after *Mad Max*, Miller returned to the Australian desert with Mel, Spence (the Gyro Pilot), more vehicles, more dough, more "juice" and even more insane ideas (like ole Humongous and the Feral Kid, for instance). This seminal post-apocalyptic actioner wins hands down for ridiculously stupefying stunts.

Those Magnificent Men in Their Flying Machines 1965

Stars: Stuart Whitman, Sarah Miles, James Fox, Robert Morley, Terry Thomas, Eric Sykes, Alberto Sordi, Gert Frobe, Jean-Pierre Cassel, Irina Demick, Benny Hill, Red Skelton; Director: Ken Annakin; Screenplay: Ken Annakin, Jack Davies; Music: Ron Goodwin

Here's proof that making tuba sounds or flapping your arms like a chicken can be high art, damnit! Red Skelton renders some brilliant bookends in this wonderfully silly account of a 1910 London-to-Paris air race. The international airmen are clichéd to hysterical perfection and never go anywhere without their signature soundtracks. Through it all, Terry Thomas manages to steal scene after scene as the insufferable, gap-toothed nasty. Loaded with authentic flying replicas of keepers and clunkers from the dawn of flight. Block out five hours and watch this with Stanley Kramer's *It's a Mad, Mad, Mad, Mad World* (1963).

The Adventures of Robin Hood 1938

Stars: Errol Flynn, Olivia de Havilland, Basil Rathbone, Alan Hale, Una O'Connor, Claude Raines, Eugene Pallette, Patric Knowles, Montagu Love; Director: Michael Curtiz; Screenplay: Norman Reilly Raine, Seton I. Miller; Music: Erich Wolfgang Korngold

Robin of Locksley is, in the words of Prince John, "a saucey fellow." Made in 1938 for the then astonishing sum of two million dollars, this is Errol Flynn's signature film. Also marks the beginning of Eugene Pallette's storied frog-voiced friar career—"Give me back my mutton joint!" Born to be baddies Basil Rathbone, Montagu Love and Claude Rains join Olivia de Havilland, Alan Hale and Una O' Connor to round out this killer cast. Over the magnificent Erich Wolfgang Korngold score, the film peaks in epic style with Robin and Sir Guy matched in one of the screen's great sword fights. Gushing with gusto, this is where the Flynn flame burns brightest.

The Flight of the Phoenix 1965

Stars: James Stewart, Richard Attenborough, Peter Finch, Hardy Kruger, Ernest Borgnine, Dan Duryea, George Kennedy, Ian Bannen; Director: Robert Aldrich; Screenplay: Lucas Heller

Far and away the greatest film premise any bloody genius ever came up with. Nothing about that here for those new to this one, but it does involve a plane wreck, the desert, about a dozen guys, a case of dates, a dead camel and a monkey. A film that makes it perfectly clear why guys consider Ernest Borgnine a true god. (Where can you find that beautiful song that comes on his radio?) Also watch for Ian Bannen as Rat Bags. Thirty years later he's the rotting and thoroughly rotten leprosy-stricken mean old bastard and otherwise very unpleasant dad of Robert the Bruce in *Braveheart*.

Monty Python and the Holy Grail 1975

Stars: Graham Chapman, John Cleese, Terry Gilliam, Terry Jones, Eric Idle, Michael Palin; Director: Terry Gilliam, Terry Jones; Screenplay: All of 'em

The Pythonification of King Arthur's court. A wedding massacre, bludgeoned octogenarians, sex-crazed shut-ins, poop-covered peons, a nice nod to *Night of the Lepus* (1972) and all the other Capra-esque comedy essentials. King Arthur's encounter with the Black Knight (now known as Mat) is even funnier than anything directed by Herschell Gordon Lewis. Also a favorite of cat lovers everywhere. Lines from this film continue to serve as Pythonian passwords. Followed by their delightfully waggish paean to Noel Coward, Monty Python's *The Meaning of Life* (1983). (Special note: This film inspired the International Hurling Society, which created a long overdue public forum for the serious discussion of cow-throwing devices.)

Captains Courageous 1937

Stars: Spencer Tracy, Lionel Barrymore, Freddie Bartholomew, Melvyn Douglas, John Carradine, Mickey Rooney, Charley Grapewin; Director: Victor Flemming; Screenplay: John Lee Mahin, Marc Connelly and Dale Van Every (based on the novel by Rudyard Kipling)

Freddie Bartholomew is on

the nosey as the rotten, snotty brat Harvey. Plucked from the sea by a fishing schooner and teamed with a simple Portuguese (Spencer Tracy), he learns the ways of men and honest labor during a semester at sea, Gloucester fashion. Melvyn Douglas, impossible to dislike under any circumstances, is the wealthy neglectful father. Some great hand line fishing tips and spectacular sailing sequences as Captain Disko heels over his beautiful gaff-rigged schooner, *We're Here*. "If Walt Cushman beats me into Gloucester," barks Barrymore, "I'll hang myself with an eel!" John Carradine is terrific as the hot-headed Long Jack. Powerful, genuine and heartbreaking (if this film doesn't move you, then kill yourself).

S.O.B. 1981

Stars: Richard Mulligan, Julie Andrews, William Holden, Robert Preston, Robert Webber, Shelley Winters, Robert Vaughn, Larry Hagman, Stuart Margolin, Loretta Swit; Director: Blake Edwards; Screenplay: Blake Edwards; Music: Henry Mancini

Would someone please really piss off Blake Edwards again so he can make another ragingly funny attack like this one? Hollywood gets hacked by the master, who appears in the guise of Felix Farmer, played to lunatic perfection by Richard Mulligan. The authors would wear diamond-tipped chansonette bras and chaps without pants for the rest of their lives if it could bring back guys like Preston and Holden.

She Wore a Yellow Ribbon 1949

Stars: John Wayne, Joanne Dru, John Agar, Ben Johnson, Harry Carey, Jr., Victor McLaglen, Mildred Natwick, George O'Brien, Arthur Shields; Director: John Ford; Screenplay: Frank S. Nugent, Laurence Stallings (from the story "War Party," by James Warner Bellah); Music: Richard Hageman

Here's cavalry comportment for you. Together with *Fort Apache* (1948) and *Rio Grande* (1950), Ford's trilogy of toughness provides just the right slap in the face and kick in the pants when deserved the most. All three were based on short stories by James Warner Bellah that appeared in the *Saturday Evening Post. Time* magazine once said of Bellah that he ". . . wrote about the West as if he had won it in a poker game." Ford called him "America's Kipling." His extraordinary life of adventure deserves A&E's "Biography" treatment. Wayne's role as Captain Nathan Brittles was his favorite.

The Mark of Zorro 1940

Stars: Tyrone Power, Linda Darnell, Eugene Pallette, Basil Rathbone; Director: Rouben Mamoulian; Screenplay: John Taintor; Music: Alfred Newman

Tyrone, you beauty! Pretty much follows the same cast and storyline of Robin Hood but without the tights and merry men. Features poor ole Basil Rathbone getting frustrated, insulted and skewered again; Montagu Love as the dad and Eugene Pallette back in his familiar fat-fatty froggy friar togs. Tyrone Power stars as the foil-flailing masked avenger and part-time pansy, slashing his way through a host of oppressors to protect the innocent in the name of niceness. European fencing champ Rathbone considered Power, not Flynn, the best of the Hollywood swordsmen. Many actresses poled did not concur.

The Outlaw Josey Wales 1976

Stars: Clint Eastwood, Chief Dan George, Sondra Locke, Matt Clark, John Vernon; Director: Clint Eastwood, Philip Kaufman; Screenplay: Philip Kaufman

"You gonna pull those pistols or whistle 'Dixie'?" If you're a bad guy and you ride onto Josey Wales' ranch, kill his family and burn his house down, it's a mistake that'll head your "Things I'll Never Do Again" list for the rest of your very short life. Snarling, bloodthirsty "red leg" Bill McKinney (that voice!) finally gets the point. Eastwood took over direction from screenwriter Philip Kaufman in the middle of filming this brutal Civil War saga of betrayal, revenge and renewal. Standouts for Clint, Chief Dan George and Sam Bottoms, with an unforgettable stream of genuine characters and detail that leaves audiences wanting to see a film about everyone in it. Called "the last of the great Westerns" until Eastwood's own *Unforgiven* sixteen years later.

Aliens 1988

Stars: Sigourney Weaver, Michael Biehn, Lance Henriksen, Bill Paxton, Paul Reiser; Director: James Cameron; Screenplay: James Cameron, Walter Hill; Music: James Horner

"Get away from her, you BITCH!" Slam-O sequel to the tension-drenched *Alien* and the most relentless monster movie ever made—a testament that sometimes more is, in fact, gooder. Creates ultra-foamy rabid anticipation when one of the characters figures the creepy eggs have been laid by "something we haven't seen yet." Oh boy, oh boy, oh boy! Watch Sigourney Weaver slip on the Caterpillar "Gobot" suit and go mano-a-monster against Queen Critter. Gripping direction by James Cameron and convincing work from Weaver, Michael Biehn and Lance Henrikson ("Watch your fingers"). Also, nobody wigs out like Bill Paxton. *It! The Terror From Beyond Space*, a 1958 sci-fi thriller budgeted for about half a buck, provided the storyline for the *Alien* trilogy.

Theo's Bead Head Stone Fly™

Patton 1970

Stars: George C. Scott, Karl Malden, Stephen Young, Michael Strong; Director: Franklin Schaffner; Screenplay: Francis Ford Coppola, Edmund H. North; Music: Jerry Goldsmith

Produced just in time to help sustain us through the world's most embarrassing decade. Scott rages like a Shakespearean king through his mountainous portrayal of Old Blood & Guts, making it the only role besides Dirty Harry we can be grateful that the Duke passed on.

The Man Who Would Be King 1975

Stars: Sean Connery, Michael Caine, Christopher Plummer, Saeed Jaffrey, Shakira Caine; Director: John Huston; Screenplay: Gladys Hill, John Huston (based on the novel by Rudyard Kipling); Music: Maurice Jarre

Kipling probably wouldn't relish the title of Literary Father of the Buddy Film, but he'd jump back into his grave if he saw how they were making them today. Or, for that matter, if he read that previous sentence. But he would have loved watching the bluff and bluster pouring out of Connery and Caine in this Shriner special. All is vanity, ladies and gentlemen, and thou art mortal. Includes instructions on how to play polo with the head of your enemy. Ford once called Huston a "faker." What the hell was he talking about?

Gunga Din 1939

Stars: Cary Grant, Victor McLaglen, Douglas Fairbanks Jr., Sam Jaffe, Joan Fontaine, Montagu Love, Eduardo Ciannelli, Annie the Elephant; Director: George Stevens; Screenplay: Fred Guiol and Joel Sayre (based on the poem by Rudyard Kipling); Music: Alfred Newman

Sabu couldn't play the title role, so naturally they turned to Sam Jaffe. What!? But he's terrific, and don't ever miss his turbanless turn in *The Asphalt Jungle* (1950). And then of course there's Ciannelli as the malevolent cult leader by way of Florence. The three stars called each other by their character names for the rest of their lives: Cutter (Grant), MacChesney (McLaglen), and Ballentine (Fairbanks). You want balls? Watch Cutter arrest 5,000 thuggees. The pesky Cali cult turns up again in *Indiana Jones and The Temple of Doom*. Annie the Elephant—never better.

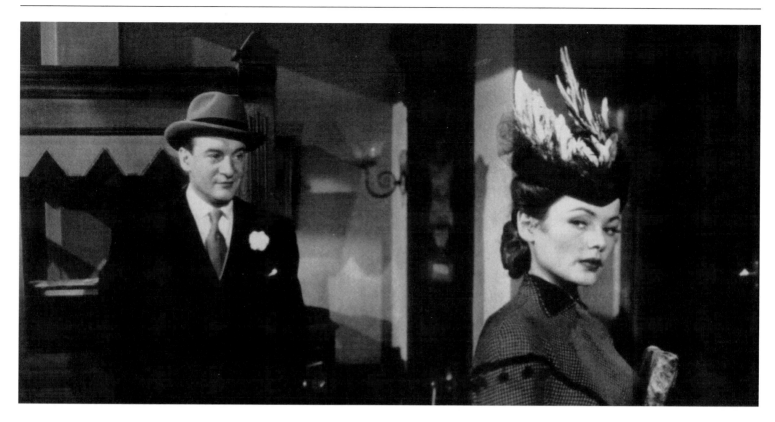

The Ghost and Mrs. Muir 1947

Stars: Rex Harrison, Gene Tierney, George Sanders, Edna Best, Anna Lee, Vanessa Brown; Director: Joseph L. Mankiewicz; Screenplay: Phillip Dunne (based on the novel by R.A. Dick); Music: Bernard Herrmann

No cars, swords, deserts or splashy heroics—just the greatest chill factor film of all time. Herrmann's genius as film composer at full bore, with themes in step with Puccini. Gene Tierney is ferociously desirable as the poised and independent lonely widow—so startling that a look could change lesser men into rhesus monkeys. Not Rex Harrison and George Sanders, however, representing the two sides of all men, captain and cad. The male animal is the romantic creature on this planet, and this is our love story.

North Dallas Forty 1979

Stars: Nick Nolte, Mac Davis, Charles Durning, Bo Svenson, John Matuzak, Dayle Haddon, G.D. Spradlin, Steve Forrest; Director: Ted Kotcheff; Screenplay: Peter Gent, Frank Yablans, Kotcheff (based on Gent's novel)

It's John Matuzak, man! It's THE TOOOOZ! Big John speaks for sports lovers *everywhere* when he rips into Charles Durning's character about his disgust with shabby, blue-suited, joy-killing commercialization. Kill, Tooz, KILL!! Almost 20 years old and still the greatest movie on The Game. No man alive will ever forget the scenes of Nolte waking up. Follow with a *Caveman* (1981) chaser.

Captain Horatio Hornblower 1951

Stars: Gregory Peck, Virginia Mayo, Robert Beatty, Denis O'Dea, Christopher Lee; Director: Raoul Walsh; Screenplay: Ivan Goff (based on the novel by C.S. Forester)

Rip-roaring Raoul Walsh delivers what may well be the greatest turn-of-the-century (19th Century, that is) sea battle ever filmed (and it occurs in the Pacific!). If Napoleon had received a fax showing Greg Peck in his Royal Navy frock, he wouldn't have pestered anybody. With terrific irony, Captain Hornblower and his gutsy crew of the HMS *Lydia* have to take on the swollen Spanish Natividad twice. The second time is a complete gas. "Beat to quarters and clear for action! Fire as your guns bear!" Hornblower, as created by C.S. Forester, is the image of poise, instinct, intelligence and grace under fire. The greatest pub we'll never get to drink at: Gunner Quist's "The Hornblower Arms." A quid bet on what Peck utters when he sees Virginia Mayo. Huba.

"Wait till you see the weird part."

NORTH DALLAS FORTY

Chironomia Pupa™

FILM CATEGORIES BEST FILMS OR SCENES ON THE SUBJECT OF...

(Note: Other than belonging to the same category, forget about finding an order to these lists; just check stuff out as you please.)

BOXING: *The Set Up* with Robert Ryan; *Requiem for a Heavyweight* with Anthony Quinn (film) or Jack Palance (TV); *Champion* with Kirk Douglas; *Gentleman Jim* with Errol Flynn; *Raging Bull* with Robert DeNiro; *Rocky* and *Rocky III* with Sylvester Stallone; *City for Conquest* with James Cagney; *Somebody Up There Likes Me* with Paul Newman; *Golden Boy* with Bill Holden; *The Champ* with Wallace Beery; *Jack Johnson* (a documentary on the great fighter, with a score by Miles Davis!); *The Life of Jimmy Dolan* with Douglas Fairbanks and *The Harder They Fall* (Bogie's last and another great).

GOLF: *Banning*; *Follow the Sun* (not the greatest but, after all, it's Glenn Ford playing Ben Hogan); *Tin Cup*; *The Dentist* and *You're Telling Me* (both with W.C. Fields).

TRACK: *Blackbeard's Ghost*; *Gallipoli*; *Chariots of Fire* and *The Bob Mathias Story* (with Ward Bond and Mathias playing himself).

HOCKEY: *Slapshot* with Paul Newman and the Hanson Brothers (when released in Japan, it was called *The Cursing Roughhouse Rascal Who Plays Dirty*) and *The Deadliest Season* (a TV movie).

FOOTBALL: *North Dallas Forty* (with the late great John Matuzak); *Jim Thorpe—All American*; *Knute Rockne—All American*; *The Longest Yard*; *M*A*S*H*; *Horsefeathers* (with The Marx Brothers) and *Navy, Blue and Gold* (the great Annapolis football story, from 1937).

RUGBY: *This Sporting Life* (a brutal portrayal of the sport; with Richard Harris).

BASEBALL: *Pride of the Yankees*; *Bull Durham*; *Bad News Bears*; *The Natural*; *It Happens Every Spring*; *Pride of St. Louis*; *Bang the Drum Slowly* and *The Babe Ruth Story* (unintentionally the most hilarious baseball movie ever made). Also special mention for *Walking Tall*; Walter Hill's *The Warriors*; Robert De Niro as Al Capone in *The Untouchables* and *Casino* (ouch).

BASKETBALL: *Hoosiers*; *Hoop Dreams*; *Go, Man, Go!* (a great story about the origin of the Harlem Globetrotters); *The Great Santini* and *The Absent Minded Professor*.

RACING: *Genevieve*; *Death Race 2000*; *The Last American Hero* (Jeff Bridges and some amazing driving scenes); *Le Mans* and *Winning*.

BULLFIGHTING: *Bullfighter and the Lady* (the Duke produced and Budd Boetticher directed); *Blood and Sand* (all three versions) and *The Sun Also Rises*.

MOUNTAIN CLIMBING: *The Crawling Eye* and *The Abominable Snowman of the Himilayas* (both featuring Forrest Tucker).

FLYING: *Those Magnificent Men in Their Flying Machines*; *Flying Leathernecks*; *Things to Come*; *Flight of the Phoenix*; *Airplane!*; *Thirty Seconds Over Tokyo* (Spencer Tracy as Jimmy Doolittle); *The Great Waldo Pepper*; *The High and the Mighty*; *Wings* (don't let any film book tell you that this is anything but a "must see"—William Wellman, a World War I flyer, made this exciting and heartbreaking classic); *Hell's Angels* from Howard Hughes; *Memphis Belle* (the 1944 William Wyler documentary); *Air Force*; *Twelve O'Clock High*; *Only Angels Have Wings* (with Clark Gable) and *The Giant Claw* (another fine product of 1957).

FISHING: *Captains Courageous*; *The Old Man and the Sea*; *Islands in the Stream*; *A River Runs Through It*; *Jaws* and *Waterworld*.

HUNTING: *The Naked Prey*; *Tarzan, the Ape Man* (with the original Great White Hunter, C. Aubrey Smith); *The Macomber Affair* (Gregory Peck in a great adaptation of Hemingway's work) and *White Hunter, Black Heart* (Clint directs Clint on John Huston).

DOGS: *Call of the Wild*; *Lassie Come Home*; *The Thin Man*; *After the Thin Man* (the noble Asta's best part); *Shadow of the Thin Man*; *Courage of Lassie*; *Lady and the Tramp*; *101 Dalmatians*; *Beethoven*; *The Biscuit Eater* (catch it if you can); *The Ugly Dachshund*; *Old Yeller* and *Frankenweenie*.

HORSES: *Phar Lap*; *Kentucky* (Walter Brennan as the greatest judge of horse flesh who ever lived); the chariot race in William Wyler's *Ben-Hur* (staged by Yakima Canutt and directed by Andrew Marton) and the countryside race in *The Quiet Man*.

POKER: *Cincinnati Kid*; *Kaleidescope*; *The Sting*; *House of Games*; *Lifeboat* and *Mississippi* (the great W.C. Fields with five aces).

CRAPS: *Guys and Dolls* (street craps); *The Only Game in Town* and *Any Number Can Play* (bank craps).

POOL: on the serious side, there's *The Hustler* and only *The Hustler*. Otherwise; you can't beat Peter Sellers playing against George Sanders in *A Shot in the Dark* or W.C. Fields as sheriff and stickman in *Six of a Kind*.

BARROOM BRAWL: *North to Alaska*; *Destry Rides Again* (the greatest cat fight ever features Marlene Dietrich tearing at Una Merkel); the Duke and Lee Marvin battle the Aussies in *Donovan's Reef*; *The Devil's Brigade* and, of course, Clint driving a train into a saloon in *Joe Kidd*. Special, if brief, mention must be made of the sheer intensity of the bar fight in *Lady Takes a Chance*. Made in 1943; it's a pretty flawless piece of

Kaufmann Lake Dragon™

entertainment starring John Wayne and Jean Arthur. He's the rugged rodeo star "from the West" (great stock rodeo footage) and she's a wide-eyed gal "from the East" on a bus tour (guided by Phil Silvers!). The Duke, and in this film he's called "Duke," does his best to deflect the unwelcome advances to Arthur made by a drunk, but the insistent pest throws a sucker punch and Duke has to clobber him. It's a beautiful roundhouse that sends the hapless schmo skidding across the floor in a collapsed chair. The requisite hell breaks loose, and what follows is some high-end choreography of pain inflicting. The inspired falls, flying fists and mid-air collisions make this one a Wince-O-Rama. The Duke, ever the gentleman, escorts his date out the second story window and into a hay wagon.

FIGHT SCENE (one-on-one):
F/X (Bryan Brown's incredibly scary encounter with a deadly agent); *The Quiet Man*; *Lethal Weapon*; *From Here to Eternity*; *Any Which Way You Can*; *The Spoilers* (mythic matchup between the Duke and Randolph Scott) and *The Treasure of the Sierra Madre* (two-on-one and brief, but one of the most realistically painful).

SEA BATTLE:
Captain Horatio Hornblower.

SWORDPLAY:
The Adventures of Robin Hood; *The Princess Bride*; *Romeo and Juliet*; *The Mark Of Zorro* (both the amazing silent with Douglas Fairbanks and the remake with Tyrone Power, featuring Basil Rathbone's agonizingly realistic death scene); *The Last of the Mohicans* (with Daniel Day Lewis as Hawkeye and Russell Means as the deadly Chingachagook, including the most excruciating compound fracture, for Wes Studi as Magua, since *Deliverance*—some sounds you just never forget—this one buries the needle on the Squirm-O-Meter); *Cyrano de Bergerac* (both versions, with Jose Ferrer and Gerard Depardieu); *The Black Shield of Falworth* (with Torin Thatcher as the supreme combat mentor, Sir James); *El Cid* (Chuck Heston's trial by combat); *Ivanhoe* (another great trial by combat, this time between George Sanders with mace and Robert Taylor with battle ax); *Scaramouche* (said to be the longest swordfight in film history—Stewart Granger obviously having a ball with this one); *Monty Python and the Holy Grail* (King Arthur vs. the annoyingly persistent Black Knight—to a draw) and the knife fight in *Butch Cassidy and the Sundance Kid.*

PRISON:
I Am a Fugitive From a Chain Gang (Paul Muni at his best); *The Bridge on the River Kwai*; *Cool Hand Luke*; *Shawshank Redemption*; *White Heat*; *The Big House* (the granddaddy of 'em all, with Wallace Beery); *Brute Force* (Burt Lancaster; Hume Cronyn; Charles Bickford—incredible); *Escape From New York*; *Papillon*; *An Innocent Man*; *Midnight Express*; *The Last Gangster* (terrific, with Edward G.); *The Hill* (with Sean Connery); *20,000 Years in Sing Sing*; *The Great Escape* and *Stalag 17.*

SUBMARINE:
Run Silent, Run Deep; *Das Boot*; *The Hunt for Red October*; *49th Parallel*; *Destination Tokyo*; *The Enemy Below*; *We Dive At Dawn* & *Above Us the Waves* (British); *Operation Petticoat*; *20,000 Thousand Leagues Under the Sea*; *Mysterious Island*; *Men Without Women* (a film that is pre-

sumed lost, with Ford directing and the Duke getting his first decent bit part—this footage convinced Raoul Walsh to star him in *The Big Trail*).

BEST "SARGE":
the pug-nosed Louis Wolheim in *All Quiet on the Western Front*; Jack Webb in *The D.I.*; the Duke in *Sands of Iwo Jima*; Louis Gossett, Jr., in *An Officer and a Gentleman*; Lee Ermey (a real D.I.) in *Full Metal Jacket*; Victor McLaglen in *Wee Willie Winkie* (MacDuff), *Fort Apache* (Mulcahy), *She Wore a Yellow Ribbon* and *Rio Grande* (Quincannon); Burt Lancaster in *From Here to Eternity* (good); Ernest Borgnine in *From Here to Eternity* (bad); Forrest Tucker (well, hell, yes) in "F-Troop" and Vic Morrow in "Combat."

"DEAD GUY" MOVIES:
Bill Holden in *Sunset Blvd.*; Rex Harrison in *The Ghost and Mrs. Muir*; Lou Costello in *The Time of Their Lives*; Charles Laughton in *The Canterville Ghost*; Paul Muni in *Angel on My Shoulder*; Cary Grant in *Topper*; Robert Montgomery in *Here Comes Mr. Jordon*; Rex Harrison in *Blithe Spirit*; Warren Beatty in the remake *Heaven Can Wait*; Edmond O'Brien in *D.O.A.*; David Niven in *Stairway to Heaven*; Albert Brooks in *Defending Your Life*; Boris Karloff in *Frankenstein* and Bela Lugosi in *Dracula.*

"DEATH GUY" MOVIES:
Sir Cedric Hardwicke in *On Borrowed Time*; Fredric March in *Death Takes a Holiday* and the bony specter who points out the salmon mousse in *Monty Python's Meaning of Life.*

GREATEST BADDEST BAD GUY:
Lee Van Cleef as "Angel Eyes" in *The Good, the Bad, and the Ugly*; Al Lettieri in anything, but particularly as the snarling "Frank" in *Mr. Majestyk*; Bill McKinney in *The Outlaw Josey Wales* and *Deliverance*; Richard Boone in *Big Jake* and in Budd Boetticher's *The Tall T* with Randolph Scott; Burt Lancaster in *Vera Cruz*; Clint Eastwood in *Unforgiven*; Robert Shaw in *From Russia With Love*; John Colicos as "Koor" in "Star Trek" (it's the way he says, "vegetable"); Michael Ironside in *Scanners*; Henry Fonda (amazingly, and to the point of hurting his career) in Leone's *Once Upon a Time in the West*; Bruce Dern's sadistically vicious character who kills the Duke in *The Cowboys*; whip-wielding Walter Matthau in *The Kentuckian* (directed by star Burt Lancaster).

GREATEST FILM FEATURING A GUY WITH A CHAINSAW FOR A HAND:
Sam Raimi's *Army of Darkness*, starring Bruce Campbell.

MOST MEMORABLE FILM SCENE FEATURING CHARLES BRONSON GETTING HIS ARM RUN OVER BY A TANK:
Battle of the Bulge (in Wince-O-Rama).

GREATEST ALL-TIME MOVIE WITH EVERYONE EITHER DEAD OR GETTING DEAD:
George Romero's 1968 *Night of the Living Dead.*

Bead Head Zug Bug

FILMS FOR GUYS

Ace in the Hole aka *The Big Carnival*—Stars: Kirk Douglas, Jan Sterling, Bob Arthur; Director: Billy Wilder; Screenplay: Billy Wilder

The African Queen 1951—Stars: Humphrey Bogart, Katharine Hepburn, Robert Morley; Director: John Huston; Screenplay: John Huston, James Agee

Air Force 1943—Stars: John Garfield, John Ridgely, Gig Young, Arthur Kennedy, Harry Carrey, George Tobias, Faye Emerson; Director: Howard Hawks

All Quiet on the Western Front 1930—Stars: Lew Ayres, Louis Wolheim, John Wray, Slim Summerville, Walter Gleason; Director: Lewis Milestone; Screenplay: Lewis Maxwell, Maxwell Anderson, Del Andrews and George Abbott

The Americanization of Emily 1964—Stars: James Garner, Julie Andrews, Melvyn Douglas, James Coburn, Judy Carne, Keenan Wynn; Director: Arthur Hiller; Screenplay: Paddy Chayefsky

Angels With Dirty Faces 1938—Stars: James Cagney, Pat O'Brien, Humphrey Bogart, Ann Sheridan, George Bancroft, the Dead End Kids; Director: Michael Curtiz; Screenplay: John Wexley; Music: Max Steiner

Barry Lyndon 1975—Stars: Ryan O'Neal, Marisa Berenson, Patrick

Theo's Bead Head Pheasant Tail™

Magee, Hardy Kruger, Gay Hamilton; Director: Stanley Kubrick

Ben-Hur 1926—Stars: Ramon Navarro, Francis X. Bushman, May McAvoy, Betty Bronson, Claire McDowell; Director: Fred Niblo

The Big Heat 1953—Stars: Glenn Ford, Gloria Grahame, Jocelyn Brando, Lee Marvin, Carolyn Jones, Jeanette Nolan; Director: Fritz Lang

Big Jake 1971—Stars: John Wayne, Richard Boone, Maureen O'Hara, Patrick Wayne, Chris Mitchum; Director: George Sherman; Music: Elmer Bernstein

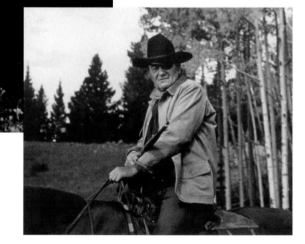

The Big Sky 1952—Stars: Kirk Douglas, Dewey Martin, Arthur Hunnicut, Elizabeth Threat, Jim Davis; Director: Howard Hawks; Screenplay: Dudley Nichols

The Big Red One 1980—Stars: Lee Marvin, Robert Carradine, Mark Hamill; Stephane Audran; Director: Samuel Fuller; Screenplay: Samuel Fuller

The Big Sleep 1946—Stars: Humphrey Bogart, Lauren Bacall, John Ridgely, Martha Vickers; Director: Howard Hawks; Screenplay: William Faulkner,

Jules Furthman, Leigh Brackett

The Big Trail 1930—Stars: John Wayne, Marguerite Churchill, El Brendel, Tully Marshall, Tyrone Power Sr., Ward Bond, Helen Parrish; Director: Raoul Walsh

Big Wednesday 1978—Stars: Jan-Michael Vincent, Gary Busey, William Katt, Lee Purcell; Director: John Milius; Screenplay: John Milius Music: Basil Poledouris

The Black Shield of Falworth 1954—Stars: Tony Curtis, Janet Leigh, Torin Thatcher; Director: Rudolph Mate; Based on the novel by Howard Pyle

The Black Swan 1900—Stars: Tyrone Power, Maureen O'Hara, Thomas Mitchell, George Sanders, Anthony Quinn; Director: Henry King

Blade Runner 1982—Stars: Harrison Ford, Rutger Hauer, Sean Young, Daryl Hannah, M. Emmett Walsh; Director: Ridley Scott; Screenplay: Hampton Fancher, David Peoples; Music: Vangelis

Breaker Morant 1980—Stars: Edward Woodward, Jack Thompson, John Waters, Bryan Brown; Director: Bruce Beresford; Screenplay: Jonathon Hardy, David Stevens, Bruce Beresford

Brute Force 1947—Stars: Burt Lancaster, Hume Cronyn, Charles Bickford, Yvonne De Carlo; Director: Jules Dassin; Screenplay: Richard Brooks

Butch Cassidy and the Sundance Kid 1969—Stars: Paul Newman, Robert Redford, Katharine Ross, Jeff Corey, Strother Martin; Director: George Roy Hill; Screenplay: William Goldman Music: Burt Bacharach (try not to listen)

The Caine Mutiny 1954—Stars:

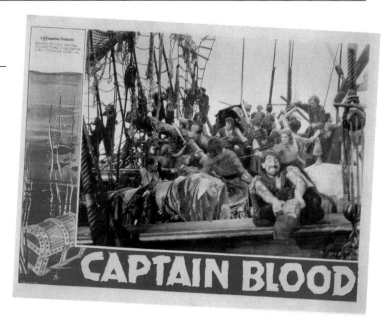

Humphrey Bogart, Jose Ferrer, Van Johnson, Fred MacMurray, Lee Marvin, Claude Akins, E.G. Marshall, Tom Tully; Director: Edward Dmytryk; Screenplay: Stanley Roberts; Music: Max Steiner

The Call of the Wild 1935—Stars: Clark Gable, Jack Oakey, Loretta Young; Director: William Wellman; Based on the novel by Jack London

Captain Blood 1935—Stars: Errol Flynn, Olivia de Havilland, Basil Rathbone, J. Carrol Naish, Lionel Atwil; Director: Michael Curtiz; Based on the novel by Rafael Sabatini; Music: Erich Wolfgang Korngold

Champion 1949—Stars: Kirk Douglas, Arthur Kennedy, Marilyn Maxwell, Ruth Roman, Lola Albright; Director: Mark Robson

The Charge of the Light Brigade 1936—Stars: Errol Flynn, Olivia de Havilland, David Niven, Nigel Bruce, C. Aubrey Smith, Donald Crisp; Director: Michael Curtiz; Music: Max Steiner

Citizen Kane 1941—Stars: Orson Welles, Joseph Cotten, Everett Sloane, Dorothy Comingore,

It's Terrific! ORSON WELLES CITIZEN KANE

COUNTRY OF ORIGIN U.S.A. 4012/562

Ruth Warrick, George Coulouris, Ray Collins, William Alland, Paul Stewart, Erskine Sanford, Agnes Moorehead, Alan Ladd; Director: Orson Welles; Screenplay: Orson Welles, Herman J. Mankiewicz; Music: Bernard Hermann

A Clockwork Orange 1971—Stars: Malcolm McDowell, Patrick Magee, Adrienne Corri, Michael Bates, Warren Clarke, Aubrey Morris, David Prowse; Director: Stanley Kubrick; Screenplay: Stanley Kubrick

Cool Hand Luke 1967—Stars: Paul Newman, George Kennedy, J.D. Cannon, Strother Martin, Dennis Hopper, Joe Don Baker, Anthony Zerbe; Director: Stuart Rosenberg; Screenplay: Frank Pierson; Music: Lalo Schifrin

The Cowboys 1972—Stars: John Wayne, Roscoe Lee Browne, A. Martinez, Bruce Dern, Colleen Dewhurst, Slim Pickens, Robert Carradine; Director: Mark Rydell; Screenplay: Harriet Frank Jr.,

Irving Ravetch, William Dale Jenning, based on the novel by Jenning; Music: John Williams

Cyrano de Bergerac 1950—Stars: Jose Ferrer, Mala Powers, William Prince, Elena Verdugo; Director: Michael Gordon; Screenplay: Carl Foreman Music: Dimitri Tiomkin

The Deer Hunter 1978—Stars: Robert

THE DEER HUNTER

EMI Films presents ROBERT DE NIRO in A MICHAEL CIMINO film THE DEER HUNTER

co-starring JOHN CAZALE · JOHN SAVAGE · MERYL STREEP · CHRISTOPHER WALKEN

Music composed by STANLEY MYERS · Director of Photography VILMOS ZSIGMOND A.S.C. Associate Producers MARION ROSENBERG · JOANN CARELLI Production Consultant JOANN CARELLI Story by MICHAEL CIMINO, DERIC WASHBURN and LOUIS GARFINKLE, QUINN K. REDEKER Screenplay by DERIC WASHBURN · Produced by BARRY SPIKINGS · MICHAEL DEELEY · MICHAEL CIMINO and JOHN PEVERALL

Directed by MICHAEL CIMINO

Technicolor® · Panavision® Stereo Distributed by EMI Films Limited © 1978 by EMI Film, Inc.

De Niro, Christopher Walken, Meryl Streep, John Savage, Amy Wright; Director: Michael Cimino; Screenplay: Deric Washburn, Michael Cimino; Music: John Williams

Destry Rides Again 1939—Stars: James Stewart, Marlene Dietrich, Brian Donlevy, Billy Gilbert, Jack Carson; Director: George Marshall; Screenplay: Gertrude Percell, Felix Jackson and Henry Meyers

Dirty Dingus Magee 1970—Stars: Frank Sinatra, George Kennedy, Anne Jackson, Lois Nettleton, Michele Carey, Jack Elam, Harry Carey Jr.; Director: Burt Kennedy; Screenplay: Joseph Heller

The Dirty Dozen 1967—Stars: Lee Marvin, Ernest Borgnine, Charles Bronson, Jim Brown, George Kennedy, John Cassavetes, Clint Walker, Telly Savalas, Robert Ryan, Richard Jaeckel; Director: Robert Aldrich

Dirty Harry 1971—Stars: Clint Eastwood, Harry Guardino, Andrew Robinson; Director: Donald Siegel; Music: Lalo Schifrin

Dodsworth 1936—Stars: Walter Huston, David Niven, Mary Astor; Director: William Wyler; Screenplay: Sidney Howard, based on the novel by Sinclair Lewis

Drums Along the Mohawk 1939—Stars: Claudette Colbert, Henry Fonda, Edna May Oliver, Arthur Shields, Ward Bond; Director: John Ford; Screenplay: Lamar Trotti, Sonya Levien, based on the novel by Walter Edmonds

El Cid 1961—Stars: Charlton Heston, Sophia Loren, Raf Vallone, Genevieve Page; Director: Anthony Mann; Screenplay: Phillip Yordan; Music: Miklos Rozsa

El Dorado 1967—Stars: John Wayne, Robert Mitchum, James Caan, Charlene Holt, Ed Asner, Christopher George; Director: Howard Hawks; Screenplay: Leigh Brackett

Elmer Gantry 1960—Stars: Burt Lancaster, Shirley Jones, Jean

Kaufmann's Stone Bead Head™

Simmons, Dean Jagger, Arthur Kennedy; Director: Richard Brooks; Screenplay: Richard Brooks; Music: Andre Previn

The Endless Summer
1966—Stars: Mike Hynson, Robert August; Director: Bruce Brown; Screenplay: Bruce Brown; Music: Theme by The Sandals

The Endless Summer 2
1994—Stars: Robert "Wingnut" Weaver, Pat O'Connell, Robert August; Director: Bruce Brown; Screenplay: Bruce Brown, Dana Brown; Music: Gary Hoey, Dick Dale

Escape From New York
1981—Stars: Kurt Russell, Lee Van Cleef, Ernest Borgnine, Donald Pleasance, Isaac Hayes, Adrienne Barbeau, Harry Dean Stanton; Director: John Carpenter; Screenplay: John Carpenter, Nick

Castle; Music: John Carpenter

The Fastest Gun Alive
1956—Stars: Glenn Ford, Jeanne Crain, Broderick Crawford, Russ Tamblyn, Leif Erickson; Director: Russel Rouse; Screenplay: Russel Rouse, Frank D. Gilroy; Music: Andre Previn

Fighting Seabees
1944—Stars: John Wayne, Susan Hayward, Dennis O'Keefe, William Frawley; Director: Edward Ludwig; Screenplay: Bordon Chase, Aeneas MacKenzie

Ffolkes
1979—Stars: Roger Moore, James Mason, Anthony Perkins; Director: Andrew V. McLaglen

A Fistful of Dollars
1964—Stars: Clint

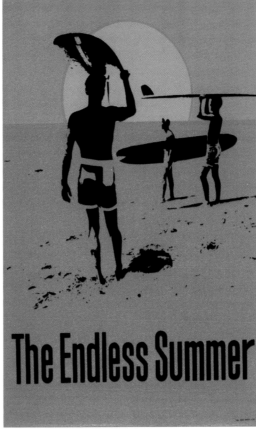

Eastwood, Gian Maria Volonte, Marianne Koch, Wolfgang Lukschy, Carol Brown; Director: Sergio Leone; "Spaghetti Western" remake of Kurosawa's *Yojimbo*

Fort Apache
1948—Stars: John Wayne, Henry Fonda, Shirley Temple, John Agar, Ward Bond, Victor McLaglen; Director: John Ford; Screenplay: Frank S. Nugent, based on the short story by James Warner Bellah; Music: Richard Hageman

The Fountainhead
1949—Stars: Gary Cooper, Patricia Neal, Raymond Massey, Henry Hull; Director: King Vidor; Screenplay: Ayn Rand, based on her novel; Music: Max Steiner

The Four Feathers
1939—Stars: John Clements, Sir Ralph Richardson, Sir C. Aubrey Smith, June Duprez, Donald Gray, Clive Barker; Director: Zoltan Korda; Screenplay: R. C. Sherriff; Music: Miklos Rozsa

The Four Musketeers
1975—Stars: Michael York, Oliver Reed, Richard Chamberlain, Frank Finlay, Raquel Welch, Faye Dunaway, Charlton Heston; Director: Richard Lester; Music: Lalo Schifrin

From Here to Eternity
1953—Stars: Burt Lancaster, Montgomery Clift, Frank Sinatra, Deborah Kerr, Donna Reed, Ernest Borgnine; Director: Fred Zinnemann; Screenplay: Daniel Taradash; Music: George Duning

Gabriel Over the White House
1933—Stars: Walter Huston, Karen Morley, Franchot Tone, C. Henry Gordon, Jean Parker; Director: Gregory La Cava

Gallipoli
1981—Stars: Mel Gibson, Mark Lee, Bill Kerr, David Argue, Tim McKenzie, Robert Grubb; Director: Peter Weir; Screenplay: David Williamson, Peter Weir

Kaufmann Krystal Bugger™

Gentleman Jim 1942—Stars: Errol Flynn, Alan Hale, Alexis Smith, Jack Carson, Ward Bond, Arthur Sheilds, William Frawley; Director: Raoul Walsh

Glengarry Glen Ross 1992—Stars: Al Pacino, Jack Lemmon, Ed Harris, Alec

Baldwin, Alan Arkin, Kevin Spacey, Jonathan Pryce; Director: James Foley; Screenplay: David Mamet; Music: James Newton Howard

Glory 1989—Stars: Matthew Broderick, Morgan Freeman, Denzel Washington, Cary Elwes, Andre Braugher, John Finn; Director: Edward Zwick; Screenplay: Kevin Jarre; Music: James Horner

Gone With the Wind 1939—Stars: Clark Gable, Vivien Leigh, Olivia de Havilland, Leslie Howard, Thomas Mitchell, Butterfly McQueen; Director: Victor Fleming; Screenplay: Sidney Howard; Music: Max Steiner

The Good, the Bad, and the Ugly 1967—Stars: Clint Eastwood, Eli Wallach, Lee Van Cleef; Director: Sergio Leone; Screenplay: Sergio Leone; Music: Ennio Morricone

Goodbye, Mr. Chips 1939—Stars: Robert Donat, Greer Garson, Paul Henreid, John Mills; Director: Sam Wood; Screenplay: R.C.

Sherriff, Claudine West, Eric Maschwitz, based on the novel by James Hilton

The Great Santini 1980—Stars: Robert Duvall, Blythe Danner, Michael O'Keefe, Julie Ann Haddock; Director: Lewis John Carlino; Screenplay: Lewis John Carlino

The Great Train Robbery 1903—Star: 'Broncho Billy' Anderson; Director: Edwin S. Porter

The Great Waldo Pepper 1975—Stars: Robert Redford, Susan Sarandon, Margot Kidder, Geoffrey Lewis, Edward Herrmann; Director: George Roy

Hill; Screenplay: William Goldman; Music: Henry Mancini

The Grey Fox 1983—Stars: Richard Farnsworth, Jackie Burroughs, Wayne Robson, Timothy Webber; Director: Phillip Borsos

Gunfight at the O.K. Corral 1957—Stars: Burt Lancaster, Kirk Douglas, Rhonda Fleming, John Ireland, Lee Van Cleef, Earl Holliman; Director: John Sturges; Screenplay: Leon Uris

The Guns of Navarone 1961—Stars: Gregory Peck, David Niven, Anthony Quinn, Richard Harris, Stanley Baker, James Darren; Director: J. Lee Thompson; Screenplay: Carl Foreman, based on the novel by Alistair MacLean

The Heartbreak Kid 1972—Stars: Charles Grodin, Cybill Shepherd, Eddie Albert, Jeannie Berlin; Director: Elaine May; Screenplay: Neil Simon

Heaven Can Wait 1978—Stars: Warren Beatty, Julie Christie, Charles Grodin, Dyan Cannon, James Mason; Directors: Buck Henry, Warren Beatty; Screenplay: Warren Beatty

The Heiress 1949—Stars: Olivia de Havilland, Montgomery Clift, Ralph Richardson, Miriam Hopkins; Director: William Wyler; Music: Aaron Copland

Hellfighters 1968—Stars: John Wayne, Vera Miles, Katharine Ross, Jim Hutton,

Kaufmann Krystal Bugger™

Bruce Cabot; Director: Andrew V. McLaglen

Hell's Angels 1930—Stars: Jean Harlow, Ben Lyon, James Hall, John Darrow; Director: Howard Hughes; Screenplay: Harry Behn, Howard Estabrook, Joseph Moncure March

The High and the Mighty 1954—Stars: John Wayne, Claire Trevor, Robert Stack, Lorraine Day; Director: William Wellman; Screenplay: Ernest K. Gann; Music: Dimitri Tiomkin

High Noon 1952—Stars: Gary Cooper, Grace Kelly, Lloyd Bridges, Lon Chaney Jr., Lee Van Cleef; Director: Fred Zinnemann; Screenplay: Carl Foreman; Music: Dimitri Tiomkin, Ned Washington (sung by Tex Ritter)

Hondo 1953—Stars: John Wayne, Geraldine Page, Ward Bond, James Arness; Director: John Farrow; Screenplay: James Edward Grant, based on a story by Louis L'Amour

Hoosiers 1986—Stars: Gene Hackman, Barbara Hershey, Dennis Hopper, David Neidorf, Fern Parsons; Director: David Anspaugh; Screenplay: Angelo Pizzo; Music: Jerry Goldsmith

How the West Was Won 1962—Stars: Henry Fonda, George Peppard, Jimmy Stewart, Gregory Peck, Debbie Reynolds, John Wayne, Raymond Massey, Walter Brennan, Carroll Baker, Henry Morgan, Agnes Moorehead, Russ Tamblyn, Andy Devine, Ken Curtis, Karl Malden, Richard Widmark, tons of others and narration by Spencer Tracy; Directors: John Ford, Henry Hathaway, George Marshall, Richard Thorpe; Screenplay: James R. Webb, John Gay; Music: Alfred Newman, Ken Darby

The Hustler 1961—Stars: Paul Newman, Jackie Gleason, Piper Laurie, George C. Scott; Director: Robert Rossen; Screenplay: Rossen, Sidney Carroll, based on the novel by Walter Tevis

I Am a Fugitive From a Chain Gang 1932—Stars: Paul Muni, Glenda Farrell, Helen Vinson, Preston Foster; Director: Mervyn LeRoy; Screenplay: Howard J. Green

The Informer 1935—Stars: Victor McLaglen, Margot Grahame, Joseph Sawyer, Preston Foster, Una O'Conner; Director: John Ford; Screenplay: Dudley Nichols

In Which We Serve 1943—Stars: Noel Coward, John Mills, Bernard Miles, Kay Walsh, Richard Attenborough; Directors: Noel Coward, David Lean; Screenplay: Noel Coward; Music: Noel Coward

If I Were King 1938—Stars: Ronald Colman, Frances Dee, Basil Rathbone; Director: Frank Lloyd; Screenplay: Preston Sturges

Jerimiah Johnson 1972—Stars: Robert Redford, Will Geer; Director: Sydney Pollack; Screenplay: Edward Anhalt, John Mills

Kaufmann Krystal Bugger™

Jim Thorpe-All American
1951—Stars: Burt Lancaster, Charles Bickford, Phyllis Thaxter, Steve Cochran; Director: Michael Curtiz; Screenplay: Douglas S. Morrow

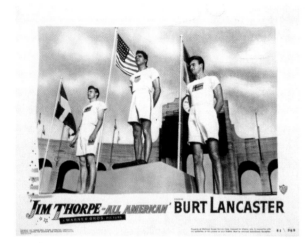

The Killer
1990—Stars: Chow Yun-fat, Sally Yeh, Danny Lee; Director: John Woo; Screenplay: John Woo

The Killing
1956—Stars: Sterling Hayden, Marie Windsor, Elisha Cook Jr., Vince Edwards, Timothy Edwards, Timothy Carey, Coleen Gray; Director: Stanley Kubrick; Based on the novel by Lionel White

King Kong
1933—Stars: Robert Armstrong, Fay Wray, Bruce Cabot; Director: Ernest B. Schoedsack; Music: Max Steiner

The Last of the Mohicans
1920—Stars: Wallace Beery, Clarence Brown, Barbara Bedford; Director: Maurice Tourneur; Based on the novel by James Fenimore Cooper; Music: R. J. Miller in restored special edition

The Last of the Mohicans
1936—Stars: Randolph Scott, Binnie Barnes, Heather Angel, Henry Wilcoxon, Bruce Cabot; Director: George B. Seitz; Screenplay: Philip Dunne

The Last of the Mohicans
1992—Stars: Daniel Day-Lewis, Madeleine Stowe, Russell Means, Wes Studi ; Director: Michael Mann; Screenplay: Mann, Christopher Crowe

The Leopard
1963—Stars: Burt Lancaster, Alain Delon, Claudia Cardinale; Director: Luchino Visconti

The Life and Death of Colonel Blimp
1943—Stars: Roger Livesey, Deborah Kerr, Anton Walbrook, Ursula Jeans; Directors: Michael Powell, Emeric Pressburger; Screenplay: Emeric Pressburger

Little Big Man
1970—Stars: Dustin Hoffman, Faye Dunaway, Chief Dan George, Martin Balsam, Richard Mulligan; Director: Arthur Penn; Screenplay: Calder Willingham, based on the novel byThomas Berger

Lonely Are the Brave
1962—Kirk Douglas, Gena Rowlands, Walter Matthau, Michael Kane, Carroll O'Connor, William Schallert, George Kennedy; Director: David Miller; Screenplay: Dalton Trumbo, based on the novel *Brave Cowboy* by Edward Abbey

Lonesome Dove
(TV) 1989—Stars: Robert Duvall, Tommy Lee Jones, Danny Glover, Anjelica Huston; Director: Simon Wincer; Screenplay: William D. Wittliff, based on the novel by Larry McMurty; Music: Basil Poledouris

The Longest Day
1962—Stars: John Wayne, Richard Burton, Robert Mitchum, Robert Ryan, Sean Connery, Rod Steiger; Director: Ken Annakin; Screenplay: Bernhard Wicki; Music: Maurice Jarre

The Lost Patrol
1934—Stars: Victor McLaglen, Boris Karloff, Wallace Ford, Reginald Denny, Alan Hale; Director: John Ford; Screenplay: Dudley Nichols, based on the novel by Philip MacDonald

Hard Body Ant

Mad Max 1979—Stars: Mel Gibson, Hugh Keays-Byrne, Joanne Samuel, Steve Bisley; Director: George Miller; Screenplay: George Miller

The Magnificent Seven 1960—Stars: Yul Brynner, Steve McQueen, James Coburn, Charles Bronson; Director: John Sturges; Screenplay: William Roberts; Music: Elmer Bernstein

A Man Called Horse 1970—Stars: Richard Harris, Judith Anderson, Jean Bascon, Manu Tupou, Corinna Tsopei, Dub Taylor; Director: Elliot Silverstein Screenplay: Jack DeWitt

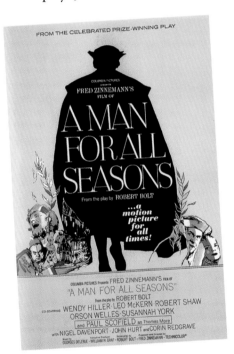

A Man For All Seasons 1966—Stars: Paul Scofield, Robert Shaw, Orson Welles, Susannah York, John Hurt; Director: Fred Zinnemann; Screenplay: Robert Bolt; Music: Georges Delerue

The Man From Snowy River 1982—Stars: Kirk Douglas, Tom Burlinson, Terence Donovan; Director: George Miller

The Man Who Shot Liberty Valance 1962—Stars: James Stewart, John Wayne, Vera Miles, Lee Marvin; Director: John Ford; Screenplay: Willis Goldbeck, James Warner Bellah, based on the story by Dorothy Johnson

The Mark of Zorro 1920—Stars: Douglas Fairbanks, Marguerite De La Motte, Noah Beery

The Mark of Zorro 1940—Stars: Tyrone Power, Linda Darnell, Eugene Pallette, Basil Rathbone; Director: Rouben Mamoulian; Screenplay: John Taintor; Music: Alfred Newman

M*A*S*H 1970—Stars: Donald Sutherland, Elliott Gould, Tom Skerritt, Sally Kellerman, JoAnn Pflug, Robert Duvall; Director: Robert Altman; Screenplay: Ring Lardner Jr.

The Master of Ballantrae 1953—Stars: Errol Flynn, Roger Livesey, Anthony Steel; Director: William Keighley; Based on the novel by Robert Louis Stevenson

Moby Dick 1956—Stars: Gregory Peck, Richard Basehart, Orson Welles; Director: John Huston; Screenplay: Ray Bradbury, John Huston, based on the novel by Melville

Mrs. Miniver 1942—Stars: Greer Garson, Walter Pidgeon, Teresa Wright; Director: William Wyler; Screenplay: George Froeschel, James Hilton, Arthur Wimperis, Claudine West; Music: Herbert Stothart

Mr. Lucky 1943—Stars: Cary Grant, Laraine Day, Charles Bickford; Director: H.C. Potter

Mr. Majestyk 1974—Stars: Charles Bronson, Al Lettiere, Linda Cristal, Lee Purcell; Director: Richard Fleischer; Screenplay: Elmore Leonard; Music: Charles Bernstein

Mr. Robinson Crusoe 1932—Stars: Douglas Fairbanks Sr., William Farnum, Maria Alba; Director: Edward Sutherland; Screenplay: Douglas Fairbanks Sr.; Music: Alfred Newman

The Moon and Sixpence 1943—Stars: George Sanders, Herbert Marshall, Doris Dudley; Director: Albert Lewin; Based on the novel by Somerset Maugham

Mutiny on the Bounty 1935—Stars: Clark Gable, Franchot Tone, Charles Laughton, Donald Crisp; Director: Frank Lloyd; Screenplay: Talbot Jenning, Jules Furthman, Carey

Wilson, based on the Nordhoff-Hall book; Music: Herbert Stothart

My Darling Clementine 1946—Stars: Henry Fonda, Victor Mature, Walter Brennan, Linda Darnell, Tim Holt, Ward Bond; Director: John Ford; Screenplay: Samuel G. Engel, Winston

Kaufmann Mini Leech™

Miller, based on the story by Sam Hellman and book by Stuart N. Lake

My Fair Lady
1964—Stars: Rex Harrison, Audrey Hepburn, Stanley Holloway, Wilfrid Hyde-White; Director: George Cukor; Music: Alan Jay Lerner & Frederick Loewe, adapted by Andre Previn

The Naked Prey
1966—Stars: Cornel Wilde, Gertrude Van Der Berger, Ken Gampu; Director: Cornel Wilde

Napoleon
1927—Stars: Albert Deiudonne, Antonin Artaud, Pierre Batcheff, Gina Manes, Armand Bernard; Director: Abel Gance; Music: Carmine Coppola

Network
1976—Stars: Faye Dunaway, Peter Finch, William Holden, Robert Duvall, Ned Beatty; Director: Sidney Lumet; Screenplay: Paddy Chayefsky

North by Northwest
1959—Stars: Cary Grant, Eva Marie Saint, James Mason, Leo G. Carroll, Martin Landau; Director: Alfred Hitchcock; Screenplay: Ernest Lehman; Music: Bernard Herrmann

North to Alaska
1960—Stars: John Wayne, Stewart

Granger, Ernie Kovacs, Capucine; Director: Henry Hathaway

Objective Burma!
1945—Stars: Errol Flynn, James Brown, William Prince, George Tobias, Henry Hull; Director: Raoul Walsh; Screenplay: Ranald MacDougall, Lester Cole; Music: Franz Waxman

On the Waterfront
1954—Stars: Marlon Brando, Eva Marie Saint, Rod Steiger, Lee J. Cobb, Karl Malden; Director: Elia Kazan; Screenplay: Budd Schulberg; Music: Leonard Bernstein

Once Upon a Time in America
1984—Stars: Robert De Niro, James Woods, Elizabeth McGovern, Joe Pesci; Director: Sergio Leone; Music: Ennio Morricone

Once Upon a Time in the West
1968—Stars: Henry Fonda, Jason Robards Jr., Charles Bronson, Claudia Cardinale, Keenan Wynn, Woody Strode; Director: Sergio Leone; Screenplay: Sergio Leone, Bernardo Bertolucci, Dario Argento; Music: Ennio Morricone

Only Angels Have Wings
1939—Stars: Cary Grant, Thomas Mitchell, Richard Barthelmess, Jean Arthur, Noah Beery; Director: Howard Hawks; Screenplay: Jules Furthman; Music: Dimitri Tiomkin

Papillon
1973—Stars: Steve McQueen, Dustin Hoffman, Victor Jory, Anthony Zerbe; Director: Franklin J. Schaffner; Screenplay: Dalton Trumbo and Lorenzo Semple Jr., based on the autobiography of Henri Charriere; Music: Jerry Goldsmith

Paths of Glory
1957—Stars: Kirk Douglas, Adolphe Menjou, George Macready, Ralph Meeker, Richard Anderson, Bert Freed; Director: Stanley Kubrick; Screenplay: Calder Willingham, Stanley Kubrick

Posse 1975—Stars: Kirk Douglas, Bruce Dern, Bo Hopkins, James Stacy, Luke Askew, David Canary; Director: Kirk Douglas; Screenplay: William Robert

The Private Lives of Henry VIII 1933—Stars: Charles Laughton, Binnie Barnes, Elsa Lanchester, Robert Donat; Director: Alexander Korda; Screenplay: Arthur Wimperis, Lajos Biro

The Professionals 1966—Stars: Burt Lancaster, Lee Marvin, Claudia Cardinale, Jack Palance, Robert Ryan, Woody Strode; Director: Richard Brooks; Screenplay: Richard Brooks

Raising Arizona 1987—Stars: Nicolas Cage, Holly Hunter, John Goodman, William Forsythe, Randall "Tex" Cobb; Director: Joel Coen; Screenplay: Ethan Coen, Joel Coen; Music: Carter Burwell

The Red Badge of Courage 1951—Stars: Audie Murphy, Bill Mauldin, Douglas Dicky Devine with narration by James Whitmore; Director: John Huston; Based on the novel by Stephen Crane

Red Dust 1932—Stars: Clark Gable, Jean Harlow, Mary Astor, Donald Crisp; Director: Victor Fleming; Screenplay: John Lee Mahin

Red River 1948—Stars: John Wayne, Montgomery Clift, Walter Brennan, Joanne Dru, John Ireland, Noah Beery Jr.; Director: Howard Hawks; Screenplay: Borden Chase, Charles Schnee; Music: Dimitri Tiomkin

Ride the High Country 1962—Stars: Randolph Scott, Joel McCrea, Mariette Hartley, Edgar Buchanan, Warren Oates; Director: Sam Peckinpah; Music: George Bassman

The Right Stuff 1983—Stars: Ed Harris, Dennis Quaid, Sam Shepard, Scott Glenn, Fred Ward, Kathy Baker; Director: Philip Kaufman Screenplay: Philip Kaufman, based on the novel by Tom Wolfe

Rio Grande 1950—Stars: John Wayne, Maureen O'Hara, Ben Johnson, Victor McLaglen, Chill Wills; Director: John Ford; Screenplay: James Kevin McGuinness, based on the story by James Warner Bellah; Music: Victor Young, The Sons of the Pioneers

Rio Lobo 1970—Stars: John Wayne, Jorge Rivero, Jennifer O'Neill, Jack Elam, Chris Mitchum, one line from George Plimpton; Director: Howard Hawks; Music: Jerry Goldsmith

Rollerball 1975—Stars: James Caan, John Houseman, Moses Gunn; Director: Norman Jewison; Music: Andre Previn

Romeo and Juliet 1968—Stars: Olivia Hussey, Leonard Whiting, Michael York, Milo O'Shea; Director: Franco Zeffirelli; Music: Nino Rota

Run Silent, Run Deep 1958—Stars: Burt Lancaster, Clark Gable, Jack

Warden, Don Rickles; Director: Robert Wise; Screenplay: John Gay

Sahara 1943—Stars: Humphrey Bogart, Dan Duryea, Lloyd Bridges, J. Carrol Naish; Director: Zoltan Korda

Sands of Iwo Jima 1949—Stars: John Wayne, Forrest Tucker, John Agar, Richard Jaeckel, includes appearances by three of the vets who raised the flag on Mt. Suribachi; Director: Allan Dwan; Screenplay: Harry Brown, James Edward Grant; Music: Victor Young

Scaramouche 1952—Stars: Stewart Granger, Eleanor Parker, Janet Leigh, Mel Ferrer; Director: George Sidney

Screenplay: Ronald Millar, George Froeschel, based on the novel by Sabatini

The Sea Hawk 1940—Stars: Errol Flynn, Claude Rains, Donald Crisp, Alan Hale, Flora Robson; Director: Michael Curtiz; Screenplay: Howard Koch, based on the Sabatini novel; Music: Erich Wolfgang Korngold

The Sea Wolf 1941—Stars: Edward G. Robinson, Alexander Knox, John Garfield, Ida Lupino, Gene Lockhart, Barry Fitzgerald; Director: Michael Curtiz; Screenplay: Robert Rossen, based on the novel by Jack London

The Searchers 1956—Stars: John Wayne, Jeffrey Hunter, Vera Miles, Natalie Wood, Ward Bond; Director: John Ford; Screenplay: Frank Nugent, based on the novel by Alan LeMay; Music: Max Steiner

Sergeant York 1941—Stars: Gary Cooper, Walter Brennan, Joan Leslie, George Tobias; Director: Howard Hawks; Screenplay: Abem Finkel, Harry Chandlee, Howard Koch, John Huston from true WWII experiences of Alvin York; Music: Max Steiner

The Set-Up 1949—Stars: Robert Ryan, Audrey Totter, George Tobias, Alan Baxter; Director: Robert Wise; Screenplay: Art Cohen, based on a poem (if you can believe it) by Joseph Moncure March

Seven Samurai 1954—Stars: Toshiro Mifune, Takashi Shimura, Yoshio Inaba, Ko Kimura, Seiji Miyaguchi; Director: Akira Kurosawa; Screenplay: Kurasawa; Music: Furnio Hayasaka

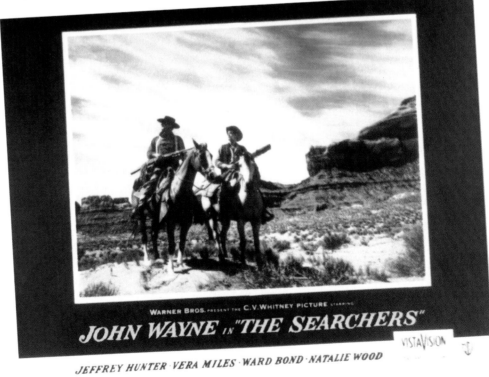

Kaufmann Floating Dragon™

Shane 1953—Stars: Alan Ladd, Jean Arthur, Van Heflin, Ben Johnson, Jack Palance; Director: George Stevens; Screenplay: A.B. Guthrie Jr., based on the novel by Jack Schaefer; Music: Victor Young

Shogun (TV) 1980—Stars: Richard Chamberlain, Toshiro Mifune, Yoko Shimada, Frankie Sakai, John Rhys-Davies, Yuri Meguro and narration by Orson Welles; Director: Jerry London; Based on the novel by James Clavell; Music: Maurice Jarre

The Shootist 1976—Stars: John Wayne, Lauren Bacall, Ron Howard, James Stewart, Richard Boone, Sheree North; Director: Donald Siegel; Screenplay: Miles Hood Swarthout, Scott Hale, based on the novel by Glendon Swarthout; Music: Elmer Bernstein

The Sons of Katie Elder 1965—Stars: John Wayne, Dean Martin, Earl Holliman, Michael Anderson Jr.; Director: Henry Hathaway; Screenplay: William H. Wright, Allan Weiss, Harry Essex; Music: Elmer Bernstein

Stagecoach 1939—Stars: John Wayne, Claire Trevor, Thomas Mitchell, John Carradine, Andy Devine; Director: John Ford; Screenplay: Dudley Nichols, based on a short story by Ernest Haycox; Music: Richard Hageman, W. Franke Harling, John Leipold, Leo Shuken, Louis Gruenberg from early American folk songs

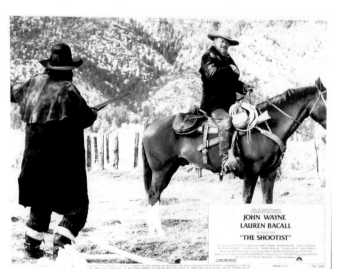

Stairway to Heaven 1946—Stars: David Niven, Kim Hunter, Raymond Massey, Roger Livesy, Richard Attenborough; Directors: Michael Powell, Emeric Pressburger; Screenplay: Emeric Pressburger, Michael Powell

The Sullivans 1944—Stars: Anne Baxter, Thomas Mitchell, Ward Bond, Bobby Driscoll; Director: Lloyd Bacon

Sunset Blvd. 1950—Stars: William Holden, Gloria Swanson, Erich von Stroheim, Nancy Olson, Buster Keaton, Cecil B. DeMille; Director: Billy Wilder; Screenplay: Billy Wilder, Charles Brackett, D.M. Marshman Jr.; Music: Franz Waxman

Swept Away 1975—Stars: Giancarlo Giannini, Mariangela Melato; Director: Lina Wertmuller; Screenplay: Lina Wertmuller

Tall in the Saddle 1944—Stars: John Wayne, Ella Raines, "Gabby" Hayes, Ward Bond; Director: Edwin L. Marin

Taxi Driver 1976—Stars: Robert De Niro, Jodie Foster, Harvey Keitel, Cybill Shepherd; Director: Martin Scorsese; Screenplay: Paul Schrader; Music: Bernard Herrmann

The Ten Commandments 1956—Stars: Charlton Heston, Yul Brynner, Anne Baxter, Edward G. Robinson, Yvonne DeCarlo, Cedric Hardwicke, Woody Strode; Director: Cecil B. DeMille

Tender Mercies 1983—Stars: Robert Duvall, Tess Harper, Betty Buckley, Ellen Barkin, Wilford Brimley; Director: Bruce Beresford; Screenplay: Horton Foote; Music: George Dreyfus with songs written by Duvall

Thief 1981—Stars: James Caan, Tuesday Weld, Willie Nelson, James Belushi, Robert Prosky; Director: Michael Mann; Screenplay: Michael Mann; Music: Tangerine Dream

Three Comrades 1938—Stars: Robert Taylor, Margaret Sullavan, Franchot Tone, Robert Young, Lionel Atwill; Director: Frank Borzage; Screenplay: F. Scott Fitzgerald

They Died With Their Boots On 1941—Stars: Errol Flynn, Sydney Greenstreet, Anthony Quinn, Hattie McDaniel, Olivia de Havilland, Arthur Kennedy; Director: Raoul Walsh

They Were Expendable 1945—Stars: Robert Montgomery, John Wayne, Donna Reed, Jack Holt, Ward Bond; Director: John Ford Screenplay: Frank "Spig" Wead

The Thief of Bagdad 1924—Stars: Douglas Fairbanks Sr., Snitz Edwards, Charles Belcher, Anna May Wong; Director: Raoul Walsh; Music: Carl Davis

The Thief of Bagdad 1940—Stars: Sabu, John Justin, June Duprez, Conrad Veidt, Rex Ingram; Directors:

Michael Powell, Ludwig Berger, Tim Whelan; Music: Miklos Rozsa

Throne of Blood 1957—Stars: Toshiro Mifune, Isuzu Yamada, Takashi Shimura, Minoru Chiaki; Director: Akira Kurosawa; Screenplay: Hideo Oguni, Shinobu Hashimoto, Riyuzo Kikushima, Akira Kurosawa; Music: Masaru Sato

Thunderbolt and Lightfoot 1974—Stars: Clint Eastwood, Jeff Bridges, Geoffrey Lewis, Gary Busey; Director: Michael Cimino; Screenplay: Michael Cimino; Music: Dee Barton

The Tin Star 1957—Stars: Henry Fonda, Anthony Perkins, Betsy Palmer, Neville Brand, Lee Van Cleef; Director: Anthony Mann; Music: Elmer Bernstein

To Have and Have Not 1944—Stars: Humphrey Bogart, Lauren Bacall, Walter Brennan, Sheldon Leonard; Director: Howard Hawks; Screenplay: William Faulkner, Jules Furthman, based on the novel by Hemingway

To Kill a Mockingbird 1962—Stars: Gregory Peck, Brock Peters, Philip Alford, Robert Duvall; Director: Robert Mulligan; Screenplay: Horton Foote, Music: Elmer Bernstein

Tombstone 1993—Stars: Kurt Russell, Val Kilmer, Michael Biehn, Sam Elliott, Dana Delany, Bill Paxton, Billy Zane, Powers Boothe; Director: George P. Cosmatos; Screenplay: Kevin Jarre; Music: Bruce Broughton

Tora! Tora! Tora! 1970—Stars: Martin Balsam, Soh Yomamura, Joseph Cotten, E.G. Marshall; Director: Richard Fleischer, Toshio Masuda, Kinji Fukasaku; Music: Jerry Goldsmith

Treasure of the Sierra Madre 1948—Stars: Humphrey Bogart, Walter Huston, Tim Holt, Robert Blake; Director: John Huston; Screenplay: John Huston; Music: Max Steiner

True Grit 1969—Stars: John Wayne, Glen Campbell, Kim Darby, Robert Duvall; Director: Henry Hathaway; Based on the novel by Charles Portis; Music: Elmer Bernstein

Twelve O'Clock High 1949—Stars: Gregory Peck, Hugh Marlowe, Gary Merrill, Millard Mitchell, Dean Jagger; Director: Henry King; Screenplay: Sy Bartlett and Bernie Lay Jr.

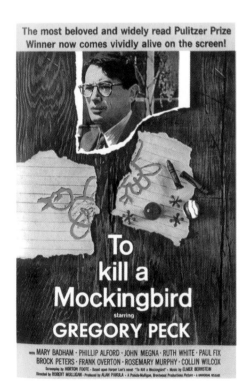

The most beloved and widely read Pulitzer Prize Winner now comes vividly alive on the screen!

To kill a Mockingbird starring GREGORY PECK

WITH MARY BADHAM · PHILLIP ALFORD · JOHN MEGNA · RUTH WHITE · PAUL FIX BROCK PETERS · FRANK OVERTON · ROSEMARY MURPHY · COLLIN WILCOX

The Unforgiven 1960—Stars: Burt Lancaster, Audrey Hepburn, Lillian Gish, Audie Murphy, John Saxon, Charles Bickford; Director: John Huston

Unforgiven 1992—Stars: Clint Eastwood, Gene Hackman, Morgan Freeman, Richard Harris; Director: Clint Eastwood; Screenplay: David Peoples; Music: Lennie Niehaus

The Vikings 1958—Stars: Kirk Douglas, Tony Curtis, Janet Leigh, Alexander Knox; Director: Richard Fleischer; Screenplay: Calder Willingham

The Virgin Queen 1955—Stars: Bette Davis, Richard Todd, Joan Collins, Herbert Marshall; Director: Henry Koster

The War Wagon 1967—Stars: John Wayne, Kirk Douglas, Howard Keel, Robert Walker Jr.; Director: Burt Kennedy

The Westerner 1940—Stars: Gary Cooper, Walter Brennan, Doris Davenport, Dana Andrews, Forrest Tucker, Charles Halton; Director: William Wyler

The Wild Bunch 1969—Stars: William Holden, Ernest Borgnine, Robert Ryan, Warren Oates, Strother Martin, Edmond O'Brien; Director: Sam Peckinpah; Screenplay: Walon Green, Sam Peckinpah

Wings 1927—Stars: Clara Bow, Charles "Buddy" Rogers, Richard Arlen, Gary Cooper; Director: William Wellman

Young Mr. Lincoln 1939—Stars: Henry Fonda, Alice Brady, Marjorie Weaver, Eddie Collins, Ward Bond; Director: John Ford; Screenplay: Lamar Trotti

Zorba the Greek 1964—Stars: Anthony Quinn, Alan Bates, Irene Papas, Lila Kedrova; Director: Michael Cacoyannis; Based on the novel by Kazantzakis; Music: Mikis Theodorakis

Zulu 1964—Stars: Michael Caine, Jack Hawkins, Nigel Green and narrated by Richard Burton; Director: Cy Endfield; Music: John Barry

COMEDY

The Three Stooges
Airplane!
Amazon Women on the Moon
Animal House
Army of Darkness
Bedazzled
Beneath the Valley of the Ultra Vixens
Benny Hill

Blazing Saddles
Lenny Bruce
Bugs Bunny and Termite Terrace
Caddyshack
Charlie Chaplin
Dr. Strangelove
Get Shorty
God help us, the "Duke &

Cookie" tape
The Gods Must Be Crazy
Goin' South
The Heartbreak Kid
Heaven Can Wait
The Holy Grail
Hope and Crosby
The In-Laws
It's a Mad, Mad, Mad, Mad World
Buster Keaton
Laurel and Hardy
Larceny, Inc. (also with kids)
Tom Lehrer
M.A.S.H.
The Man Who Came to Dinner
The Marx Brothers
The Meaning of Life
Monty Python
My Favorite Year
Network
P.G. Wodehouse on golf, "The Great Game"
Paint Your Wagon

The Princess and the Pirate (with Bob Hope, Virginia Mayo, Walter Brennan as Featherhead and Victor McLaglen as a pirate!)
Raising Arizona
S.O.B.
Allen Sherman
Some Like It Hot
The Sting
The Thin Man
Those Magnificent Men in Their Flying Machines
Victor, Victoria
W.C. Fields
Way Out West (with Laurel and Hardy)
What's Up, Tiger Lily?
Young Frankenstein

A GLORIOUS GALLERY OF GUTS,

Walter Brennan

Jack Elam

Robert Montgomery with James Gleason

Arthur Hunnicutt

Strother Martin

Thomas Mitchell

Eugene Pallette

GEORGE "GABBY" HAYES—He'd have been the first inductee into the Sidekicks Hall of Fame, if there was such a thing. Bearded, toothless, with a face like an apple puppet, Hayes delivered his lines with a tongue that must have been the size of a Polish sausage. He pretty much appeared in every Western from 1932-1950, and was parodied with hilarious success in *Blazing Saddles*.

RHYS WILLIAMS—Williams' the guy you want teaching your kid the manly art of boxing (he taught Roddy McDowall in *How Green Was My Valley*). Williams was also outstanding in *Mrs. Miniver*, *The Inspector General*, *The Farmer's Daughter*, *Hills of Home* and *The Corn Is Green*.

EUGENE PALLETTE—Pallette is best remembered as the well-fed friar in *The Adventures of Robin Hood*. His barrel shape and bullfrog voice are unforgettable. Born in Winfield, Kansas, he began his film career in 1910. Pallette served in the Army Air Corps in World War I and was actually once a jockey.

THOMAS MITCHELL—Mitchell's best known as the swillin' Doc Boone in *Stagecoach* and as the hapless Uncle Billy in *It's a Wonderful Life*. Born in Elizabeth, New Jersey, he started in films in 1934, going on to liven up *Lost Horizon*, *Gone With the Wind*, *The Long Voyage Home*, *The Outlaw*, *High Noon* and *Mr. Smith Goes to Washington*.

JAMES GLEASON—Terrific as Max Corkel, the fight manager in *Here Comes Mr. Jordan*, Gleason is splendid in everything. Called "140 pounds of Irish dynamite," he's the all-time great sourpuss and perfect sarge. ("Stop holdin' up the woik!") Gleason appeared in *The Last Hurrah*, *The Life of Riley*, *Meet John Doe*, *Arsenic and Old Lace*, *Crash Dive* and *Tycoon*.

ARTHUR HUNNICUTT—Born in Gravelly, Arkansas, Hunnicutt came to Hollywood in 1942. He was unbelievably great in *The Big Sky* as the lanky, wise ole hoss in buckskins, a character he pretty much reprised in *El Dorado*. He can also be seen in *Broken Arrow*, *The Red Badge of Courage* and *Lust For Gold*.

HENRY HULL—Born In Louisville, Kentucky, Hull was tremendous as the cynical cigar-chomping millionaire in *Lifeboat* who loses one of the greatest poker matches ever. Look for him, too in *Stanley and Livingston*, *Werewolf of London*, *Jesse James*, *The Great Gatsby*, *Kentucky Rifle*, *High Sierra* and *The Fountainhead*.

PERCY HELTON—Born 1894 in New York, Helton was blessed with the great raspy voice of the huckster. Listen for it in *How to Marry a Millionaire*, *Fancy Pants* and *A Star Is Born* (19??).

RUSSELL SIMPSON—Simpson was born near San Francisco

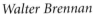

GUZZLERS, GRIT & GRIZZLE

Alan Hale Sr., Eugene Pallette

George "Gabby" Hayes

Percy Helton

Henry Hull

John Qualen

Russell Simpson

Rhys Williams

Chill Wills

in 1800 and spent some time hunting for gold in the Yukon, coming to Hollywood in 1917. He was probably best loved for his role in *The Grapes of Wrath*. He was also in *My Darling Clementine, Seven Brides for Seven Brothers, The Last Command* and *Saddle Tramp*.

ALAN HALE SR.—Flynn's constant companion and the original big lug, Hale was a master of bluff and bluster. Born in Washington, D.C., he achieved all kinds of success in many endeavors, from writing and singing to inventing things like folding theater seats and hand-held fire extinguishers. *The Sea Hawk, Sante Fe Trail, Dodge City, It Happened One Night, Gentleman Jim*—he played too many solid support roles to name. And, yes, he's the father of Alan Hale Jr., the Skipper from "Gilligan's Island."

WALTER BRENNAN—Mr. Grit and Grizzle himself was born in Massachusetts in 1894. Depend on him to be great in everything—*The Pride of the Yankees, The Westerner, Kentucky, Red River, Sergeant York*, and on and on. A true god.

CHILL WILLS—He's the guy the audience could count on to supply nick-of-time pearls of wisdom to the Duke or Rock Hudson. (Check out *Kentucky Rifle, Pat Garrett and Billy the Kid* or *Giant*.) In 1961, Wills lobbied so tastelessly for an Oscar for his role in *The Alamo* that the whole of Hollywood, including John Wayne, turned their backs on him. All was forgiven two years later, however, when Wayne signed him on to

play his sidekick in *McLintock!*

STROTHER MARTIN—Martin always seems to play the guy who treats Paul Newman like a blithering idiot—remember "What we have here is a failure to communicate" from *Cool Hand Luke*? When Newman teams up with Robert Redford in *Butch Cassidy and the Sundance Kid*, Martin nails both of them: "Morons. . . I've got morons on my team." A great character in *The Man Who Shot Liberty Valance, McLintock!, Rooster Cogburn, Slap Shot* and *The Wild Bunch*.

JACK ELAM—With Elam's gap-toothed grin and wandering eye, it was apparently against the law to make a Western without him—*Rio Lobo, The Rare Breed, Pony Express Rider, Support Your Local Sheriff!, Once Upon A Time in the West* (whose opening shot features the screen's second-best scene ever with a fly).

JOHN QUALEN—Born in Vancouver in 1899, Qualen was known to most of us as Swede. No one around can say "yumpin' yiminy" like this guy. He was in all kinds of great stuff—*The Long Voyage Home, The Fugitive, Casablanca, The Grapes of Wrath, Hans Christian Andersen, The Searchers, Two Rode Together*.

Poxy Biot Nymph™

P-38

Kaufmann's Bead Head Scud™

Damn near everyone's favorite fighter, Lockheed's twin-boomed beauty was designed by 27-year-old Clarence L. "Kelly" Johnson in 1937 and first flown on January 27, 1939. The US Army Air Corps wanted a fast interceptor/fighter and this was it. The RAF nicknamed her the Lightning but the Germans had another name—*der Gabelschwänz+Teufel*—the fork-tailed devil. It was equally feared in the Pacific theater, where it destroyed more Japanese aircraft than any other plane.

The P-38 had the greatest range and bomb-load capacity (two 2,000-pound bombs) of any fighter at the time. She sped along at over 420 mph but was once clocked at close to 800 mph in a dive! She had buzz saw firepower in the nose from a 20mm cannon and four .50-caliber Browning machine guns. Some of the pilots wired the two firing buttons together—and one touch would unleash a vicious forward assault. Richard Bong, America's top ace with 40 confirmed kills, scored them all in the Lightning.

Take any opportunity that arises to get close to one—you'll be struck by the size. For a single-seat fighter, she's a big airplane—52 feet across. Sadly, there are only about half a dozen of these babies still flying.

Lindy and the Lightning—Charles Lindbergh fought against the US involvement in World War II, but when it was declared he vowed to support the effort and do his bit. He was an incredibly gifted pilot, but past 40 and he had never seen combat. FDR wanted to keep it that way. He didn't want our "national treasure" at risk, so denied him a commission. Determined, Lindbergh took the back door and got an aircraft company to send him to the Pacific as a technical advisor. He was leading a Lightning squadron in a combat test run when attacked. Lindy, twice the age of the other pilots and a civilian, engaged and shot down a Japanese Zero. The victory remains "unofficial."

LOCKHEED P-38

950 LOCKHEED P-38

KEEP 'EM FLYING!

ARMY

Kaufmann's Bead Head Scud™

267079

Kaufmann's Bead Head Scud™

Theo's Black Devil Bead Head™

LOCKHEED'S

SKUNK WORKS

Former Secretary of Defense Caspar Weinberger said it best: "Every administration since Eisenhower's has counted on their skill and ability that gave us important advantages over our adversaries in a very dangerous world. The Skunk Works kept us preeminent."

The term *skunk works* has become generic for any high-tech secret operation, but the prototype—Lockheed Advanced Development Co.—started in 1943. The Army Air Corps had caught sight of experimental German jets and knew they had to play some catch-up—fast.

The significance of the jet threat late in World War II cannot be overstated. Fortunately, as advanced as Germany was, Hitler hadn't advanced things any further. This strategic error may well have saved our bacon. The Jet Age just missed the dance, but in 1943, the Allies were rightly nervous as cats.

Lockheed turned to Kelly Johnson, designer of the P-38. Johnson hand-picked his team and set up his top-secret operation inside a high-security. . . uh, rented circus tent. The proximity of the location to a stinky plastics factory in Burbank cried out for a nickname. Al Capp's *Li'l Abner* comic strip offered just the thing: its moonshiner character, Injun Joe, concocted his famous "Kickapoo joy juice" in a still called the Skonk Works—so named thanks to ingredients like dead skunks and old sneakers. The design crew adopted the name, and it stuck.

Kelly's team delivered the first of many successes: the P-80 Shooting Star. In Korea, it won the first-ever jet-on-jet dogfight by dusting a MiG. Thousands of P-80s went into production, and Skunk Works was rewarded with a real factory and the government's toughest "black budget" top-secret contracts.

Its achievements under Johnson and later, Ben Rich, are legend.

Some highlights:

U-2— This "spooky" high-altitude spy plane designed for the CIA, first flew on August 4, 1955. It remained a secret until Gary Powers was shot down in 1960 (in the first-ever surface-to-air missile victory). The U-2 is the most potent intelligence-gathering airplane of all time. During Desert Storm, its eight-hour-plus deep-penetration flights were brutal—pilots said they ran out of ass before they ran out of gas.

SR-71—The monstrously advanced titanium Blackbird has been the fastest plane in the world for 35 years—officially. It has outrun missiles and never been shot down. The Blackbird was clocked at Mach 3.3 (2,193 mph), but her top speed is

Kelly Johnson (At right) demonstrates his "hands on" style; (Opposite) Test pilots Dave Ferguson (F-117A) and Tony LeVier (P-38) share a moment in history.

classified. It's staggering to look on this incredible airplane and realize that its development began way back under Ike's administration. It first flew in late April, 1962. Rumors persist that a "black project" replacement plane, perhaps the Aurora, may have broken Mach 10 (6,600 mph, or coast-to-coast in something like 20 minutes) but has experienced numerous problems. That might explain why the SR-71, retired in 1990, was recently reactivated.

The following incident is described by SR-71 pilot Lt. Col. William Burk, Jr. in *Skunk Works*, by Ben Rich and Leo Janos. It occurred in 1983 during a recon of Lebanese terrorist bases, ordered by President Ronald Reagan after the Marine barracks bombing at Beirut International Airport. The mission from England was a long one, because France had refused permission to cross their airspace (check it out on your atlas).

U-2

"We completed our pass over Beirut and turned toward Malta, when I got a warning low-oil-pressure light on my right engine. Even though the engine was running fine, I slowed down and lowered our altitude and made a direct line for England. We decided to cross France without clearance instead of going the roundabout way. We made it almost across, when I looked out the left window and saw a French Mirage III sitting 10 feet off my left wing. He came up on our frequency and asked us for our Diplomatic Clearance Number. I had no idea what he was talking about, so I told him to stand by. I asked my backseater, who said, 'Don't worry about it. I just gave it to him.' What he had given him was 'the bird' with his middle finger. I lit the afterburners and left that Mirage standing still. Two minutes later we were crossing the Channel."

SR-71

F117-A

F117-A—The faceted Stealth Fighter was another case of the Skunk Works coming upon conventional aircraft design and clubbing it to death. Desert Storm may have been a bullying rout, but it was damn good for our American soul to kick butt that sorely deserved it. It was also an excellent proving ground for the life-saving tactical ghost called the Nighthawk. Often referred to by pilots as the Black Jet, it actually operates as an invisible precision bomber. As Ben Rich put it, "The overriding fact of Desert Storm was that the only way the enemy knew the F-117-A was in the sky above was when everything around him began blowing up."

Bird's Nest Brown

The YB-49 Flying Wing—Jack Northrop's tragic masterpiece—remains the most beautiful airplane ever built on Earth. The granddaddy of the B-2 Stealth Bomber (they share the exact same wingspan), the Flying Wing first flew as the prop configured XB-35 on June 25, 1946. A 50th anniversary event was held at the Hawthorne Airport takeoff site, which was rededicated as Jack Northrop Air Field. It was a bittersweet gathering.

Jack Northrop's contribution to aviation is uncontested—every modern airplane bears something that Jack and his team designed. Yet Jack's dream was to advance the purest concept of flight: the Wing. Nothing about it would fight the air it was made to conquer—no tubular fuselage or bulky engine nacelles. Every aspect of his design would contribute to efficiency of lift, speed and range—the cleanest aerodynamics imaginable. But the bureaucracy and demands of his client, the US government, may have doomed the project from the start.

Jack's early success with flying wing designs led to his 1941 contract to build a heavy, long-range bomber capable of carrying 10,000 pounds 10,000 miles. In other words, a plane capable of dropping the atomic bomb on Berlin. Fifteen of the 172-foot airframes were constructed, and six of them were flown in varying configurations.

Every takeoff was an event. Employees and local residents turned out by the thousands. Witnesses today practically tear up thinking about it—the sight was unforgettable. When the YB-49 roared into the air with its eight jet engines, it was the most powerful plane in the world. People absolutely loved this airplane.

Into pop culture jetted the Flying Wing, inspiring design—and pulp fiction. Takeoff footage was used in *The War of the Worlds*, and air travelers anticipated sleek, all-wing commercial transports. It wasn't to be. Politics, timing and some performance problems combined to kill the plane. Big Wings were salvaged for scrap, and Jack Northrop never fully recovered from the blow.

Sweet vindication appeared at that anniversary celebration in 1996. A low and slow flyover by the Northrop *Spirit* B-2 Stealth Bomber had the Hawthorne crowd cheering like kids again. Another feat resonated even deeper. The N-9MB, the only survivor of four scale models constructed before the giant bomber, was parked next to the dais. Ed Maloney of the Chino Air Museum and a devoted restoration team had accomplished the impossible. Life had been restored to a highly complex but decaying hulk. The little plane looked, many of the old guard remarked, better than she ever had. The N-9MB made several flybys before returning to Chino. On the last pass the pilot performed a wing rock, and a chill rippled through the crowd below. It was a farewell and a salute to Jack. His dream, shared by so many who knew and respected him, soared again.

(Clockwise from above) Flying Wing inspired Foster Flight Band case. The jet powered YB-49; the B-2 Spirit Stealth Bomber; first flight, June 25, 1946—test pilot Max Stanley eases up the XB-35 from Northrop Field.

LaFontaine Emergent Sparkle Pupa™

FLYING WING

LaFontaine Emergent Sparkle Pupa™

B-17 FLYING FORTRESS

Boeing's rugged workhorse has deservedly won the highest respect bestowed on any warplane. These resilient bombers were famous for getting shot to pieces but still bringing their crews back home.

Development was initiated by the U.S. Army Air Corps in 1934. At the roll out less than a year later, a reporter for the *Seattle Daily Times* described the heavily fortified big silver beauty as a "flying fortress"—and she was christened for life.

The B-17 was designed for long-range high-altitude precision daylight bombing, and featured the famous Norden bomb sight. It could carry up to 16 M2 .50-caliber Browning machine guns, 10,000 rounds of ammunition and more than 8,000 pounds of bombs.

The flexible airframe underwent many changes and configurations. The 1941 B-17E introduced a signature feature: the Sperry ball turret. The "ball gunner" had one of the hairiest jobs in the war, and deservedly earned a certain distinction. Smaller, nonclaustrophobic guys either chose—or were chosen—for the cramped space. The two Brownings were fixed, and the gunner, using foot pedals, pivoted and turned the entire ball. The noise from the guns was deafening. In the event of damaged landing gear, the turret could be jettisoned for "belly" landings.

Olive Flash Back Pheasant Tail

What a Beauty! The late model B-17G with Bendix chin turret and "Cheyenne" tail gun turret. (Inset) The ballsiest gunner station. A B-17E Sperry ball turret from 1942.

LOWER TURRET EXT (CHANGE BEGINS ON SHO

"Mission Regensburg"
copyright 1994—Artist Gil
Cohen suspends a moment
from 1943 aboard the B-17
Just a-snappin', *of the
"Bloody 100th" Bomb
Group. The image is one of
several limited edition
prints based on the 8th Air
Force and available from
Aeroprint, P.O. Box 154,
Spofford, New Hampshire
03462.*

MACK TRUCKS

songs and movies, the truth is these guys have a grueling, tiresome job. It might give something in terms of adventure, but it also offers plenty of greasy spoons, endless delivery deadlines and goofy-twanged divorced gals named Flo. Only the drivers know for sure what it's all about, and they'd probably have trouble explaining its attraction.

However, the drivers *would* say they appreciate Mack trucks. With their chrome bulldogs riding strong on the hood, these workhorses have established a reputation for helping truckers get the job done—wherever, whenever and however they have to.

In 1890, John "Jack" Mack took a job at the carriage and wagon firm of Fallesen & Berry, in Brooklyn, New York. Jack and his brother Augustus (Gus) bought the company in 1893, and a year later, brother William (and a couple of other Macks) brought a skill in wagon building to the family operation. Carriage making was phased out, and the brothers focused on wagons and on experimenting with steam and electric motor cars.

In 1900, the brothers finally produced their first motorized vehicle—a bus used for touring Brooklyn's Prospect Park. This 20-passenger bus, Old No. 1, was powered by a Mack-built 40-horsepower gasoline engine, with chain drive. Old No. 1 would serve in the New York area for 17 straight years, becoming the first in a long line of Mack trucks to rack up a million miles of service. Mack's commercial motor vehicles proved to be more successful than their horse-drawn vehicles, and in 1905, production moved to Allentown, Pennsylvania, still the company's world headquarters. By 1910, the nameplates on the trucks had been changed to "Mack."

They continued to add innovations, like a constant meshing of gears (1905) to prevent stripping, cab-over-engine design (1905), air cleaners and oil filters (a truck first, pre-1920s), power brakes (1920) and four-wheel brakes (1930s),

Mack trucks, all right. Tough, reliable trucks. Tough as nails. Tough as their drivers. If there's a single open-road, maverick profession left in this day and age, it's probably truckin'. Glamorized into some overly romantic image by various all of which added safety and performance to these vehicles' already rugged demeanor. The famous Mack AC model, introduced in 1915, had a successful production run all the way through 1937, totaling more than 55,000 units.

These workhorses were put to use in World War I, as British military trucks were built by Mack, and 4,470 ACs were sent with American doughboys to France. Tenacious, they took the abuse of the roughest terrain and came back for more. With their blunt, bulldoglike snub noses, when a lesser truck became stuck, it's said that the British Tommies would yell, "Aye! Bring one of them bulldogs in!" The name stuck, and in 1922, the bulldog became the Mack corporate symbol.

Models were built for specific needs, such as the BJ and BB in 1927, boasting larger capacity and higher speed haulage; the E series in 1936, with gross vehicle weight ratings ranging up to 23,000 pounds; an assortment of 30,000 Macks were to serve in World War II; the L series in 1940 to 1956 added clean timeless styling; the H series in the 1950s, known as Cherry Pickers because of their high short cabs, were designed to accommodate 35-foot trailers and meet 45-foot overall legal limits; and the rounded sexy B series in 1953 created a new standard of styling. The MC/MR series and various Cruise Liners and Super Liners have carried the tradition to the present, where these state-of-the-art vehicles, with their customized paint jobs and their chrome bulldogs shining, win gawks and thumbs-up from people up and down every interstate they travel. And if it's possible, they become a little cooler-looking with a pair of mud flap girls dancing on the rear end.

If the flagships on the highway aren't enough, check out some of these fun opportunities: a Mack Museum at the Macungie, Pennsylvania, assembly facility, and trucking museums (see sidebar) and shows in all regions. And be warned: if there's a good lookin' lass present at a show, you just might hear somebody exclaim, "Darn! She's built like a Mack truck!!"

The living quarters in a Mack truck have gotten state of the art: refrigerators, TVs, stereo equipment—even a "burrito-tested ventilation system."

Old Trucks Never Die. . .

One of the largest collections of antique trucks in the United States

HAYS ANTIQUE TRUCK MUSEUM

Hays Antique Truck Museum

2000 East Main Street, Woodland, California 95776 (916) 666-1044

Trucks from 1901 though 1954 on display on more than two acres

Open daily except Wednesdays; Thanksgiving; December 24, 25 and 31; and January 1.

American Truck Historical Society

P. O. Box 531168, Birmingham, Alabama 35253-1168 (205) 870-0566

Dedicated to the collection and preservation of the history of trucks, the trucking industry, and its pioneers.

Dues: $25 per year, includes bimonthly magazine Wheels of Time.

Prince Bead Head

GEORGE BARRIS

The King of the Kustomizers brought some of the world's wildest rides to the car shows and the pages of mags like Hot Rod and Rod & Custom. Don't think that he's slowed down—the Riverside, California, shop is still churning out the product, and the man is a blur. Recent jobs include the custom Ford Explorers in Jurassic Park, the latest James Bond beemer and the new Batman vehicles. (The original Batmobile was transformed in three weeks from a Lincoln Futura dream car.)

Barris was born to customize. As a kid in Sacramento he won awards for balsa wood models and, before he could drive, was cutting into the real thing. In 1944, he hit L.A. in a cool '36 Ford and learned all he could from the local chop shops. Pretty soon a teenage businessman, he rode the

postwar boom. The "Barris look" emerged, to be copied in Detroit and all over the world. The legendary "James Dean" Mercury Monterey ('49-'51) remains an icon for the era.

Hollywood came calling, turning Barris into a brand-name. Cars for the stars included personalized rigs for (among others) Gable, Elvis, Sinatra, Hope, Crosby and Travolta. Yes, delivery of a customized Barris makes for some serious leg-jiggling anticipation.

WANTED: HAVE YOU SEEN THIS CAR?

This one-off George Barris creation, the XPAK 400 air car, disappeared years ago from a warehouse near LAX. Contact Barris Kustom in North Hollywood, CA with any info.

SALT WATER
Mayfly Thorny Bead

Harley J. Earl

FATHER OF THE FIN

Harley J. Earl (1893-1969) is one of the true automotive design gods. Born in L.A., the teenage Harley dug clay from the backyard to sculpt his first cars. In 1927, he went to Motor City. A big imposing guy weighing in at 6'4", 230 lbs., Earl, with his design team at GM, rocked the car world for more than 30 years. Some of their innovations were as simple as two-tone paint. Others, like embracing aircraft design, became an entire movement. In 1939, Earl led his team, including 'vette designer Bill Mitchell, on a specially arranged field trip to check out the latest product from design colleague Clarence "Kelly" Johnson. At an airfield near Detroit, they were allowed inside a secured hangar to see a radically new top-secret pursuit fighter, the Lockheed P-38. Johnson may not have appreciated their reaction, which was something like, "Wow! This baby would look really great on the *road!*" The influence of the twin boom P-38 became evident after the war, when the GM gang could again afford to be indulgent. The 1948 Cadillac introduced the tailfin, actually not much more than a taillight bump. Front bumper overriders, jutting like breasts (or like the Lightening nose), became a standard feature. The postwar crowd couldn't get enough. By 1959, the Caddie had turned into a Sailfish.

CLAY SMITH

Known as "the man who talked to engines," he was the greatest racing mechanic of his day, yet he had no formal training in engineering. He had a natural gift under the hood which allowed him to instantly diagnose problems and tweak just a little more go out of any engine he laid his magic hands on. With his ever present cigar set in a wide infectious grin, Smith brought a confidence and good humor that extended to those around him. The 1954 death of the well loved 39-year-old mechanical genius had a shattering effect on the racing community. In a freak accident at the track, Smith was killed instantly. He died in the pit. He died doing what he loved.

But his innovations became legend. He juiced up Johnny Mantz' V8 midget at Balboa Stadium in San Diego, and Mantz promptly blew the doors off circuit hot shots Walt Faulkner and Bill Vukovich. With egg dripping off his face, Faulkner wrongly filed a protest claiming that the victory must have been due to the use of an oversized engine.

Even manufacturers started scratching their heads. The Smith/Bill Stroppe team won a major power boat race on the Detroit River by a margin of two minutes. Smith's V-8 succeeded at 5000 rpms when Ford engineers had guaranteed detonation of the little 135 cubic inch engine at 4500. Clay shifted his cigar and explained with a smile, "Well, we just go by 4500 so fast it doesn't have a chance to do any damage."

A partnership with Danny Jones began in a small Long Beach, CA, cam grinding shack in the 30's and a caricature of Clay, called Mr. Horsepower, became their popular figurehead. Decals of the cigar chompin' icon began turning up everywhere from the Indy 500 to high school lockers. When Walter Lantz introduced Woody Woodpecker in 1940, an agreement was reached to allow the cartoon to continue since the business was unrelated.

Clay Smith Engineering keeps the legend alive with trophy winning custom ground camshafts and high performance parts.

Von Dutch:

FATHER OF THE FLAME

The vehicular flame is yet another nod to aircraft inspiration. On a crude airstrip during WWI, some moth-headed genius was watching an open cockpit crate prepare for take-off. He smiled as black smoke and stabs of flame belched from the exhaust ports. Pretty. . . Painting it on for permanent effect was only natural.

The idea turned up in crude fashion on racers and jalopies through the 30's. But the guy who really brought flames and pin stripping into the realm of high art was L.A. born Kenneth Howard, aka Von Dutch.

Born in 1929, his independent spirit quickly earned him a family nickname—the kid was stubborn as a Dutchman. Von Dutch inherited the steady hand of his father, a sign painter and the man who created the mallet-wielding tuxedo-clad Western Exterminator logo. He landed a job with George Barris striping cars in his unique way and soon everybody was lining up to get their rods "Dutched." Credited as the inventor of "Kandy Apple Red," Von Dutch earned a most notorious footnote when he flamed a Gullwing.

Kaufmann's Marabou Damsel™

AMPHICAR

Everybody could use an amphicar—to break up those dull Sunday afternoons, get you across the English channel when the Chunnel is crowded, and more importantly, to give a fella a new vehicle to toss great trolling lures out of. While the mixing of two great technologies—cars and boats—has proven to be very difficult to engineer successfully and affordably, a number of these versatile crocodiles are still running. And it's great evidence that man, in his never-ending search for glory, or at least something real nifty, will improvise and actually create working things that many would have called him an idiot for even considering.

In the late 1950s Hanns Trippel, who had designed some amphibious military transports for Germany, set his eye on the consumer market. He came up with a convertible with two propellers tucked under the rear bumper and a streamlined front end. The front tires worked as rudders, as much as is possible, and some 2500 Amphicars were produced between 1961 and 1967, many being shipped to the U.S. Alas, with a hefty price at the time of $3395, and with poor performance for a boat in the water and a car on land, and a tendency to rust after a couple of dunkings, these ducks are difficult to find in the average garage. Have you ever seen one?

But do not underestimate man's resolve: the French Hobbycar and the German Amphi-Ranger gave it a run, and as recently as 1994 *Popular Mechanics* reported on a fiberglass duck—the "Aquastrada Delta." Developed in Northern California, the Delta is fueled by a 245-hp Ford engine, reportedly churning out 100-mph on land and 45-mph at sea. Something romantic leads man to want to perch on the bow of his car—or indeed to *catch* a perch on the bow of his car—cutting smoothly through the whitecaps, the sea air in his nostrils, a great gal baiting up his line next to him. . . Good luck building your own, and relish this guy's little sea worthy roadster.

Figurehead

SWIM 7CS

Mini Puff

Aft

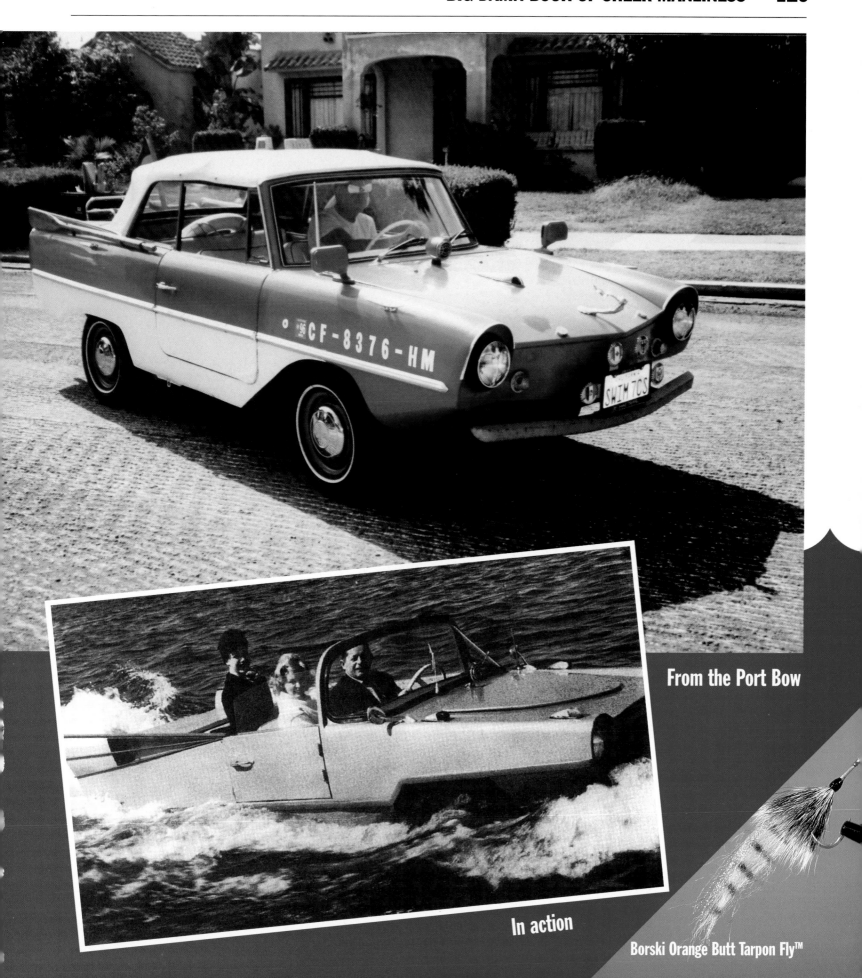

From the Port Bow

In action

Borski Orange Butt Tarpon Fly™

Clouser's Minnow Sliver Shiner™

BAJA 500
&
BAJA 1000

Are you kidding me? Ripping down a snaky, rock-clogged dirt path, alone in a perfectly tuned vehicle with nothing but cactus and pain and foul water between you and the finishing line more than one thousand miles away. It's a dream—and a nightmare, of sorts. A total harebrained fantasy. And folks are planning right now on doing it sometime soon down in the Baja 1000.

The Baja 500 and Baja 1000 are two grueling examples of off-road marathon races, traveling through the lion's share of the Baja Peninsula in Mexico. In 4 x 4 trucks, buggies, motorcycles or whatever, wild folks traverse hundreds of miles of incredibly hostile terrain, honored to take on this race's challenge. A guy named Ed Pearlman, a founding father of off-road racing culture and the seminal organization NOORA, conceived many races, including the Mexican 1000 in 1967 (which became the Baja 1000) and, in 1971, the Baja 500. Today, we enjoy great events and the resulting great off-road, motorcycle and racing coverage on ESPN,

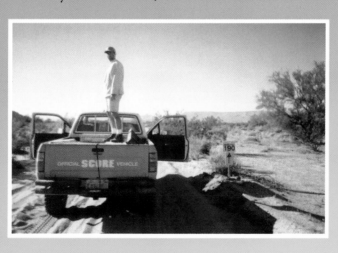

ESPN2 and others due largely to the efforts of innovators like Ed.

The Baja 500 and 1000 are currently run by SCORE International, the sanctioning body and promoter of the legendary races. SCORE's phone number is (818) 583-8068. The 1000—the Big Un—is held every November, and the 500 every June.

Parnelli Jones described the big race as "an all-day plane crash." SCORE's Paul Fish says, "The Baja 1000 will always be considered more of an adventure than a race." More than 300 slightly off-center participants from all walks of life and all over the world compete in 15 car and truck classes and eight motorcycle classes. And while there's a 45-hour time limit, the real goal is to finish the race.

Regular Guy Mark Smith: "Riding in the 1000"

Beyond raw driving skill and endurance, a racer needs some good luck, as ordinarily crappy silt beds and rocky scrub are made worse by flash floods, brushfires, mud holes, big rocks, cows, horses and nasty booby traps. A motorcycle guy named Mark Smith went solo for the 1000 in 1995, on his 92 XR 600. After meeting with Stewart "Dogmeat" Powell, a D-37 expert and the first ironman at the last peninsular 1000, Mark trained for six months perfecting survival techniques. Here's his account:

Four o'clock in the morning, and there was no stopping it—today is the day I find out how I do. Rustled the family from their slumber and sat down for as big a breakfast as I could squeeze into me. We all finished loading my truck, and then I put on half my gear: knee braces and ankle braces, sport tape for the wrists and a Texas catheter so I can go while I go. If it wasn't comfortable in the first two hours, it wasn't going to be for the next 44. . . . But it was pretty cool being in line behind Ty Davis, Johnny Campbell, Chuck Miller and Malcolm Smith. I'm sure as they looked around they wondered who that threat was back there in the 73rd position. After clearing some early morning booby traps, SCORE let the first racer out at 8:20 A.M.

As I got closer to the starter there were rumors of guys already going down and crowds lining the course for 15 miles. Total silence. All I could hear was my heartbeat and the announcer calling my name out in Spanish. . . . The green flag dropped, and I was outta there. Now I could hear my motor and the cheer

from my family. The excitement was exhilarating. How do I keep my front wheel down? Everybody is waving to me—I want to wave back.

Down the rio for the escape into the mountains. . . . What I had heard was true, there were people for 15 miles, all the way to the foothills near Rodriguez Dam. Then the show was over, and it was time to get down to business. Get relaxed, shake off the nervous tension, find your pace and pick up a rhythm.

The initial goal was to get to San Felipe without being exhausted. Bruce Ogilvie had told me that from there on out it was smooth and fast. Piece of cake—100 miles of mountain roads and 200 miles of sand whoops. I began to see visions of Fud as an angel. I thanked him for all the great D-38 races that had prepared me for this. Am I already hallucinating? No, I'm in the sand whoops, and that is thorny cactus I see.

I had anticipated darkness by mile 260, where check three was. So my headlights were waiting for me there. I was early, but that was no problem. I ate some fruit, sucked down a drink and was off ahead of schedule. The sand whoops going up the Mini Summit and the rocky decline after that was nothing I expected. This is where I had to be most conservative. But I must admit it drained a lot out of me. . . .

This race is made of extremes. There are tens of miles of rocks, tens of miles of whoops, tens of miles of sand. The turns are tight, the hills are steep and there are thousands and thousands of elated spectators. And, yes, there are tens of miles of sweet, rolly, sweepy stuff through the cactus forests. Under the eerie light of the moon and beam of your head-

Then it was fast and smooth, with big wide turns all the way down the moon lit Gulf Coast to Gonzaga. I don't think I got it over 60 here—I didn't want any surprises. Meanwhile, the leaders were *averaging* 60. . . . Someone with a broken collarbone was heading out. If he can do it, no problem. I never did find the easy way out. . . .

I was too tired to try all the alternate lines and roads around the miles of mud. I kept it straight and paddled my way through. I might have lost a lot of time, but at least I wasn't lost. Then came the rock garden: softball-sized rocks that were scattered on the roadbed and through hills, washes and turns for about 20 miles. I couldn't hold a line. I just followed my front wheel.

light, Tim Morton had called it surreal. He was right. It had become a different race, a different country. . . .

But you don't get to enjoy it. You are reminded you are racing when a truck roars up behind you and casts shadows on the rocks as if they were headstones. You scramble across the road in panic, then launch off the course into darkness. . . anywhere is better than being in front of him.

Nine o'clock at night I pulled into pit two. I'm only two hours behind the main pack and am quite satisfied. I mow down some of Patty's pasta, get a hug from Ally, rub my eyes and I'm back on the road.

Couple of miles down the road I encounter the strangest dirt I have ever seen. It was wet silt. Not dusty or muddy, but deep wet silt. Miles of first-gear meandering down a deep thick pancake-mix wash. . . .

The spectators were almost angry at me for not buzzing by. My eyes were barely open. If I went any faster, I would surely do a face plant. What are these people doing here anyway? They should have seen me earlier. . . . I am past the halfway mark, starting to come back to life, and Paul Krause is

Clouser's Crayfish™

Kaufmann's Interceptor™

already pulling into La Paz. I only have 500 more miles to go. I couldn't keep the bike on the center hump of the road, so I had to ride down in the tire rut on the side. One handlebar was always in the cactus, hitting it, and once my bar hit something solid and turned my bike 90 degrees. . . . I snapped the bike straight, just escaping the cactus wall. . . . [Mark continued through similar situations up toward the end of the race.]

I was getting pretty beat and starting to lose the battle. This is where the unimaginable happened. The race course made a U-turn and started heading north. For as far as I could see there were whoops and cactus. I slowed to a disgusted crawl. What cruel and heartless person would put this route in a 1,150-mile race? I have already gone 1,000 miles. Haven't I proved my mettle yet? I was all alone, it was the middle of the day and I realized why Baja is such a legend. I had to continue. It was the only way out.

I suffered every whoop and cactus till it cleared out at checkpoint 10. . . . The legend was far from over. I had to go through another deep silt section right in front of a big pit. Waving from a hilltop was my cherished friend, David Wade, pointing me in the right direction. About 18 hours behind the leader, I finally showed up at Honda pit 20. I could never thank them enough for their commitment. I tried closing my eyes but couldn't. Only 100 miles to go.

Off I go into the rain, which was more of a nuisance than a downpour. My final wind arrived just before I reached the "little silt." The little silt was a couple of miles long, 100 yards wide and 3 feet deep. I tried my way around it to no avail. So I chose to dive into a rut and let it be my autopilot, stopping only to pick up distress notes from fellow racers with expired motors. I would deliver the notes to their pits so that they could get help, all the while knowing that it would be tomorrow before the downed rider would be unburied from his resting place. . . .

I arrived at Honda 21, my last pit stop. . . . I stopped at every pit, asking if they had seen my chase crew, until

I came upon the Kawasaki pit. They said my job was to go to La Paz. Everyone knew I was going to La Paz. Go to La Paz.

Here the course became a dream. No more silt. No more rocks. No more whoops. Good dirt, bumps, ruts and turns. . . . If I wasn't so exhausted, this would have been my favorite section. . . .

The sight of La Paz was like seeing Las Vegas. All the locals had come out and lit bonfires and were lighting the main highway with their car lights. Everybody was whistling and spinning, their T-shirts standing out in the road. I came to a junction and was totally confused. My guardians grabbed me by my shoulder pads, turned me in the right direction and hit my helmet. Laughing or cheering, they couldn't decide. They only wanted one thing and that was to see me finish. They didn't know who I was or care that I was struggling for 53rd place. They just wanted good racing. It was a short stint down to the highway, ahh pavement! Police everywhere, guarding me.

I had the right of way. Cars were parked perpendicular to the road with their lights on, honking and flashing, for five miles all the way into La Paz. I made the turn onto the final stretch to the finish palisade. People were pressed four-deep against the fence, cheering my arrival. I ascended onto the finisher's platform and was caught in the arms of my little sister.

I had finished the Baja 1000 solo, didn't hit any big rocks and didn't blow any corners. *Cycle News* didn't interview me. Honda didn't have a contract for me to sign, and there was definitely no trophy. My prize was the extra beat in my heart and sitting on the ground with my son on my lap, surrounded by my family.

Now I know why this race is so legendary.

—Mark Smith, 1996

Mark finished in a respectable 53rd place, out of 108. Today, he says he isn't sure if he's crazy enough to enter the race again or not.

Nix's Epoxy Root Beer™

A Tribute to The Dog

The one absolutely unselfish friend that man can have in this selfish world, the one that never deserts him, the one that never proves ungrateful or treacherous, is his dog.

A man's dog stands by him in prosperity and in poverty, in health and in sickness. He will sleep on the cold ground, where the wintry winds blow and the snow drives fiercely, if only he may be near his master's side.

He will kiss the hand that has no food to offer; he will lick the wounds and sores that come in encounter with the roughness of the world.

He guards the sleep of his pauper master as if he were a prince.

When all other friends desert, he remains.

When riches take wing and reputation falls to pieces, he is as constant in his love as the sun in its journey through the heavens.

Senator George Vest, 1870

Rag Head Crab

Who the hell is that genius who painted
THE POKER DOGS?

Remington schlemington! What about Coolidge, the greatest painter of nonfishing, nonflying guy stuff who ever lived? Case in point: true dog lovers will admit to finding one canine feature a real puzzler. How is it that dogs evolved such a wide range of facial expressions? (People, usually single dames pushing 40, claiming the same of cats should be slapped repeatedly about the face.) Just the eyebrows on a dog can dance through a whole sack full of subtleties. Coolidge puzzled over and was inspired by that exact very same damn thing. Maybe he was anyway. His art sure captures some stuff difficult to put into words.

Cassius Marcellus Coolidge (1844-1937) was from a well-off family that operated a large farm near Antwerp in upstate New York. He loved hunting, fishing and bicycling, and worked variously as caricaturist, sign painter and teacher. Before choosing the life of an artist, Cash, as he was called, pursued a wide range of interests. He started both the first bank and the first newspaper in Antwerp, and wrote a comic opera about a New Jersey mosquito epidemic. His real success, however, came from an invention you will recognize. Coolidge created those amusement park cardboard caricatures that you could stick your head through to be

photographed as a muscle man or a fat lady. He called them Comic Foregrounds, and sold smaller versions mail-order.

While living in Manhattan some time in the mid-1870s he began to caricature dogs—in the manner that he had done of people for years. The sight of our canine counterparts at card night, in the club car or at the track obviously appealed to him in a big way, and he produced a series of oils. The local tobacconists loved his paintings and had prints made up as giveaways. Later, he signed a contract with Brown & Bigelow of St. Paul, a printer/advertising agency that commissioned more "dog theme" portraits. The "poker dogs" entered pop culture as the company turned out hundreds of thousands of posters, calendars and prints (a prized kitsch favorite sometimes found at garage sales is the out-of-print rendering on black velvet).

Coolidge hit a nerve, particularly with the 19th-century sport. He knew dogs and the domains of men. His details were genuine, and guys today still recognize a pal among those bowser bachelors.

Coolidge was a single bohemian until his marriage at age 65. His only child, daughter Marcella, was born the following year. He lived a modest life with his small family first in Brooklyn, then on Staten Island, where he died in 1937. Brown & Bigelow owned several of his oils, but the prints, normally 2 x 3 ft., were all given away as gifts to various lucky clients. An original Coolidge may well be the ultimate adornment for your game room. May be? Hell, if you got one, it is.

Prints and related licensed products are still available through Brown & Bigelow. Additionally, Marcella Coolidge, together with De Marco Productions, has made available some inspired new Coolidge items. Most excitingly, Ms. Coolidge recently uncovered the wonderful portraits of her father seen here. This is, to your author's knowledge, the first time they have publicly appeared. Could there be a more satisfactory looking gent behind such a unique body of work?

Lefty's Deceiver™

Cassius Marcellus Coolidge in rare photographs courtesy of DeMarco Productions. (His paintings from opposite right) "Kelly Pool", "One to Tie, Two to Win", "Dog of a Bachelor."

CARDS

7♣ 7♣

The big year for cards was 1423. Card playing was already 100 years old by this time (it started in either Italy or China), but it hadn't really caught on. It needed something. Enter a pious Franciscan friar named St. Bernard. Now, ole Bernie detested idle gaming of any kind. He decided to target a small fry and snuff out this card playing business for good. His mission took him all over the countryside. In a booming voice, he'd announce that cards were an invention of the devil himself! An industry was born.

Borski's Super Swimming Shrimp™

(Following pages) "A Bold Bluff"

Who Was Hoyle?

The Book of Hoyle is the last word in any gaming dispute, but the meaning has grown beyond any individual work. To perform a task "according to Hoyle" is to play fair and square, within the rules. It is to do something "by the book." What book? The Book Of Hoyle, already!

Fig. 26

Edmond Hoyle was an Englishman born in 1672 who loved the gaming life. His later years were devoted to teaching fashionable games to the ladies and gentlemen of London. At the age of 72, he published the authoritative text, called *A Treatise on the Game of Whist*, on that precursor of bridge. This highly successful handbook was followed by others standardizing the play of backgammon, chess, faro and numerous card games.

Thus, Hoyle's rule books became the final word and arbiter of all gaming disputes. A generic usage developed and, as the 1911 Britannica puts it so nicely, the name of Hoyle "gained currency as a general proverb." Since Hoyle's death at the age of 97, his name has been appropriated by any number of gaming rule book authors in England and America. The name "Hoyle" figures prominently in their titles, and such a reference is simply called "a Hoyle." In sum, Hoyle's life is a testament to the old saw, "It's never too late."

POKER RULES

ANACONDA, THE SNAKE

Six players are optimal. The minimum is five. A high-low game is played with the best five out of seven cards. The dealer deals out seven cards to each player. Players then pass three cards to the left or right, dealer's choice. (Because all passes go in the same direction for the duration of the game, this pass is generally followed by a series of groans and oaths as some players realize that they've been screwed.) In this game, the object is to make do with the other guy's trash, so don't be surprised if, when attempting a perfect low, you end up with ace, two, three, four, jack, queen, king.

Bet—Always begin with the player to the left of the dealer. Players then pass two cards in the same direction.

Players pass one, no bet, discard three, arrange their best five remaining cards in the order they are to be revealed. Once on the table, the order cannot be changed. The players simultaneously roll their cards one at a time and bet after each. After the fourth card is revealed, it's time to declare whether the player is going high, low or both ("pig"). Normally, the perfect low is ace, two, three, four, six. However, the Snake can be played with the "wheel," that is, a perfect low of ace, two, three, four, five. This, of course, is a straight, but used in this fashion it allows the player to declare both high and low or pig. However, if you declare pig, you must win both hands outright. If you tie or lose one of the hands, you lose all. Players declare by placing chips in their hands, concealed under the table: none for low, one for high, two for both ways. Once ready, players place their closed fists into the center of the table and reveal the contents at the count of three.

If a player happens to be lucky enough to be the sole player going high or low, he has a "lock." In other words, he's guaranteed half of the pot, so he's best off to bet the ranch. Also, as the lock, he initiates the first bet. If there is no lock, the player with the highest hand initiates. Players then raise, fold or call. Players split their half of the pot in the event of a tie.

"Ace up his sleeve"—Card cheats are popularly, though erroneously, shown producing a fifth or sixth ace from their coat sleeves. Hidden aces are more likely stolen from the deck in play. A cheat will keep an ace from an otherwise poor hand, fold the hand and use the ace later. Players rarely notice that the discarded hand contains only four cards. This trick was often accomplished with an ingenious device called a "hold-out," a jointed armature worn under clothes. By simply moving the legs apart, a cheat could extend a card-grabbing clip down the wrist to a palmed ace. Bringing the legs back together retracted the card safely up the sleeve. This device was invented in the early 1900s by a man named Kepplinger, who was caught using it—by prudent gentlemen who neither killed him nor worked him over. Rather, each demanded a hold-out of his own.

Lefty's Deceiver™

Now, if you think about it, with all the passing going on, you're really playing with 13 cards, so the quality of the hands is usually pretty high. Generally, a full house will win the high (although

four of a kind is not unusual), and a six will win the low. Going for pig is a highly ballsy move, but with four cards revealed, a player should be able make a pretty informed call. Either way, anytime someone goes for the all the marbles, it charges up the game in a big way.

Strategy—Let's say a player has a full house of queens over 10s. At the reveal, he may want to roll the three queens first to create the impression he's got four of them. The thinking here is that if a player rolls two queens and then two 10s, the best he could possibly have is a boat. When revealing the low, it's usually best to show the highest card last. There are exceptions, of course. For example, if his low is ace, two, three, five, six, a player will want to roll the five last to create the possibility that he has the perfect low. Always keep opponents guessing. Scaring the other guy is the whole point and makes the Snake a great game of guts and glory.

SHIFTING, WHISPERING SANDS

No game is dealt in more ways than the "Shifter." Here's *our* way. (When you write your book, you can explain yours.) Basically, the game's six-card stud, high-low, with a 50¢ buy at the end. Playing with the wheel is the dealer's option. He antes as usual. The dealer deals a down card to everyone and then an up card to the player to his left. That player then has the option of keeping that card, along with his down card, or, for a nickel, passing either to the player to *his* left. Each card passed always becomes an up card. The player may then keep both of his cards or, as the player preceding him did, pass either to the player to his left. This continues until everyone has had the opportunity to pass or stay (the dealer has the option of passing, by taking a card from the top of the deck; if he "burns" his hole card, it must be shown to the rest of the table). Those who pass receive a new card from the dealer, a down card for a down and an up for an up.

Bet—Always starting with the high hand, the passing procedure continues until everyone has one card down and four cards up (betting after each round).

Card Trick

Hide the seven of clubs and eight of spades on the top and bottom.

Show the seven of spades and eight of clubs to the mark and ask him to place them anywhere in the deck. Hold the deck with thumb and forefinger. Dramatically slam down the deck while squeezing it to retain the top and bottom card, while the other cards fall in a pile.

Show in your hand the remaining two cards, which you have miraculously drawn from within. Most won't notice the switch. Key elements are speed, flair and alcohol.

Players are then given their sixth card down. There is no more passing.

For 50¢, each player now has the option of replacing one of his cards, up or down, for a new one.

All declare (none for low, one for high, two for pig).

As always, the lock bets first. If there is none, then the honor is passed to the highest hand.

LOW IN THE HOLE ROLL YOUR OWN

A seven-card game played either with a high-low split or a high-only winner (dealer's option). The lowest hole card and any other like it in a hand is wild. Although in the end it will look like a game of seven-card stud, all cards are dealt face down, with the player deciding which cards are to be rolled up. The strategy here is simple: let's say a player is dealt a pair of fours and a two on his first three cards—he'll want to roll the two, making the two fours wild. In order to keep them wild, he'll want to roll any subsequent card that's lower than a four. The only downside to all of this is that the seventh card dealt stays down, so if a player is unlucky enough to hit a river card that's lower than a four. . . well, frankly, he's screwed and it may be a good time to switch from beer to Jack Daniel's.

PASS THE TRASH

Not to be confused with Anaconda. Pass the Trash is not related to any game of poker—however, due to its simplicity and innate silliness, it makes a welcome addition to any card game.

At the risk of sounding cryptic, let me begin by saying that the sole object of the game is not to win but not to lose. (Confused? Well, wipe the dopey look off your face and keep reading.) Everyone puts three 1$

stacks in front of him. This is the total amount a player is allowed per game. Players are dealt one card only. The highest card is the king of spades, the lowest the ace of clubs. This is one of the few games suits come in to play. Starting to the left of the dealer, the player decides if he wants to keep his card. If not, he trades cards with the player to his left, who has no say in the matter, unless he has a king. In that case, the player to his right is stuck with whatever dreck he was trying to unload. Then, it's the next player's turn.

Everyone has a chance to exchange cards until it's the dealer's turn. If he's not happy with the card he ends up with, the dealer takes one off the top of the deck. When all the passing is done, everyone turns up their card, and the player with the lowest card puts one of his stacks into the pot. The cards used are "burned," and the process is repeated. Whoever loses all three stacks is out of the game. The process is again repeated, until only one person is left with any of his stacks—this player sweeps the pot.

Now to explain what I meant by the object of the game being not to lose. Let's say that the player to the right passes another player the two of spades, and the second player gives the first the two of clubs. The second player will want to "stick," because the two of spades is higher than the two of clubs, so he can't lose. No matter how rotten the card, if a player has one guy beat, he can't lose. (I can't tell you how many guys never seem to get this. Time and again they'll have their guy beaten, pass anyway, end up with the ace of clubs and lose. It makes you want to stick their face in a blender.)

FOLLOW THE BITCH

Some people call this game Follow The Queen—they're people who haven't played it much. The queen in question rarely acts the lady. In play she's the Bitch, the Mop Squeezer or something less flattering, but she can be a Beauty or a Lassie.

This is an easy-to-learn relative of seven card stud dealt two down, four up, one down.

Lefty's Deceiver™

Dealer antes and begins by dealing two down cards to each player, followed by one up card. These up cards are highly anticipated by the players, as queens, up or down, are always wild. In addition, any up card dealt directly after a queen is also wild. Say the guy to your right gets a queen and the dealer gives you a duck. Now all queens and quackers, up or down, are wild. This remains the case unless another queen is dealt up. Then, the card following the new queen is now wild and your wild ducks revert to plain old Deuces again. If no queens are dealt up, then only queens are wild. Also, if the last up card to the dealer is a queen, then only queens are wild. Bets follow each of the up cards initiated by the high hand. (Note: With only one card up, a king or an ace will initiate before a wild queen. Thereafter, naturals don't take precedence, i.e., an ace-queen pair equals a pair of queens or aces, so first pair bets.) The last card is dealt down and the high hand initiates the final round of betting. The best hand made with five cards (often five-of-a-kind with two wild cards) wins all. In the event of a tie, house rules prevail. Since this is a seven-card game, the leftover two cards in a player's hand are not considered—the pot is simply split between the tied hands.

HIGH CHICAGO

Also known as High Moriah. Seven-card stud (dealt two down, four up, one down), with the player with the high hand splitting the pot with the player who has the highest spade in the hole . . . . And that, my friend, is the whole enchilada.

Strategy here is simple: if you're dealt the ace of spades in the hole, bet the ranch.

BURNERS

We recommend that this game be played at night's end. The reason is simple: even a player who's been the night's big winner can be turned into a pauper in about five hands.

Burners is played with three cards dealt two down, one up. The player with the highest card up is burned and must stay in. Then, starting with the player to his left, each player decides whether he's in. Straights and flushes don't count. Ace-king is a good hand. A pair is better. Three of a kind is almost unbeatable. Ten, two, four is an automatic win. (Don't look for any hidden logic regarding why these three cards make the perfect hand—they were arbitrarily chosen by the poker gods years ago when the world was young.) The highest hand wins, and the losers match the pot. (If the average is more than one loser per hand, it's pretty easy to see how the take can quickly escalate in size.) The game ends when the burned player is the only one "in," and he then sweeps the pot.

There's really very little strategy. However, a set of brass-plated, hot-air-balloon-size cajones would come in handy.

CHALLENGE

This is another game best played toward the end of the night. It's also similar to Burners in that the pot can grow at an alarming rate. (I've personally been in games where Challenge was responsible for whole fortunes circumnavigating the table.)

Everyone is dealt two cards. This hand is to be played low. The perfect low is ace, two. One at a time and starting to the dealer's left, each player is asked if he is in. The first to say "yes" opens a challenge by putting his hand face down in the middle of the table. He now must accept all challengers.

Starting to the opener's left, each player wishing to accept the challenge will exchange hands with the opener. They now know who of the two has the winning hand. This is kept secret until the end, when each loser pays the winner a quantity equal to the pot. If the opener is challenged by several players and he loses all of them, it's easy to see how money can be won and lost in a hurry.

Now, each player is dealt a third card. This hand is played "high" (no straights or flushes). Ace, king is good. A pair is better. Three of a kind is almost always a winner. After this hand is played out, players are dealt a fourth card. This hand is played low.

For the final round, players are dealt a fifth card. This hand is played high, following the regular rules of poker (straights and flushes are now in play).

The game ends when no one challenges the opener.

FARO

The cowpokes played it; Wyatt Earp and "Doc" Holiday dealt it; gunfire erupted over it; green felt, chips and cards were involved; the saloons in old westerns always seem to have a game going. . . Question is, what the hell is it?

Faro is one of the simplest card games ever devised. First off, suits are irrelevant. The dealer deals out two cards at a time from a standard deck and the players bet on which number will appear. The first card's a loser and the second a winner. The thirteen possible values, ace through king, are depicted on a green felt layout. Bets are then placed on one or more of the thirteen.

Also known as Pharo, Pharoah, Pharoan, its name derives from early French playing cards that bore the likeness of an Egyptian king. The game was hugely popular in France during the early 1600s but is probably several hundred years older. French colonists brought it to the U.S., where it spread from New Orleans parlors to become the hottest game in the Wild West.

Sadly, faro may be extinct. Though still an approved game, it hasn't been played in the casinos of Las Vegas or elsewhere in Nevada for more than 15 years. Faro has never been allowed in Monte Carlo (some say because the odds are too fair), and it's doubtful that the game is extant in any of the new gambling venues.

Comb's Sea Habit Bucktail™

HOW TO LOOK AND SOUND LIKE YOU KNOW WHAT YOU'RE DOING WHILE PLAYING POKER IN VEGAS,

Kaufmann Christmas Isl. Special™

Let's see if this sounds familiar: For the past ten years you've consistently been the big winner at your local, bimonthly, nickel-dime-quarter poker game. On particularly good nights, using guile, acute powers of observation and a stone cold poker face, you've been known to fleece your poor overmatched cronies for fortunes sometimes exceeding *$25!* So, it's time to try your luck in Vegas. You walk confidently into the nearest casino, sit down at a poker game and 10 minutes later you're $300 in the hole. . . . What went wrong? Simple. . . . You're now playing *real* poker. The rules are different. The strategy is different. The stakes are much higher. And the players are usually much better. Aside from knowing what hand beats what, very few homespun poker skills will work here. For instance: At home in a typical game of "night baseball" if, after five cards, you're *only* two cards away from filling an inside royal flush, it seems to make sense to play the hand to the end because practically every other card is *wild.* At home everyone hates to fold. In Vegas, in a correctly played game of seven card stud, you will fold after your first three cards *90* percent of the time. Here's a helpful hint that could save you millions in seven stud: If after your first three cards you don't have three to a straight, three to a flush or a good pair, *fold.* . . . Case closed! Seven stud is a very conservative game. Aside from the rules, the lingo is also different. Notice that the seasoned players and the dealer all seem to speak a foreign language.

Don't be surprised if you hear something like this: "Well, I had sixes in the pocket, a nine on third and hit my third on sixth street but I had a four-flusher sitting at seven hitting pretty hard so I just called instead of betting the come. Well, I hit a nine on the river, filling me up so I put the hammer down and came out swinging. The flush on seven raised, I raised, he called, I flipped over my love boat and after the rake and throwing some sugar to the dealer, pulled in about 80 fish." *Translation*: "Well, my first two cards were sixes, my third card was a nine and I got my third six after six cards. Now, the guy sitting in the No. 7 seat had four up-cards to a flush and was betting pretty heavily so instead of raising him, I just called. On the last card I got a nine that gave me a full house of sixes over nines so I bet it. The guy sitting in the seventh seat obviously had a flush because he raised me. Well, I raised him back which must have scared him because he just called. I turned over my full house, which beat his flush and after the dealer took a percentage of the pot and I tipped him, I won about $80."

POKER-PHRASES-TO-ENGLISH DICTIONARY

"aces rolled up"	Your first three cards are aces.
"aces pocketed"	Your first two down cards are aces.
"third street"	the third card dealt to you
"fourth street"	the fourth card dealt to you
"fifth street"	If you need the answer to this one, you probably wore black socks in gym class.
"sixth street"	(see "fifth street")
"the river"	the last card dealt to you
"rats and mice"	a full house consisting of three threes over two twos
"love boat"	a full house consisting of three sixes over two nines
"four-flusher"	four cards to a flush
"betting the come"	betting a hand that isn't yet made
"catching it down the river"	making your hand on the last card
"all blue"	a club flush
"gizmo"	a hand going nowhere
"possible pair"	see "gizmo"
"fisherman"	a bad poker player who stays in every hand
"liar"	a player who likes to bluff
"bug"	one or both jokers inserted into the deck and acting as limited wild card filling aces, straights and flushes
"cowboys"	kings
"johnnys"	jacks
"hooks"	jacks
"ladies"	queens
"bitches"	queens
"mop squeezers"	queens
"killer tomatoes"	pair of tens
"dead man's hand"	two pair consisting of aces and eights
"asshole"	asshole!
"spoiler"	a neophyte

aka HOW TO SPEAK VEGAS

Krystal Flash Charlie

THE DEAD BROTHER POEM

O*ne day, in the middle of the night, two dead boys went out to fight. Back to back they faced each other, took their swords and shot each other. A deaf policeman heard the noise and went to shoot the two dead boys. If you don't think this story's true, ask the blind man he saw it too.*

Playing any dice game is often called "rolling the bones." While it's true that long ago dice were made from bone or ivory, the reference is even earlier. Bones of the human hand or the ankle bones of sheep, colored or knicked with a blade, may have been the oldest known gaming tools. Yes, dem bones is mighty old, but even the familiar six-sided dice are ancient—the Bible tells us that soldiers played dice for Jesus' robe at the foot of his cross. It's even believed that cube-shaped gaming dice evolved independently in many parts of the ancient world.

The most popular dice game—and the most representative of Las Vegas—is craps. Hollywood loves to portray the roaring, wild-eyed excitement around a craps table, and the myth holds up. The ear will easily lead you from the electronic warbling and metallic clatter of the slots and video poker banks through the gaming tables to the crap shooters. It's not always that way, of course—disgusted murmurs hang like a shroud over a cold table—but the action explodes when somebody gets hot.

So it's the big game in Sin City—is that reason enough to learn craps? No, don't bother on that account. Vegas is a very silly town and should never direct any decision on personal development. For instance, Vegas celebrated the new year of 1997 in typical fashion: It blew up a 900-room hotel to make space for a 4,000-room resort. After all, the hotel was already 10 years old. And, of course, there's still no water out there. But what the hell? The symbol of the city may have shifted from Sammy to the sky crane, but it's still an original—if strange—town, with a wild history. You can't beat that anything-can-happen anticipation and aura of naughtiness that hangs over the place (of course, that's during the first half of your visit, while you still have some of your money left). The mob stories have their fascination, but Vegas is also the place where "Doc" Holiday got into one of his many barroom shoot-outs. That connection with the Old West is probably the best and truest way to view today's casinos and megaresorts. They're just a bunch of saloons—hysterically enlarged by some mad scientist's growth hormone concoction drawn from the testicles of P.T. Barnum, Bugsy Seigel and Liberace.

So why learn craps? Just why is it incumbent upon the sporting gentleman to develop at least a working knowledge of what W.C. Fields called the "galloping dominoes"? For one reason alone: Played smart, it's still the best game in town.

Kaufmann Maribou Shrimp™

Just how does a game get a name like craps anyhow? Well, it could be worse. Craps is descended from an old dice game called Hazard. One of the throws was called "crabs." The foul and most foreign French who brought the game to New Orleans corrupted the name to "creps," later "craps." But we can be thankful—playing craps beats the hell out of playing crabs.

Your basic crap game can be played anywhere. All you need is dice, tender and a few sports. Nathan Detroit didn't have to worry about $4,000 oak tables, green felts and stickmen. Traditional settings are the same as your basic cheap sex venues: alleys, coat rooms, dorms, barracks, boiler rooms, sewers, Salvation Army halls, church basements. Shooters play against each other and, in an honest game, everyone has an equal chance to win. In the casino version, "bank craps," players play against the house, which holds a slight advantage. There are detailed rules in any Hoyle but, for your edification, the basics of each version follow.

Street Craps

To Begin Play—Each player rolls the dice and the high number becomes the "shooter." The shooter takes the dice and lays out some cash, say $20. Called the "center bet," this represents how much the shooter is willing to risk. The other players may cover, or "fade," the shooter's bet, up to a total of $20. If three players put in $5 each, then only $15 of the center bet is covered and the shooter removes the extra "fin." The pot is right and the shooter shoots. One of three things can happen:

The Shooter Wins—If the shooter rolls a seven or an 11 (called a "natural"), he's a winner and the pot is his. He can pocket the $30 and pass the dice or leave any portion of it as a new center bet, invite the players to fade him and shoot again. Note: The odds that you will lose as the shooter are 251 to 244. The odds are against you but not by much. This gives you an idea of why craps is the best game in town.

The Shooter Loses—If the shooter rolls a two, a three, or a 12 (called "craps"), he's a loser and the other players pick up their $5, plus $5 from the center bet. The first player to the left at the table becomes the next shooter.

The Shooter Rolls a Point—If the shooter rolls one of the remaining numbers (a four, a five, a six, a eight, a nine or a 10), then that number becomes his "point." The shooter now needs to roll his point again ("pass") to win. He can keep trying unless he rolls a seven. A seven means he has

Kaufmann Christmas Isl. Special™

"crapped out" and is a loser. Why a seven? The number seven in dice is the number that works most for you—and against you. The reason is that there are more ways to roll a seven (six ways) than any other number.

That's your basic craps. The play gets a bit more complicated from here. To keep things interesting, side bets between players about whether the shooter will make his point and how—mostly these involve a variety of sucker bets.

Try It Out Before Reading Further

—You're now a crapshooting neophyte who needs to roll the bones. Grab some dice, some monopoly money or some matches and at least two other bodies (kids love to learn this game with mom and dad). Write the winning, losing and point numbers down as a guide, find a wall and start the action. As the "money" begins to move, the ancient subtleties of the game will gradually reveal themselves. Revelations will be imparted as if from ghosts of crapshooters past. You will begin to realize, for instance, that a 10 point is a little harder to make than a six. And that this game's a bitch on the knees and lower back.

Bank Craps

The same basic rules apply in a casino crap game except that all bets are against the house (this creates a great "us against them" spirit), the drinks are free, your knees feel better and the gaming felt reads like complete gibberish. Don't panic! The sucker bets are out in force on the bank craps felt—you can ignore most of them. But there are a few new terms to learn.

Remember that in private craps the shooter is betting he'll win and the other players are betting he'll lose. In bank craps a player can bet either that the shooter will win (be a "right bettor") or lose (be a "wrong bettor"), but all bets are made with the house. These win/lose bets are represented on the table layout as "pass," "don't pass," "come" and "don't come" (no off-color cracks now—pay attention, ya bum).

The Pass Line

—This is a bet that the shooter will win (roll a seven or an 11) or make his point. The player lays down his bet before the shooter's first roll (his "come out"). The house pays even money ("five'll getcha 10").

The Don't Pass Line

—This is a bet that the shooter will lose (roll a two, a three or a 12) or not make his point. The house pays even money. (Note: To "bar" a number is one of the differences in bank craps. On the casino felt you'll see the word "bar" followed by dice representing either the two, the three or the 12. If the shooter rolls the barred number, he still loses but your "wrong" bet is not a winner—it's a tie.)

Come

—This is a great idea for a bet but a little confusing at first. A bettor can lay his money down on the "come" portion of the felt any time after the shooter's first roll ("come out"). A bet on the "come" treats every roll by the shooter as if it were his first. Now what the hell does that mean? The best way to think about it is to imagine that every bet on the "come" makes you the shooter. No matter what the actual shooter may be going for, treat his roll after your bet like your first. Let's say the shooter has established a four as his point. He's trying to roll another four before he craps out, right? You bet the come. The shooter rolls an 11. That number means nothing to the shooter but you win (just as if you had just rolled yourself for the first time, get it?). If the shooter rolls a seven, then he's crapped out but you're a winner. Say the shooter (still trying to make his four point) rolls a five (or any other point number). Such a roll means nothing to the shooter, who keeps trying for that four, but the five has just become your point. Pretty cool, eh? Like any great game, it only gets better the more you play and understand it. For instance, even if you don't play the long shots, you'll at least be in a position to appreciate them when they come in for somebody else. That's the beauty of craps—for the most part everyone's rooting for each other and every player's united in a grand and glorious effort to kill, kill, KILL THE HOUSE!

Don't Come

—This is the opposite of the above bet, which makes it a little weird. You're still treating any roll after this bet like a "come out" but you're betting on a loser. Any number barred in "don't pass" is barred here as well.

With lots of different players betting the "come/don't come" at different times, you begin to appreciate that the

---

Talkin' Crap

1,1	Snake Eyes
3	Tray, Trays (from *tres*)
Any 4	Little Joe, Little Joe From Kokomo
Any 5	Phoebe
Any 8	Eighter From Decatur
Any 9	Nine-a From Carolina
Any 10	Big Dick (from *deca* or *dix*)
6,6	Box Cars

Possible Rolls & Their Odds

2	1,1						35 to 1
3	1,2	2,1					17 to 1
4	1,3	3,1	2,2				11 to 1
5	1,4	4,1	2,3	3,2			8 to 1
6	1,5	5,1	2,4	4,2	3,3		6.2 to 1
7	1,6	6,1	2,5	5,2	3,4	4,3	5 to 1
8	2,6	6,2	3,5	5,3	4,4		6.2 to 1
9	3,6	6,3	4,5	5,4			8 to 1
10	4,6	6,4	5,5				11 to 1
11	5,6	6,5					17 to 1
12	6,6						35 to 1

dealers have a lot to keep track of and need to be pretty damn sharp—they are... bet on it. And don't forget to kick 'em back something when you win. The gaming gods favor good sports looking for fun but they piss on any shmo who's there trying to make his rent. The main thing is to remember that old Boy Scout creed, "Be prepared." The casino crap game is fun as hell, but it's the big time and it can be intimidating. Learn at home with friends, low stakes and a cheap felt, drum the procedures into your head and stick to the smart money bets mentioned above.

What About Cheating?
—The crooked gambler figures prominently in fiction but these bad fellows did, and do, exist. An infamous English dice cheat named John Outlawe, in fact, lent his name to our vernacular. If dice are our oldest gaming implements, then it stands to reason that crooked dice came second. Cheating at a casino, saloon or private game may have a romantic angle but it's a highly dangerous business. The cheat may feel that he's just being clever by working the odds in his favor but what he's really doing is working them at someone else's expense. That someone, upon discovery, could respond in the traditional manner—by breaking the cheat's thumbs or kicking his teeth in. Back in the days of the riverboat gambler, vigilantes would pursue a cheat, or "sharper," to "do him up." This popular euphemism meant to gouge out his eyes, pull his ears off, and stomp his face. So how does someone cheat with dice? Lend me your eyes and ears, brother:

Loaded Dice
—The dice are weighted, or "loaded," to roll a particular way. This is accomplished by drilling into the side opposite to the one that you want to turn up. A discreet cavity is made by drilling into one or more of the dots. Special vises and hand drills have been made for just this purpose. The space is then filled with a heavy substance (gold is the traditional favorite), the hole repaired and the dot repainted.

These dice tend to land weighted side down and thus affect the outcome of the game. Glass and the current clear red plastic dice have rendered this technique obsolete.

Shaved or Gaffed Dice
—The shape of the dice can be altered in numerous ways to affect throws. One or more of the sides may be shaved to create a larger face. The corners may be rounded or altered. Certain faces of "beveled" dice bulge slightly outward so that the dice tend to land on the flatter surfaces.

Mismarked Dice
—Opposing sides of any dice should always add up to seven. However, crooked dice that are custom-made may change these sums, or leave a number off entirely. While it seems insane to attempt anything so obvious, when dice are viewed on a table only three sides are visible. Mismarked dice can therefore appear perfectly legit.

Cheating With the House Dice
—The basic problem crooked dice present is how to work them into an otherwise honest game. There are a few ways that an experienced dice cheat may manipulate honest dice. Not to sound too reverential, but this is where low cheating may approach high art. "The end-over-end" roll throws the dice in such a way that the side numbers have no chance of appearing. "The slide" is truly remarkable. With this throw, the dice do not tumble but rather skid down the felt—the top numbers never change. A modified slide is less obvious—only one of the dice slides while the other tumbles alongside, giving the impression that both are behaving normally. Be forewarned! These tricks have been defeated at the casinos by installing little speed bumps under the felt or insisting that shooters throw over a string or bounce the dice off a backboard.

Kaufmann Maribou Shrimp™

BASS PRO

Ask any bass angler for directions to mecca and he'll point the way to Springfield, Missouri. The town has long been famous among Wild West aficionados as being the site of an honest-to-goodness, classic showdown. On July 12, 1861, Wild Bill Hickok met and killed Davis Tutt in Market Square. The dispute, over cards or a woman, resulted in one of the few actual *High Noon*-type confrontations in history.

Today, thanks to the magnificent headquarters of Johnny Morris' Bass Pro Shops, fishermen have made Springfield the largest tourist attraction in Missouri. Morris' Outdoor World showroom, at more than 170,000 square feet and growing, is one of the Seven Wonders of the Fishing World.

The enormous selection of outdoor and sporting equipment runs through an amazing complex that simulates the great outdoors. The 140,000-gallon aquarium system features ponds, streams and a four-story waterfall. Various live fish and game birds inhabit the premises and readily reproduce indoors. Ethel, the largest bass in captivity, lived out the last of her 20 years here. A world-famous collection of big game mounts and a two-story log cabin are also among the sights.

Crazy Charlie

Bass Pro Shops, the sportsman's paradise; (Above) The lovely and legendary Ethyl the bass; (Right) The 4-story indoor waterfall at the Bass Pro Shops Outdoor World national headquarters in lucky Springfield, Missouri.

Crazy Charlie

LORDS OF THE FLY
RANDALL KAUFMANN

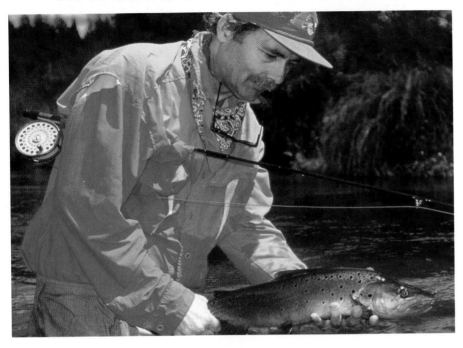

Live to fish, fish to live. It's the fantasy of all die-hard fishermen and a reality that best describes the life of Randall Kaufmann. Anyone who gets the *Kaufmann's Streamborn* catalog knows at least one thing about him—he leads an enviable life. The cover photo more often than not features him in some far-off angler's paradise holding up an absolutely fantastic fish just taken on the fly. Even the fish seem to be smiling....Anyway, they don't look unhappy. Experience with the Kaufmann Co. and the terrific books that he's written add admiration to envy.

Randall's career has been a family affair. His stepfather introduced him and his brother, Lance, to fly-fishing at a young age. The two brothers started in mail order from the garage, and their mother, Oda, helped with the accounting and shipping.

Tying and selling flies was an immediate passion for Randall and has become his singular contribution to the world of fly-fishing. His books are the standard for comprehension and clarity. A surprising feature of his catalog makes it the greatest reference bargain on the market—each fly (and there are more than 300) has its own bio. And Randall's superior flies are featured on the pages of this book, with all due appreciation.

DR. NICK CURCIONE

Maybe you've caught Nick Curcione on "ESPN Outdoors"—his appearances have been unforgettable. He's the guy who started a stampede in Southern California after showing how you could skiff-fish bonita on the fly, right in Redondo Beach Harbor. It was an incredible segment that featured Nick's skill with "shooting heads." His casts went something short of a mile, and zinged off his reel as if he'd snagged a jet ski. He displayed a super fast double-hand retrieve with the rod tucked under his arm, then hooked into a nice tail-walking fish and fought like mad to boat it before swarming seals could scarf the damn thing.

Another wild sequence had Nick going after shark on the fly. He chummed up the water, and pretty soon the gray shapes were circling. Slapping the fly on the surface, with only about 6 feet of line out, did the trick. Nick was a riot, yelling, "Oh! He ate it! He ate it! He's a grinner, sports fans!" Great stuff.

With more than 30 years experience on the water, Nick is one of the pioneers of offshore flyfishing. He's a member of the Orvis Saltwater Advisory Team, the author of the terrific *Orvis Guide to Saltwater Fly-Fishing* and a regional editor for *Flyfishing Saltwaters* magazine. His newest book is *Baja on the Fly*. Raised in New York City, he loves getting back East to sight-fish flat water for stripers. As an instructor, Nick has some of the greatest patter in the business (he sounds like he could definitely put you on to a good horse) and takes pride in his butt-ugly, but deadly, flies.

When not doing battle with seals or sharks, Dr. Nick serves as professor of sociology at Loyola Marymount University. His area of expertise is deviant behavior, another growth industry.

Clouser Deep Minnow White™

"LEFTY" KREH

Lefty is a true god of the salt. His mentor was the legendary Joe Brooks, and Kreh, in turn, has acted as mentor to lucky guys like Nick Curcione and Flip Pallett. Thanks to his videos, books and magazine articles, Kreh has probably inspired and improved the skills of more fly fishermen across the country than anyone now alive. When it comes to casting demonstrations, nobody can hold an audience like Lefty. He runs through a repertoire of precision and specialty casts so effortlessly you just want to kill him.

Armchair anglers got to check out Lefty's inner sanctum on a jaw-dropping episode of Pallett's "Walkers Cay Chronicles." Lefty led Flip down to a room that was like a treasure chamber of fishing tackle. Another room was exclusively for fly tying—a fly tying room. (This is where he tied up the now-legendary Lefty's Deceiver, the fly that now graces a U.S. postal stamp.)

Joe Brooks

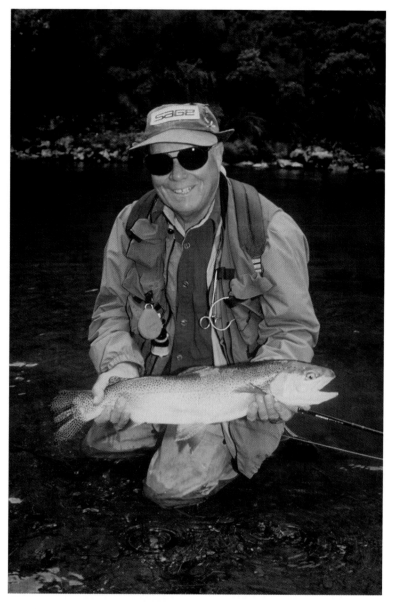

A retired outdoor editor for the *Baltimore Sun* and a one-time exhibition shooter, Lefty currently holds a staff position on six outdoor magazines and acts as consultant to *Sage*, *Scientific Anglers* and *Worldwide Sportsman*. Guys with private jets are lined up waiting to go fishing with Lefty—it's no wonder he's always got that big grin on. "Hell, I've been foolin' 'em for years!" he says.

CABELA'S

Fishermen are notorious window shoppers—but they buy from Cabela's. If you have any fishing, hunting or outdoor equipment at all, surely some of it came from the "world's foremost outfitter" (I know, I know—don't call me "Shirley").

Cabela is another great example of the kitchen-table dream coming true. It all started back in 1961, when Dick Cabela ran an enticing classified ad in the Casper, Wyoming, newspaper. It read: "12 hand-tied flies for $1." Orders went out with a mimeographed catalog that Dick put together with his wife, Mary. The appeal was instant.

Dick's younger brother, Jim, joined the company in 1963, and storage facilities moved quickly from sheds to basements to a four-story vacant John Deere building in the Panhandle.

Boasting showrooms in Kearney and Sidney, Nebraska, Cabela's now puts some 55 million catalogs a year into the grateful hands of hungry gear hounds.

(On the following pages) Paintings by renowned wildlife artist Russ Smiley. "International Game Fish of the World" and "Freshwater Fish of North America." Prints, in addition to the original painting of "Freshwater," are available from the artist at (305) 754-9526.

Blanton's Sar-Mul-Mac™

"International Game-Fish of the World" A limited edition by Ross Smiley — 850 NE 84 Ave Rd Miami, Fl 33138 ©KS 1976

A.D. Ross Smiley

Fresh Water Fish of North America
© 1993 Ros Smilley
550 N.E. 4th Ave. Rd.
Miami, Florida 33138

King Salmon
Sockeye Salmon
Humpback Salmon
Atlantic Salmon
Atlantic Salmon
Coho Salmon
Dog Salmon
Arctic Grayling
Montana Grayling
Kokanee Salmon
Landlocked Salmon
Coastal Cutthroat Trout
Steelhead Trout
Rainbow Trout
Kamloops Trout
Brown Trout
Cisco
Mooneye
Cutthroat Trout
Smelt
Brook Trout
Lake Trout
Golden Trout
Dolly Varden Trout
Saugeye Trout
Lake Whitefish
White Sucker
Rocky Mountain Whitefish
Freshwater Drum
Walleye
Yellow Perch
White Bass
Yellow Bass
Sauger
White Perch
Northern Muskellunge
Chautauqua Muskellunge
Northern Pike
Chain Pickerel
Redfin Pickerel
Grass Pickerel
Muskellunge
Warmouth Perch
Warmouth Perch
Shortnose Sturgeon
Lake Sturgeon
Alligator Gar
Florida Largemouth Bass
Northern Largemouth Bass
Northern Smallmouth Bass
Meridian Smallmouth Bass
Redeye Bass (Alabama)
Redeye Bass (Apalachicola)
Northern Bass
Alabama Spotted Bass
Neosho Spotted Bass
White Crappie
Flier Sunfish
Rock Bass
Spotted Sunfish
Channel Catfish
Black Bullhead
Flathead Catfish
Suwannee Bass
Guadalupe Bass
Bluegill
Black Crappie
Green Sunfish
Pumpkinseed
Longear Sunfish
Sacramento Perch
White Catfish
Yellow Bullhead
Blue Catfish
Brown Bullhead

THE NATIONAL FRESHWATER

THE INTERNATIONAL GAME FISH ASSOCIATION

The year 1939 remains a standout for the American male. It was a peak of industrial design as demonstrated by the New York World's Fair, theaters were packing them in with some of the greatest films of all time, planes, trains and automobiles were never prettier, and the IGFA held their first official meeting at the American Museum of Natural History.

The IGFA was founded by Michael Lerner, a powerful guy who loved nothing more than battling big billfish. At the suggestion of his Aussie pal, Clive Firth, Lerner brought a universal code of sporting ethics, conservation and competition to saltwater angling. With headquarters in Ft. Lauderdale, the IGFA produces the authoritative and invaluable *World Record Game Fishes Annual* (freshwater all-tackle and saltwater fly rodder records were added in 1979) and have established the world's largest fishing library—an amazing research facility. Call these guys for more info at (305) 467-0161.

Popovic's Surf Candy™

FISHING HALL OF FAME & MUSEUM

The next time you get within 3,000 miles of Hayward, Wisconsin, don't forget to stop in and pay your respects to the mightiest fish in the nation. The National Freshwater Fishing Hall of Fame & Museum created the ultimate shrine to anglers in 1979: the magnificent muskie museum, four and a half stories tall. It's not just the world's largest fishing museum—the viewing platform in the mouth of the big beastie also makes it the fisherman's all-time favorite photo op.

The big muskie serves as the centerpiece of a beautifully situated, six-acre sculpture garden and an authentic, informative museum complex founded by Bob Kutz in 1960 and helped along by the good folks at Jim Beam Distillers. Which is great. But just remember: It's a giant fish, a seriously giant fish *and* a fishing museum. Go. Go now.

KISS A TROUT

Or do the next best thing—join Trout Unlimited. With more than 450 chapters, it's America's leading trout and salmon conservation organization. You get their great *Trout* magazine and absolutely no fishy aftertaste. It's the Blalockian thing to do. (800) 834-2419 or trout@tu.org or www.tu.org/trout

TROUT UNLIMITED

Clouser's Deep Minnow Black™

THIS THING CALLED WHISKEY

The monks called it *aqua vitae*, and it's referred to in song as Old John Barleycorn, but the subject at hand is our uniquely American beverage. The term *American whiskey* applies to many products unique unto themselves, but generally it refers to our mellowed adaptation of the original gruffer spirits of Scotland and Ireland. Indeed, St. Pat himself is often credited with creating the first whiskey, called *Uisge beatha* (*uisge* = "water of life"; from *uisge*, we get "whiskey"), by distilling beer sometime in the fifth century. (Regarding the different spellings: the general rule is *whisky* in Scotland and Canada, and *whiskey* in Ireland and the U.S., with a few exceptions.)

What's going on in those stills? Intricacies aside, how do they make this stuff? Basically, here's the procedure:

Mash—It all starts with pure limestone-filtered spring water (as with beer, the water used is very important) and a mash. Mash is a boiled concoction of about 75 percent cornmeal combined with equal parts rye and barley grains. Natural converted sugars released from the grains are consumed by the next additive, yeast. (Drum roll, please.) This process is *fermentation*.

Yeast—The poor channel-surfing slob who blunders onto a commercial break for the Lifetime Network or for any daytime blather gets an earful about yeast. It doesn't sound pretty. Yeast is a fungus. There are countless types, with associated properties. The distiller carefully cultivates a strain he likes and keeps it safely and forever alive. When the yeast is added to the mash, a magical thing happens. The fungus devours the mash sugars and, after digestion, expels alcohol and CO_2. (You heard me right—alcohol is fungus whizz. See why they say ignorance is bliss?)

The party really rocks when the yeast is cranking and the huge fermentation vats are hissing and bubbling like mad until all released sugars are consumed.

Distilling—For most, the image of whiskey-making includes a copper pot topped with corkscrew coil and the steady drip, drip, drip of clear kickapoo joy juice. While no doubt some of these babies are still percolating away in remote corners of America, this wondrous contraption was abandoned long ago by

REGISTERED U.S. PAT. OFFICE.

MYOPIA CLUB

WHISKEY

A BLEND BOTTLED BY H.W. HUGULEY CO. BOSTON

the big boys. Commercial stills have incorporated modern design techniques, ensuring greater quality control and quantity of product. But the principle remains the same.

The fermented brew is skimmed and heated in the still. Because alcohol boils before water does, the rising vapor is what the distiller is after and must deftly control, along with assorted flavor additives. Now the crazy corkscrew, called a cooling worm, comes into play. The rising vapor is caught in the copper spiral, where it condenses and exits stage right. In the old days, what you had at this point was white lightning. Today's more subtly rendered concoction is cut with demineralized water to achieve the desired (and legally administered) proof. (The proof of the beverage represents one-half the alcohol content by volume—for example, 100 proof = 50 percent alcohol.)

Cogeners—At the risk of getting too technical, it's important to note this particular step in distilling. Cogeners are the natural and artificial additives that impart subtleties and distinctives—the unique character of your "who hit John." Remember in *Forbidden Planet* when Robby the Robot gulped down that last bit of bourbon? His chemical evaluation referred to "traces of fusel oil"—that's one of your cogeners, friend.

Aging—The young whiskey is loaded into beautiful, charred American White Oak 50-gallon barrels, and the wooden cork, called a bung, is hammered home into the, uh, bung hole. Here another magical process happens, affecting maturation and color. A minimum of two years is required (again, by legal decree). Then, out comes whiskey.

Nothing to it, right? Well, before calling a plumber buddy over to knock out a still along these lines, remember that home manufacture of distilled spirits is illegal, even if only for personal use. (Now wine, beer and cider are another matter…) Truly, the best way to experience the manufacture of American whiskey is to call up one of the pros and ask for a tour. Meet some elegant practitioners of the craft and better appreciate the rich history and art of their business. (Notice, too, that the intimate knowledge gained will impart a big informed grin on your face the next time you sample their product.) Get goin', boy.

Dooley Wilson (left) and Humphrey Bogart (in white) in a classic scene of moroseness and doubt, with man's favorite antidote: distilled spirits. The film: Casablanca (1943).

Krystal Flash Charlie

What Makes Tennessee Sippin' Whiskey Tennessee Sippin' Whiskey?

Tennessee—The home of Davey Crockett, Andy "Old Hickory" Jackson, the Cherokee and Chickamauga, famous Civil War battles, Nashville, Memphis and the Tennessee Walking Horse. The pioneer mothers and fathers of this state had a special kind of guts and independence of spirit. They've got their own way of doing things in Tennessee and that extends, thankfully, to whiskey. There are only two companies there that make it: Jack Daniel's (Black Label, Green Label, Lem Motlow, Gentleman Jack) and George Dickel (No. 8, No. 12, Special Barrel Reserve).

Tennessee's whiskeys earned their distinction with the Lincoln County Process, which involves leaching the beverage through maple charcoal before it enters the keg. At the Jack Daniel's distillery, the whiskey is poured through 10 feet of this smoothing charcoal. A legal distinction—recognized by the Feds in 1941—separates Tennessee's product from that of other distilleries, just as there is a legal distinction for Kentucky bourbon. George Dickel drives the distinction home further—they make Tennessee *whisky*, the Scottish spelling dating back to their inception. Now this gets a little confusing, but before the legal distinction, Jack Daniel's used to call their product a bourbon.

> "Whiskey on beer, never fear,
> Beer on whiskey makes you frisky."
>
> **— An Old Saying**

United Distillers, which owns George Dickel & Co., includes George Dickel Special Barrel Reserve in their Bourbon Heritage Collection.

Tennessee sure as heck is one beautiful part of the country. My yankee sister moved there with her Yankee husband. She's lived in the Northeast and in Paris, France, but you couldn't blast her out of Knoxville. Of course, that's no signal for other damn Yankees to pull up stakes and head on down. Lokka what happened to Santa Fe. Once a town of real character, history and charm, the place went to hell after the West Coast discovered "Santa Fe-style" decorating, New Age crystals, channeling, sweat lodges and all the rest of that related bullshit back in the go-go 80s, everybody looking for "spiritual" vacation homes and a new Indian best Friend. The green menace this time was cash. Swollen land prices quickly pushed out a segment of the locals, and the place became filthy with frosted-hair real estate harpies stumbling around in designer boots, wide-fit jeans and turquiose. Then up sprang rows of astronomically priced art galleries and haute cuisine Italian restaurants with pony-tailed waiters. "Isn't it just awful?" moan some of the longtime locals. You know some wasps lay their eggs in caterpillars and then the young eat their way out

JACK DANIEL'S
OLD TIME
DISTILLERY
Established 1866

COME VISIT US

DISTILLERY TOURS
8:00 a.m.–4:00 p.m. daily
(except Thanksgiving Day,
Christmas Day and New Year's Day)
Lynchburg, Tennessee
(POP. 361).

The Nine Kentucky Bourbon Distilleries

Age International/Leestown Distilling—Ancient Age, Ancient Ancient Age, Blanton's Single Barrel Bourbon, Rock Hill Farm, Hancock's Reserve, Elmer T. Lee.

Barton Brands Ltd.—Ten High, Kentucky Gentleman, Very Old Barton, Colonel Lee.

Jim Beam Brands—Jim Beam (White, Green, Black Label), Old Grand Dad and their small-batch Bourbons—Basil Hayden, Knob Creek, Baker's, Booker's.

Boulevard Distillers—Wild Turkey (four varieties, plus single-barrel Kentucky Spirit).

Brown-Forman—Early Times (technically not Bourbon, but straight Kentucky whiskey, because it is aged in used barrels), Old Forester.

Heaven Hill Distilleries—Evan Williams, Evan Williams Single Barrel, Elijah Craig, Elijah Craig 18-Year-Old Single Barrel, Henry McKenna Single Barrel, Heaven Hill.

House of Seagram—Four Roses, No. 1 Bourbon Street (export only, though Four Roses and the recent Four Roses Single Barrel Reserve can be found here in select markets.)

Maker's Mark Distillery—Maker's Mark, Maker's Mark Limited Edition.

United Distillers—I.W. Harper, W.L. Weller, Old Charter, George Dickel Special Barrel Reserve, Old Fitzgerald, Rebel Yell.

The Oscar Getz Museum is located in historic Bardstown, bourbon capital of the world and home of the annual Kentucky Bourbon Festival.

of the living host? Well, it's not really all that awful when you put it in perspective. But the author digresses. . . go get some Tennessee Whiskey or some Tennessee Whisky.

JACK DANIEL'S OLD-TIME DISTILLERY

Our nation's oldest registered distillery was established in 1866 in Lynchburg, Tennessee (population 361). The good folks at Jack Daniel's are proud of the diminutive—and stable—size of their town. With a touch of country humor, the population tally adorns every bottle. Any discussion of the company and their historic legacy is normally handled by Mr. Roger Brashears (c/o the Jack Daniel Barrelhouse), and a finer communications pointman can't be imagined. The richness of this guy's deep mellow voice falls right in step with the company product. (Thanks are in order to you, sir, for all the help.)

The Daniel family boasts some great stories, and how they came to America is no exception. Jack's English-born grandfather, Joseph, was the coachman for a wealthy Scottish family, the Calaways. In a scenario reminiscent of *Wuthering Heights*, young Joseph and the Calaway's 15-year-old daughter, Elizabeth, fell in love. Alas, typical patrician attitudes prevailed: Elizabeth's parents disapproved of an unpropertied suitor for their daughter and immediately objected to the union. The young lovers were resolute, however, and eloped, traveling to the much-talked-about land they believed would welcome them—America. Heading south, they settled in South Carolina. Their timing could have been better—the year was 1772, and Joseph was soon fighting for their new country's independence in the Revolutionary War.

Krystal Flash Charlie

Jack's father, Calaway Daniel, was the eighth child in the new American generation produced by Joseph and Bettie. Calaway married a local gal named Lucinda Cook, who bore him 10 children. Jasper Newton "Jack" Daniel, born in 1846 (probably on September 7), was No. 10.

By this time, the family lived in Lincoln County, Tennessee. At age seven, Jack went to work on the farm of a local Lutheran preacher named Daniel Houston Call. The young lay preacher, all of 17 years old, had recently inherited the property, including ownership of a country store. The whiskey sold at the store was made at the preacher's own still near the farm. This was not as unusual as it may seem. Whiskey was commonly used as tender for real property or wages, and even preachers might be paid, in part, with whiskey. (Abe Lincoln's pappy sold his farm for several barrels of the stuff, plus cash. This by no means meant that Honest Abe's dad was a heavy drinker—whiskey was simply a commodity used for trade of other goods.)

Life at the farm transformed Jack Daniel. Dan's wife, Mary Jane, taught the boy his ABCs, and Preacher Call took him on as apprentice, teaching him the whiskey trade. The story goes that Dan rewarded the boy with this privilege after Jack saved his life by killing a striking rattlesnake.

Changing attitudes eventually persuaded the preacher to abandon the business. Jack, meanwhile, had come to love the whiskey trade and was figuring out ways to expand distribution. Preacher Call admired the boy's pluck and sold him the business—lock, stock and barrels, one might say. Jack Daniel was then 13 years old.

Shortly thereafter, Jack moved his operation to the present sight of the Old Time Distillery. Cave Spring in the Hollow had just the water he was looking for. An old beech tree nearby had once been used to hang two deserters from Gen. Andrew Jackson's army. The "lynching tree" gave rise to the name of the community—Lynchburg (actually, there are other theories, but they don't beat this one). At the Hollow, Jack had time to refine his manufacturing technique and build up the business. It's said that the fire at Jack's still burned for 35 years straight.

Uncompromising quality was central to Jack Daniel's philosophy. "By, God, every day we make it, we're going to make it the best we can," he was known to say. That commitment carries on to this day in the hills of Tennessee, where the Old Time Distillery produces one of the world's great sippin' whiskeys.

Read More About It—*Jack Daniel's Legacy*, by Ben A. Green, is the one and only biography of Mr. Daniel and the company. This is one helluva great American story. You can find the book for sure at the Lynchburg Hardware & General Store, Lynchburg, TN 37352; (615) 759-4200. The cost is about three bucks—this bargain can't be beat. Give 'em a call—they're nice folks.

Bourbon—Some bourbon is made outside of Kentucky and some of it is very fine, but when you're talking about bourbon, you're usually talking Kentucky Bourbon. There is a legal distinction for this beverage—in 1964, "bourbon" became "Bourbon." Now, Bourbon sounds kinda French, doesn't it? Well, most of Kentucky was called Bourbon County back in 1785, named after King Louis XVI, a member of the Bourbon family. That was back when the French were actually helpful as allies. In fact, America's struggle for independence from King George III was accomplished with the help of French forces. In gratitude, many colonies duly honored that nation,

by Ben A. Green

resulting in several French-sounding towns today. (Now, what smarty out there can explain how Louisville got it's name?)

WHAT MAKES BOURBON BOURBON?

Whiskey is considered Bourbon when it is distilled from a fermented mash of corn (over 50 percent), rye and barley, and aged in new charred oak barrels a minimum of two years. Sometime around 1800 or perhaps earlier, folks down in Old Kentuck got the idea of firing the inside of the cooper's craft when storing their product. The practice is often attributed to a Bourbon County Baptist minister named Elijah Craig. In fact, a super-premium 12-year-old Bourbon produced by the Heaven Hill Distillery bears the name of this inspired man of God. (Isn't it great how preachers keep figuring into these stories?) Whether for sanitary reasons, as an accident, or as an experiment in flavor enhancement, storage in charred oaken kegs was a highly successful practice. Aside from giving the whiskey a unique color, this aging technique mellowed the spirits considerably. Kegged whiskeys continue to lose their harsh qualities over time; older means smoother. Producing whiskey in this fashion became regular practice in the area, and Bourbon-style whiskey was shortened over time to simply Bourbon.

The Kentucky Bourbon Festival—Held in Bardstown, the Bourbon Capital of the World, usually the second week of September. A week of great events and a must for Bourbon lovers: tours, black-tie dinners, history, cooperage demonstrations, performers and games.

Rye—Defined as being made with a mash of at least 51 percent rye rather than corn. When one of the authors came of age, he wanted to drink his grandmother's favorite drink with her—J&B Scotch—but couldn't get it down. His mother, amused by this notion, indulged him with an introduction to a great "beginner's" whiskey cocktail—the Rye Presbyterian (rye whiskey and ginger ale on the rocks)—a fine starter and still a good drink. Most of the rye is made in Pennsylvania and Maryland, where the soil is accommodating to this grain. The Father of Our Country cooked up some fine rye as well as peach brandy right at Mt. Vernon.

Corn Whiskey—Defined as made with a mash of at least 80 percent corn and usually considered the traditional product of moonshiners.

Now, Abraham Lincoln was well acquainted with whiskey. Kentucky's famous son operated a tavern in New Salem, Illinois, in 1833, charging 6 cents a glass. In a speech some years later, Honest Abe expressed his opinion on the subject with typical intelligence and common sense: "If people are injured from the use of liquor, the injury arises not from the use of a bad thing but from the abuse of a very good thing."

Suggested Reading—*The Book of Classic American Whiskeys,*

Mom and Dad's Mint Julep

The Mint Julep is the traditional summer Bourbon beverage of the gods. Be warned: Tradition demands that you take the high road with this one. Not unimportantly, it is *the* drink of the Derby. Though born in and identified with the genteel South, this heat-beater boasts such sheer-delightful splendidness that it was probably being served in New England and parts West within days, perhaps hours, of its birth. Fancy accoutrements are optional, but the authors' folks like to do things in style, so this recipe begins with chilling the sterling silver Mint Julep cups. These are plain in design, pretty as hell, hold about 10 ounces and come with silver straws with a mint leaf spoon fashioned on the end (imagine an uptown Slurpee straw—wa-a-ay uptown).

While the cups chill down, shave up some ice. Pick four or five leaves from your garden's mint plant—grown just for this purpose. Put a teaspoon of water and a rounded teaspoon of powdered sugar in each chilled cup, add the mint leaves and mash them up a bit with your muddler (also silver, and *not* a golf club). Fill the cup with fine crushed ice, add a jigger of Bourbon and stir until the ice level drops a bit. Add ice to fill, follow with a second jigger, top with a mint sprig dusted with powdered sugar, and chill in the fridge (not the freezer) for half an hour. Serve.

Suggested dress: Tennis whites, sweat-soaked after three hard sets played in August, or your favorite kelly green dress pants with the little ducks stitched in 'em. The authors' Uncle Bill's got a pair with red lips and the letters KMA stitched all over in red. (He says the letters stand for "kiss me, angel," but something in the angle of his eyebrow suggests that our chains are being yanked.)

by Mark H. Waymack and James F. Harris, Open Court Publishing Co. (1995) "These guys did one hell of a wonderful job. *The Book of Classic American Whiskeys* tells the whole story, the way it truly is, with a lot of interesting details. I've never read a better book on whiskey."—F. Booker Noe Jr., grandson of Jim Beam, Master Distiller Emeritus, James B. Beam Distilling Co.

The story is a fascinating one, but there's another benefit, as Waymack and Harris say, "the people now involved in the industry are among the most friendly, colorful and delightful people we have ever met. However, in one respect, this ought not to

Shinebou Shad Wool Head™

be very surprising since the story of American whiskey is really a story of the American people. It was the people who made American whiskey what it is, and the making of the whiskey contributed, in part, to making us the people that we are." Be sure to check out the great bibliography.

Gin—When it comes to grand and glorious origin stories, it doesn't get much worse than the invention of gin. Before the martini, before Bond, before the modern tuxedo, the cut-glass bottles, the Beefeater and controversy over British vs. American, came the humble (*exceedingly* humble) origin of gin. Simply put, about 1672, a doctor at the Netherlands' University of Leyden, trying to make a diuretic (that is, a potion to help the patient tinkle better), wound up inventing the stuff. (The author did say humble.) Juniper berries steeped in Scottish grain alcohol produced the first gin, and the process, despite adding flavor enhancers like lime and orange peel, hasn't changed much. It's basically flavored "white dog."

The French called the new brew *genièvre*, which was shortened and popularized by the British. King William III helped immeasurably by deciding to tax French wine right out of the country. As a result, his countrymen turned to this cheaper, more potent beverage and the Gin Epidemic began. So much hell broke loose that the beverage was outlawed in 1736, but it proved so easy to make at home that the decree lasted only six years. (Another fizzled stab at prohibition.) *Dry* means, as it does with wine, less sweet.

The Perfect Martini—Believe it or not, the original recipe called for two parts gin to one part vermouth, with olive. (*Vermouth* refers to a dry specialty herb-flavored white wine—unless "sweet" vermouth, usually red and Italian, is called for.) The reverse martini calls for just a drop or two of vermouth in the glass, swirled around, any excess to be poured out before filling with gin.

For the absolutely guaranteed driest martini, wave the vermouth bottle over the glass. The author's cool old dial-a-drink cocktail shaker suggests the following for a "dry martini": $5/8$ part dry gin, $1/4$ part dry vermouth, $1/8$ part Italian vermouth, a dash of Angostura bitters, and ice (bitters are any of a group of bottled alcoholic beverages, like Campari, produced with bitter herbs for that characteristic dry

Dixie Devil

bite. Angostura, the most common, hails from Trinidad). Or you can throw out both the gin and vermouth, pour in vodka and still call it a martini.

Which is right? Personal choice through trial and error is always the right call. The famed "21" Club in Manhattan set the standard with the Ballantini ($1 3/4$ oz. Ballantine's gin to $1/4$ oz. vermouth, plus an olive). Popular garnishes include onion or lemon, orange or lime peel, but novelties like glass eyes, salmon eggs, pollywogs or bull testicles are real conversation starters.

The Martini and Bond, James Bond—What exactly is Bond after when he utters the famous tag line (in *You Only Live Twice*), "shaken, but not stirred"? The answer is something of a puzzler, because the only time the author remembers the screen Bond offering an explanation was when he remarked that this technique wouldn't "bruise the gin." Now wouldn't shaking bruise more than stirring? W. Somerset Maugham is credited with having said, "Martinis should always be stirred, not shaken, so that the molecules lie sensuously on top of one another." Was Bond simply flying in the face of tradition? It's a mystery. It just goes to show that something that sounds great doesn't always make sense.

Ray Milland tells his bartender, Howard da Silva, all about it in The Lost Weekend *(1945).*

COCKTAIL RECIPES

IRISH COFFEE

Sweeten black coffee to taste, then add a shot or so of Bushmills and float some whipped cream on top.

BULLSHOT

1 beef bouillon cube

2 ounces hot water

1 $^1/_2$ ounces vodka

dash of celery salt or lemon pepper

fresh lemon

ice

Dissolve cube in hot water. Add vodka, squeeze of lemon and dash of celery salt or lemon pepper. Stir and pour over rocks.

HANGOVER CURES

(plastic cups recommended):

SORTA VIRGIN MARY

Pour V8 over rocks in the biggest glass you can find (don't ever use one of those novelty beer mugs, as you'll probably break your foot). Add Worcestershire, Tabasco and lemon pepper. Stir well and drink about half. Make a look of disapproval as you look around for the vodka.

PRAIRIE OYSTERS

Shake some Worcestershire into a glass. Drop in an egg yolk. Use Tabasco drops to form a happy face. Give Mr. Happy a five o'clock shadow using a pinch of lemon pepper. Close your eyes and throw it back.

RED EYE

Find a half-finished brew and check it for lipstick and butts. Pour over rocks into a tall glass. Fill with V8.

"A wet night maketh a dry morning," quoth Hendyng, "rede ye right; and the cure most fair is the self-same hair of the dog that gave the bite."

—Punderson

BAR BETS

In Dan Ford's great book about his grandfather, John Ford, he tells the story about an old trick that Ward Bond once (and only once) played on the Duke. They were hanging out at the Ford place gettin' loaded and ornery. Bond held up a piece of newspaper. He bet the Duke that if they stood facing each other on opposite ends of that paper, there was no way the Duke could knock him off of it. "You're on!" said the Duke. Smiling like a kid, Bond lay the paper over the threshold of a doorway and closed the door, with the Duke on the other side. "OK, you dumb sonofabitch, now hit me!" he hollered. The Duke stood there for a moment feeling foolish, then drew back a haymaker and punched Bond, *through the door*, and off the paper.

One thing to remember about bar bets—the goal is to find some half-drunk sap in a public house, make a fool out of him and take his money. Be careful out there. Also, you may want to bone up on your presentation skills by watching *The Sting*.

Mr. Surveyor

Guys love being able to judge stuff, like the length of lumber or the size of wrench needed for a job, by sight. This "Mr. Surveyor" bar-stool scam relies on that particular vanity. Your mark will be on the stool next to you. Tell him to hold his drink in his lap for a minute—no arms or elbows on the bar. Now take out a penny, a nickel and a dime. Place the penny on the bar, and very carefully place the dime and nickel on either side of the penny, each about 18 inches from center. Add a little flair, as if you're setting up a trick pool shot. Satisfied, you say, "OK, with no measuring devices, which are furthest apart?" He'll probably say, "The penny and the dime" or "The penny and the nickel." The answer, of course, is "The dime and the nickel." (Laying your pocket tape measure on the bar really helps this one.)

Number Nine

Tell your mark that you're going to call out five numbers. The bet is that he can't name the next highest number each time. You say nine. He says 10. You say 99. He says 100. You say 999. He says 1,000. You say 9,099. Chances are very good that he'll say 10,000, which is off by a mile.

Liar

Your mark should be a guy who fancies himself a great liar, so this is a good Irish pub blarney bet. If the pub's full of Irish fishermen, all the better. Now tell the bloke that you're going to ask him seven questions and you bet that he can't answer with a lie each time. Start in and keep the pace steady: "What's your name?" "What town is this?" etc. He'll answer with an easy lie each time. After four questions you pause, think for a sec, and ask matter-of-factly, "Say, how many was that, three or four?" "Four," he's likely to say helpfully. And you will have won your bet.

Smoked Hat

This is an old one that still reels 'em in. Place a cigarette on the bar, and cover it with a hat. If it's a baseball cap, have the brim face your mark so that the cigarette cannot be seen. Now you bet anyone that you can pick up the cigarette without touching the hat. When the bets are in, you go into an elaborate magician's act. Sprinkle a few drops of beer over the hat, light a match and wave it above, cover and

Chunkin machines have witnessed a glorious progression. Medieval catapults and trebuchets share the field with giant slingshots made from telephone poles and surgical tubing (one fired a punkin 493 feet). Then you get to the hairiest-looking contraptions on the field: the centrifugals. "When one of these starts," advises a chunker, "you gotta be outta the way." Agrees Bill Thompson, "All this stuff is mechanically incorrect. You don't want to be around it 'cause it could come apart at any time." The punkin is held in a bucket at the end of a propellerlike arm attached to an A-frame. The big smoke-belching chain-driven whirlygigs spin like mad before launching the punkin (hopefully) down range.

Melson was an early and innovative centrifugalist, but the desire for more distance gnawed at him. He also wanted the title back from Ellsworth. The sight of Ellsworth driving around in his punkin-orange '68 Caddie was too much. In '94, Melson showed up with a radically new beast that blew away the competition. It was the Universal Soldier, the first of the air cannons. As slack-jawed spectators milled around his machine, Melson grinned, "I've come down off the porch to dethrone his ass." He did, with a distance of 2,508 feet.

The howitzerlike pneumatic guns are the standard now. Like giant pea shooters, they feature big compressed air tanks connected to long barrels (no rifling, yet). The different breech designs are ingenious.

Gunners are naturally accorded all appropriate respect. Capt. Speed, champion of 1995, solemnly moves among the bowed heads, a hand raised in benediction. His air cannon, Mello Yello, hit 2,655 feet.

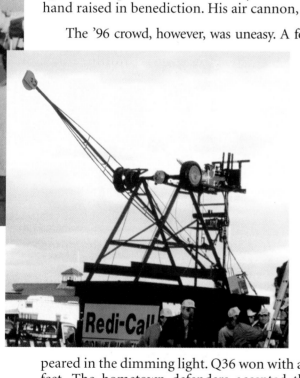

The '96 crowd, however, was uneasy. A formidable-looking stranger pulled into town from far-off Illinois. The mystery gun, called the Aludium Q36 Pumpkin Modulator (Duck Dodgers fans?), had laser guidance, an onboard computer and corporate sponsorship (Caterpillar, no less). The competition's worst fears were soon realized. On the accuracy test, Q36 didn't just hit the target, it blew a hole right through it.

The shoot-off for distance ended in controversy as several punkins, including one from Melson's cannon, disappeared in the dimming light. Q36 won with a verified distance of 2,710 feet. The hometown defenders accepted the results graciously, but curiosity led Melson back to the field a few days later. He came upon a punkin impact crater and smiled. The ID markings on the few surviving pieces were his. "Next year," he mused to himself. The distance? Unofficially, over 3,200 feet.

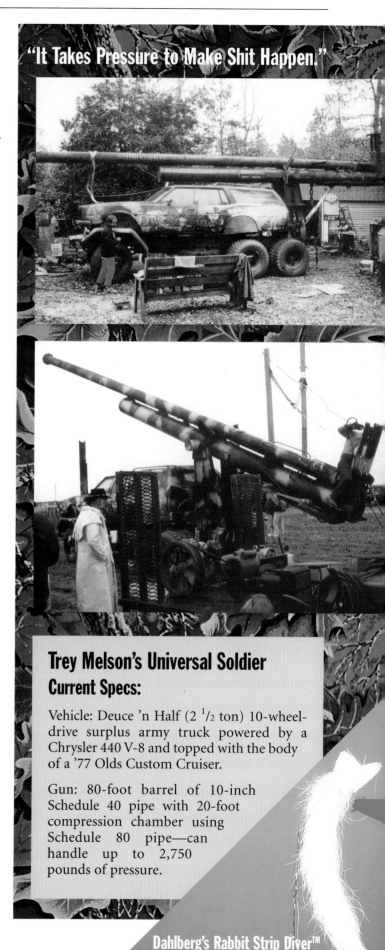

"It Takes Pressure to Make Shit Happen."

Trey Melson's Universal Soldier
Current Specs:

Vehicle: Deuce 'n Half (2 $\frac{1}{2}$ ton) 10-wheel-drive surplus army truck powered by a Chrysler 440 V-8 and topped with the body of a '77 Olds Custom Cruiser.

Gun: 80-foot barrel of 10-inch Schedule 40 pipe with 20-foot compression chamber using Schedule 80 pipe—can handle up to 2,750 pounds of pressure.

Dahlberg's Rabbit Strip Diver™

INSTRUCTIONS FOR BUILDING A POTATO CANNON "SPUD GUN"

WARNING: This gun could seriously injure someone if fired directly at them. And, it's illegal in some states, a minor detail that may or may not be of interest.

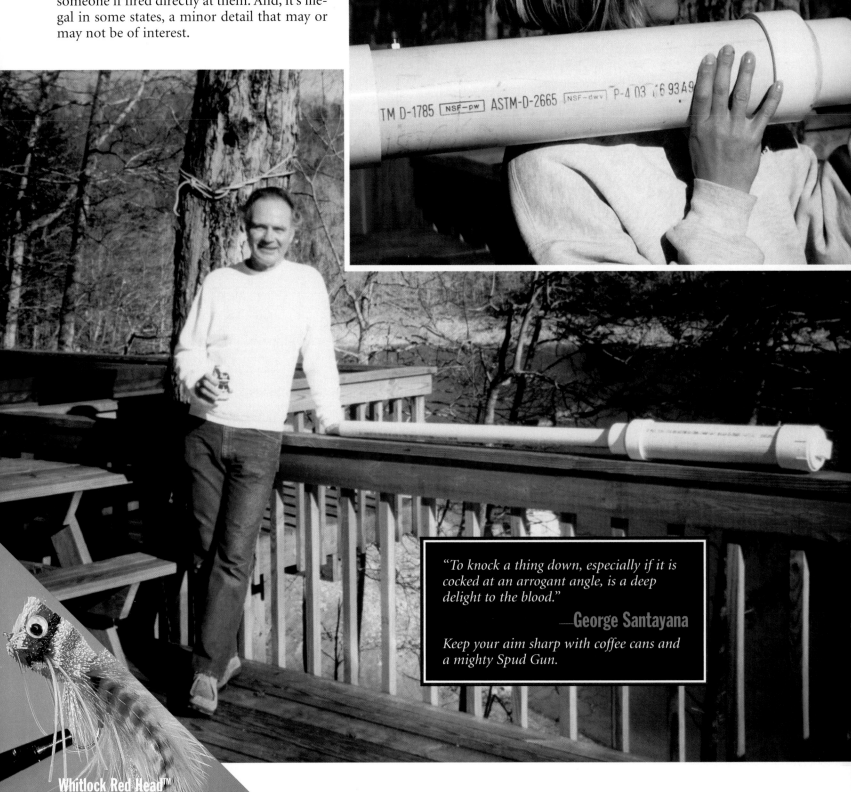

"To knock a thing down, especially if it is cocked at an arrogant angle, is a deep delight to the blood."

—George Santayana

Keep your aim sharp with coffee cans and a mighty Spud Gun.

Whitlock Red Head™

SPUD GUN

MATERIALS

PVC piping—280 PSI, schedule 40 pipe

    4" pipe cap screw

    4" diameter x 1.5'–2' pipe

    Reducer: 4" to 2"

    2" diameter x 4' pipe (or so)

    (Lengths of pipe can vary)

PVC glue

Lantern igniter

$2\frac{1}{2}$" screw, and bolt for end

CANNON ASSEMBLY

Bore hole through 4-inch pipe, a few inches from screw cap.

Install igniter into pipe.

Bore second hole in 2-inch pipe toward end that will be joined with 4-inch pipe (this will stop the potato once it has been loaded into the barrel; use screw and bolt to secure in place).

Sharpen the far edge of the 2-inch pipe (this will help to cut and peel the potato as you're loading it into the cannon).

Use a broom handle or long stick to stuff the potato down into the barrel—think "musket gun."

Screw, and glue pipes together.

Use combustable anti-rust spray or hairspray as igniter.

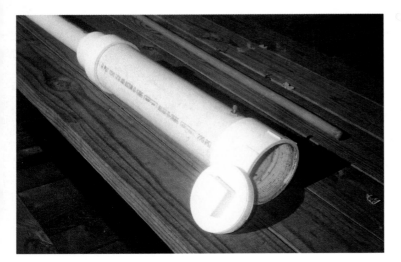

TO FIRE CANNON

Remove screw cap from igniter end. Stuff potato down barrel of cannon, using broom handle if necessary. Potato will come to rest at point in barrel where screw is. Spray the combustable spray or hairspray into igniter end of cannon—keep spray five inches away from opening. Spray for three or five seconds or so. Do not saturate inside of pipe. Quickly close screw cap.

Aim cannon in direction you wish it to fire.

Quickly flick igniter to fire cannon. Spark generated by igniter inside pipe will ignite chemical and launch potato. The spud gun made to these specifications will launch a potato 400 to 500 feet. Have fun.

SALMON/STEELHEAD
Hunter's Ponoi Green™

Rusty Rat

Hell Squash

Professional racing has undergone tremendous development over the years, and the American legacy is a deservedly rich one. And yet, somehow, we don't know how, a glaring omission persists. Racing fans for years have clamored about the stubborn refusal of the so-called "legitimate" organizations to create a category for pumpkins. Despite the outcry, the recalcitrant racing establishment has failed to create even one title.

But while these elitist snobs are content in perpetuating such a festering blemish, some brave gentlemen in California (yes, there are a few) decided to take the bull in their teeth and do something about it. It's called the Pumpkin Races. This popular Halloween event is entering its seventh year at the appropriately inclined residence of John Holliday. Holliday and Michael Aaker maintain the tradition started by Carl Rogers, about whom there are now many songs.

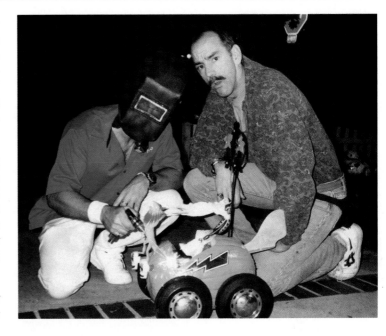

Hundreds of costumed kids of all ages (including many cigar-smoking ones) line the Manhattan Beach hill street for the soapbox derby-a-squash. Competitors may fashion a generic brand entry on the spot but most bring their own customized cruiser. Pumpkins are released from the starting line using the one-finger hold, and the officiating is impeccable. No prefab chassis of any kind is allowed—offending vehicles meet swift justice at the hands of a large masked enforcer wielding a baseball bat.

PUMPKIN RACES

Screamin' Skull

Sky Komish

PANTS AND

What strange force drives men to detrouserfy their brothers? What mad insistent inner voice demands of us to make no pants where once there were pants? It is a mystery and yet, it is good.

My fondest memory regarding what was known in ancient times as "the Dropage of the Trouwe" recalls one of the many bastions of higher learning that I had the pleasure, if only briefly, to attend. My mark, of course, was a pal—a sweeter-than-hell big lug named Jonesy. Jonesy was a guy everybody liked—good-looking, great at sports, hit the books, considerate, blah blah blah. Don't get me wrong, this was no namby-pamby Dudley Doright—he was part of our party planning corps called "the Matteson Animals" and a regular guy all the way. He also had several inches (height, that is) and about 30 pounds on me—I was really tempting the Gods of Pain with this one.

But when I saw him enter the dining room, fresh from the track, wearing an old T-shirt and a baggy pair of sweats, that old devil inspiration hit me—such was my death wish. After alerting some compadres, I waited until he had his tray and was making his way across open space to a table. Hundreds of students were facing in that direction.

I untied one of my shoelaces and got up with my tray to meet him midway. We were standing there and I started some casual BS about this and that and then, indicating my lace, handed poor Jonesy my tray "for a sec." Here he was, holding two trays and at my mercy—a thing of beauty to my squirming, sick brain.

Silver Hilton

GETTING PANTSED

In a flash, I stepped behind him and dropped his sweats right to his ankles. Now a wiser man may have instantly fled at this juncture, but the scientist in me took hold and I just stepped back with a big shit-eating grin to observe the results. The whole place was roaring, and Jonesy, standing there in his jock strap and trying for a hilarious moment to figure out how to get hold of his pants, was redder than my dog's johnson.

I was unfit for escape anyhow 'cause I was crying from laughing so hard. This was a bad thing because Jonesy soon realized that he could just put those trays on the floor—a real bad thing. Jonesy, yelling "I'm goin' to kill you, man!" chased my ass outta there. I didn't make it too far before he had me on the ground, pounding away. Fortunately he let up because I was such a defenseless tub of guts at this point.

Now a couple of weeks later, I'm waiting in line for chow at the front of the dining hall. Folks are milling around, it's noisy as hell. . . the usual scene. As it happens, I was wearing my own pair of baggy sweats at the time. Next thing I know, Whoosh! They're down to my ankles and I'm feeling the breeze—a rather distinct breeze as it turns out. Jonesy, looking for payback, had seized the opportunity but, to his horror, I wasn't wearing a damn thing under my sweats. My biggest laugh came from watching good ole Jonesy, embarrassed all to hell, trying desperately to get my pants back up. Like I said, he was a real gent.

Kaufmann's Ferry Canyon™

For any lover of fireworks, that is, the roadside variety, the name Black Cat represents the standard against which all others are measured. The label says simply, The Best You Can Get, and there's no need to argue the point. Experience confirms the truth of that statement.

quite different. One of four things usually goes wrong (any fireworks user has probably experienced them all): 1– a smoker—no show and no go, 2– a fizzler—travels just a few feet and gives a pathetic pop, 3– the traditional dud—fuse burns down to a tiny pinhead of red that lingers for a maddeningly long time before going out completely, 4– the zip-bang—blows up as soon as the match gets near it, making the user jump like a rabbit and become the rightful object of the scorn and big yucks of pals.

A lit fuse holds a promise. If that promise is broken, there's hell to pay. Black Cat keeps their promise, every time.

FIREWORKS
& The Black Cat Story

Who Are Those Guys?—The Chinese have the longest-running tradition of celebrating events with fireworks (pretty logical considering they invented them), though the practice is based on one that predates the 2,000-year-old discovery of gunpowder. Bamboo was burned to celebrate the coming Chinese New Year—the cracking and popping sounds that resulted were believed to drive away evil spirits. Firecrackers—whose ancient name, *pao chuk*, means "burst bamboo"—eventually replaced bamboo in these celebrations. Firecrackers remain today as spectacular climaxes for weddings, festivals, business openings and even funerals.

Fireworks are among those products that develop kids into passionate consumers. There's no greater joy than walking the aisles of a well-stocked emporium, recognizing old favorites among beautifully colored boxes and packages, making new discoveries, reminiscing with the proprietor about long-gone classics like torpedoes (and at the same time, feeling out his/her haggling quotient), and always, always, trying to work a few extra bucks out of the folks.

There's nothing worse than a dud. Fizzled firecrackers provoke as much disgust as a kid can muster. Bottle rockets are a perfect example. The idea is beautifully simple: you light the thing, it takes off, it blows up—cool. With a cheapo brand, however, the customer gets something

Fireworks are one of the premier products, along with garments and toys, from Li & Fung, the largest Chinese multinational trading company. With modern headquarters in Hong Kong, the company carries on a business tradition of supplying goods to the West that reaches back over centuries, to the silk and spice caravans. Cargo jets and huge container vessels have replaced camels and those beautiful clipper ships, though the actual manufacture of fireworks remains relatively unchanged.

Hunter's Ponoi Red™

Undertaker

Fireworks Reference

Pyrotechnics Guild International, Inc.

Ed Vanasek, PGII Sec.—Treasurer
18021 Baseline Avenue
Jordon, MN 55352
$25 annual membership includes
quarterly Bulletin.
The PGI is composed of pyro enthusiasts
from all walks of life, amateur to profes-
sional, technical experts, label collectors
and those who just love to learn more
about this ancient art. Following the first
Friday in August, the PGI holds their
annual convention (huge flea market,
etc.). Locations vary. The group has
become famous for their traditional
"Super String"—a deafening ignition of
millions of firecrackers. On the amateur
enthusiast circuit, this is The Event.

Western Pyrotechnic Association, Inc.

2230 Aralia Street
Newport Beach, CA 92660
$30 annual membership includes WPA
newsletter.
The WPA holds their annual Winterblast
Convention over Presidents' Day weekend
(mid Feb.) in Lake Havasu City, Arizona.
The 3-day event, open to WPA members
in good standing, features nightly aerial
and ground displays, designated shooting
areas for Class B and C fireworks, a flea
market of hard-to-find collectibles and a
variety of seminars and workshops.

American Fireworks News

HC 67 Box 30
Dingmans Ferry, PA 18328-9506
John M. Drewes, Editor (717) 828-8417
E-Mail: AMERFWKNWS@aol.com
Subscription: $19.95 per year
This monthly newsletter tracks the

pyrotechnic world with articles about the
National Fireworks Association, American
Pyrotechnics Association, Pyrotechnics
Guild International, How-To's,
Safety, History and collectibles. They also
publish the International Fireworks
Trade Directory and offer a terrific list of
books, videos and symposium proceedings
for the serious enthusiast.

The Hot Sheet

Burning Sage Publications
4247 Alder Drive
San Diego, CA 92116
Bob Weaver, Editor (619) 284-3784
E-Mail: rjweaver@sd.2net.com
Subscription: $12.95 per year
This quarterly newsletter is targeted to the
consumer fireworks lover. Ratings and
reviews of the new and old combine with
entertaining articles and interviews with
enthusiasts sharing their experiences.
Burning Sage has also published
Fireworks For Everyone—*a guide and*
reference book covering fireworks types,
ratings and state by state legislation. A
U.S. dealer directory is due out soon.

Monochio Enterprises

P.O. Box 2010
Saratoga, CA 95070
(408) 996-1963
Dennis Monochio, Jr. operates a monthly
auction of rare fireworks labels, toys and
collectibles. Advance flyers depicting these
unusual items are sent out and bids
accepted by phone, mail or fax.

Southerners, who traditionally have a
great affection for fireworks, set off large
displays to celebrate the New Year. Many
stopped July 4th celebrations after 1861.

The first use of Black Cat was on February 23, 1952. Today's image is a polished and glossed-over version of the original. Early labels featuring a mangy and deranged-looking critter have become highly collectible. While black cats are a symbol of luck in China, emblazoning them on the packaging is a marketing idea that could have gone belly up, considering Western superstition. Nevertheless, the image has been anything but unlucky. Black Cat dominates the business.

While China produces between 80 and 90 percent of the world's fireworks, the United States has invariably been the destination for most of them. When a trade embargo was imposed in 1950, following the outbreak of the Korean War, Li & Fung concentrated their operations in Macao. Any fireworks you had as a kid probably came from there or from right here at home. A few U.S. fireworks companies are operating today, but the Child Protection Act of 1966 killed much of the business. The old-time classics like M-80s, ashcans, cherry bombs and torpedoes were given the hook, and the world became a quieter, duller place. When President Richard Nixon normalized relations with China in 1972, the trade embargo was lifted. China's cheaper manufacturing costs brought the companies back, closing all but one or two of the Macao factories.

Today, Black Cat is still the preeminent fireworks brand. But while American regulatory agencies closely monitor these products and the Consumer Product Safety Commission is responsible for the familiar warning labels on every package (Light Fuse, Leave the state), the consistent quality of the brand is due to the standards of Li & Fung. All their fireworks are routinely tested and strictly controlled for safety. (Now there's a dream job—quality control at Black Cat.)

The safety factor is the reason why firecracker manufacturing is one of the few industries in the world to have resisted

automation. Assembly-line machinery would mean a lack of control, and that lack of control could spell disaster. Many of the larger items, like big cones and mortars, are made in the

U.S., but most come from areas like the Hunan province of China, where small family operations create all the fireworks by hand, as they have for centuries. The base chemicals are mixed, fuses are cut, paper tubing is rolled and the labels are glued on one at a time. The red sticks connected to our beloved bottle rockets have all been carefully dyed, bundled in flowerlike balls and dried in the Eastern sun.

General Practitioner

Sam Colt (1814-1862) is responsible for producing the first practical, percussion-type revolver. This rather specific legacy follows Col. Colt around because he did not, as some might imagine, invent the revolver. He made it a functional reality. (The same may be said about the breech loading-metallic cartridge of Horace Smith and Daniel B. Wesson.) Adding to Colt's accomplishment is the fact that revolvers had been around for hundreds of years, and generations of inventors had taken a crack at the idea before he

got it right. Initially, Colt's company and gun had failed too.

Lack of a government contract and trouble raising money led to the closing of Colt's Paterson, New Jersey, plant in 1843. At the time, most civilians were content to carry a pepperbox—a handgun with revolving barrels. But, of course, attitudes differed out West. The Texas Rangers swore by the early Paterson Colt model and dispatched Capt. Samuel H. Walker to ensure that it resumed production. Colt subsequently modified the gun to

SHOOTING STAR OF INDUSTRIAL DESIGN

44 Magnum Colt Anaconda

44 Magnum Colt Anaconda Realtree

Colt manufactures the Walker Colt as part of its Sam Colt Signature Series of authentic black powder arms. For information regarding the complete line of these historic and beautifully crafted firearms, get on the Colt Black Powder mailing list by calling 718/499-4678.

The definitive books on Colt firearms, written by R.L. Wilson and available along with a killer variety of licensed products, are available from Colt Wear at 800/962-COLT. Wilson's titles include *The Book of Colt Firearms, Colt: An American Legend* and *The Peacemakers: Arms and Adventure in the American West.*

Ranger specifications, earning the more powerful 1847 model the name "Walker Colt," first of the real "hand cannons." This was the break Colt needed. The Army adopted the gun, and the United States became the first country to issue revolvers as standard equipment.

Colt lived only to the age of 47, but he lived intensely and had one helluva good time while he was here. He enjoyed enormous success but, more important, laid a formidable foundation for the future. His revolutionary Hartford factory, completed in 1855, was the world's finest armory and a model for the industrial revolution. The Colt name is linked with an amazing series of successes, including the .45-caliber Peacemaker, the double-action Thunderer, the Gatling gun, the BAR and Colt .45 sidearm from design genius John Browning, the Thompson Submachine Gun, the 357 Magnum/38 Special Python and the AR15/M16.

Check out the ferocious Double Action 44 Magnum Colt Anaconda. This incredible new hand cannon is also available in a special Realtree edition featuring camo finish, eight-inch barrel and precision scope.

Walker Colt

Truly one of our indelible American icons. She's the metal mama, the trucker's temptress, our bright shining sweetheart, the hard cold queen of the road, bolted to the body or flapping suggestively in her accustomed setting behind a rumbling 18-wheeler. You probably first saw her on a road trip from the backseat of your parent's station wagon (a site of many future revelations). Your face pressed against the cool glass as your jaw worked the words, "Oh, wow." Sure, she's got some miles on her, several million in fact, but we love her all the same. Why? Because she combines two of the elements most adored by men: chrome and the female form.

THE MUD FLAP GIRL

She's leaning back on her hands, rocking along, doing her happy little mud flap dance. Seductively undulating to the rhythm of the road, dangerously teasing the cruel blurs of rubber and concrete that fly just under her tush at 80 miles an hour. She's catching the sun and sending brilliant flashes back your way—"follow me, boys. . . follow me, boys." She's got those big breasts and big hair, and tiny waist and feet. Could be that she can't stand at all, and the pose just means she fell on her ass again, but we don't care. One look and you're sure of one thing—somebody out there really knows how to punch metal. She deserves a song about her by God. . . maybe by Johnny Cash, Elvis Costello or the Fabulous Thunderbirds.

From whence have you come, o mud flap gal? She's everywhere, yet strangely elusive. So we set off to find out who originally forged this beauty. No luck at the local Pep Boys or Kragen Auto Parts—damn disappointing. It's certainly the first product we'd put on the shelves. Truck stops? Fortunately America has a council or association for everything. One toll-free call to the National Auto Truck Stops Association put us in touch with a delightful gal ready with phone numbers for several big-rig havens in the area.

Kaufmann Dredger™ Green

Now, when you're calling a busy truck-stop store to ask who supplies their mud flap gals you've gotta hope for bemused compliance, but expect to have your sanity called into question. We encountered nothing but the former. In fact, the helpful enthusiasm of some empathetic souls warmed out hearts —we had struck a chord. . . the world supported our quest. You've gotta take your grails where you find 'em these days. . . whatever the hell that means.

As it turns out, there are a lot of distributors of the mud flap gal and no single manufacturer. While some are made here in the U.S.A., the majority come from Taiwan. As Jim Rogers of J.R. Enterprises explained, "The EPA discourages the use of the heavy acids you need to etch the metal prior to plating, so the better chroming is done outside the US." As to the origin of the saucy vixen? "Well," Jim said, "You're apt to find as many stories about her as there are distributors. She's been around at least 25 years. The way I heard it, a woman had designed it for her husband's truck years back. It caught on, the Taiwanese picked it up, and they've been crankin' 'em out ever since."

Big Jim Iler of the Trucker's Toy Store believes it was a company called Truck Mate in Los Angeles that got her started— figures that she's a California girl. Unfortunately, Truck Mate went out of business years ago. The mud flap girl seems to be a public entity with many suppliers but no one company laying rightful claim to her. Perhaps that's as it should be—she's a Mustang Sally, wild and free, an untamed American beauty jostling over the open road.

Bright Roe Chartreuse

Bright Roe

THE QUIET MAN

BY MAURICE WALSH

(reprinted as it first appeared to John Ford in the *Saturday Evening Post*, February 11, 1933)

SHAWN KELVIN, a blithe young lad of 20, went to the States to seek his fortune. And 15 years thereafter he returned to his native Kerry, his blitheness sobered and his youth dried to the core, and whether he had made his fortune or whether he had not, no one could be knowing for certain. For he was a quiet man, not given to talking about himself and the things he had done. A quiet man, under middle size, with strong shoulders and deep-set blue eyes below brows darker than his dark hair—that was Shawn Kelvin. One shoulder had a trick of hunching slightly higher than the other, and some folks said that came from a habit he had of shielding his eyes in the glare of an open-hearth furnace in a place called Pittsburgh, while others said it used to be a way he had of guarding his chin that time he was a sort of sparring-partner punching bag at a boxing camp.

Shawn Kelvin came home and found that he was the last of the Kelvins, and that the farm of his forefathers had added its few acres to the ranch of Big Liam O'Grady, of Moyvalla. Shawn took no action to recover his land, though O'Grady had got it meanly. He had had enough of fighting, and all he wanted now was peace. He quietly went amongst the old and kindly friends and quietly looked about him for the place and peace he wanted; and when the time came, quietly produced the money for a neat, handy, small farm on the first warm shoulder of Knockanore Hill below the rolling curves of heather. It was not a big place but it was in good heart, and it got all the sun that was going; and, best of all, it suited Shawn to the tiptop notch of contentment; for it held the peace that tuned to his quietness, and it commanded the widest view in all Ireland—vale and mountain and the lifting green plain of the Atlantic Sea.

There, in a four-roomed, lime-washed, thatched cottage, Shawn made his life, and, though his friends hinted at his needs and obligations, no thought came to him of bringing a wife into the place. Yet Fate had the thought and the dream in her loom for him. One middling imitation of a man he had to do chores for him, an ex-navy pensioner handy enough about house and byre, but with no relish for the sustained work of the field—and, indeed, as long as he kept house and byre shipshape, he found Shawn an easy master.

Shawn himself was no drudge toiler. He knew all about drudgery and the way it wears out a man's soul. He plowed a little and sowed a little, and at the end of a furrow he would lean on the handles of the cultivator, wipe his brow, if it needed wiping, and lose himself for whole minutes in the great green curve of the sea out there beyond the high black portals of Shannon Mouth. And sometimes of an evening he would see, under the glory of the sky, the faint smoke smudge of an American liner. Then he would smile to himself—a pitying smile—thinking of the poor devils, with dreams of fortune luring them, going out to sweat in Ironville, or to bootleg bad whiskey down the hidden way, or to stand in a bread line. All these things were behind Shawn forever.

Market days he would go down and across to Listowel town, seven miles, to do his bartering; and in the long evenings, slowly slipping into the endless summer gloaming, his friends used to climb the winding lane to see him. Only the real friends came that long road, and they were welcome—fighting men who had been out in the "Sixteen": Matt Tobin the thresher, the schoolmaster, the young curate—men like that. A stone jar of malt whiskey would appear on the table, and there would be a haze of smoke and a maze of warm, friendly disagreements.

"Shawn, old son," one of them might hint, "aren't you sometimes terrible lonely?"

Waller Walker™

"Like hell I am!" might retort Shawn derisively. "Why?"

"Nothing but the daylight and the wind and the sun setting like the wrath o' God."

"Just that! Well?"

"But after the stirring times beyond in the States—"

"Ay! Tell me, fine man, have you ever seen a furnace in full blast?"

"A great sight."

"Great surely! But if I could jump you into a steel foundry this minute, you would be sure that God had judged you faithfully into the very hob of hell."

And then they would laugh and have another small one from the stone jar.

And on Sundays Shawn used to go to church, three miles down to the gray chapel above the black cliffs of Doon Bay. There Fate laid her lure for him.

Sitting quietly on his wooden bench or kneeling on the dusty footboard, he would fix his steadfast deep-set eyes on the vestmented celebrant and say his prayers slowly, or go into that strange trance, beyond dreams and visions, where the soul is almost at one with the unknowable.

But after a time, Shawn's eyes no longer fixed themselves on the celebrant. They went no farther than two seats ahead. A girl sat there. Sunday after Sunday she sat in front of him, and Sunday after Sunday his first casual admiration grew warmer.

She had a white nape to her neck and short red hair above it, and Shawn liked the color and wave of that flame. And he liked the set of her shoulders and the way the white neck had of leaning a little forward and she at her prayers—or her dreams. And, the service over, Shawn used to stay in his seat so that he might get one quick but sure look at her face as she passed out. And he liked her face, too—the wide-set gray eyes, cheek bones firmly curved, clean-molded lips, austere yet sensitive. And he smiled pityingly at himself that one of her name should make his pulse stir—for she was an O'Grady.

One person, only, in the crowded chapel noted Shawn's look and the thought behind the look. Not the girl. Her brother, Big Liam O'Grady of Moyvalla, the very man who as good as stole the Kelvin acres. And that man smiled to himself, too—the ugly, contemptuous smile that was his by nature—and, after another habit he had, he tucked away his bit of knowledge against a day when it might come in useful for his own purposes.

The girl's name was Ellen—Ellen O'Grady. But a truth she was no longer a girl. She was past her first youth into that second one that had no definite ending. She might be 30—she was no less—but there was not a lad in the countryside who would say she was past her prime. The poise of her and the firm set of her bones below clean skin saved her from the fading of mere prettiness. Though she had been sought in marriage more than once, she had accepted no one, or, rather, had not been allowed to encourage anyone. Her brother saw to that.

Big Liam O'Grady was a great, raw-boned, sandy-haired man, with the strength of an ox and a heart no bigger than a sour apple. An overbearing man given to berserk rages. Though he was a churchgoer by habit, the true god of that man was Monday—red gold, shining silver, dull copper—the trinity that he worshipped in degree. He and his sister Ellen lived on the big ranch farm of Moyvalla, and Ellen was his housekeeper and maid of all work. She was a careful housekeeper, a good cook, a notable baker, and she demanded no wage. All that suited Big Liam splendidly, and so she remained single—a wasted woman.

Big Liam himself was not a marrying man. There were not many spinsters with a dowry big enough to tempt him, and the few there had acquired expensive tastes—a convent education, the deplorable art of hitting jazz out of a piano, the damnable vice of cigarette smoking, the purse-emptying craze for motor cars—such things.

But in due time, the dowry and the place—with a woman tied to them—came under his nose, and Big Liam was no longer tardy. His neighbor, James Carry, died in March and left his fine farm and all on it to his widow, a youngish woman without children, a woman with a hard name for saving pennies. Big Liam looked once at Kathy Carey and looked many times at her broad acres. Both pleased him. He took the steps required by tradition. In the very first week of the following Shrovetide, he sent an accredited emissary to open formal negotiations, and that emissary came back within the hour.

"My soul," said he, "but she is the quick one! I hadn't 10 words out of me when she was down my throat. 'I am in no hurry,' says she, 'to come wife to a house with another woman at the fire corner. When Ellen is in a place of her own, I will listen to what Liam O'Grady has to say.'"

"She will, by Jacus!" Big Liam stopped him. "She will so."

There, now, was the right time to recall Shawn Kelvin and the look in his eyes. Big Liam's mind corner promptly delivered up its memory. He smiled knowingly and contemptuously. Shawn Kelvin daring to cast sheep's eyes at an O'Grady! The undersized chicken heart, who took the loss of the Kelvin acres lying down! The little Yankee runt hidden away on the shelf of Knockanore! But what of it? The required dowry would be conveniently small, and the girl would never go hungry, anyway. There was Big Liam O'Grady, far descended from many chieftains.

The very next market day at Listowel he sought out Shawn Kelvin and placed a huge, sandy-haired hand on the shoulder that hunched to meet it.

"Shawn Kelvin, a word with you! Come and have a drink."

Shawn hesitated. "Very well," he said then. He did not care for O'Grady, but he would hurt no man's feelings.

They went across to Sullivan's bar and had a drink, and Shawn paid for it. And Big Liam came directly to his subject—almost patronizingly, as if he were conferring a favor.

"I want to see Ellen settled in a place of her own," said he.

Shawn's heart lifted into his throat and stayed there. But

that steadfast face with the steadfast eyes gave no sign and, moreover, he could not say a word with his heart where it was.

"Your place is small," went on the big man, "but it is handy, and no load of debt on it, as I hear. Not much of a dowry ever came to Knockanore, and not much of a dowry can I be giving with Ellen. Say 200 pounds at the end of harvest, if prices improve. What do you say, Shawn Kelvin?"

Shawn swallowed his heart, and his voice came slow and cool: "What does Ellen say?"

"I haven't asked her," said Big Liam. "but what would she say, blast it?"

"Whatever she says, she will say it herself, not you, Big Liam."

But what could Ellen say? She looked within her own heart and found it empty; she looked at the granite crag of her brother's face and contemplated herself a slowly withering spinster at his fire corner; she looked up at the swell of Knockanore Hill and saw the white cottage among the green small fields below the warm brown of the heather. Oh, but the sun would shine up there in the lengthening spring day and pleasant breezes blow in sultry summer; and finally she looked at Shawn Kelvin, that firmly built, small man with the clean face and the lustrous eyes below steadfast brow. She said a prayer to her God and sank head and shoulders in a resignation more pitiful than tears, more proud than the pride of chieftains. Romance? Wellaway!

Shawn was far from satisfied with that resigned acceptance, but then was not the time to press for a warmer one. He knew the brother's wizened soul, guessed at the girl's clean one, and saw that she was doomed beyond hope to a fireside sordidly bought for her. Let it be his own fireside then. There were many worse ones—and God was good.

Ellen O'Grady married Shawn Kelvin. One small statement; and it holds the risk of tragedy, the chance of happiness, the probability of mere endurance—choices wide as the world.

But Big Liam O'Grady, for all his resolute promptness, did not win Kathy Carey to wife. She, foolishly enough, took to husband her own cattleman, a gay night rambler, who gave her the devil's own time and a share of happiness in the bygoing. For the first time, Big Liam discovered how mordant the wit of his neighbors could be, and to contempt for Shawn Kelvin he now added an unreasoning dislike.

Shawn Kelvin had got his precious, red-haired woman under his own roof now. He had no illusions about her feel-

ings for him. On himself, and on himself only, lay the task of molding her into a wife and lover. Darkly, deeply, subtly, away out of sight, with gentleness, with restraint, with a consideration beyond kenning, that molding must be done, and she that was being molded, must never know. He hardly knew, himself.

First he turned his attention to material things. He hired a small servant maid to help her with the housework. Then he acquired a rubber-tired rub cart and a half-bred gelding with a reaching knee action. And on market days, husband and wife used to bowl down to Listowel, do their selling and their buying, and bowl smoothly home again, their groceries in the

well of the cart and a bundle of secondhand American magazines on the seat at Ellen's side. And in the nights, before the year turned, with the wind from the plains of the Atlantic keening above the chimney, they would sit at either side of the flaming peat fire, and he would read aloud strange and almost unbelievable things out of the high-colored magazines. Stories, sometimes wholly unbelievable.

Ellen would sit and listen and smile, and go on with her knitting or her sewing; and after a time it was sewing she was at mostly—small things. And when the reading was done, they would sit and talk quietly in their own

Blue Charm

quiet way, for they were both quiet. Woman though she was, she got Shawn to do most of the talking. It could be that she, too, was probing and seeking, unwrapping the man's soul to feel the texture thereof, surveying the marvel of his life as he spread it diffidently before her. He had a patient, slow, vivid way of picturing for her the things he had seen and felt. He made her see the glare of molten metal, lambent yet searing,

made her feel the sucking heat, made her hear the clang; she could see the roped square under the dazzle of the hooded arcs with the curling smoke layer above it, understand the explosive restraint of the game, thrill when he showed her how to stiffen wrist for the final devastating right hook. And often enough the stories were humorous, and Ellen would chuckle, or stare, or throw back her red, lovely curls in laughter. It was grant to make her laugh.

Shawn's friends, in some hesitation at first, came in ones and twos up the slope to see them. But Ellen welcomed them with her smile that was shy and, at the same time, frank, and her table was loaded for them with scones and crumpets and cream cakes and heather honey; and at the right time it was she herself that brought forth the decanter of whiskey—no longer the half-empty stone jar—and the polished glasses. Shawn was

proud as sin of her. She would sit then and listen to their discussions and be forever surprised at the knowledgeable man her husband was—the way he would discuss war and politics and the making of songs, the turn of speech that summed up a man or a situation, and sometimes she would put in a word or two and be listened to, and they would look to see if her smile commended them, and be a little chastened by the wisdom of that smile—the age-old smile of the matriarch from whom they were all descended. In no time at all, Matt Tobin the thresher, who used to think, "Poor old Shawn! Lucky she was to get him," would whisper to the schoolmaster: "Herrin's alive! That fellow's luck would astonish nations."

Women, in the outside world, begin by loving their husbands; and then, if fate is kind, they grow to admire them; and, if fate is not unkind, may descend no lower than liking and enduring. And there is the end of lawful romance. Look now at Ellen O'Grady. She came up to the shelf of Knockanore and in her heart was only a nucleus of fear in a great emptiness, and that nucleus might grow into horror and disgust, but, glory of God, she, for reason piled on reason, presently found herself admiring Shawn Kelvin; and with or without reason, a quiet liking came to her for this quiet man who was so gentle and considerate; and then, one great heart-stirring dark o' night, she found herself fallen head and heels in love with her own husband. There is the sort of love that endures, but the road to it is a mighty chancy one.

A woman, loving her husband, may or may not be proud of him, but she will fight like a tiger if anyone, barring herself, belittles him. And there was one man that belittled Shawn Kelvin. Her brother, Big Liam O'Grady. At fair or market or chapel that dour giant deigned not to hide his contempt and dislike. Ellen knew why. He had lost a wife and farm; he had lost in herself a frugally cheap housekeeper; he had been made the butt of a sly humor; and for these mishaps, in some twisted way, he blamed Shawn. But—and there came in the contempt—the little Yankee runt, who dared say nothing about the lost Kelvin acres, would not now have the gall or guts to demand the dowry that was due. Lucky the hound to steal an O'Grady to hungry Knockanore! Let him be satisfied with that luck!

One evening before a market day, Ellen spoke to her husband: "Has Big Liam paid you my dowry yet, Shawn?"

"Sure there's no hurry, girl," said Shawn.

"Have you ever asked him?"

"I have not. I am not looking for your dowry, Ellen."

"And Big Liam could never understand that." Her voice firmed. "You will ask him tomorrow."

"Very well so, agrah," agreed Shawn easily.

And the next day, in that quiet diffident way of his, he asked Big Liam. But Big Liam was brusque and blunt. He had no loose money and Kelvin would have to wait till he had. "Ask me again, Shawneen," he finished, his face in a mocking smile, and turning on his heel, he plowed his great shoulders through the crowded market.

His voice had been carelessly loud and people had heard. They laughed and talked amongst themselves. "Be-gobs! The devil's own boy, Big Liam! What a pup to sell! Stealing the land and keeping a grip on the fortune! Ay, and a dangerous fellow, mind you, the same Big Liam! He would smash little Shawn at the wind of a word. And devil the bit his Yankee sparring tricks would help him!"

A friend of Shawn's, Matt Tobin the thresher, heard that and lifted his voice: "I would like to be there the day Shawn Kelvin loses his temper."

"A bad day for poor Shawn!"

"It might then," said Matt Tobin, "but I would come from the other end of Kerry to see the badness that would be in it for someone."

Shawn had moved away with his wife, not heeding or not hearing.

"You see, Ellen?" he said in some discomfort. "The times are hard on the big ranchers, and we don't need the money, anyway."

"Do you think Big Liam does?" Her voice had a cut in it. "He could buy you and all Knockanore and be only on the fringe of his hoard. You will ask him again."

"But, girl dear, I never wanted a dowry with you."

She liked him to say that, but far better would she like to win for him the respect and admiration that was his due. She must do that now at all costs. Shawn, drawing back now, would be the butt of his fellowmen.

"You foolish lad! Big Liam would never understand your feelings, with money at stake." She smiled and a pang went through Shawn's breast. For the smile was the smile of an O'Grady, and he could not be sure whether the contempt in it was for himself or for her brother.

Shawn asked Big Liam again, unhappy in his asking, but also dimly comprehending his woman's object. And Shawn asked again a third time. The issue was become a famous one now. Men talked about it, and women too. Bets were made on it. At fair or market, if Shawn was seen approaching Big Liam, men edged closer and women edged away. Some day the big fellow would grow tired of being asked, and in one of his terrible rages half kill the little lad as he had half killed other men. A great shame! Here and there, a man advised Shawn to give up asking and put the matter in a lawyer's hands. "I couldn't do that," was Shawn's only answer. Strangely enough,

none of these prudent advisers were amongst Shawn's close friends. His friends frowned and said little, but they were always about, and always amongst them was Matt Tobin.

The day at last came when big Liam grew tired of being asked. That was the big October cattle fair at Listowel, and he had sold 20 head of fat, polled Angus beeves at a good price. He was a hard dealer and it was late in the day before he settled at his own figure, so that the banks were closed and he was not able to make a lodgment. He had, then, a great roll of bills in an inner vest pocket when he saw Shawn and Ellen coming across to where he was bargaining with Matt Tobin for a week's threshing. Besides, the day being dank, he had had a drink or two more than was good for him and the whiskey had loosened his tongue and whatever he had of discretion. By the powers!—it was time and past time to deal once and for all with this little gadfly of a fellow, to show him up before the whole market. He strode to meet Shawn, and people got out of his savage way and edged in behind to lose nothing of this dangerous game.

He caught Shawn by the hunched shoulder—a rending grip—and bent down to grin in his face.

"What is it, little fellow? Don't be ashamed to ask!"

Matt Tobin was probably the only one there to notice the ease with which Shawn wrenched his shoulder free, and Matt Tobin's eyes brightened. But Shawn did nothing further and said no word. His deep-set eyes gazed steadily at the big man.

The big man showed his teeth mockingly. "Go on, you whelp! What do you want?"

"You know, O'Grady."

"I do. Listen, Shawneen!" Again he brought his hand clap on the little man's shoulder. "Listen, Shawneen! If I had a dowry to give my sister, 'tis not a little shrimp like you would get her. Go to hell out o' that!"

His great hand gripped and he flung Shawn backwards as if he were only the image of a man filled with chaff.

Shawn went backwards, but he did not fall. He gathered himself like a spring, feet under him, arms half raised, head forward into hunched shoulder. But as quickly as the spring coiled, as quickly it slackened, and he turned away to his wife. She was there facing him, tense and keen, her face pale and set, and a gleam of the race in her eyes. "Woman, woman!" he said in his deep voice. "Why would you and I shame ourselves like this?"

"Shame!" she cried. "Will you let him shame you now?"

"But your own brother, Ellen—before them all?"

"And he cheating you—"

"Glory of God!" His voice was distressed. "What is his dirty money to me? Are you an O'Grady, after all?"

That stung her and she stung him back in one final effort. She placed a hand below her breast and looked close into his face. Her voice was low and bitter, and only he heard: "I am an O'Grady. It is a great pity that the father of this my son is a Kelvin and a coward."

The bosses of Shawn Kelvin's cheek bones were like hard marble, but his voice was as soft as a dove's.

"Is that the way of it? Let us be going home then, in the name of God!"

He took her arm, but she shook his hand off; nevertheless, she walked at his side, head up, through the people that made way for them. Her brother mocked them with his great, laughing bellow.

"That fixes the pair of them!" he cried, brushed a man who laughed with him out of his way, and strode off through the fair.

There was talk then—plenty of it. "Murder, but Shawn had a narrow squeak that time! Did you see the way he flung him? I wager he'll give Big Liam a wide road after this. And he by way of being a boxer! Thart's a pound you owe me, Matt Tobin."

"I'll pay it," said Matt Tobin, and that is all he said. He stood wide legged, looking at the ground, his hand ruefully rubbing the back of his head and dismay and gloom on his face. His friend had failed him in the face of the people.

Shawn and Ellen went home in their tub cart and had not a single word or glance for each other on the road. And all that evening, at table or fireside, a heart-sickening silence held them in its grip. And all that night they lay side by side, still and mute. There was only one subject that possessed them and on that they dared speak no longer. They slept little. Ellen, her heart desolate, lay on her side, staring into the dark, grieving for what she had said and unable to unsay it. Shawn, on his back, contemplated things with a cold clarity. He realized that he was at the fork of life and that a finger pointed unmistakably. He must risk the very shattering of all happiness, he must do a thing so final and decisive that, once done, it could never again be questioned. Before morning, he came to his decision, and it was bitter as gall. He cursed himself. "Oh, you fool! You might have known that you should never have taken an O'Grady without breaking the O'Gradys."

He got up early in the morning at his usual hour and went out, as usual, to his morning chores—rebedding and foddering the cattle, rubbing down the half-bred, helping the servant maid with the milk in the creaming pans—and, as usual, he came in to his breakfast, and ate it unhungrily and silently, which was not usual. But, thereafter he again went out to the stable, harnessed his gelding and hitched him to the tub cart. Then he returned to the kitchen and spoke for the first time.

"Ellen, will you come with me down to see your brother?"

She hesitated, her hands thrown wide in a helpless, hopeless gesture. "Little use you going to see my brother, Shawn. 'Tis I should go and—and not come back."

"Don't blame me now or later, Ellen. It has been put on me, and the thing I am going to do is the only thing to be done. Will you come?"

"Very well," she agreed tonelessly. "I will be ready in a minute."

And they went the four miles down into the vale to the big farmhouse of Moyvalla. They drove into the great square of cobbled yard and found it empty.

On one side of the square was the long, low, lime-washed dwelling house; on the other, 50 yards away, the two-storied line of steadings with a wide arch in the middle; and through the arch came the purr and zoom of a threshing machine. Shawn tied the half-bred to the wheel of a farm cart and, with Ellen, approached the house.

A slattern servant girl leaned over the kitchen half door and pointed through the arch. The master was out beyond in the haggard—the rickyard—and would she run across for him?

"Never mind, achara," said Shawn, "I'll get him. . . Ellen, will you go in and wait?"

"No," said Ellen, "I'll come with you." She knew her brother.

As they went through the arch, the purr and zoom grew louder and, turning the corner, they walked into the midst of activity. A long double row of cone-pointed corn stacks stretched across the yard and, between them, Matt Tobin's portable threshing machine was busy. The smooth-flying, 8-foot driving wheel made a sleepy purr and the black driving belt ran with a sag and a heave to the red-painted thresher. Up there on the platform, bare-armed men were feeding the flying drum with loosened sheaves, their hands moving in a rhythmic sway. As the toothed drum bit at the corn sheaves it made an angry snarl that changed and slowed into a satisfied zoom: The wide conveying belt was carrying the golden straw up a steep incline to where other men were building a long rick; still more men were attending to the corn shoots, shoulders bending under the weight of the sacks as they ambled across to the granary. Matt Tobin himself bent at the face of his engine, feeding the fire box with sods of hard black peat. There were not less than two score men about the place, for, as was the custom, all Big Liam's friends and neighbors were giving him a hand with the threshing—"the day in harvest."

Big Liam came round the flank of the engine and swore. He was in his shirt sleeves, and his great forearms were covered with sandy hair.

"Hell and damnation! Look who's here!"

He was in the worst of tempers this morning. The stale dregs of yesterday's whiskey were still with him, and he was in the humor that, as they say, would make a dog bite its father. He took two slow strides and halted, feet apart and head truculently forward.

"What is it this time?" he shouted. That was the un-Irish welcome he gave his sister and her husband.

Shawn and Ellen came forward steadily, and, as they came, Matt Robin slowly throttled down his engine. Big Liam heard the change of pitch and looked angrily over his shoulder.

"What the hell do you mean, Tobin? Get on with the work!"

"To hell with yourself, Big Liam! This is my engine, and if you don't like it, you can leave it!" And at that he drove the throttle shut and the purr of the flywheel slowly sank.

"We will see in a minute," threatened Big Liam and turned to the two now near at hand.

"What is it?" he growled.

"A private word with you. I won't keep you long." Shawn was calm and cold.

"You will not—on a busy morning," sneered the big man. "There is no need for private words between me and Shawn Kelvin."

"There is need," urged Shawn. "It will be best for us all if you hear what I have to say in your own house."

"Or here on my own land. Out with it! I don't care who hears!"

Shawn looked round him. Up on the thresher, up on the straw rick, men leaned idle on fork handles and looked down at him; from here and there about the stackyard, men moved in to see, as it might be, what had caused the stoppage, but only really interested in the two brothers-in-law. He was in the midst of Clan O'Grady, for they were mostly O'Grady men— big, strong, blond men, rough, confident, proud of their breed. Matt Tobin was the only man he could call a friend. Many of the others were not unfriendly, but all had contempt in their eyes, or, what was worse, pity.

Very well! Since he had to prove himself, it was fitting that he do it here amongst the O'Grady men.

Shawn brought his eyes back to Big Liam—deep, steadfast eyes that did not waver. "O'Grady," said he—and he no longer hid his contempt—"you set a great store by money."

"No harm in that. You do it yourself, Shawneen."

"Take it so! I will play that game with you, till hell freezes. You would bargain your sister and cheat; I will sell my soul. Listen, you big brute! You owe me 200 pounds. Will you pay it?" There was an iron quality in his voice that was somehow awesome. The big man, about to start forward overbearingly, restrained himself to a brutal playfulness.

"I will pay it when I am ready."

"Today."

"No; nor tomorrow."

"Right. If you break your bargain, I break mine."

"What's that?" shouted Big Liam.

"If you keep your 200 pounds, you keep your sister."

"What is it?" shouted Big Liam again, his voice breaking in astonishment. "What is that you say?"

"You heard me. Here is your sister Ellen! Keep her!"

"Fires o' hell!" He was completely astounded out of his truculence. "You can't do that!"

"It is done," said Shawn.

Ellen O'Grady had been quiet as a statue at Shawn's side, but now, slow like doom, she faced him. She leaned forward and looked into his eyes and saw the pain behind the strength. "To the mother of your son, Shawn Kelvin?" she whispered that gently to him.

His voice came cold as a stone out of stone face: "In the face of God. Let him judge me.

"I know—I know!" that was all he said, and walked quietly across to where Matt Tobin stood at the face of his engine.

Matt Tobin placed a hand on her arm. Give him time, colleen," he whispered urgently. "Give him his own time. He's slow, but he's deadly as an ogre when he moves."

Big Liam was no fool. He knew exactly how far he could go. There was no use, at this juncture, in crushing the runt under a great fist. There was some force in the little fellow that defied dragooning. Whatever people might think of Kelvin, public opinion would be dead against himself. Worse, his inward vision saw eyes leering in derision, mouths open in laughter. The scandal on his name would not be surrounded by the four seas of Erin. He must change his stance while he had time. These thoughts passed through his mind while he thudded the ground three times with iron-shod heel. Now he threw up his head and bellowed his laugh.

"You fool! I was only making fun of you. What are your dirty few pounds to the likes of me? Stay where you are." He turned, strode furiously away, and disappeared through the arch.

Shawn Kelvin was left alone in that wide ring of men. The hands had come down off the ricks and thresher to see closer. Now they moved back and aside, looked at one another, lifted eyebrows, looked at Shawn Kelvin, frowned and shook their heads. They knew Big Liam. They knew that, yielding up the money, his savagery would break out into something little short of killing. They waited, most of them, to prevent that savagery going too far.

Shawn Kelvin did not look at anyone. He stood still as a rock, his hands deep in his pockets, one shoulder hunched forward, his eyes on the ground and his face strangely calm. He seemed the least perturbed man there. Matt Tobin held Ellen's arm in a steadying grip and whispered in her ear: "God is good, tell you."

Big Liam was back in two minutes. He strode straight to Shawn and halted within a pace of him. "Look, Shawneen!" In his raised hand was a crumpled bundle of greasy bank notes. "Here is your money. Take it, and then see what will happen to you. Take it!" He thrust it into Shawn's hand. "Count it. Make sure you have it all—and then I will kick you out of this haggard—and look"—he thrust forward a hairy fist—"if ever I see your face again, I will drive that through it! Count it, you spawn!"

Shawn did not count it. Instead he crumpled it into a ball in his strong fingers. Then he turned on his heel and walked, with surprising slowness, to the face of the engine. He gestured with one hand to Matt Tobin, but it was Ellen, quick as a flash, who obeyed the gesture. Though the hot bar scorched her hand, she jerked open the door of the fire box and the leaping peat flames whispered out at her. And forthwith, Shawn Kelvin, with one easy sweep, threw the crumpled ball of notes into the heart of the flame. The whisper lifted one tone and one scrap of burned paper floated out of the funnel top. That was all the fuss the fire made of its work. But there was fuss enough outside.

Big Liam O'Grady gave one mighty shout. No, it was more an anguished scream then a shout: "My money! My good money!" He gave two furious bounds forward, his great arms raised to crush and kill. But his hands never touched the small man.

"You dumb ox!" said Shawn Kelvin between his teeth. That strong, hunched shoulder moved a little, but no one

THE QUIET MAN

John Ford's classic adaptation of the Maurice Walsh short story is the greatest collection of scene stealers in the history of modern cinema. From bit-player Elizabeth Jones as the Widow Telland's housemaide, who looks like she's just under 4 feet tall but just over a thousand years old, to Barry Fitzgerald's perpetually pie-eyed Michaeleen Oge Flynn, the author defies anyone to name a film that matches *The Quiet Man* actor for actor in sheer number of colorful performances.

In this Irish tale of love and honor, John Wayne stars as Sean Thornton, a retired heavyweight contender fighting in America under the name Trooper Thorn, who returns to his native Ireland after fatally knocking out fellow pugilist Tony Gadello.

Smitten almost immediately by Mary Kate Danaher (Maureen O'Hara), a brazen beauty with fiery red hair, a quick temper and a roundhouse right, Sean courts and ultimately marries the temperamental stunner. (If after viewing O'Hara's performance, any man doesn't suffer from hormonal overload and believe that she represents the culmination of all that is the perfect woman, you'd do well to put on a nice housedress and call it a day.)

In a true battle of titans, the film climaxes in a spectacular fistfight, pitting Sean against the gargantuan Red Will Danaher, brother of Mary Kate (played with proper bluster by crater-faced Victor McLaglen), who reneged on the financial portion of his sister's dowry.

In the end, amidst all the mud and the blood and the beer, all's well that ends well. This film is an absolute must-see.

there could follow the terrific drive of that hooked right arm. The smack of bone on bone was sharp as a whip crack, and Big Liam stopped dead, went back on his heels, swayed a moment and staggered back three paces.

"Now and forever! Man of the Kelvins!" roared Matt Tobin.

But Big Liam was a man of iron. That blow should have laid him on his back—blows like it had tied men to the ground for the full count. But Big Liam only shook his head, grunted like a boar, and drove in at the little man. And the little man, instead of circling away, drove in at him, compact of power.

The men of the O'Gradys saw then an exhibition that they had not knowledge enough to appreciate fully. Thousands had paid as much as $10 each to see the great Tiger Kelvin in action, his footwork, his timing, his hitting; and never was his action more devastating than now. He was a thunderbolt on two feet and the big man a glutton.

Big Liam never touched Shawn with clenched fist. He did not know how. Shawn, actually 40 pounds lighter, drove him by sheer hitting across the yard.

Men for the first time saw a 200 pound man knocked clean off his feet by a body blow. They saw for the first time the deadly restraint and explosion of skill.

Shawn set out to demolish his enemy in the briefest space of time, and it took him five minutes to do it. Five, six, eight times he knocked the big man down, and the big man came again staggering, slavering, raving, vainly trying to rend and smash. But at last he stood swaying and clawing helplessly,

and Shawn finished him with his terrible double hit—left below the breastbone and eight under the jaw.

Big Liam lifted on his toes and fell flat on his back. He did not even kick as he lay. Shawn did not waste a glance at the fallen giant. He swung full circle on the O'Grady men and his voice of iron challenged them:

"I am Shawn Kelvin, of Knockanore Hill. Is there an O'Grady amongst you thinks himself a better man? Come then." His face was deep-carved stone, his great chest lifted, the air whistled through his nostrils; his deep-set flashing eyes dared them. No man came.

His face was still of stone, but his voice quivered and had in it all the dramatic force of the Celt: "Mother of my son, will you come home with me?"

She lifted to the appeal, voice and eye: "Is it so you ask me, Shawn Kelvin?"

His face of stone quivered at last. "As my wife only—Ellen Kelvin!"

"Very well, heart's treasure." She caught his arm in both of hers. "Let us be going home."

"In the name of God," he finished for her.

And she went with him, proud as the morning, out of that place. But a woman, she would have the last word. "Mother of God!" she cried. "The trouble I had to make a man of him!"

"God Almighty did that for him before you were born," said Matt Tobin softly.

Hecho
... mano

Coffret
Humistat 70

Pluton

ROMEO y JULIETA

O lovely cigar boxes with your handcrafted beauty. . . . All our treasures were stored long ago yet we continue to bring you home. Me thinks we have a sickness and the wife is certain. (Above) Skilled artisans of The Las Vegas Cigar Company—an obligatory stop.

Cañones   IMPORTED

PARTAGAS Y C.ᵃ
1845
FABRICA DE CIGARROS PUROS
SUPERIORES IMPORTADOS
HECHOS A MANO

Superior imported cigars manufactured by hand
Cigares supérieurs importés et fait à la main

FLOR   FINA

THE LORE OF PAIN
UNUSUAL & PAINFUL JOB SITE & INDUSTRIAL ACCIDENTS

The smallest injury on a job site invariably leads to lunchtime one-upmanship regarding the Lore of Pain.

Scaffolding is Pain Central on most job sites. Scrambling up and down the stuff like a monkey builds your confidence but pushes your luck. Most hard hats will tell you that putting it up and tearing it down is the hairiest thing about it—watching one of these crews blast the stuff out can be amazing. Tom from Montana had a scaffolding experience like I'd never heard. He was climbing the outside support of the seventh level when one of the planks slid and he lost his footing. He didn't have time to grab anything and started falling straight down to a certain death. Amazingly, he didn't go far before he was jolted to a stop. His arms and legs were dangling but, in relief mixed with agony, he realized what had happened. One of the metal crossbar pegs had dug under his ribcage and hooked him. His full weight was hanging on a two-inch finger of steel jabbed under a rib. They got him down but his whole side was a sick black-and-blue for weeks.

Tom had another crazy mishap during one of those frozen Montana winters. He and an impatient buddy were loading a stake-bed truck and then had to put up the gates to enclose it. They were moving fast because Tom didn't have any gloves on and his hands were getting numb. The long side gates were made of heavy plywood. As they were guiding it into place his buddy dropped it sooner than Tom had figured and it slammed into place. Back in the cab, Tom blew on his cupped hands to warm up. That's when he noticed that the end of his pinky was missing. The bone was there sticking out at him, but the nail and whole outer tip was gone. When he found it out on the truck bed he said it "looked like a macaroni shell." He got back in the truck with his dumbfounded pal and slipped it back over the bone. It never hurt a bit because of the cold. They sewed it back on at the ER.

Mike had a visor snap on his motorcycle helmet that wouldn't give. He held it on the ground between his knees with his left hand. He stuck a flathead screwdriver under the snap and put all of his weight on it using his right hand. When it slipped he heard himself screaming, "Shiiit!!" The screwdriver had stabbed clear through the index finger on his left hand. It looked like the blade had even pierced the bone but it apparently just pushed the bone aside as it went through the meat between his first and second joint. It was hardly bleeding at all. A taxi got him to the ER where he walked up to the attendant at the chest high counter. When he held up his hand with a little wave she just about puked. They got it out all right but he said the worst part about it was the cab ride. He figured the guy wouldn't charge him for the short hop but fat chance. Mike said trying to work that money out of his wallet was a real bitch.

Another time Mike was doing some concrete work next to a hospital. It was a medium-sized job so he had one of those diesel-powered mixers. The three big mixing blades whirred in a clockwise motion inside the tilted barrel while the machine chugged away. Mike was shoveling in more sand when he noticed a big clump stuck on the inside. Naturally he stuck the shovel head in to dislodge it. One of the blades immediately snagged the shovel against the mixer wall. The handle was now navigating a circle but Mike held on trying to pull it out. At the bottom of its arc, the butt end of the handle snagged his belt and lifted him into the air. Rounding the top, his boots were dangling about four feet off the ground. He took another three turns around before he got off the thing. His immediate response, of course, was to look around quick to see if anyone had seen him. About a dozen nurses were behind those hospital windows laughing their asses off.

A 24-year-old Detroit man needed 16 stitches on his penis after apparently shooting himself with a semiautomatic pistol while asleep, police said Tuesday. The man, whom police did not identify, was sleeping with a loaded pistol when the incident occurred early Saturday, said Lt. Al Zielinski of the Sterling Heights Police Department. "He states he heard a loud noise and when he awoke discovered he had shot himself in the penis," Zielinski said.

The man, who sleeps in the basement of his parents' home, drove himself to the hospital, which then notified police, Zielinski said. No one else in the home was aware the gun had gone off, and the man told police he did not know how the semiautomatic pistol discharged, Zielinski said. "There's no permanent damage other than a scar," he added.

Bomber

The Darwin Awards

The Darwin award is the annual honor given to the (deceased) person who did the gene pool the biggest service by killing themselves in the most extraordinarily stupid way. Last year's winner was the fellow who was killed by a Coke machine that toppled over on him as he was attempting to tip out of it a free soda.

And this year's nominee? The Arizona Highway Patrol came upon a pile of smoldering metal embedded into the

(Jet Assisted Take Off—actually a solid-fuel rocket), used to provide heavy military transport planes with an extra "push" for takeoff from short airfields. He had driven his 1967 Chevy Impala out into the desert and found a long, straight stretch of road. He attached the JATO unit to his car, jumped in, achieved some speed and fired off the rocket.

The facts, as could best be determined, are that the operator of the Impala hit the ignition at a distance of approximately three miles from the crash site. This was established by the prominently scorched and melted asphalt at that location. The JATO, if operating properly, would have reached maximum thrust within five seconds, in that time propelling the Chevy to speeds well in excess of 350 mph, continuing at full power for an additional 20 to 25 seconds. The driver, soon to be pilot, most likely would have experienced G forces usually reserved for dog-fighting F-14 jocks under full afterburners—basically causing him to become insignificant for the remainder of the ride. Nonetheless, the automobile remained on the straight highway for another 2.5 miles/15 to 20 seconds before the driver applied—and completely melted—the brakes, blowing the tires, leaving thick rubber marks on the road and becoming airborne for an additional half mile before impacting the cliff face at a height of 125 feet, leaving a blackened crater three feet deep.

Most of the driver's remains were not recoverable; however, small fragments of bone, teeth and hair were extracted from the crater, and fingernail and bone shards were removed from debris believed to have been a portion of the steering wheel.

This is what a JATO bottle does.

side of a cliff rising above the road at the apex of a curve. The wreckage resembled a crashed airplane but was, in fact, a car. The type of car, unidentifiable at the scene, was finally determined, along with what had happened to it. Apparently, the driver had commandeered a JATO unit

Bomber

(*A West Virginia surfer buddy named Reechard tells this joke better than anybody—try to give the miner a semi-Southern surfer twang*):

This old crusty miner had been working his claim up in the foothills for years without a break and figured it was time to hit town, so he saddles up his mule and off he goes. Hitchin' his mule, he stomps into the saloon, pounds his leathery fist on the bar and bellows, "By God, bartender, gimme a whiskey!" Bartender lays the whiskey down, the miner slams it back and, arching his brow, sez, "Say, ye got any wimmin' round here?" Bartender sez, "Nah, we ain't had no women fer a year or more... but a 'course there's Old Joe in the back...." "What's that, ye dang fool?" cries the miner. "I ain't inta that shit!" and off he storms back up into the hills. Some years later, he gets a hankerin' for company agin so back down he goes and stomps into the same saloon. "By God, bartender, gimme a whiskey!" he sez. "Now listen here—ye got any wimmin round here yet?" "No," sez the bartender, "but we got Old Joe out back...." "By thunder, I told ye I ain't inta that shit!" and off the miner goes. Some time passes and his need for companionship is just gettin' unbearable, so off into town he goes. "By god, bartender, gimme a whiskey!" Bartender lays the whiskey down. "So tell me," sez the old coot, "ye got any wimmin round here yet?" "Heck no," the bartender sez, spitting, "but we still got Old Joe in the back." "Dang it, I ain't inta that shit! But, uh, now tell me," sez the desperate miner, "if'n I was to go wid Old Joe, who's a gonna know 'bout it?" "Well," sez the barkeep, "there'd be me, you, Old Joe, o'course, an' the two other guys...." "Two other guys? What fer we need two other guys?" demanded the miner. "Well, to hold down Old Joe," sez the barkeep. "He ain't into that shit, neither!"

* * *

Lady Hotbottom returned to her elegant estate late one evening after a dinner party and was met at the door by her faithful butler, Wellington. Giving him a long look, she said, "Wellington, I would like you to come up to my bedroom." "Yes, Madam," replied the servant. She had him close her door and directed him near the bed. "Now Wellington, I would like you to remove my dress." "Yes, Madam." "Now Wellington, I would like you to remove my slip." "Yes, madam." "Now, Wellington, my Wonderbra, please." "Yes, madam." "Now, Wellington, I would like you to take off my silk panties and leather pumps." "Yes, madam", replied the servant. Satisfied, Lady Wellington gathered up the clothes and said, "Now, Wellington, if I ever catch you wearing my things again, you're fired!"

* * *

JOKES

Oil Fire—Buck Austin had a mishap on his oil field, one of the wells exploding into flames that shot several hundred feet into the air. Now in Texas, of course, there's only one name that comes to mind when you've got an oil fire—Red Adair. Buck called him up and got the estimate: $1 million. "There's just no way I can afford that," Buck said to himself. Desperate, he picked up the yellow pages. Only two names were listed under "Oil Fires": Adair and another company called Pedro's Budget Oil Fire Service. Buck called Pedro for an estimate, and Pedro showed up in an hour to look the well over. "You've never seen anybody work like my crew," said Pedro. "I can have 'em here at 7 A.M. to get your fire out, guaranteed. The fee is $10,000." Buck bit his cigar in half and sputtered, "Ya gotta deal." The two men were already on the site when Pedro's crew showed up. A stakebed truck roared past them, with about 30 guys howling like banshees. "They certainly are enthusiastic," said Buck. The truck plowed straight into the inferno and slammed against the melting tower. "Good Christ!!" Buck yelled. The men immediately jumped outta the truck and started fighting the blaze. They kicked dirt, beat the fire with their jackets, pissed on it, spit, anything—it was the most frightening thing the oilman had ever seen. Incredibly, they got the fire out and staggered, looking like ghosts, toward the two men. "That's either the bravest or most insane display I've ever seen," Buck said. "Here's your check, a lot of money for a day's work. What are you going to do with it?" "Well, first," said Pedro, "I'm going to get the brakes fixed on that goddamn truck!"

* * *

One day, Mike noticed that he couldn't keep any weight on. He was eating three, sometimes four, full meals a day, but nothing. Worried, he went to the doctor. The doc gave him a full exam and discovered that he had a tapeworm. "No problem," said the doc, "I've got just the cure for these guys. Come back tomorrow and bring an apple and a lemon cookie." Mike thought the doc was nuts but showed up as promised. "OK," said the doc, "now drop your trousers, bend over and hold steady." The doc stuffed the apple and lemon cookie right up Mike's butt. "*Yeowch!*" Mike yelled. But the doc just said, "Trust me—this will work. Now come back next week with an apple and a lemon cookie." Mike glumly returned twice more for the "treatments" but then told the doc he couldn't take it any more. "Don't worry, I promise you, we're almost there," said the doc. "Now come back next week, but this time bring an apple and a hammer." Mike shook his head but returned the next week as instructed. He dropped his trousers, climbed on the table and assumed the position. The doc shoved the apple up his butt. "Now lie on your stomach and be still," said the doc. He grabbed the hammer and stared intently at Mike's ass. After a few minutes the tapeworm stuck his head out and said, "Hey! Where's my lemon cookie?" WHAM!

A man asked his doctor what he knew of the new penis extension surgery. "Why, I do it myself," said the doc, "and have had wonderful success grafting on sections of elephant trunk." The man thought the doc was nuts, but a round of referrals backed up the doc's claim. So the man went for it and, after four weeks, healed up perfectly. Eager to try out his new large-caliber weapon, he phoned up a lady friend, who met him at a favorite restaurant. The waiter seated them, and a basket of fresh rolls were brought to the table. Their conversation was interrupted when the elephant trunk appeared from beneath the table, grabbed a roll and withdrew. The woman stared in amazement. "Was that what I think it was?" "It was," he replied, rather flustered. "That's the most amazing thing I've ever seen," she gasped. "Can you do it again?" "Trouble is," the guy said, shifting in his chair, "I'm not sure if I could take another roll up my ass."

* * *

Flanagan, a new recruit in the French Foreign Legion, asked the sergeant if there were any chance to get laid. "Now don't fret yourself," said the sergeant, "we're provided for." "But we're just 100 men in the middle of the desert," Flanagan protested, "and no woman or town in sight!" "You'll see now, young pup," assured the sergeant, "you'll see. We've got a special treat at the end of the month, don't you worry." Well, Flanagan asked the old-timers, but all he got was a wink and a thumbs up.

Finally, at month's end, the sergeant ordered all of the Legion's camels into the courtyard and blew his whistle. The soldiers came flying out of the barracks, whooping it up and racing across to meet the camels. In moments, they had their uniforms off and were screwing like madmen. Flanagan caught up with the sergeant and said, "Gee, now I guess I know what you meant. But tell me something. There's gotta be more than 300 camels out here—why in hell is everyone rushing?" "What?" puffed the sergeant, "and get stuck with an ugly one?"

A new Foreign Legion recruit asked one of the soldiers what they did for sex way out in the desert. "Well, we just use ole Gloria over there," said the soldier. The recruit followed the other guy's gaze to a crusty old female camel chewing her cud near the wall. "Oh, jeez, no way. . . I'm not that hard up!" said the disgusted recruit. The soldier bristled and raised his eyebrows. "Hey, don't knock ole Gloria," he said. "She gives a fine ride." "Sure, OK, sure. . . whatever," the recruit said, backing down. Perhaps, he figured, it was some kind of badge of honor to bang the filthy animal.

Weeks passed and the recruit often noticed one of the soldiers leaving the compound with Gloria. Can't be all that bad, he figured. So one day, he led the camel just outside the gate and proceeded to vigorously screw her under a tree. Greatly satisfied and a bit proud, he noticed that the commandant and several of the soldiers had lined the wall to witness his initiation. He was flushed when reentering the fort. "Boy, were you right," smiled the sweaty recruit, "ole Gloria here is one helluva ride!" "Just the same," approached the now queasy commandant, "let's confine our rides to the village cathouse like everyone else, shall we?"

* * *

A young country couple was checking into a scenic hotel. The front desk manager could tell with a glance that they were on their honeymoon. "Bridal suite?" he inquired with a knowing smile of the young lady. "Gosh, no thanks, Mister," she giggled, "I'll just hold his ears."

* * *

There was a guy sitting next to a woman on an airplane. She was apparently suffering from some kind of killer flu. After every sneeze, her eyes closed, her body trembled and a low groan escaped from her tightly clenched jaw. She caught his worried look. "I'm sorry, but don't worry—I'm not contagious. Actually, it's a little embarrassing," she confided in a low voice, "but you see, I've developed a kind of crazy condition where I have an orgasm every time I sneeze." "That's the craziest thing I've ever heard," the guy replied. "Are you taking anything for it?" "Oh sure," she nodded, "Right now, black pepper and snuff."

* * *

An elderly Chicago couple pulled into a Missouri gas station. The attendant, Bob, asked if he should fill it up. "WHAT'D HE SAY!?" asked the wife in a loud, grating voice. "HE ASKED IF WE WANT GAS," the annoyed husband replied and gestured Bob to go ahead. "Check under the hood, Pal?" "WHAT'D HE SAY!?," again asked the half-deaf wife. "HE'S ASKED IF HE SHOULD CHECK UNDER THE HOOD!" the husband repeated for her, and so it continued. Presently, Bob finished and was wiping his hands on a rag while the man counted out some cash. "I see you folks are from Illinois," remarked Bob, adding in a low voice, "You know, buddy, I gotta tell ya, I met a gal from Chicago once, and brother, she was the worst lay I think I ever had." "WHAT'D HE SAY!? WHAT'D HE SAY!?" demanded the wife. The husband rolled his eyes, "HE SAYS HE KNOWS YOU!"

An elderly pioneer couple was on the dole, and the husband was frustrated by every attempt to get them back on their feet. Things were desperate, and the wife, an ex-soiled dove, suggested she go back to work. "But, honey," said the husband, "you're pushing 70. Who's going to want you now?" That hit the old pro right in her pride. "Well, we'll just see about that," she sniffed. "And besides, what choice do we have?"

So she painted herself up and went out into the night, returning late the next day, disheveled and dog tired. "Here you go, I guess you were right," she said and handed her husband $5.25. "Well hold on now, honey, it's a start," replied the hopeful husband. "But, tell me, who gave you the $0.25?" "Everybody," she said.

* * *

A tour bus was making its way through northern Nevada when the driver announced, "We are now passing the famous Mustang Ranch, largest cathouse in the nation." A guy in the back was heard to ask, "Why?"

* * *

Sign in a Nevada cathouse: It's A Business Doing Pleasure With You.

LIMERICKS

The Olde Time Dirty Limerick traditionally is distinguished by its high reach and low aim. Not just crudely contrasted, like dog crap on fine china, of course, but a Byronesque, bawdy-to-bestial pleasing puree of the patrician and the pornographic. Bryan Brown still holds the Greatest On-Screen Dirty Limerick title for *Breaker Morant*. Humbly submitted are the following, which we deem worthy to join that limerick masterpiece "The Man From Nantucket."

An upstart who gained notoriety
Is shunned by the cream of society,
For his foul ventral breezes
He voids as he pleases,
In tones of fantastic variety.

A Middle Age monk, St. Augustin,
His penis a boy's bottom thrust in.
Said old Father Ignatius,
"I say, really! Good gracious!
Your conduct is really disgusting."

Quipped the hip L.A. hostess at tea,
"Say, dude, do you fart when you pee?"
Replied I with fair wit,
"Do you burp when you shit?"
On the coast that was one up for me.

It takes little strain and no art
To bang out an echoing fart.
The reaction is hearty
When you fart at a party,
But the sensitive persons depart.

A cowboy down in Oklahoma
Had a cock that could sing "La
Paloma,"
But his sweetness of pitch
Couldn't offset the hitch
Of impotence, size and aroma.

There was a young stud from
Saskatchewan
Whose johnson was, jeez, gargantuan.
It was good for large whores
Or small dinosaurs,
And sufficiently rough to scratch a
match upon.

From *The Autobiography of Alice* by Charles L. Dodgson:

There once was a naughty old
lesbian
Who went into a bookstore for cat
food.
But the ceiling fell down
And she died of a stroke,
And nobody came to the funeral
except the immediate family.

NOTICE

OF

PENILE REVOCATION

KNOW YE THIS . . .

Let it be known that by these articles fair and true and after grave and pretty much legally sober consideration of a kind most grievous and irksome, notice hereby and for all just purposes has been duly served forthwith to the blackguard, toadie, worm, pain in the ass, all-round jerkified, lowly crawfish and insufferable yutz, once called by the name

_____

and who is herein and hereafter to be referred to as "NEUTER-BOY."

AND THAT . . .

Whereas, the aforementioned NEUTER-BOY has been rightfully found by The Society Of Maledom to have charted a shabby course of life consistent with those offenders habitually guilty of any of a number of crimes repugnant to our brotherhood, including but not limited to: gutlessness, shameless cowering or ass-kissing, unsportsmanlike conduct, unfair business practices, ducking a confrontation, shoddy parenting, gross inconsideration and selfishness, actions not befitting a gentleman, shirking of duty, whining, betraying a pal or a sworn confidence, disgracing your family, running crying to a lawyer, behaving like a prick at a Little League game, taking the low road, putting your dingus in Whoopi Goldberg, etc.

AND THAT . . .

Therefore, consistent with the unwritten laws of comportment accepted by The Society and extending back over the countless generations to the Great Hairy Nomad and First Regular Joe himself, be it known that the aforementioned NEUTER-BOY, having been found pitiable, unworthy and unfit to carry The Societal Staff, and in keeping with the Revocation Terms of said offender's Appendage Lease as covered in the Johnson Clause, section III, paragraph VI, shall and will at once forfeit said appendage. Please return it in the envelope provided for your convenience.

_____
Eminent Regular Guy Arbiter

_____
Date

A Sheer Manliness List

NAMES FOR THE WONDROUS FEMALE BREAST

1. Abbondanzas (Meyer)
2. Abundance
3. B-52 s
4. Balcony
5. Balloons
6. Bazooms
7. Bazoongies
8. Beauts
9. Begonias
10. Bells
11. Berks
12. Big Brown Eyes
13. Biscuits
14. Bobbers
15. Bolt-Ons
16. Bongos
17. Boobahs
18. Boobies
19. Boobs
20. Boondogglers
21. Bosoms
22. Boulders
23. Boy Toys
24. Breasts
25. Bristols
26. Bubbles
27. Buffers
28. Bulbs
29. Bumpers
30. Bust
31. Butter Bags
32. Cans
33. Cantaloupes
34. Challoopas
35. Charms
36. Chee-chees
37. Chest
38. Cleavage
39. Cleave
40. Cream Pies
41. Cupcakes
42. Dairies
43. Droopers
44. Dumplings
45. Eyes
46. Fried Eggs
47. Front
48. Fun Bags
49. Gazongas
50. Giganzos (Meyer)
51. Gland Canyon
52. Globes
53. Gobdobblers
54. Golden Bozos
55. Grandstand
56. Grapefruits
57. Handwarmers
58. Hangers
59. Happy Sacks
60. Headlights
61. Hemispheres
62. Hogans
63. Honeydews
64. Honkers
65. Hooters
66. Jersey Cities
67. Jiggly Bits
68. Joy Boys
69. Jugs
70. Kanakas
71. Kettledrums
    (Yes, Kettledrums)
72. Knicknacks
73. Knobs
74. Knockers
75. Lactallicas
76. Lemons
77. Love Bubbles
78. Love Fruit
79. Lungs
80. Mammoth Mammary Monuments
81. Mams
82. Manchesters
83. Marshmallows
84. Melons
85. Mezzanine
86. Milk Bottles
87. Milk Cans
88. Milky Way
89. Missiles
90. Molonies
91. Moo-Moos
92. Mountains
93. Muffins
94. Nubbies
95. Num-Nums
96. Nungas
97. Orbs
98. Pair
99. Peaches
100. Pillows
101. Pink-nosed Puppies
102. Playground
103. Rack
104. Rib Rack
105. Sacks
106. Set
107. Shelf
108. Swingers
109. Ta Tas
     (as in Bodacious ___)
110. Teacups
111. Teats
112. Tits
113. Titties
114. Tomatahs
115. Tracts o' Land"
     (as in Holy Grail)
116. Twin Towers
117. Twins
118. Udders
119. Upper Deck
120. Veiled Twins
121. Wallopies
122. Wangdoodles
123. Watermelons
124. Whoppers
125. Winnebagoes
126. Yabahos

A Sheer Manliness List

NAMES FOR YOUR JOHNSON

1. Adam's arsenal
2. Appendage
3. Arbor Vitae
4. Artist's Brush
5. Bagpipe
6. Bald Headed Mouse
7. Balls & Bat
8. Baloney
9. Banana
10. Bat
11. Bauble
12. Bayonet
13. Bean
14. Beef
15. Bell Rope
16. Best Leg
17. Big Jim & the Twins
18. Big Uncle
19. Bishop's Hat
20. Blood Sausage
21. Blue Veiner
22. Bobbie's Helmet
23. Boner
24. Bop Gun
25. Bowsprit
26. Breakfast Boner
27. Bushwhacker
28. Butter Knife
29. Callibistris
30. Candle
31. Cane
32. Captain Standish
33. Carrot
34. Chicken Wing
35. Chod
36. Chubby
37. Chum
38. Cock
39. Cod
40. Coral Branch
41. Crank
42. Credentials
43. Dawk
44. Diamond Cutter
    (Cat couldn't scratch it)
45. Dick
46. Ding Dong
47. Dingle Dangle
48. Dingus
49. Dirk
50. Do-Dad
51. Doohickey
52. Dong
53. Donkey's Ear
54. Doodle Dandy
55. Dork
56. Drumstick
57. Elephant's Trunk
58. Family Jewels
59. Fiddle Bow
60. Fire Poker
61. Fishing Rod
62. Flapdoodle
63. Flute
64. Foreman

65. Frigamajig
66. Gadget
67. Gap Stopper
68. Giggle Stick
69. Girlometer
70. Gladius
71. Goober
72. Gooseneck
73. Hammer
74. His Eminence
75. Horn
76. Hose
77. Hot Dog
78. Instrument
79. Irish Root
80. Iron Bar
81. Jiggling Bone
82. Jing Jang
83. John Thomas
84. John Willie
85. Johnson
86. Johnson County
87. Joint
88. Jones
89. Joy Stick
90. Joy Toy
91. Junior
92. Key
93. Kick Stand
94. Knob
95. Kracken
    (as in Unleash The ...!)
96. Lance
97. Length
98. Lickin' Stick
99. Little Brother
100. Little Colonel
101. Little Davey
102. Little Fireman
103. Little General
104. Little Man with the
     Helmet
105. Lizard
106. Love Dart
107. Love Muscle
108. Magic Twanger
109. Magic Wand
110. Main Vein
111. Majestic Spire
112. Man Fruit
113. Manhood
114. Manliness
115. Man Root
116. Master Cylinder
117. Master of
     Ceremonies
118. Meatstick
119. Meat Whistle
120. Member
121. Monkey
     (Spank the...)
122. Mr. Happy
123. Mr. Johnson
124. Mr. Merrymaker
125. Mr. Tom

126. Nimrod
127. Old Blind Bob
128. Old Fella
129. Old Hornington
130. One-Eyed Milkman
131. One-Eyed Pocket
     Trout
132. One-Eyed Trouser
     Snake
133. Organ
134. Peacemaker
135. Pecker
136. Pee Pee
137. Pen
138. Pencil
139. Pendulum
140. Pepperoni
141. Perch
142. Pestle
143. Peter
144. Phallus
145. Piccolo
146. Pickle
147. Pied Piper
148. Pile Driver
149. Pindle
150. Pink Torpedo
151. Pipe
152. Piston
153. Plaything
154. Pleasure Piston
155. Plug
156. Po Po (Yes, Po Po)
157. Pointer
158. Poker
159. Pole
160. Pony
161. Porkeroon
162. Pork Sword
163. Post
164. Priapus
165. Prick
166. Pride and Joy
167. Privates
168. Probe
169. Prod
170. Prong
171. Pud
172. Pump Handle
173. Purple Headed
     Warrior
174. Putz
175. Quarter Master
176. Quill
177. Quimstake
178. Radish
179. Red Cap
180. Rhubarb
181. Rod
182. Rolling Pin
183. Rooster
184. Root
185. Ruddèr
186. Saber
187. Saint Peter

188. Salam
189. Scepter
190. Schlong
191. Schvance
192. Schvanschtucker
193. Screwdriver
194. Shaft
195. Shillelagh
196. Short Arm
197. Sir Martin Wagstaff
198. Skin Flute
199. Spindle
200. Spout
201. Staff
202. Stalk
203. Stanley
204. Stargazer
205. Stem
206. Stiffy
207. Strap
208. Sword
209. Tackle
210. Tallywhacker
211. Tassel
212. Tee Tee
213. Tent Stake
214. Thing
215. Thingamabob
216. Third Leg
217. Thorn
218. Throbber
219. Tickle Tail
220. Tickler
221. Tinker
222. Tool
223. Toy
224. Tube Steak
225. Ugly
226. Uncle Dick
227. Unemployed, The
228. Unit
229. Upright Citizen
230. Veinous Maximus
231. Wang
232. Wang Dang Doodle
233. Wankle
234. Wares
235. Waterworks
236. Wazoo
237. Weapon
238. Wedding Kit
239. Weenie
240. Weiner
241. Whacker
242. Whistle
243. Whizzer
244. Wick
245. Wife's Best Friend
246. Wigga Wagga
247. Willy
248. Winkle
249. Woody
250. Worm
251. Ying Yang
252. Zubrick

THE CHICKEN RANCH

You have to hand it to Nevada—still the only state in this "enlightened age" with guts enough to reasonably address "the world's oldest profession." Licensed, regulated, health inspected, taxed—the state legislature allows the rural counties the choice, and it works. The two most legendary cathouses today are the Mustang Ranch and the Chicken Ranch.

The Legend of the Chicken Ranch as told by the Chicken Ranch

Sure, you've heard of the hit show *The Best Little Whorehouse in Texas*, but how many folks really know about the best little whorehouse in Texas? Yes, there was such a place; yes, the show is based on a true story; and yes, the legacy of this grand old bordello carries on to this day in Pahrump (pronounced "Pah-rump"), Nevada, about 60 miles outside of Las Vegas.

Definitions

Appetizers
generally used as foreplay or preludes to sex

1. Massage · the lady rubs and massages a man for relaxation and/or masturbating him to climax.
2. Exchange Massage · same as above except the man also rubs and massages the lady.
3. Breast Massage · a man kisses, rubs, and massages the ladies' breasts or lady massages man's body using her breasts.
4. Lingerie Show · the lady models sexy underwear, such as nighties, garter belts with nylons, crotchless panties, etc.
5. Bubble Bath · a lady prepares a hot bubble or mineral bath for the man. The couple may bathe together, if desired.
6. Hot French Oil Massage · the lady warms a French massaging oil and massages the man with oil.

A La Carte
a primary sex activity generally leading to the man's climax

7. Body French · the lady kisses, licks, caresses the man with her tongue, about his neck, shoulders, nipples and stomach.
8. Bondage · the man is submissive while a dominating woman has sex with him while he is passively restrained.
9. Dominance · the man is submissive to a dominating woman.
10. Drag Party · the man dresses up in women's clothing.
11. Hot and Cold French · the lady performs oral sex holding liquids of different temperature in her mouth to give different sensations.

Ranch Specialties
complete course of fun and sex

12. VIP Lounge · a special separate room with a water bed, mirrors, and passion chair, video tape player with porno movies, etc. · where couples or group sex occurs.
13. Movies · video tape player with a large selection of pornographic tapes.
14. In Date · a man may stay for extended periods of time, such as over night, with a lady in her room at the Ranch.
15. Audio Delight · unique travels into the pleasures of sound. Listen to different fantasies while enjoying your favorite appetizer.
16. Passion Chair Party · available in the VIP Lounge. A novelty chair where either the man or lady sits, while the other performs oral sex. And that's not all . . . use your imagination.
17. Jacuzzi · couples and groups

Entrees
a main sex activity generally leading to the man's climax

18. Straight Lay · conventional missionary intercourse.
19. Half and Half · a lady performs oral sex, bringing the man to erection, but not climaxing, then conventional missionary intercourse with man climaxing.
20. Reversed Half and Half · beginning with conventional intercourse, climaxing with oral sex.
21. Two Girl Show · two ladies perform with each other while the man watches.
22. Two Girl Party · two ladies attending to the man.
23. Vibrator · let me titillate you . . . or you can do me.
24. Fantasy Session · basically, you can get what you want.

Desserts
more fun

25. Creme de Menthe French · the lady wets her mouth with a creme de menthe liqueur and then performs oral sex on the man.
26. Frappe French · a lady wets her mouth with a cold or icy liquid and then performs oral sex on the man.
27. Shower Party · before or after sex, the couple takes a shower together.
28. Seduction · A cocktail or two . . . then to my boudoir . . . soft music . . . let me tease you and please you.

The Chicken Ranch was established about the time Texas became a state, at a little trading post on the beautiful Colorado River in La Grange, Texas. It catered to local farmers, ranchers and soldiers; generals to privates stopped during the Civil War for a bit of relaxation. Later, there were the great cattle drives with the cattle barons and cowboys; the cool waters and green pastures of the Chicken Ranch were a welcome sight to the footsore longhorns and saddle-sore cowboys heading north to the railheads in Kansas. Later on, the cowboys were followed by the beneficiaries of the explosive oil booms of central Texas. The ranch attracted millionaires and roughnecks alike. It survived the hardships of the Great Depression, and in World War II its customers were the fighting men from the military bases in the La Grange/San Antonio area. The reputation of the ranch grew worldwide, as the proprietors maintained a high ethical standard that none questioned. The Chicken Ranch became so much a part of the history of the Southwest that Texas-born President Lyndon B. Johnson once paid a publicized visit to the Ranch—for its historic value.

Where did the name "Chicken Ranch" come from? Hard cash was difficult to come by in the 1840s, and the local ranchers and farmers often used a barter system. The common item of barter for the favors of the bordello's ladies in residence was chickens, so by and by, the enterprise was known as the Chicken Ranch.

And what of the beautiful ladies who come and go as residents of the ranch? Well, they're mostly just sweet young girls who end up marrying, raising families and living happily ever after.

Things ran peacefully, even though the operations of the Chicken Ranch had been illegal for nearly 130 years. Sadly, however, in 1973, after a massive public awareness campaign mounted by Marvin Zindler, a moralistic Houston television reporter, Governor Dolph Briscoe ordered Sheriff T.J. Flourney to close the Ranch, and a chapter of Texas history closed with it.

But the Chicken Ranch and those three men were revived in 1978, bigger and better than ever, in the Broadway show *The Best Little Whorehouse in Texas*. Having played in most major cities nationwide, it tells, in a musical way, the history of the ranch.

After the Chicken Ranch was closed in Texas, an enterprising capitalist established a legal, licensed brothel in Nevada, just a ways outside of Las Vegas. His research led him to acquire 41 acres right on the Clark County line, which makes the new Chicken Ranch the most convenient brothel to Las Vegas. Yes, the Best Little Whorehouse in the West is located as close as legally possible to the Entertainment Capital of the World: Las Vegas, Nevada. A lot of the more than 2 million friendly visitors to Vegas each month drop by

the Chicken Ranch to say hello. (The bartering item is now money or charge cards, not chickens.)

A new chapter in the Chicken Ranch's history began in early 1982. Instead of a madam, the ranch is now run by Russell Reade, previously a biology teacher in Northern California. Going from teaching to managing a brothel caused quite a fuss at Russ' old school and in the California and Nevada papers. Russ is turning the Chicken Ranch into quite a progressive brothel. The parlor, where you meet the ladies is exquisitely decorated, the perfect atmosphere for romantic introductions. The ladies dress in evening gowns, and are the most beautiful, talented women practicing their art in the State of Nevada.

The majority of the Chicken Ranch's customers are mature, intelligent gentlemen, who often have questions about the ladies' "protective" practices. Now, the ladies are the cleanest, most health-conscious women you will ever meet.

All customers are required to use condoms, and the ladies receive weekly checks from the local doctor as well as a monthly blood test. In fact, the ladies are well trained in these matters, so visitors are invited to go right ahead and ask any questions they may have.

The ranch menu offers sexual fare for the most discriminating connoisseur. The ladies thoroughly review the menu with each visitor so that everyone's dreams can come true.

The ranch is a short drive over the beautiful Mt. Springs Summit Pass, which at night gives you a sparkling, panoramic view of Las Vegas. Ask any taxi driver about the ranch—he'll be glad to bring you out and back.

Well, the Chicken Ranch has come a long way. It's been a part of the Old West for years, and is still making history today. Drop by for a visit so you can say, "I've been to the Best Little Whorehouse in the West."

World Famous MUSTANG RANCH

This storied bordello, which dates back to the 1940s, is the largest cathouse in the world, lying less than ten miles outside of Reno, Nevada.

It offers legal, disease-free, fun, consensual sex. While so many "modern women" are making it such an incredible pain in the ass to get some "sexual healing" as Mr. Gaye put it, here the girl of your choice will simply take you by the hand and escort you to her room. . . .

"I enter a whorehouse with the same interest as I do the British Museum or the Metropolitan—in the same spirit of curiosity. Here are the works of man, here is an art of man, here is his eternal pursuit of gold and pleasure. I think I can truthfully say that my behavior in whorehouses has been exemplary. These are about the only institutions I never have been ejected from."

—Errol Flynn

"The Miners came in '49, the whores in '51,
     They rolled upon the barroom floor, then came the native son."

—old San Francisco quatrain from the Barbary Coast days

"A man who wouldn't cheat for a poke don't want one bad enough."

—Robert Duvall as Capt. Augustus McCrae/*Lonesome Dove*

"You're a *hooker*!?! I just thought I was doing great with you!"

—Dudley Moore, in *Arthur*

IF PROHIBITION COULDN'T CURB ALCOHOL, HOW CAN IT STOP SOMETHING LIKE THIS?

Unfortunately, suppressing human desires doesn't make them go away. It just makes them go underground. Much like prohibition in the Twenties, outlawing prostitution created a whole industry of vice, complete with disease, poverty and drugs. After two centuries of crackdowns, it's apparent that these laws aren't working. Because prostitutes still are.

THE MARGO ST. JAMES TASK FORCE ON PROSTITUTION.
The more you know, the more you'll support decriminalization.

"To be able to fulfill a need of a fellow human being and profit by it, is good business, besides being an act of faith and, sometimes, charity."—Margo St. James, COYOTE

Beyond the titillation aspect, if you're interested in the serious issue of prostitution rights, contact COYOTE.

A MANLY CALENDAR

Long Range Historic Artillery Match

Angola Prison Rodeo

This calendar does not claim to be complete or authoritative! But in addition to the classic TV events, it should help remind readers of some of the great stuff out there inviting them to join the party. Getting your tail somewhere out of town for a good time—maybe once per month—is strongly recommended. A quick call to a city's chamber of commerce opens the door.

Check out regional events and festivals too.

January

College Football Bowl Games,
    early January

Quandrantids Meteor shower, January 3

NFL Playoffs, mid-January

Super Bowl, late January

Senior Skins Game, January (date varies)

February

Mardi Gras, second Tuesday in February,
    call Arthur Hardy's Carnival Times
    504/838-6111

Valentine's Day, February 14;
    make a point of it, you schmuck

Presidents' Day, February 17
    (3-day weekend)

Western Pyrotechnic Association Winter
    Blast Convention, Presidents' weekend
    in Lake Havasu City, AZ; write: WPA
    2230 Aralia Street, Newport Beach, CA
    92660

Daytona 500, mid-February,
    Daytona Beach, FL

March

St. Patrick's Day, March 17

NCAA Basketball tournament (aka March
    Madness), weekends throughout
    March, with the Final Four contested
    the third weekend of play [late March
    or early April], sites rotate

South x Southwest Music Festival, Austin,
    Texas, mid-March

U.S. [Amateur] Boxing Championships,
    every March, Colorado Springs

April

Masters golf, Augusta, GA, early April

NBA Playoffs, begin early April,
    Finals in late May

Boston Marathon, mid-April

NHL Playoffs, begin mid-April,
    Finals in mid-May

World Championship Poker Tourney,
    Benny Binion's Horseshoe Club, Las
    Vegas, 800-237-6537, mid-April to
    mid-May

Jazz & Heritage Music Fest, New Orleans,
    late April to early May

May

Kentucky Derby, Louisville,
    first Saturday in May

Cinco de Mayo, May 5th,
    abundant Mexican fiestas

Mother's Day, second Sunday in May

Preakness Stakes, Baltimore, mid-May

NHL Finals, mid-May

North-South Skirmish Association Spring
    National Competition, "black powder
    events," musket & cannon
    competitions, third Friday in May,
    Winchester, VA 810/258-9007

Memphis In May World Championship
    BBQ Cooking Contest,
    third weekend in May

Armed Forces Day, third Saturday in May

Memorial Day, May 26 (3-day weekend)

Indianapolis 500, late May

NBA Finals, late May

June

Back To The 50's Hot Rod Show,
    Minneapolis

Belmont Stakes, Elmont, NY, early June

Baja 500 road race, Baja, Mexico,
    early June

College World Series, early June

U.S. Open golf, sites rotate, mid-June

Father's Day, third Sunday in June

Wimbledon tennis, late June to early July

Rhinebeck Aerodrome Museum Weekend
    Air Shows, beginning in June and
    continuing through mid-October,
    914/758-8610

July

Independence Day, Fourth of July; don't under-celebrate this one

Dam Rod Run, hot rod race, Mossy Rock, WA, second weekend in July

British Open, mid-July

Annual Long Range Artillery Invitational Match, third weekend of July, Grayling MI, it's a competition for owners of artillery pieces designed before 1898 and fired with black powder, call 313/243-6347 August

Sturgis, South Dakota Rally & Races, motorcycles, first full week in August, 605/347-6570

Goodguys Carlisle Rod & Custom Classic, early August, Carlisle, PA, 717/243-7855

Logger's Jubilee, over 50 years old, cuttin' and climbin' and lawnmower races, Morton, WA, second weekend in August

Pyrotechnics Guild International, Inc. Annual Fireworks Convention, second week in August, sites rotate, 800/650-8071

Perseids Meteor Shower, August 12

Travers Stakes at Saratoga, late August

Hot August Nights Hot Rod Show, hot August nights, Reno, NV

U.S. Open tennis, Flushing Meadow, NY, late August-early September

September

Labor Day, September 1 (3-day weekend)

Route 66 Rendezvous, San Bernardino, third Saturday in September, 800/TO RTE 66

Great American Beer Festival (nation's largest), late September in Denver, CO

October

Baseball Playoffs, early October, World Series, late October

North-South Skirmish Association Fall National Competition, "black powder events," musket & cannon competitions, first Friday in October in Winchester, VA, 810/258-9007

International Chili Society World

Championship Chili Cookoff, first weekend in October in Reno, Nevada, 714/631-1780

Antique Auto Club of America Fall Meet, world's largest auto show and flea market, second weekend in October, Hersheypark Grounds, Hershey, PA, 717/545-1457

Edwards Air Force Base Open House, third Saturday in October 805/277-1110

Halloween, October 31

Angola Prison Rodeo, Louisiana, every Sunday in October

Lewes, Delaware Punkin Chunk, first weekend past Halloween

November

Baja 1000, road race, Baja, Mexico, early November

Wick Fowler-Frank X. Tolbert Memorial Chili Cookoff at the West Texas Big Bend ghost town of Terlingua, early November

Love Ride, Glendale, CA: sounds corny, but 20,000 motorcycles cruising to Lake Castaic to raise a million bucks each year for muscular dystrophy isn't; plus, Peter Fonda rides; call 818/246-5618 or 818/896-3934, November 9

Veterans Day, November 11

New York City Marathon, mid-November

Bob Marriott Annual Fly Fishing Fair, weekend before Thanksgiving

Skins Game, weekend after Thanksgiving

December

National Finals Rodeo, Las Vegas, early December

Pipeline Masters surfing tournament, mid-December, Hawaii (there's also an Eddie Aikau memorial contest in December there, but 20 foot waves have to smash in for eight hours straight for the contest to begin, and that's only happened 3 times in the last ten years)

Geminids Meteor Shower, December 15

College Bowl Games, mid/late December to early January

New Years' Fiestas, December 31

Love Ride

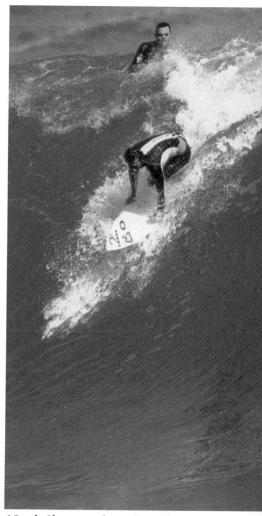

North Shore madness (Pipeline, etc.)

River Beer

River Bloody

Uncle Grumpy sez a proper BBQ has a trailer hitch

Ozark Turtle Trappers

Welcome men of Earth. With any luck you have found something herein to inform, entertain, annoy or offend you. If, however, you are unsatisfied for any reason, please return the book with your store receipt and the authors will have a good laugh. We're ALL unsatisfied you silly yutz, but that's a good thing. If you're not confused or pissed off or worried about something then you're probably dead. But can you say "I'm Spartacus"? Got a Mythic Haunt? A good Lore of Pain story or Art of Screwing Off event? The authors want to hear from you. E-Mail the boys at BDBOOKS@aol.com.

Caution: Do Not Put Explosives In Your Pants

The von Hoffmann Brothers

Authors at Work

Author's Bride

Author's Kid

B-17 at Chino Air Museum

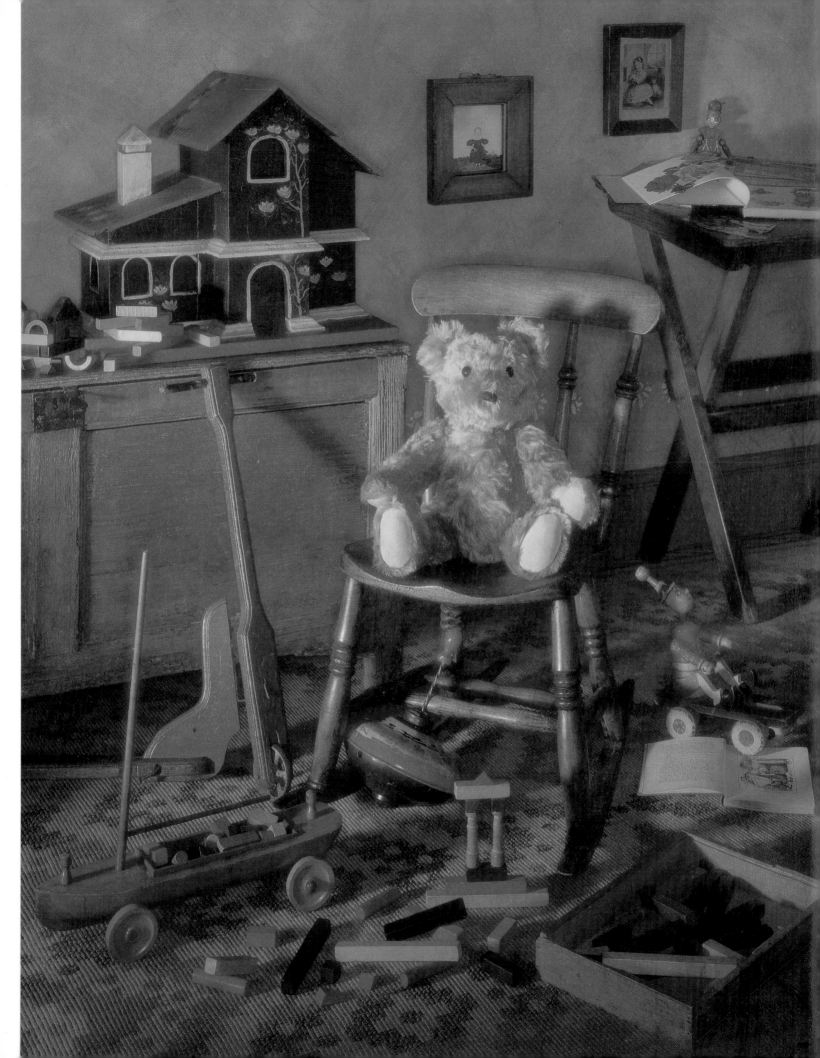

CLASSIC BEARS

HOW TO MAKE 14 HEIRLOOM BEARS

·JULIA JONES·

BROCKHAMPTON PRESS
LONDON

This edition published 1999 by Brockhampton Press,
a member of Hodder Headline PLC. Group

ISBN 1-86019-196-7

For Charlotte Brandrick and her brother George

First published in Great Britain in 1994 by Anaya Publishers Ltd,
Strode House, 44-50 Osnaburgh Street, London NW1 3ND

Text and designs © Julia Jones 1994
Illustrations © Anaya Publishers Ltd 1994
All photography © Anaya Publishers Ltd 1994
except for those listed on page 112

Designer: Clare Clements
Photographer: Jon Stewart
Front cover picture: Tim Hill
Stylist: Barbara Stewart
Artwork: Anthony Duke

British Library Cataloguing in Publication Data
Jones, Julia
Classic Bears: How to make 14 Heirloom Bears
I. Title
745.592

Typeset in Great Britain by Litho Link Ltd, Welshpool, Powys
Colour reproduction by J. Film Process, Singapore
Printed at Oriental Press, Dubai, U.A.E.

Page 1: A rare Steiff teddy bear circa 1906.
Page 2 (opposite title page): Julia Jones' 1920s German Bear.
See pages 48 to 53 for instructions.
Page 3 (title page): Julia Jones' American Bear.
See pages 82 to 87 for instructions.

CONTENTS

INTRODUCTION

The earliest advertisement for teddy bears appeared in 1909. The Christmas novelty gift offered by Morrells of Oxford Street, London, that year was 'Old Mistress Teddy that lived in a shoe', together with twelve baby bears, a sledge, ladder and even some bottles and bowls, all packaged together in a large crimson shoe.

The wonderful, lovable, loyal and friendly teddy bear is probably one of the most enduring treasures of childhood. Even most adults would not be embarrassed to admit their secret fondness for an old, worn bear. Ever since teddy bears gained popularity in the early part of the century, they have appeared as mascots and talismans; going into battle with their owners, facing the stresses of examinations and featuring in countless songs, books and verse.

The teddy bear came into the world in 1903. Since its conception it has been made in all shapes, sizes and colours with numerous expressions and capable of a wide range of actions.

This book looks at the classic bear and how it has evolved over the years. On the following pages, bears reminiscent of early examples can be made using modern materials and traditional methods. No complex needlework skills are necessary to produce wonderful collectors' bears, just straightforward sewing techniques.

DEFINING A CLASSIC BEAR

A classic bear has well-defined characteristics. It has slightly curved paws, which taper at the ends. Its feet are long in relation to its overall height; to the purist this ratio is set at 5:1. High quality felt or velvet oval or triangular pads complete the feet. It either has no claws or ones stitched in black wool or cotton thread. Its head is rather small and triangular – it may or may not have a central gusset – with a long, pointed muzzle. Its head and limbs are invariably attached to its body with hardboard or cardboard discs and split pins. Black boot button eyes are the hallmark of a traditional bear, with a nose and mouth either embroidered with black thread or conveyed by an oval of black leather.

TEDDY BEAR HISTORY

Although there are numerous stories surrounding the birth of the bear, it is probably accurate to attribute the lovable teddy to two simultaneous sources: America and Germany.

The American tale is perhaps the most entertaining, although not strictly documented. Certainly, a Russian immigrant shopkeeper, Morris Michtom, conceived the idea for a cuddly bear after seeing the now famous cartoon of President Roosevelt refusing to shoot a tethered bear cub. As Michtom's wife was a skilled toymaker, she set about creating what we now refer to as a Michtom teddy (see page 36).

The legend runs that the enterprising Michtom sent one of her bears to the president with the request to name the bear 'teddy' after Roosevelt's first name, Theodore. The President allegedly consented and 'Teddy's bear' was born.

Meanwhile, in Germany a young seamstress had begun to make soft toys. The girl was Margarete Steiff and so popular were her designs that by the close of the 19th century, she had become firmly established as a leading toymaker. It was her nephew Richard who brought the idea

A rare Steiff teddy bear made circa 1903.

of a soft toy bear to Margarete's attention. Looking for a boy's alternative to the doll, Richard thought a bear might be the answer. After various modifications and some setbacks, the Steiff factory produced 'Friend Petz' in time for the Leipzig Toy Fair of 1903.

Evidently no one seemed interested in little Friend Petz until the last day of the Fair. Hermann Berg, an American buyer for a New York company, approached the Steiffs, complaining that there was little new or interesting that year. Richard showed him the small bear and it is said that he was so delighted he placed an order for 3,000.

And so the teddy bear had arrived. The new toy had such an impact that suppliers just could not keep up with demand. By the 1920s, and despite the interruption of World War I, firms in Britain had sprung up to manufacture these creatures. While US bears stayed more or less at home, German bears were exported around the world.

The shape of bears has evolved gradually over the years and makers have experimented with different colours, shapes and fabrics. The modern bear has mostly lost its jointed limbs and hump, and its body and face is rounder, but the basic appeal remains the same.

COLLECTING BEARS

Today, old bears have become most collectable and many are quite valuable. The main factors governing the price of a bear are its condition, quality, rarity value and desirability. In older bears look for the soft colours of old mohair (black being the exception), straw or wood wool stuffing and wooden boot button eyes which should be deeply set. The body should display a well-defined hump. As early bears were designed to stand on all fours, they should have long arms, extending half way down their legs.

Personal preferences for bears vary considerably from collector to collector. Only you can decide the style and decade which appeals most, but always beware of impulse buys. Check the facts before making a decision and determining a fair price. But when the choice has been made, make the most of the bear you have the privilege of owning!

MAKING BEARS

There is now a growing interest worldwide, not only for collecting bears but also making them in the traditional manner. On the following pages, you will find 14 bears – all with full patterns and clear instructions.

Even complete beginners will achieve remarkable success with their first bear by following the step-by-step instructions closely, while experienced bear-makers will find the useful tips contained throughout this book a stimulus to their creativity.

There is also scope to vary each bear, so that a tremendous range and variety of styles can be achieved, needing only a little imagination and confidence. Once the basic steps have been mastered, the desire to experiment will naturally develop. Making any bear and watching its personality develop as you work is rewarding and great fun.

However, when first making a particular bear, it is best to use the recommended fabric. Bears made up in different fabrics or colours will look quite unlike the ones illustrated. For the more experienced this can be one of the delights of making your own Classic Bears!

The classic bears in this book are not designed as toys for small children. If, however, one of them is to be made for a small child, it must conform to all toy safety standards.

Manufacturers were quick to realize the marketing potential of the endearing 'teddy' bear and over the years its form has appeared in the trademarks of many companies. Teddies have been used to promote all manner of produce, as widely diverse as ladies' hosiery, balloons and coal!

MATERIALS
AND EQUIPMENT

Occasionally a nose moulded from leather or gutta-percha (a natural resin exuded from various Malaysian trees) can be found on a classic collectors' bear.

Classic bears have always been made from natural materials such as wool, mohair, angora and cashmere, with fillings of wood wool or straw. The eyes were almost always fashioned from black wooden boot buttons, though occasionally beads or metal discs were used. Most paw and foot pads were made from good quality felt. Other features, such as mouths and claws where included, were embroidered with simple stitches such as straight stitch, using cotton or wool embroidery threads.

During the world wars some resourceful people, faced with limited supplies of material, resorted to using sheepskin and surviving examples have a very unusual and distinctive look. A small number of early bears, with a somewhat unappealing appearance, were manufactured from 'burlap', a fabric coarsely woven from jute. This gave a hairless and slightly abrasive feel to a creature primarily designed to be cuddled.

In this section, the more recognizable and ubiquitous materials are described, together with the essential tools, equipment, materials and fittings required to make authentic collectors' bears today.

TOOLS AND EQUIPMENT

The following are all the simple tools and equipment you will need when making a classic bear using the techniques described in the section called Classic Bear-making. They are listed in the order in which they will be required.

Never use ballpoint pens when marking templates of pattern pieces, as they will leave a mark which may be transferred accidentally to the right side of the fabric and will be impossible to remove.

Graph paper The pattern pieces on grids in this book are designed to be transferred to graph paper (or pattern paper) with 1in (2.5cm) squares. Should you wish to reduce or enlarge the size of a bear, you can use smaller or larger sized squared paper.

Tracing paper Ideally use a heavy-weight tracing paper for transferring the pattern outlines when making templates. Do not be tempted to economise by buying a lighter weight tracing paper as this may distort slightly or tear during use.

Pencils A selection of hard and soft lead pencils are needed for making the pattern-piece templates and also for marking fabric. In many cases, a soft lead pencil will seem the most suitable choice for marking fabrics.

A French curve This is a flexible plastic rod which may be helpful in joining the marks smoothly when drawing pattern-piece shapes on graph paper.

When marking dark fabrics for bear-making, coloured pencils or chalk can be used.

Masking tape Masking tape is used to hold the tracing paper in position while the outlines are transferred to the templates.

Non-smudge ink pen When marking templates with a pen, it is essential to use one that will not smudge.

Card Thin white modelling card or cardboard is needed for making semi-permanent templates which can be used many times. Any type of lightweight card can be used, provided it is clean and fairly stiff.

Craft scissors Short round-ended scissors are needed for cutting paper and card or cardboard.

Tailor's chalk and dressmaker's marker pens Both tailor's chalk and dressmaker's marker pens are useful when marking fabric around the templates. Tailor's chalk is most suitable for dark fabrics and it will brush out easily after use. Dressmaker's marker pens are also used to label and mark fabric pieces. Usually pale blue in colour, they work well on most fabrics, but the manufacturer's instructions must be carefully followed to avoid leaving stains on some fabrics.

Dressmaking scissors Dressmaking scissors are used for cutting fur fabric, suedette, leather and, indeed, all other bear-making fabrics. Ideally, these should be 7–8in (18–21cm) long and have offset handles.

Embroidery scissors Fine-bladed, sharp embroidery scissors are useful for cutting around small pattern pieces, negotiating sharp angles and for all embroidery work.

Pins Long slim dressmaker's pins are required to hold seams together before tacking (basting). As an extra safety precaution, coloured glass-headed pins can be used. Either way, do count the number of pins used as you work and be sure to remove them all as soon as possible.

Sewing machine and needles Although it is perfectly possible to make any of the bears in this book without the aid of a sewing machine, it is assumed that most readers will have access to one and instructions are written accordingly. A ball-point or sharp sewing-machine needle can be used for fur fabrics, velvet and velveteens; and a wedge point for leather or suede. The machine needle size depends on the fabric thickness and a size 14 to 16 will suit most fabrics. A heavy-weight leather or suede will require a size 16 to 18.

Needles A variety of needles will be necessary for the various hand-sewing and embroidery techniques used to make a classic bear. Besides the obvious choice of sharps and embroidery needles for general work, it is necessary to use a 3in (7.5cm) darning needle which is slim enough not to snag or distort the fabric when inserting eyes. A toymaker's or packing needle is useful for ladder stitching openings after stuffing. Alternatively, a fine curved upholstery needle will serve equally well.

Seam ripper A seam ripper is useful for unpicking seams quickly to undo errors, but great care must be used not to tear or cut the fabric.

Fine crochet hook or bodkin Either a fine crochet hook or a bodkin can be used for teasing out pile trapped in machine-stitched seams. A knitting needle could also be used, but it is likely to bend during use.

Stiletto or awl A stiletto (or awl) is used for making holes in fur fabric or card templates. However, if this is not available, a fine knitting needle can be used instead.

A stuffing stick A strong stick is necessary to ensure that any filling medium can be tightly packed into even the smallest corners. A cheap alternative to a custom-made stuffing stick can be made from an 8in (20cm) length of ⅜in (1cm) dowelling, smoothly sanded before use. Stuffing sticks can also be used to assist in the turning of small limbs and the pushing out of noses and feet. Orange (manicure) sticks are useful when working on tiny bears.

Tape measure A tape measure is needed for measuring the positions for eyes, ears and nose.

Do not be tempted to cut paper with dressmaking or embroidery scissors, as this will quickly blunt their blades.

'T' pins are useful for holding bear ears in position before stitching.

Any hand-stitched seams in bear-making must be very accurately and firmly worked to withstand the pressure exerted during the stuffing process.

The handle of a wooden spoon or a chopstick could be used as stuffing stick in bear-making.

Pliers are useful for flattening the wire on the back of some glass eyes, to aid their insertion through the fabric.

If any of the bears in this book is to be made for a child, it is essential that a suitable, non-flammable fabric is used.

As synthetic fur fabrics are much cheaper than natural fur fabrics, it may be wise for a beginner to practise with these first.

The mohair plush originally used by all German makers in the manufacture of their bears is believed to have been woven exclusively in Yorkshire, England.

Pliers Long-nosed pliers are essential for bending split pins when assembling crown joints and for pulling through a needle when extra purchase is required.

Wire cutters These are used for cutting the joining wire found on some glass eyes and for cutting through wrongly assembled joints in order to release them.

Teasel brush A teasel or soft bristle nail brush is useful to help ease trapped strands from machine-stitched seams or to fluff up the pile on a finished bear. On crushed mohair it is better to use a soft nail brush, rather than the wire teasel type, as this will not disturb the distinctive antique appearance of the fabric.

FABRICS AND THREADS

There are many types of fabric to choose from, both traditional and modern, and these can vary enormously in price and quality. The work entailed when making a classic bear demands that you use the best possible material, to produce an heirloom. Fur fabrics are either woven or knitted and the materials used for the pile may be synthetic or natural. Obviously, the choice for a classic bear would be for a natural and traditional material such as mohair, wool or cashmere.

Plush The word 'plush' is a term often applied to fur fabrics. This simply means that the fabric has a nap which is softer and longer than velvet. Plush is usually manufactured from silk, cotton or wool and will produce an authentic and lovable bear.

Synthetic furs Synthetic furs are usually produced with a knitted backing, which is not ideally suited to the production of a collectors' bear. Knitted fabrics do not withstand stress and are inclined to give and pull out of shape during stuffing, whereas natural fibres such as mohair, alpaca, silk and wool have a woven backing that will withstand pressure, resulting in a better quality and firmer bear.

The pile length of each type of fabric can vary considerably, as does its quality and softness, and these factors will also determine the look of your finished bear.

Two of the bears in this book – the 1950s British Bear and the 1940s American Bear have been made with man-made fabrics. Although both bears can, of course, also be made up using an alternative, natural fabric for a more traditional appeal. If you have never made a soft toy before, use a good quality synthetic fabric and follow the step-by-step classic bear instructions carefully to produce results that should be very satisfying. Keep in mind the possibility of stretching, however, when the stuffing stage is reached.

Non-pile fabrics The patterns in this book can be also used for a modern approach to bear-making, using techniques such as quilting or patchwork and fabrics such as silk, cotton or linen. A good-quality German felt can also be used to produce a hairless bear, but in this case avoid any pattern with a very thin body, arms or legs, as the bear's thinness will be accentuated by its lack of fur!

Mohair pile fabrics Classic teddies were and still are, in general, made from mohair fabric. This is obtained from the coat of the Angora goat, which is woven into soft luxurious fabric. The process of making mohair fabrics for bears can take as long as six weeks and this explains their relatively high cost. A mohair substitute, made from a mixture of wool and cotton, is obtainable.

Fur fabric widths Fur fabric is generally woven in widths of 54in (137cm) and a 16in (41cm) bear would require ½yd (45cm) of this. If you intend to make several bears, it is possible, by careful placing of the pattern pieces, to economise on fabric, cutting several from 1yd (91cm). Different widths of fabric will, of course, need differing lengths. If in doubt, cut a sheet of paper to the required width and arrange the templates on this, measuring the depth of fabric required to cut them all satisfactorily.

Felt Traditional bears always had felt paw and foot pads, usually of beige, black or cream. Felt is easily and quickly cut and has no pile or right and wrong side. Consequently, pattern pieces can be fitted jigsaw-like onto the fabric resulting in very little waste.

To the right are some fur fabrics currently available for classic bear-making. Also shown are fabrics used for pads, such as felt and suedette.

The felt used for classic bear paws should always be the best quality. Today the best felt is manufactured in Germany.

Velveteens and Velvets Velveteen was used for paws and pads for many bears in the period from 1910 to 1940. It is a cotton pile fabric, similar in appearance to velvet, but with a much shorter nap or pile. Because velveteen is harder to find today, velvet is often used in its place on classic bears.

Suede and leather Ovals for noses, paw and foot pads can be cut from suede or leather. The most usual colours are light beige, brown or black. Old, worn gloves can be successfully recycled for this purpose. Suede could be used for any of the bear pads in this book.

Suedette This fabric is manufactured to resemble suede. It can be purchased in a variety of colours and is extremely easy to cut and sew.

Threads All-purpose sewing thread (no. 30) of the same colour as the fabric is required for machine stitching classic bears. In addition, a heavy-duty or buttonhole thread is required for some sewing jobs such as attaching the eyes and ears securely; or for machine stitching large bears, or heavy-weight leather or suede. Cotton or wool embroidery threads are the most suitable choices for embroidering features.

BEAR FILLING OR STUFFING

Wood wool was traditionally used for the heirloom bears and most modern collectors' bears are still stuffed with it. Occasionally referred to as 'Excelsior', wood wool is made of long, thin fine-quality wood shavings. Kapok, sometimes called 'silk cotton', took over from wood wool as the most popular medium for stuffing toys from the 1940s until the advent of man-made fibres.

Kapok This is a natural material similar to cotton, and is formed from the short fibres which surround the seeds of a tropical tree. If you are stuffing a large bear with kapok remember that it is relatively heavy, and it may be advisable to combine kapok, with some other medium. Asthma sufferers are advised to wear a mask when using kapok, as the fine strands and dust can prove irritating.

Sheep's wool This can be collected from hedges and barbed wire fences or bought in a fleece. With careful washing it will make a wonderful filling material and can be teased out gently to fill tiny corners. As it is possible to contract a skin complaint from unwashed sheep's wool, it is advisable to wear rubber gloves while collecting and washing. Do make sure that wool prepared at home is thoroughly dry before use.

Wood wool This can be ordered from specialist suppliers (see page 112) and will usually be packaged in a polythene bag or sack. As soon as it is delivered, it should be emptied into a large cardboard box or wooden tea chest, as storage in polythene may cause dampness and rotting.

Wood wool is sold in a semi-compressed state and the blocks should be lightly teased out to their full volume just before use. Check carefully and remove any large wood shavings, before beginning to stuff a bear.

For a smooth finish paws, feet and muzzles should be stuffed with a small amount of synthetic filling to give a softer feel, before completing the stuffing using wood wool.

Man-made fibres A variety of man-made fibres are available for soft toy making – the most commonly used is polyester or terylene (Dacron). When purchasing it is essential to specify whether a soft or firm fill is required for the bear in question. Terylene produces a loose, open and

Embroidery threads such as stranded cotton (floss) or pearl cotton are often used for embroidering the features on contemporary collectors' teddy bears.

Turn to page 112 for a list of specialist suppliers who sell classic bear fabrics, fittings, and filling or stuffing.

When buying any filling or stuffing sold for soft toys, always read the labelling on the packaging so that you are aware of the safety standard information.

fairly resilient stuffing medium, while polyester has less crimp and will need slightly more to produce the same results.

Foam rubber Never be tempted to use the brightly coloured pieces of foam rubber sold in some stores as a suitable medium for stuffing good quality toys. Although it has the advantage of being cheap, readily available and hygienic, it also has a nasty habit of sticking to the inside of the fabric and will make the finished bear very heavy and shapeless.

BEAR FITTINGS

The fittings used for classic bears – such as eyes, joints and growlers – can be purchased from specialist suppliers (see page 112). Remember that the bear instructions in this book are for traditional collectors' bears which are not suitable for small children. If you intend to make toys for children, strict safety regulations must be adhered to and only fittings which comply with these regulations can be used.

Eyes Following tradition, all classic bears made for the collector's market are fitted with boot button or glass eyes. A careful search through boxes of odds and ends at antique and bric-à-brac fairs will sometimes be rewarded by discovering wooden boot button eyes. Failing that, specialist suppliers sell reproduction boot button eyes in sizes ranging from ¼in (7mm) to ⅝in (16mm).

Safety eyes, made of plastic, can be found in handicraft shops or mail order catalogues. They range in size from ⅜in (9 mm) to 1¼in (45mm) and are made in various colours, including amber, brown and black. It is possible to purchase a special tool to help to exert pressure when assembling safety eyes. It is not essential, however, as an empty sewing cotton spool can be employed in much the same manner.

Joints Most classic bears are assembled using crown joints. These come in different sizes. Bears made for children must be fitted with the correct safety-locking plastic joints.

Growler boxes This can be fitted to most bears to provide a voice. A growler is made from a cylindrical cardboard container with holes at one end like a pepper pot. It has a weight inside which, when the bear is tipped backwards, presses on a small bellows, forcing air through its reed to produce a sound similar to a short growl. These teddy bear 'voices' were introduced in 1908, but were later replaced with cheaper, mass produced 'squeakers'.

It is wise to purchase a growler from a specialist bear supplier. Otherwise, do listen to its sound carefully – you may find that your bear sounds more like a cow or a duck!

Squeakers A squeaker comprises a small bellows, which, when pressed, forces air through a reed, emitting a high-pitched note.

Tinklers A tinkler is a simple device made from a cardboard cylinder containing steel pins of various lengths. A weight is suspended from one end and when the cylinder is rolled, this hits the pins, making a soft tinkling sound.

Musical boxes Musical boxes were first included in bears during the 1920s, when, understandably, the tune 'Teddy Bears' Picnic', was a popular choice. Today, musical boxes suitable for insertion in soft toys are enclosed in a small tin and have a key for winding which is fitted to a screw. (See page 27 for inserting a musical box in a teddy bear.)

Never use any fittings either outside or inside a teddy bear that is to be given to a child unless these fittings comply with toy safety regulations.

Growlers, tinklers and musical boxes can only be inserted into bears big enough to accommodate them. Bears containing any of these items should be well stuffed with wood wool.

CLASSIC BEAR-MAKING

The traditional techniques for making classic bears are outlined here in these detailed step-by-step instructions. Before making any of the bears featured in this book, you will need to read this chapter. Where a bear has a special feature not included in these general directions, the necessary techniques are outlined in the individual instructions.

PREPARING THE TEMPLATES

The first stage in the process of bear-making is preparing the pattern-piece templates. The pattern pieces for most of the bears in this book have been drawn on a grid with squares representing 1in (2.5cm). These pieces must be transferred onto graph paper with 1in (2.5cm) squares, then onto tracing paper and finally onto the thin, stiff template card or cardboard. To make a bigger or smaller bear than the recommended one, a graph paper with different sized squares can be used. The pattern pieces can also be reduced or enlarged on a photocopier.

The pattern pieces for the Miniature Bear and the 1980s Bear are given actual size (see pages 54 and 100).

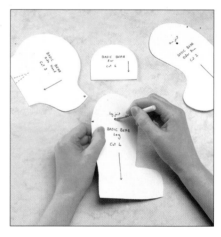

1 To transfer the pattern shapes to graph paper, first note where each curved line crosses the sides of a square. Make a light mark at these points on the graph paper before drawing in the finished curves. An artist's flexible plastic rod may be helpful in joining the marks smoothly. When all the shapes have been transferred to graph paper, transfer all pattern markings, labels and, most importantly, the name of the bear.

2 Trace each pattern shape onto tracing paper, using a soft lead pencil and a firm hand. Transfer all pattern markings in the same way. Turn over the tracing paper and lay it over a piece of card or cardboard, securing it with masking tape. Using a hard lead pencil, go over the traced outlines and markings, thus transferring them to the card. Repeat this process for each pattern shape, fitting the pieces closely together.

3 Set aside the tracing paper and, using a fine non-smudge pen, reinforce the traced lines and markings on all of the templates. Still using the pen, insert all remaining labels. Then cut out each template, using craft scissors. Cut smoothly and accurately, as the quality of the templates will affect the quality of your bear. Using a stiletto, push holes through templates at all dart points and at the positions for arm and leg joints.

TRANSFERRING PATTERN SHAPES TO FUR FABRIC

Before beginning to outline the pattern shapes onto your fur fabric, first check that you have the required number of templates. (You will notice that your templates are mirror images of the shapes in the book because the tracing paper was turned over to transfer the pieces to the template cardboard.)

The type of fabric from which each pattern piece is to be cut is clearly marked on each piece. How many pieces to cut from a template and whether to reverse a piece (for a right and left side) is also indicated. All this should be checked carefully after the pieces have been drawn, but before cutting, paying attention to the direction of the pile.

The minimum amount of fabric required for each bear is given in the Materials list accompanying each set of instructions. If more material has to be purchased than is necessary to cut a particular bear, it may be possible, by careful arrangement of the pattern pieces, to cut a second smaller bear from the surplus. In any event, do not throw the remnants and scraps away. These can be stored, for future use.

It may be necessary to try various layouts to achieve the most economical use of fabric, but experience will quickly make this apparent. It is not possible, as with dress patterns, to work on folded fabric, cutting two pieces at a time. You must therefore remember to reverse the template in order to form 'pairs' of pattern pieces where necessary.

Most of the patterns in this book require two body sections, two side head sections, one head gusset, as well as two inner arms, two outer arms, two inner legs, two outer legs, two paw pads and two foot pads. The paw and foot pad pieces will be cut from suedette, leather, velvet or felt as instructed.

Do not use a ballpoint pen to mark any fabric. It may smudge and would undoubtedly stain the material, which could spoil the finished bear. Note that all seam allowances are included in the templates.

Using templates (instead of paper patterns) allows for more accurate bear-making. Templates can also be re-used many times.

When fur fabric or velvet is stroked, the pile or 'nap' lies smoothly or it ruffles, depending on the direction in which it lies. The pile on a bear should always run downwards from head to toe, except on the top of the muzzle and the ears. If in any doubt check the direction in which the fur runs on a dog or cat!

1 First spread the fur fabric out on a large flat surface (such as a table or a clean floor), face up. Check the direction of the nap or pile by stroking the fur flat, noting the direction it runs.

2 Turn the fur fabric face down, so that the pile of the fur runs towards you. Then carefully draw a few large arrows showing the direction of the fur pile, using tailor's chalk.

3 Arrange the templates on the fabric, being sure to match the directional arrows to the direction of the pile. Pattern pieces should always be cut on a single layer of fur fabric.

4 When you have decided on the layout, you can begin tracing the shapes. Carefully holding each template firmly in place with one hand, draw around the edge of each template, using tailor's chalk, a marker pen or a soft lead pencil.

5 Transfer onto the fabric all markings for openings, arm and leg joint positions, dart points, seam labels and any notches. Then label each piece with the part name, e.g. 'inner arm', 'leg', 'head gusset', 'paw pad', 'body', etc.

6 Prepare remaining pieces in the same way, reversing templates where necessary so that there is a 'right' and 'left' side of head or an 'inner' and 'outer' arm, etc. After completion, check that you have the correct number of cut pieces.

CUTTING FABRICS

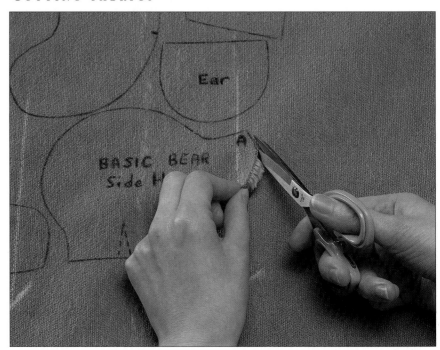

Remember that the seam allowances are already included inside the pattern-piece outlines.

When absolutely sure that the pattern pieces are drawn correctly, lay the fabric right side down on a firm surface. Then using sharp, pointed dressmaking scissors, push the point through the fabric and carefully cut out each drawn shape. Rather than cutting through both the fabric and the fur pile, try to cut only the ground fabric, leaving the fur to be teased apart. On small or complex shapes, it may be easier to use sharp, embroidery scissors.

As each piece is cut, check that it is correctly labelled and that all necessary instructions have been transferred. As you work, place all the cut pieces in a clean self-seal plastic bag or a paper bag, keeping identical pieces together.

Your bear's velvet, suedette or leather foot and paw pads should be traced onto the wrong side of the fabric in the same way as the pattern pieces were transferred to the fur, taking the direction of the nap into account in the case of the velvet. Felt has no right and wrong side and the shapes can be transferred to either side of felt.

Using small, sharp scissors, cut very carefully around each paw and foot pad shape being sure to keep closely to the outlines.

It may be advisable, when using especially soft fabrics, to cut paw and foot pads out again in a medium weight interfacing, which can then be tacked (basted) to the outer fabric to give additional body.

SEWING THE PATTERN PIECES

As fur fabric has a habit of 'slipping', all pattern pieces should be pinned together first before tacking (basting), using long slim pins placed at right angles to the seams. After careful pinning, the pieces should be tacked (basted), using long running stitches. It is helpful to tuck the pile inwards between the two edges of fabric while tacking (basting).

If the pattern pieces do not fit exactly, use pins and tacking (basting) stitches to ease the longer edge gently before machine stitching. The dense pile of fur fabric can, fortunately, be used to cover a number of minor mishaps! This does not mean, however, that anything but the greatest care should be taken when stitching, as the ultimate character of your bear will be affected by your attention to detail.

When machine stitching, added strength can be given to a seam by turning the fabric and running a second row of stitches back along the original seamline. To secure the thread ends, always backstitch at the beginning and end of a machine-stitched seam.

All seam allowances are ¼in (7mm) on bears unless otherwise stated. References to the seamline apply to an imaginary line at this distance from the cutting edge.

In the instructions given for each bear, the word 'stitch' means pin, then tack (baste) and then machine stitch, unless the instructions state otherwise.

After each seam has been machine stitched, any pile trapped in the seams should be gently teased out using a bodkin or stiletto. (See also 'teasel brush' on page 10.)

Running stitch is the simplest of the hand-stitching techniques used in bear-making. It is used for tacking (basting) and for stay stitching along some fur-fabric edges before the seams are machine stitched.

Ladder stitch is used for closing openings after stuffing. It is worked by taking a tiny stitch alternately on each side of the seam. After every few stitches the thread should be pulled firmly to close the seam.

Oversewing (overcast stitches) can be used along the raw edges of fabrics that are likely to fray. Never use oversewing stitches to close openings as they will form an ugly ridge, in which the stitches will show.

STITCHING THE BEAR'S HEAD

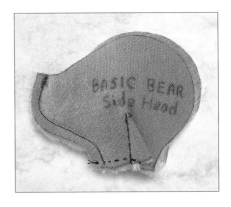

1 Some bear heads do not have shaping darts, but if there are any they may be stitched first before joining head pieces. Fold together the dart gusset of each side head section and pin. Tack (baste) outside the dart line from the tip of the dart to the fabric edge. Machine stitch the dart. Remove tacking (basting).

2 Do not slash darts, but press them down firmly (away from the muzzle) using a thumb and forefinger (index finger). Using heavy-duty thread, knotted and doubled, stay stitch along the lower neck edge with short, even running stitches. This will prevent the raw edge from stretching out of shape.

3 Place the side head sections right sides together and pin and tack (baste) the lower muzzle seam which goes from the tip of the nose to the neck. Machine stitch this seam, remembering to always start and finish each seam with a few backstitches. Remove tacking (basting) stitches.

4 If any darts appear on the head gusset pattern piece, stitch these in the manner described in Step 1. Using heavy-duty thread, stay stitch along the seamline on both long edges of the gusset. The fitting of the head gusset is critical for the finished head shape. Great care should be taken to make sure that the gusset does not stretch out of shape. (As you join the gusset, it may be helpful to turn the head right side out occasionally to check the balance and shape of the muzzle and head.)

5 Pin the head gusset to one side of the head, easing to fit where necessary. Make sure that the centre notch on the nose tip of the gusset is lined up accurately with the centre of the lower muzzle seam. When you are entirely satisfied with the fit and shape of the seam, tack (baste) the gusset and the side of the head together just inside the seamline, using small running stitches. The seam may need to taper towards the nose tip. Join on the second side of the head in the same way.

6 When completely satisfied with the easing and shaping of these seams, machine stitch from the point of the nose to the back neck edge on each side of the gusset, starting the machine stitching as close as possible to the muzzle seam on each side of the nose notch. Remove the tacking (basting) stitches and trim the seams around the nose to ⅛in (3mm) to ensure a smooth muzzle. (Be careful when trimming not to cut the seam.) Set the head section aside for stuffing later.

STITCHING THE BEAR'S BODY

1 The bear body-shapes vary, and some have an upper and lower dart on each of the two body sections. Before joining the body pieces, stay stitch along the seamline of the back opening on each of the two pieces, using heavy-duty thread and small running stitches. Place the body sections right sides together, matching any notches. If there are no darts, simply pin, tack (baste) and machine stitch body pieces together, leaving an opening for stuffing (above left). If there are body darts (above right), pin from the edges of the upper dart around to the edges of the lower dart. Tack (baste), then machine stitch centre front seam and centre back seam, each from dart to dart; leaving opening for stuffing. Remove tacking (basting).

Some bears have four body sections. In these cases, the side seams should be joined first to create a left and right body section. The general instructions can then be followed to complete the body.

2 To complete a body with darts, flatten the top body section across the seamline, placing the top dart edges together. Pin and tack (baste) this dart from the farthest point to the seam edge. Remove the pins and machine, again starting from its farther point to the seam edge. Then remove tacking (basting) stitches. The tiny space left where the four seams meet will provide the hole for the bear's head joint.

3 Flatten the dart seam towards the back of the body, using the pressure from the thumb and forefinger (index finger). Do not be tempted to slash or cut these darts as this may seriously weaken the fabric. Pin, tack (baste) and machine stitch the dart at the lower body edge in the same way. As there are no joints to be attached here, try to make all machine stitching lines coincide as closely as possible. Set body aside for stuffing later.

Most of the bears have seam allowances of ¼in (7mm). Check individual instructions for seam allowances for the two smallest bears (pages 54 and 100).

19

ATTACHING PAW PAD TO INNER ARM

Unless great care is exercised, a smooth fabric such as suedette tends to slide across the surface of a fur fabric during the pinning and tacking (basting) processes.

1 Take an inner arm and a paw pad section and, with the right sides together, pin and tack (baste) along this seamline. Machine stitch and remove tacking (basting) stitches. Trim the seam close to the machine stitching and press the seam upwards towards the top of the arm, using the thumb and forefinger (index finger).

2 Tease the pile from the seamline using a bodkin or stiletto and brush the fur lightly. If using a teasel brush, avoid scratching or pulling the fabric of the paw. This is particularly important when using suede, leather or felt. (Only use a teasel brush if instructed.) Join the second inner arm and paw pad sections in the same way.

STITCHING THE BEAR'S ARMS

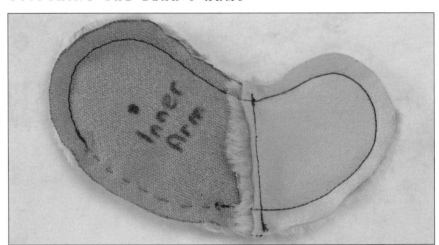

The finished seam between the paw pad and the arm should face upwards towards the top of the arm to prevent it showing through on the smooth surface of the paw.

Stay stitch the stuffing opening along the seamline on both the inner and outer arms. Place a front and back arm section right sides together, ensuring that the seamline of the paw is pressed upwards. Pin and tack (baste) all around the arm, leaving the stay-stitched edge open. Starting from the edge of the stuffing opening, machine stitch around the arm, paying particular attention to the paw seams. Trim the seams where necessary and turn the arm right side out. Tease any trapped pile from the seamline. Make the second arm in the same way and set both arms aside for stuffing later.

STITCHING THE BEAR'S LEGS

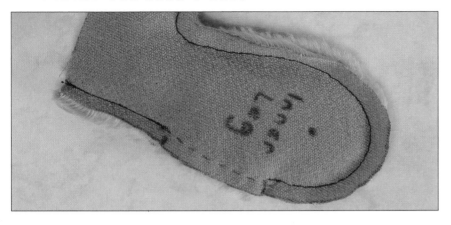

Stay stitch along the seamline of the stuffing opening on the inner and outer leg sections. Place these right sides together, and pin carefully, taking care to align each lower straight edge of the foot correctly. Tack (baste), then machine along the seamline around the leg section, leaving the lower edge and stuffing opening unstitched. Remove the tacking (basting) stitches. Turn the leg right side out and pull any trapped pile from the seamlines. Turn the leg inside out once more.

ATTACHING THE BEAR'S FOOT PADS

1 Place a foot pad within the oval formed by the lower straight edge of the foot, lining up the front and back notches with the front and back seamlines. Pin the pad in position. It may be necessary to stretch the fur fabric slightly to take in the curve of the oval smoothly. Using very small running stitches, tack (baste) around the pad, trying to maintain its oval shape as far as possible. Tack (baste) each side of the foot separately, starting and ending at a seamline and leaving seam free.

2 Remove the pins and turn the leg right side out to check that the pad is correctly placed. When you are completely satisfied, turn the leg inside out and machine stitch the pad, again working each side of the foot separately and ending and starting stitching as close as possible to the seamlines. Remove the tacking (basting) stitches, turn the leg right side out and brush out the pile on all the seams. Make the second leg in the same way and set both legs aside for stuffing later.

Before machine stitching, all stuffing openings on the bear pattern pieces are stay stitched using a heavy-duty sewing thread.

The foot-pad seam is worked in two sections on either side of the leg seams to avoid having to stitch through two thicknesses of fur fabric. The foot-pad seam allowance is tapered as it approaches the leg seams.

When positioning the bear's eyes, the aim is to achieve a pleasing symmetry and an endearing expression.

If the special 'eye tool' for inserting safety eyes is not available, a sturdy wooden sewing thread reel (spool) can be placed over the shank behind the washer to give extra purchase.

Polyester filling, or stuffing, is used in conjunction with traditional wood wool to achieve a smoother finish on your collectors' bear.

BEAR EYES

Both plastic teddy-bear safety eyes and traditional glass or boot button eyes come in various sizes. Altering the size and position of the eyes will greatly alter the expression of the finished bear. For instance, large eyes will give a bright, wide-awake look to your bear. By careful positioning these can be made to give the impression of slight surprise. Whatever the size of the eyes, try out various positions before deciding, then mark the centre position of each eye using a glass-headed pin.

Glass and boot button eyes are inserted after the head has been stuffed (see opposite page), but safety eyes are inserted before the head is stuffed. For inserting safety eyes, turn the head right side out and make a tiny hole by easing the fabric threads aside with a stiletto or bodkin. Push the shank of the eye through to the wrong side. Then press down the securing washer over the shank as firmly as possible. It is possible to purchase a small strip of metal with two small holes, known as an 'eye tool' or 'flat safety tool' which will help to give additional pressure on the washer.

STUFFING THE BEAR'S HEAD

Begin by rolling a small amount of polyester filling between the palms of your hands to form a small ball. Then, using a stuffing stick, push the ball into the muzzle of the bear to begin to shape the nose section. Continue to fill the muzzle in this way, using your hands to mould and shape the bear from the outside. When the nose and muzzle are well shaped and firm, continue to stuff the head, using wood wool and working from the muzzle upwards, outwards and downwards. When sufficient filling has been added to the head, thread a darning needle with a doubled and knotted length of heavy-duty thread. Run this around the neck opening, using medium-length straight stitches. Do not fasten off the thread.

INSERTING THE NECK CROWN JOINT

1 Assemble the first part of the larger crown joint by threading a washer and one hardboard disc on to the split pin. (While inserting the crown joint in Step 2, check that there is sufficient stuffing behind it to hold it securely in position when the neck opening is closed.)

2 Push the head of the split pin, the washer and the hardboard disc into the neck opening of the bear's head. The joint should sit above the line of running stitches. Take up the needle and heavy-duty thread and draw up the running stitches quite tightly, to hold the joint firmly in place.

3 Take long stitches backwards and forwards through the fur fabric and across the joint around the split pin. Pull these stitches tightly and secure with a few stitches, before cutting the thread. Pull the split pin firmly to ensure that its head is sitting against the enclosed hardboard disc.

FIXING GLASS OR BOOT BUTTON EYES

1 Before fixing the bear's eyes, determine the exact positions of eyes and ears. Thread a long darning needle or bodkin with a long, doubled length of heavy-duty thread, knotting this several times at the end. Take the needle through the head from the position of the left ear seamline to the position of the left eye, bringing the needle through the fabric and pulling the thread slightly to tighten the tension.

2 Using a stiletto, push aside the ground fabric warp and weft threads from around the needle thread, thus making a small hole through which the 'bail' or loop of the eye can be passed. Thread the first eye onto the needle and take it down the thread to push the 'bail' firmly through the fabric. Take the needle back through this hole and across the muzzle to surface at the position of the second eye.

3 Repeat the last step for the second eye, but finish by taking the needle through the head to the position of the seamline of the right ear. Tighten the thread to pull in both eyes, forming a slight depression in each to provide the eye socket. Anchor the thread firmly by making several small straight stitches in one place on the ear line and cut off the working thread close to the fabric.

STITCHING AND ATTACHING THE BEAR'S EARS

The ears are attached using oversewing (also called overcasting) stitches. Before stitching them in place, check that they are symmetrical and give the bear the right appearance.

Place two ear shapes right sides together. Pin, tack (baste) and machine stitch around the upper curve. Make the other ear in the same way and turn both right side out.

Then pin the back edge of each ear to the head. Using heavy-duty thread, stitch from the centre point of one ear to the outer edge, using small oversewing (overcast) stitches pulled tightly. At the outer edge, tuck in the seam edges and stitch them inside the ear line. Secure with a few stitches and cut the thread. Re-join the thread to the centre of the ear and work to the opposite edge in the same way. Turn under a tiny seam on the front edge of the ear and oversew this in position, working from the centre outwards each time. Repeat for the second ear.

PLACING THE NECK JOINT IN THE BODY

Each classic bear requires five crown joints. The four smallest are for the legs and arms and the largest, for the neck. The head is attached before the arms and legs.

1 Before the body is stuffed, the crown joints are fitted. Use a stiletto to ease aside the seam stitching gently at the centre top point of the body section. Insert the legs of the split pin through this hole and turn the top section of the body inside out.

2 Finish assembling the crown joint by threading on the second hardboard disc followed by a washer. Using sharp-nosed pliers, curl one pin over tightly, so that it sits against the washer and disc. Curl the second pin and check that the joint is firm.

STUFFING ARMS AND LEGS AND INSERTING CROWN JOINTS

1 Stuff both arms and legs to within 2in (5cm) of the joint mark. From inside push a stiletto through this joint mark, carefully easing apart the threads of the fabric. Make a hole large enough for the split pin to fit. Assemble the remaining joints, threading on a washer and a disc. Push these through the holes in the arms and legs.

2 Finish stuffing each limb, packing the filling behind and around each hardboard disc until the required shape and firmness is achieved. Using matching sewing thread, ladder stitch the stuffing openings firmly closed on both arms and both legs, pushing in extra filling with the stuffing stick or a knitting needle as required while stitching.

3 Using a stiletto as before, make holes and insert the split pins at the points marked for placing both arms and legs on the bear's body. Thread on the second hardboard disc followed by a washer. Then complete the crown joints as described in Step 2 for the neck joints (see opposite page), making sure that each joint is firm.

STUFFING AND CLOSING THE BEAR'S BODY

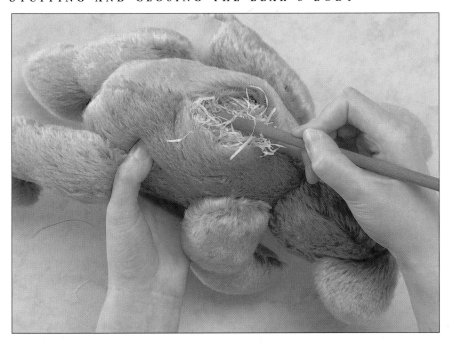

When all the joints are securely placed, stuff the body very firmly, pushing the stuffing down into position and shaping the bear as you work. (Before closing bear, see page 27 about growlers, squeakers, etc.) Ladder stitch the back opening of the bear closed, pulling the stitches firmly and fastening off securely.

The ladder stitching should not be visible on the surface of the bear.

TRIMMING THE BEAR'S MUZZLE

If it is called for in the individual bear instructions, trim the pile around the muzzle. Use fine embroidery scissors and cut a little at a time until the required effect is achieved. For a traditional look, the muzzle should be trimmed all around to the point where the face begins to spread and flatten out. If in doubt, proceed very slowly and carefully, checking from time to time that the balance is correct.

Great care should be taken when trimming any of the fur pile on your classic bear. Before beginning, test your trimming skills on a fur-fabric scrap or remnant.

EMBROIDERING THE BEAR'S FEATURES

1 Embroidering features is the last stage in the bear-making process. With embroidery thread, embroider the nose in the desired shape, using closely worked satin stitches. It may be necessary to use pliers to pull the needle through when embroidering over seamlines.

2 Using straight stitches and embroidery thread, embroider the mouth. Experience will show the style of mouth you prefer, to create the right expression for your classic bear. If in doubt, unpick the mouth stitches and try again until you are completely satisfied with the result.

Worked in satin stitch, the bear's nose is usually made in a rectangular shape, but other shapes include hearts, triangles and ovals.

GROWLERS

For the ultimate touch of nostalgia a growler could be inserted in your bear before the stuffing opening on the body is closed. Growlers are best fitted in bears filled with wood wool, which, when tightly packed, will support their weight.

To insert a growler box, cut a circle of calico of sufficient size to enclose the growler completely. Place the growler, hole-end down in the centre of the calico fabric, pulling up the edges and gathering these over the opposite end. Wrap heavy-duty thread around the ends of the fabric a few times and tie off securely.

Half-fill the body of the bear with wood wool, packing it tightly into the lower section. Insert the growler so that the flat side is against the centre back of the body. Using a darning needle and heavy-duty thread, stitch the calico neatly to the fur fabric with tiny stitches that should be invisible on the right side. Finish off firmly. Continue to stuff the bear with wood wool, making sure this is tightly packed around the growler. Close the opening in the usual way with ladder stitching (see page 25).

SQUEAKERS

Bears fitted with squeakers should be soft enough to press and should not be laundered. A squeaker should be wrapped in calico and placed inside the bear in a similar manner to a growler (see instructions above), making sure that the reed is facing outwards.

TINKLERS

A tinkler, like a growler or a squeaker, must be inserted in a teddy bear before the stuffing opening on the bear's body is closed. It should be placed right in the middle of the bear. The bear should be large and well stuffed with wood wool.

MUSICAL BOXES

Before a musical box can be inserted in a bear, a calico cover should be made for it. The cover should have a hole through which the screw can be pushed. The calico is then stitched to the back of the bear in a similar manner to a growler, with the screw facing the fur fabric. A stiletto can then be used to make a hole through which to push the screw before the key is replaced. As with other 'voices', the bear should be firmly stuffed with wood wool which will hold the movement rigidly in position.

When making collectors' bears always use the best quality bear fittings.

Below are shown (from left to right and interspersed with sewing equipment) wood wool, eyes, hardboard crown joints, a teasel brush, plastic squeakers, a growler box and a musical box.

BEAR CARE AND REPAIR

Both new and old classic bears should be looked after carefully in order to preserve them in the best possible condition. The high acid content of straw and wood wool stuffing can cause bears to rot and the natural fibres used in their textiles can dry with age, making them prone to tear at the slightest pressure.

Strong sunlight or artificial light that contains ultra-violet rays can also prove damaging, so always keep bears away from prolonged exposure.

Before attempting to use a vacuum cleaner to remove dust from a classic bear, cover the hose nozzle with a piece of net or gauze

Read the instructions for cleaning classic bears on the opposite page before brushing a valuable bear.

For a permanent display of bears it is best to use a tungsten light bulb. Fluctuations in temperature should also be avoided, so do remember to keep bears away from any source of heat, such as a radiator, convector heater or even hot water pipes.

Collectors' bears should always be handled with clean hands and in the case of valuable bears, it is wise to wear cotton gloves. The grime and acid on the hands can inflict untold damage on delicate fabrics.

CLEANING CLASSIC BEARS

Dust can also prove a problem. It too has a high acid content and bears on display should be vacuumed regularly to remove any particles that may have settled. To minimise the risk of damaging the bear, cover the hose nozzle of the vacuum cleaner with a piece of fine net or gauze, which can be held in place with an elastic band. Then run the nozzle gently over the bear, taking extra care around the eyes, over the embroidered areas and along the seams – all places where dust is most likely to settle.

It is possible to freshen the fur pile of a bear by scrubbing it gently with a soft tooth brush or natural bristle nail brush which has been dipped in a very weak solution of detergent. The liquid type used for washing delicate clothes is best. Great care must be taken not to let the water soak into the backing fabric, as this might be absorbed into the wood wool filling. The fur can then be wiped gently with a clean damp cloth until both the detergent and grime have been removed. It cannot, however, be stressed strongly enough that you should not attempt to wash a valuable bear without seeking advice from an expert such as the curator of a museum specializing in childhood toys and memorabilia. Specialist companies are now developing dry-cleaning fluids for bears and the manufacturers' instructions should always be followed carefully.

REPAIRING BEARS

Restorers who specialize in making good the wear and tear inflicted by the years can also be found. Unless you are very sure of what you are doing, or the bear is of little value, do not attempt do-it-yourself repairs.

Obviously, seams can be restitched using a good quality thread and a ladder-stitch technique and eyes can be replaced using reproduction glass boot buttons or modern amber ones. However, never make a repair or alteration that cannot be easily removed, thus restoring the bear to its original condition. This is particularly true of replacement paw and foot pads.

STORING BEARS

A well-loved collectors' bear that is beginning to show its age should be wrapped in acid-free tissue paper and stored in a sturdy cardboard box. On no account should it be wrapped in polythene or plastic. It is possible that an old bear may have had its stuffing eaten by mites, in which case the seams should be opened gently, and the remaining stuffing removed. The bear should then be treated with a suitable proprietary insect repellant before being restuffed with wood wool and its seams restitched. Again, if in any doubt, it is always wise to consult an expert before attempting any repairs.

Remember that collectors' bears and the bears in this book should not be given to small children to play with, as they do not comply with toy safety regulations.

Take good care of your traditionally made teddy bears and they will be a joy for collectors in the future.

EARLY BLACK BEAR

The bear pictured here was inspired by early black bears. Made from black bouclé woven fabric, it is 16in (41cm) tall and has a black velvet muzzle and pads.

Some years before the official birth of the teddy bear in 1903, both stuffed and wooden bears were being sold as toys. Unlike the teddies of later years, these bears were made to sound fierce and lifelike with a sinister growl; hardly the cuddly confidante of childhood!

These forerunners of the modern teddy were based on the bears of the wild. Known as 'bruins', they stood on all fours and usually had a humped back. Often they were made from real fur; they had snarling expressions and some even had clockwork mechanisms to open their mouths in a realistic growl.

Some of these lifelike bears were muzzled and chained, resembling the dancing bears of middle European countries of the time. These poor bears stared through sad eyes over the straps and harnesses used to fetter them.

By today's more enlightened standards, we look at these early examples of bears as being pathetic and miserable! They certainly were not made to be cuddled and loved.

Russian children of the time were no strangers to bears in captivity. One particular bear – Mishka – is traditional to Russian folklore and is looked upon as part of the national heritage. (More recently he appeared as the national emblem for the Moscow Olympic games held in 1980). Certainly, carved wooden bears that could perform simple tricks were produced in Russia, alongside somersaulting bears and bears that could walk across the floor. Once again, these were amusing pieces, but far removed from the teddy bear.

There was also a range of German-produced bears known as Peter bears. With their rolling eyes, moving tongues and bared teeth, they would probably have startled most adults, let alone a small child! Examples of these ferocious animals still exist; and although they post-date early teddy bear manufacture by a couple of decades (historians put their production around 1925), they are more advanced and more frightening versions of the original bruins.

Although we tend to think of teddy bears in golden plush fur

fabric, many early bears were black or dark brown. In the dawn of teddy bear production, black and dark brown bears were still popular, particularly with German manufacturers. Unlike their predecessors, these are proper teddies with all the charm of their breed. The bear featured here is reminiscent of a Steiff bear produced in 1912 which, in fact, had beige felt pads and glowing, red tinted eyes (they were shiny black buttons on circles of orange felt). The ferocious Victorian bruins would, almost without exception, have had black glass eyes and dark paw and foot pads.

Early bears were intended to issue a fierce growl, although often it sounded more as though they were mooing! Although this bear has a friendly disposition, a growling voicebox would add to its authenticity and old-fashioned appeal.

A growler can be inserted quite easily – instructions on how to do this appear on page 27.

Materials

½yd (45cm) of 54in (137cm) wide black bouclé woven fabric with man–made pile
9in (23cm) square of black velvet
Tacking (basting) thread
Matching sewing thread
Matching heavy-duty thread
One 2½in (64mm) hardboard crown joint
Four 2in (50mm) hardboard crown joints
Small amount of 'firm-fill' polyester filling (stuffing)
1½lb (680g) wood wool
Two ⅝in (17mm) black boot button eyes
One skein black 'pearl cotton' embroidery thread

MAKING THE EARLY BLACK BEAR

Before starting to make the bear, carefully read the chapter on Classic Bear-making. Following the step-by-step instructions there, make the 10 templates, cut out the fabric pieces and assemble the bear, taking into consideration the special points below. Take care to keep your working surfaces as clean as possible at all times.

This bouclé fabric is not easy to sew and beginners are advised to practice on the more usual fur pile fabrics before attempting a bear of this type. The backing fabric is quite stiff and it may be necessary to use a pair of pliers and a stronger needle (such as a darner) when hand stitching or tacking (basting). The pile is not so easily trapped in the seams, but these should be checked and any caught threads teased out using a bodkin or stiletto. Do not use a teasel brush on bouclé fabrics.

The muzzle of this bear is cut out separately in velvet. Before sewing the head gusset to the side-of-head pieces following the step-by-step instructions, join the two velvet side-muzzle pieces to the two side-of-head pieces (seams B-C). Then join the velvet top muzzle to the head gusset (seam B-B).

As velvet tends to 'slip' as it is machine sewn, it is advisable to hand stitch paw and foot pads, using a doubled thread and a firm backstitch. Tack (baste) both paw and foot pads in position as shown in the step-by-step instructions on page 21 for foot pads, using smaller and closer stitches than normal.

The eyes are placed on the head gusset seam, so that their lower edges are 1in (2.5cm) from the start of the velvet muzzle.

The ears should be set towards the back of the head across the gusset seams and at a slight angle with the lower edges tilting forwards a little.

The nose is worked in horizontal satin stitches across the seam at the end of the muzzle, forming a rectangle about ¾in (2cm) wide and ¼in (7mm) deep. Using two strands of pearl cotton, work a ½in (12mm) straight stitch downwards from the nose along the lower muzzle seam. Then work a ⅝in (18mm) straight stitch to either side to form the mouth.

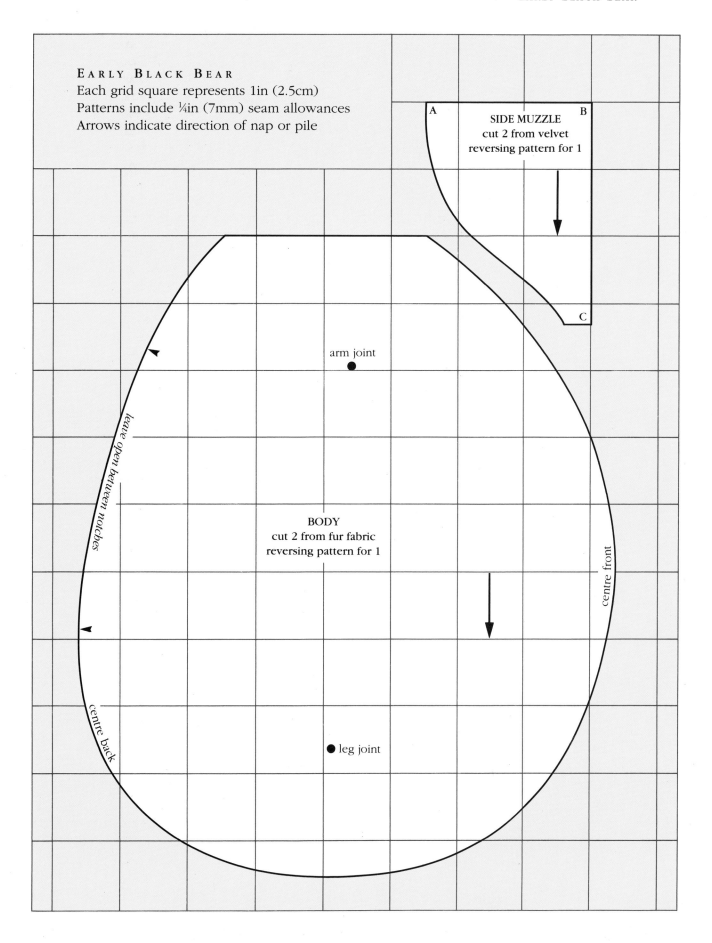

EARLY BLACK BEAR
Each grid square represents 1in (2.5cm)
Patterns include ¼in (7mm) seam allowances
Arrows indicate direction of nap or pile

A B

SIDE MUZZLE
cut 2 from velvet
reversing pattern for 1

C

arm joint

leave open between notches

BODY
cut 2 from fur fabric
reversing pattern for 1

centre front

centre back

leg joint

33

SIDE HEAD
cut 2 from fur fabric
reversing pattern for 1

B

C

TOP MUZZLE
cut 1 from velvet

B   B

A

leg joint
*(mark on 2 'inner' leg
pieces only)*

LEG
cut 4 from fur fabric
reversing pattern for 2

leave open between notches

EAR
cut 4 from fur fabric
reversing pattern for 2

PAW PAD
cut 2 from velvet

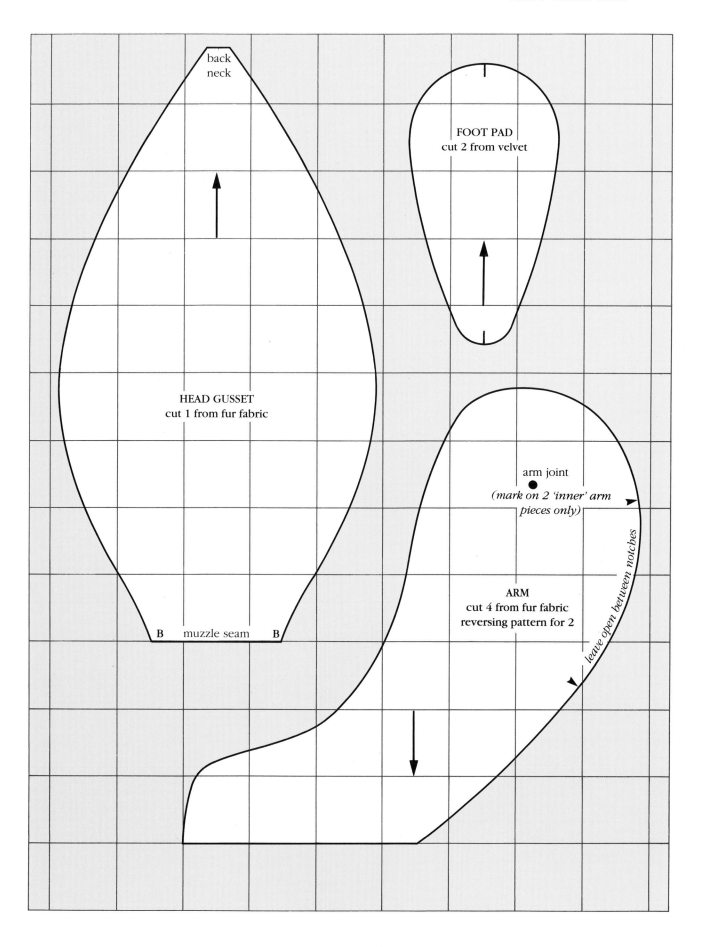

back
neck

FOOT PAD
cut 2 from velvet

HEAD GUSSET
cut 1 from fur fabric

arm joint
●
*(mark on 2 'inner' arm
pieces only)*

ARM
cut 4 from fur fabric
reversing pattern for 2

leave open between notches

B   muzzle seam   B

MICHTOM BEAR

The bear pictured here was inspired by Michtom bears. Made from honey-gold mohair pile fabric, it is 18in (46cm) tall and it has mushroom-coloured suedette paw and foot pads.

The creation of a jointed, mohair pile bear, was the inspiration of a Russian immigrant to the United States named Morris Michtom.

Michtom ran a small candy store in Brooklyn with his wife, Rose, a skilled toymaker and seamstress. Many of her toys adorned the shop window to encourage customers inside.

The enterprising Mr Michtom seized upon the idea of the toy bear while reading the *Washington Evening Post* one November day in 1902. A political cartoon, showing President Theodore Roosevelt refusing to shoot a tethered bear cub, gave Michtom the idea for an endearing toy bear. Michtom persuaded his wife to make a prototype cuddly bear. It was to be the first of many.

The original Michtom bear was made from golden plush mohair. It stood 21in (53cm) tall, with long, rather thin, arms and legs which had pale felt paws embroidered with black, straight-stitched claws. The bear's large, rounded ears were set on the sides of its head and it viewed the world from small, black, boot button eyes. The rather pensive and woebegone expression of Rose Michtom's toy bear proved an instant success.

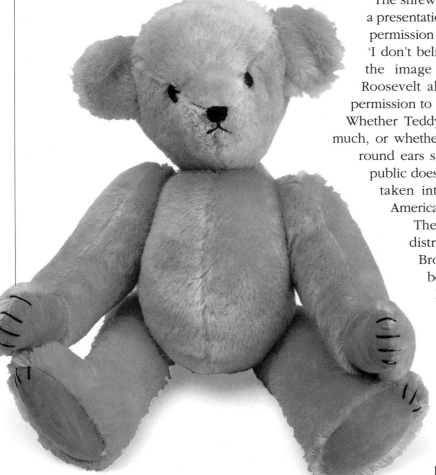

The shrewd Mr Michtom, so the story goes, sent a presentation bear to the White House asking for permission to name it in honour of the President. 'I don't believe that my name will do much for the image of your stuffed bear,' President Roosevelt allegedly replied, 'but you have my permission to use it'.

Whether Teddy Roosevelt's name did, in fact, do much, or whether the lovable little bear with its big round ears simply caught the imagination of the public does not really matter. 'Teddy's bear' was taken into the hearts and homes of many American families.

The Michtom bear was soon being distributed through wholesalers Butler Brothers and from these simple beginnings the hugely successful Ideal Novelty and Toy Company was formed in Brooklyn.

In fact, so successful was the Michtom's teddy, that many imitators jumped on the bear bandwagon, producing teddy bear lookalikes.

Certainly, by 1907, teddy bears had taken America by storm. Although teddy bear history is poorly documented, evidence of

these creatures' popularity was immortalized in the much-loved music, *Teddy Bears' Picnic*, composed in this year by W J Bratton. The lyrics to the piece were added later.

One of the original Michtom bears now resides at the Smithsonian Institute in Washington, DC, but you can make your own version displaying some of its charming characteristics by using the following pattern instructions.

The Michtom bear, in common with most bears in this book, can be stuffed with either a polyester or wood wool filling (stuffing). The latter creates a lot of dust, so asthma sufferers would be advised to wear a mask when using it.

Materials

*½yd (45cm) of 54in (137cm)
  wide honey-gold mohair
  with ⅜in (9mm) pile*
*Small square of mushroom-
  coloured suedette*
Tacking (basting) thread
Matching sewing thread
Matching heavy-duty thread
*One 2in (50mm) hardboard
  crown joint*
*Four 1⅜in (36mm)
  hardboard crown joints*
*Small amount of 'firm-fill'
  polyester filling (stuffing)*
1½lb (680g) wood wool
*Two ½in (14mm) black
  buttons for eyes*
*One skein black 'stranded
  cotton' embroidery thread*

MAKING THE MICHTOM BEAR

Before starting to make the bear, carefully read the chapter on Classic Bear-making. Following the step-by-step instructions there, make the 10 templates, cut out the fabric pieces and assemble the bear, taking into consideration the special points below. Take care to keep your working surfaces as clean as possible at all times.

When using wood wool, always stuff the point of the muzzle, the feet and front paws with polyester filling (stuffing) first. This will ensure a smooth and even shape. Additional wood wool can be added to give extra firmness, but the smoother polyester should always remain as a protective layer beneath the fabric.

After stuffing and before finally closing the back opening, use polyester filler to pad out the hump and back curve fully.

If you wish to use black buttons for the eyes, it may be necessary to enlarge the stiletto hole by carefully cutting a few strands of ground fabric to enable the shank of the button to slip through. The eyes should be set just below the head gusset seam lines, level with the lower edge of the ears.

The claws are formed by embroidering three straight stitches on each foot pad and four straight stitches on each paw pad, using six strands of black stranded cotton embroidery thread.

The ears should be positioned from the head gusset seam downwards following the stitching line of the lower dart.

The nose is worked in horizontal satin stitches across the seam at the end of the muzzle, forming a rectangle about ⅝in (16mm) wide and ½in (12mm) deep. Using 6 strands of stranded cotton, work a ¼in (7cm) straight stitch downwards from the nose along the lower muzzle seam; then work a ½in (12mm) straight stitch to either side to form the mouth.

Finally, trim the fur pile back close around the whole of the muzzle. The pile around the teddy bear's eyes should also be trimmed lightly to expose them fully.

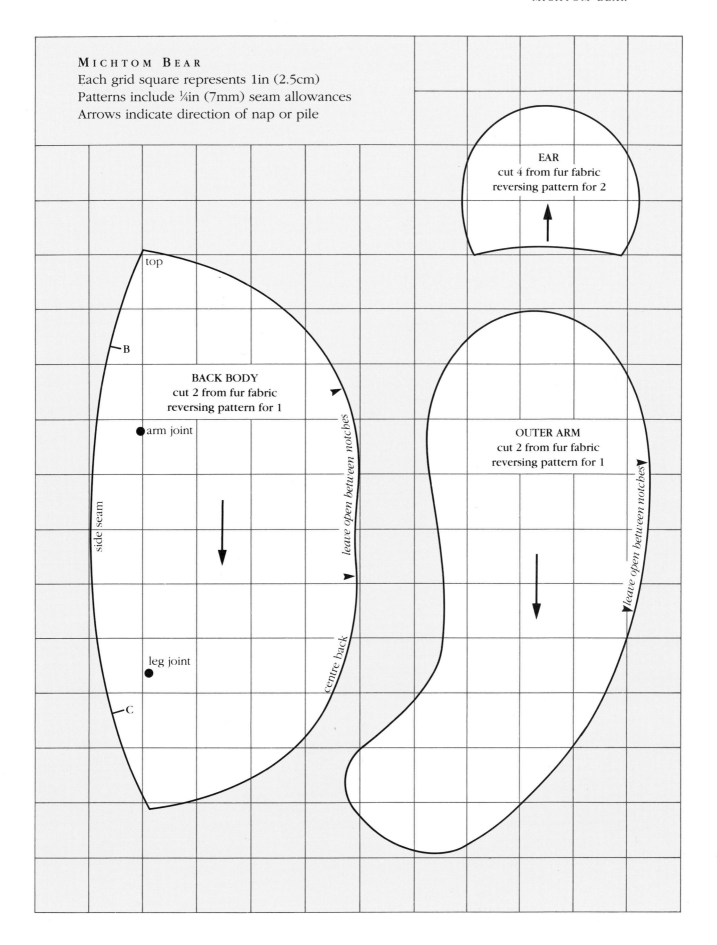

MICHTOM BEAR
Each grid square represents 1in (2.5cm)
Patterns include ¼in (7mm) seam allowances
Arrows indicate direction of nap or pile

EAR
cut 4 from fur fabric
reversing pattern for 2

top

B

BACK BODY
cut 2 from fur fabric
reversing pattern for 1

● arm joint

side seam

leave open between notches

centre back

● leg joint

C

OUTER ARM
cut 2 from fur fabric
reversing pattern for 1

leave open between notches

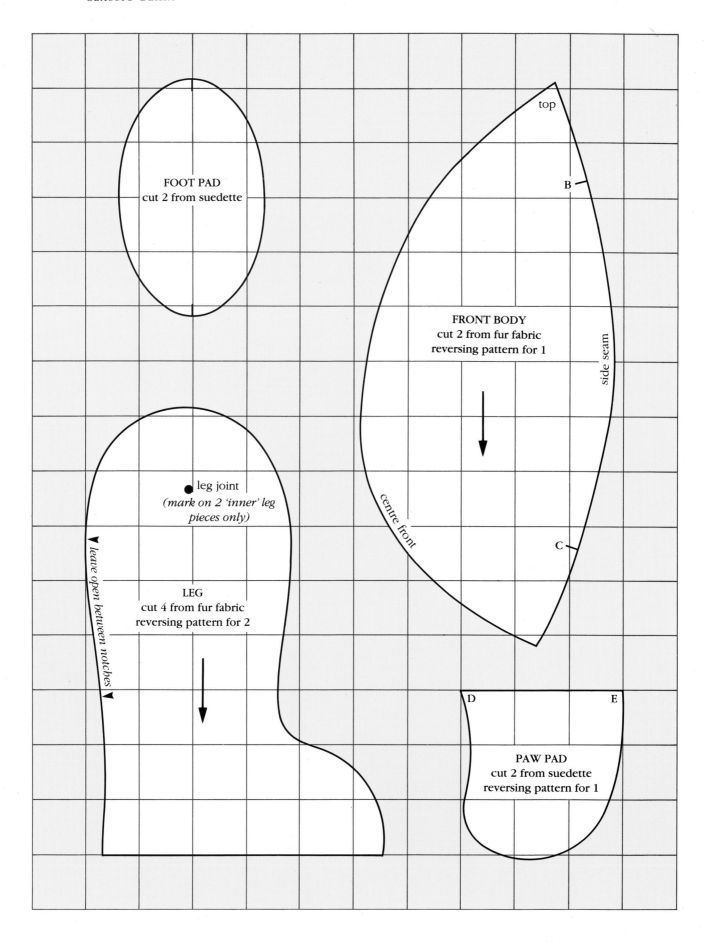

FOOT PAD
cut 2 from suedette

top

B

FRONT BODY
cut 2 from fur fabric
reversing pattern for 1

side seam

centre front

C

leg joint
(mark on 2 'inner' leg
pieces only)

leave open between notches

LEG
cut 4 from fur fabric
reversing pattern for 2

D   E

PAW PAD
cut 2 from suedette
reversing pattern for 1

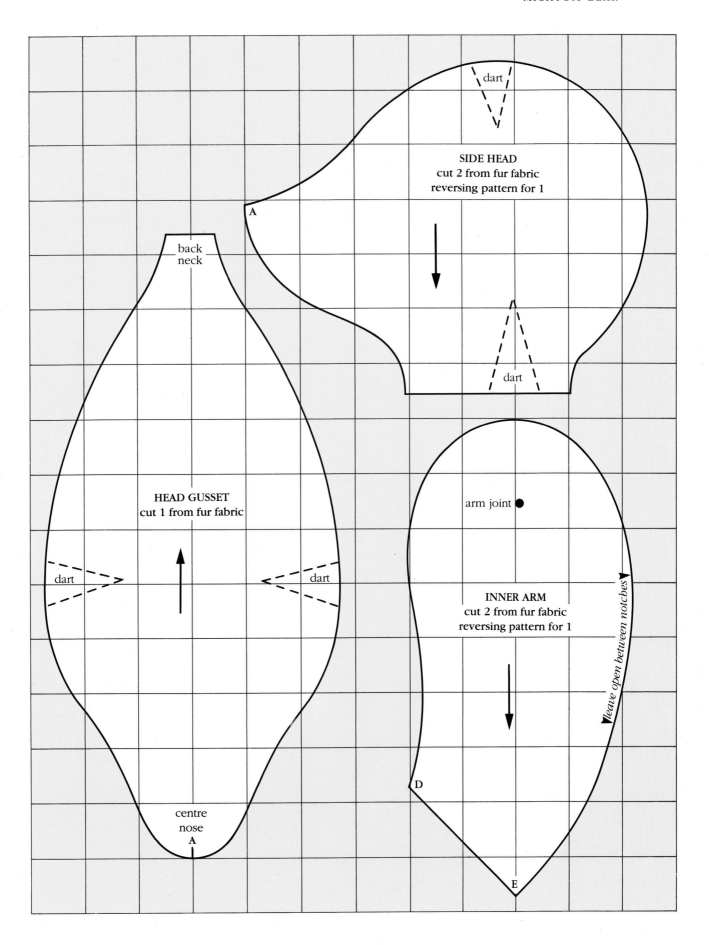

SIDE HEAD
cut 2 from fur fabric
reversing pattern for 1

dart

dart

back
neck

A

HEAD GUSSET
cut 1 from fur fabric

dart

dart

centre
nose
A

arm joint ●

INNER ARM
cut 2 from fur fabric
reversing pattern for 1

leave open between notches

D

E

EARLY GERMAN BEAR

The bear pictured here was inspired by early German bears. Made from honey-beige distressed pile mohair fabric, it is 14½in (37cm) tall and has pale beige suedette paw and foot pads.

Although disabled from childhood by polio, German-born Margarete Steiff conquered her disability to become a world-renowned toy maker. And it is for the Steiff teddy bears that she is probably best known. Without doubt, the toy bears created by the Steiff factory in the early part of this century are the great-grandfathers of today's teddies.

History is still slightly confused over the origins of the Steiff bear, although it is commonly thought the toy was the brainchild of Margarete's nephew, Richard, who often sketched bears at Stuttgart Zoo.

It evidently took several years to persuade Margarete Steiff that bears with movable joints and plush fur were the toy of the future, but after setbacks and various modifications, the first Steiff bear – called Friend Petz – was completed in time for the Leipzig Toy Fair of 1903. Even then, it looked as though the bear was destined for the reject pile, as no one showed any particular interest. On the last day of the Fair, a leading New York toy importer approached the Steiff stand. It is said he was disappointed that there were no really new or exciting toys that year. Friend Petz was brought to his attention by Richard and so enthralled him that he placed an order for 3,000 bears there and then. The Steiff legend was born!

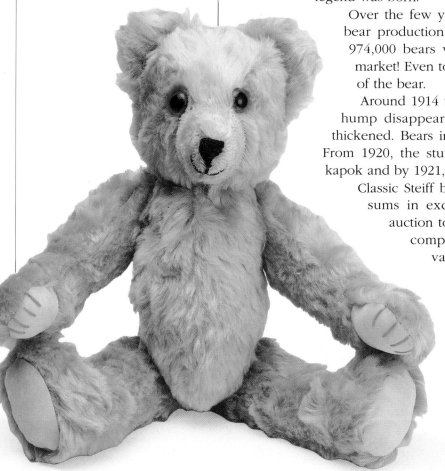

Over the few years following the Leipzig Toy Fair, bear production rose rapidly. By 1907 an amazing 974,000 bears were produced. Steiff led the bear market! Even today, this is remembered as the year of the bear.

Around 1914 the Steiff style began to change; the hump disappeared and the muzzle shortened and thickened. Bears in general took on a friendlier form. From 1920, the stuffing changed from wood wool to kapok and by 1921, glass eyes replaced boot buttons.

Classic Steiff bears can now be expected to fetch sums in excess of four figures when sold at auction today. All bears manufactured by the company before 1910 are extremely valuable and the few with their growlers still working prove particularly desirable.

The record price for a bear at auction is held by the 1920s Steiff bear, 'Happy', made in dual plush fabric. Originally purchased in Ireland, it had been with the same family for some time. It was bought for a staggering £55,000 ($81,000) by the chairman of a modern teddy bear manufacturer on behalf of a

The Steiff button label above is dated circa 1910.

Materials

½yd (45cm) of 54in (137cm) wide honey-beige distressed pile mohair with ½in (12mm) pile

Small square of pale beige suedette

Tacking (basting) thread

Matching sewing thread

Matching heavy-duty thread

One 1⅜in (35mm) hardboard crown joint

Four 1in (25mm) hardboard crown joints

Small amount of 'firm-fill' polyester filling (stuffing)

1lb (450 g) wood wool

Two ⅝in (16mm) amber and black glass boot button eyes

One skein black 'soft cotton' and one skein terracotta 'stranded cotton' embroidery thread

friend. (By the time you read this, this record price for a teddy bear at auction might easily have been surpassed.)

It was as early as 1905 that the firm of Steiff protected its products by registering its now famous 'button in the ear' trademark. Although other companies tried to imitate this, legal action prevented them from doing so.

This delightful bear has some of the characteristics of a Steiff creation of around 1904. It has a marked hump and long, slim, curved arms with claws embroidered in terracotta thread on its paw pads. Its nose is worked in satin stitch onto a thin, tapering muzzle and its rounded ears are set vertically across the head gusset seams. Instead of wooden boot buttons, it has amber glass eyes, set rather close together, and it is made in long pile distressed honey-beige mohair to provide a classic effect.

MAKING THE EARLY GERMAN BEAR

Before starting to make the bear, carefully read the chapter on Classic Bear-making. Following the step-by-step instructions there, make the 9 templates, cut out the fabric pieces and assemble the bear, taking into consideration the special points below. Take care to keep your working surfaces as clean as possible at all times.

Unlike other bears in this book, those made from distressed pile mohair should not be brushed with a teasel brush, as this is likely to alter the characteristics of the fabric.

The claws are formed by embroidering four straight stitches on each of the bear's two paw pads, using six strands of terracotta stranded cotton embroidery thread.

The eyes are placed just below the head gusset seam, so that their lower edges are 2in (5cm) from the tip of the muzzle.

The muzzle is trimmed back slightly unevenly, and a small amount of pile is cut away around the eyes to improve their appearance.

The ears should be set at the top of the head across the gusset seams and about 1½in (4cm) apart.

The nose is worked in horizontal satin stitches across the tip of the muzzle, using black soft cotton embroidery thread and forming a triangle. Using two strands of black soft cotton embroidery thread, work a ¼in (7mm) straight stitch downwards from the tip of the nose along the lower muzzle seam. Then using a single strand of the same thread, work a ½in (12mm) straight stitch upwards to either side to form the smiling mouth.

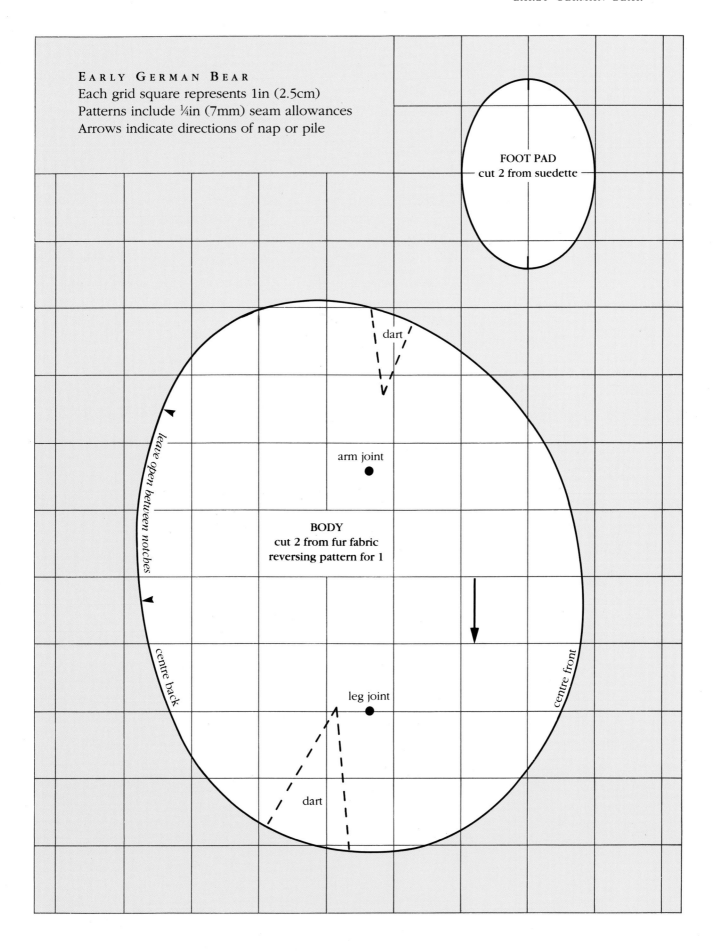

EARLY GERMAN BEAR
Each grid square represents 1in (2.5cm)
Patterns include ¼in (7mm) seam allowances
Arrows indicate directions of nap or pile

FOOT PAD
cut 2 from suedette

dart

leave open between notches

arm joint

centre back

BODY
cut 2 from fur fabric
reversing pattern for 1

centre front

leg joint

dart

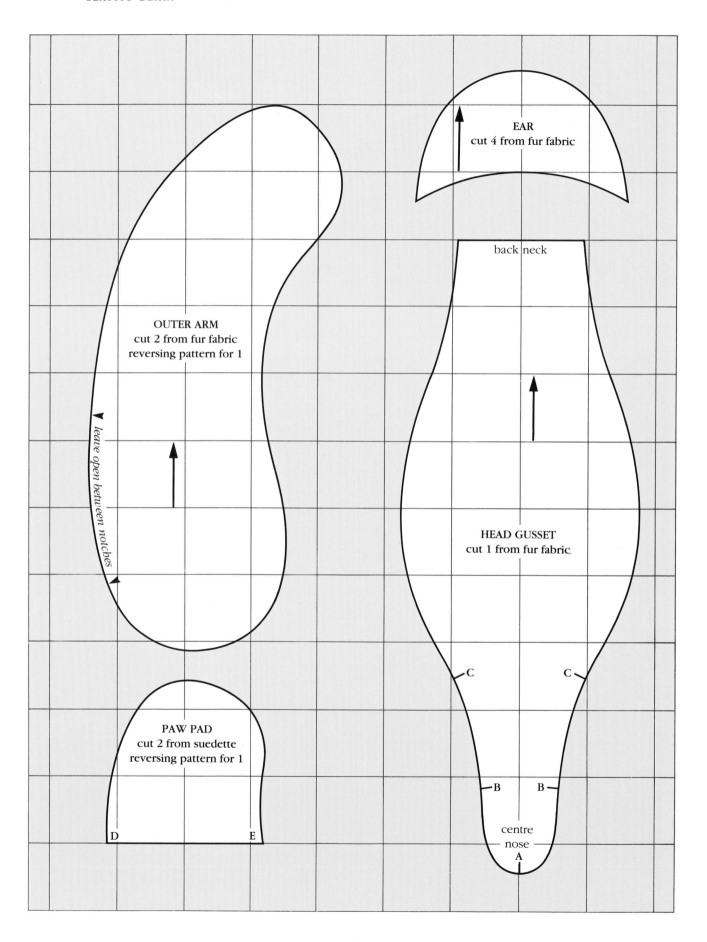

EAR
cut 4 from fur fabric

back neck

OUTER ARM
cut 2 from fur fabric
reversing pattern for 1

leave open between notches

HEAD GUSSET
cut 1 from fur fabric

C   C

PAW PAD
cut 2 from suedette
reversing pattern for 1

D   E

B   B

centre
nose
A

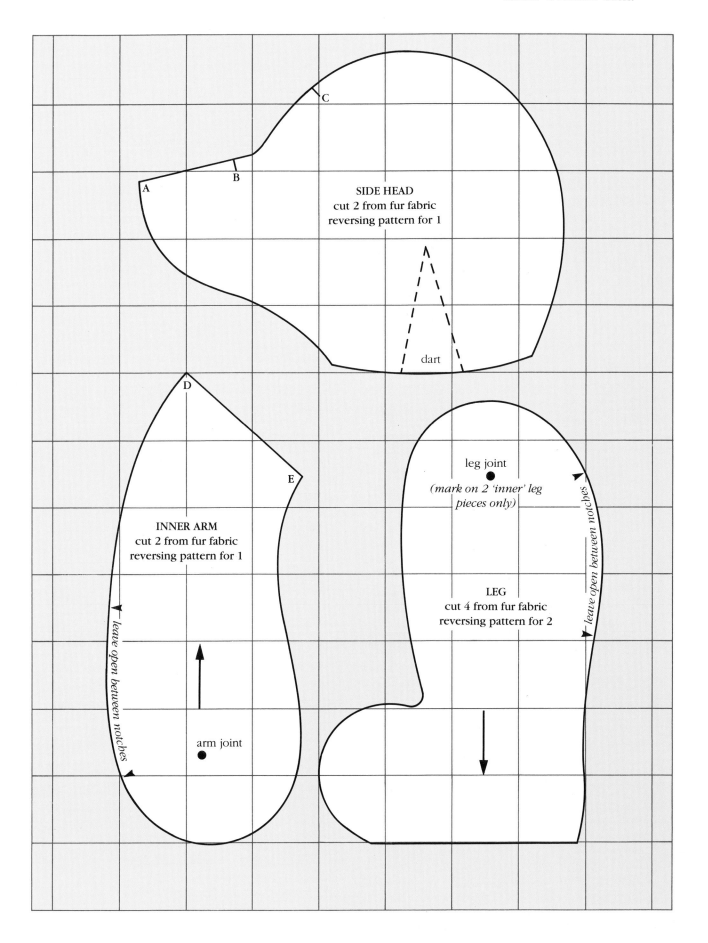

SIDE HEAD
cut 2 from fur fabric
reversing pattern for 1

dart

INNER ARM
cut 2 from fur fabric
reversing pattern for 1

arm joint

leave open between notches

leg joint
(mark on 2 'inner' leg
pieces only)

LEG
cut 4 from fur fabric
reversing pattern for 2

leave open between notches

1920s GERMAN BEAR

Up until the outbreak of World War I in 1914, the basic teddy bear had changed little from its early beginnings. However, the war brought disruption to trading and production, and it wasn't until the turn of the decade that bears again began to fill the shelves.

By the 1920s, German bears were once more exported in large numbers. Factories such as Bing, Gebrüder Hermann, Gebrüder Sussenguth and, of course, Steiff, were all in evidence.

Bing bears, as they came to be known, were mechanical and often colourfully dressed. Gebrüder Sussenguth produced the rather ferocious Peter bears already discussed on page 30. Hermann bears, on the other hand, closely resembled the famous Steiff bears. In fact, the Hermann company was founded in 1907 specifically to make bears. It was only in later years that the company widened its range to include other toys.

However, by the 1920s, the German manufacturers were up against stiff competition from a growing number of toy companies in other countries manufacturing teddy bears for the first time.

In Britain, Chad Valley had made use of the war, which blocked German imports, to firmly establish itself as a soft toy manufacturer. Its teddy bears did not roll off the production line though till 1920.

Like Steiff bears, the Chad Valley ones bore a metal trade button quite often clipped to the ear.

Other major manufacturers included Dean's and J K Farnell in Britain and the Ideal Toy Company and Knickerbocker Toy Company in America.

By the 1920s, bears were evolving into a more modern design. Glass eyes were replacing boot buttons, the hump was beginning to lessen in size, the limbs began to shorten and the torso grew more rotund. In other words, the bears became more cuddly than they had been before. The stuffing for bears had also changed as they evolved.

Many bears manufactured in the 1920s were stuffed with a substance known as 'Aerolite'. This was the trade name for kapok, a natural fibre which can be mixed with wood wool or sawdust (and indeed it was) to create a softer feel.

One of the most famous bears from the early 1920s is surely Winnie-the-Pooh, a character created by A A Milne and almost certainly inspired by

This German bear (1910-20) is only 8in (20cm) tall.

Materials

½yd (45cm) of 54in (137cm) wide gold crushed pile mohair (with ¾in (21mm) pile

Small square of tight beige suedette

Tacking (basting) thread

Matching sewing thread

Matching heavy-duty thread

One 3in (76mm) hardboard crown joint

Four 2in (50mm) hardboard crown joints

2lb (1kg) 'firm-fill' polyester filling (stuffing)

Two ⅝in (17mm) black glass boot button eyes

One skein black 'pearl cotton' embroidery thread

a J K Farnell bear. However, the illustrations of Pooh, drawn by Ernest Shepard, are modelled upon a Steiff bear called Growler.

The other notable bear of the period is 'Happy', a brown-tipped, beige, dual plush mohair bear from the Steiff factory. Happy was sold at auction in 1989 for a record sum of £55,000 ($81,000), making it the most expensive teddy bear in the world to date.

The bear featured here has large, narrow feet in the classic style and large round ears set wide apart. It has long, slim arms and light beige suedette foot and paw pads. Although toy bears were evolving at this time, German manufacturers, more than others, continued to make the traditional long-muzzled bears.

This bear has black glass boot button eyes and a black embroidered nose, but brown glass eyes and a brown embroidered nose and mouth could be substituted to achieve a closer resemblance to Happy. The famous bear's pads were made from a yellowish, beige felt; velveteen or suedette would make an acceptable substitute.

MAKING THE 1920s GERMAN BEAR

Before starting to make the bear, carefully read the chapter on Classic Bear-making. Following the step-by-step instructions there, make the 9 templates, cut out the fabric pieces and assemble the bear, taking into consideration the special points below. Take care to keep your working surfaces as clean as possible at all times.

When working with extra long pile mohair, great care must be taken at the cutting stage. Use small, pointed and very sharp scissors, ensuring that only the backing fabric is cut. As each piece is finished, pull it away from the fabric carefully, separating the mohair strands as you do so.

As the pattern pieces are pinned and then tacked (basted) together, try using the flat of the pin or needle to push the pile inwards. This will help when the seams are machine stitched, preventing excessive amounts of pile being caught in the stitches.

The muzzle of this bear is left untrimmed. However, it may be advisable to trim away the pile in the area of the nose, before stitching. This will give a much neater effect and make working easier. Some pile may be trimmed from around the eyes if preferred.

The eyes are placed on the head gusset seam, so that their lower edges are 2½in (6.5cm) from the centre of the tip of the nose.

The ears should be set about 2in (5cm) apart across the gusset seams and at a slight angle with the lower edges tilting forwards a little.

The nose is worked in vertical satin stitches across the seam at the end of the muzzle, forming a rectangle about ¾in (2cm) wide and ½in (12mm) deep. The bear has no embroidered mouth.

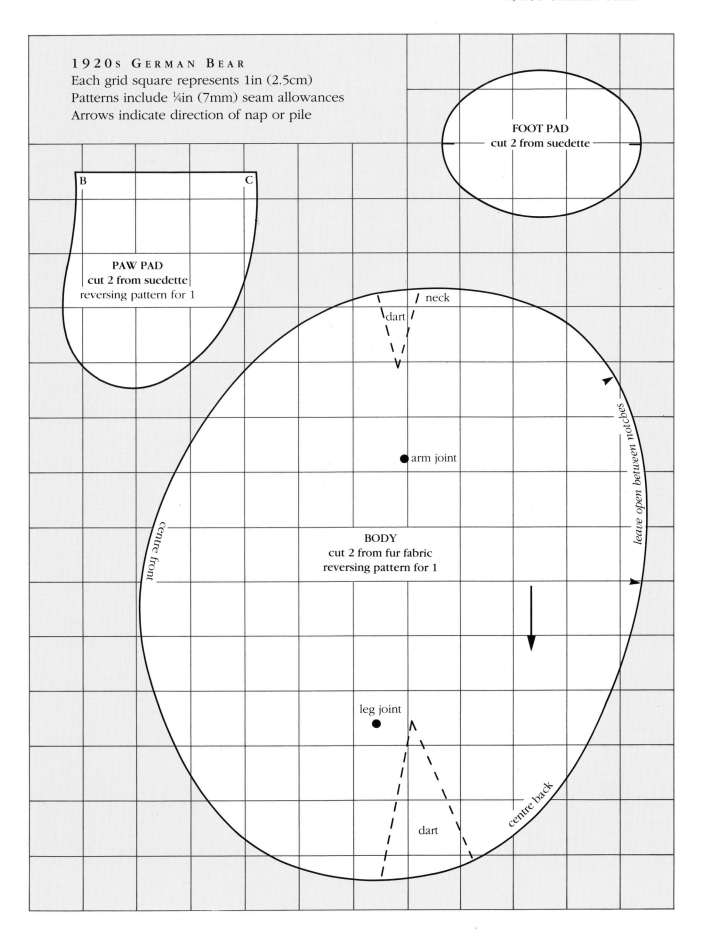

1920s GERMAN BEAR
Each grid square represents 1in (2.5cm)
Patterns include ¼in (7mm) seam allowances
Arrows indicate direction of nap or pile

FOOT PAD
cut 2 from suedette

B   C

PAW PAD
cut 2 from suedette
reversing pattern for 1

neck

dart

arm joint

centre front

BODY
cut 2 from fur fabric
reversing pattern for 1

leave open between notches

leg joint

centre back

dart

SIDE HEAD
cut 2 from fur fabric
reversing pattern for 1

A

dart

● leg joint
(mark on 2 'inner' leg
pieces only)

arm joint

INNER ARM
cut 2 from fur fabric
reversing pattern for 1

leave open between notches

LEG
cut 4 from fur fabric
reversing pattern for 2

leave open between notches

B

C

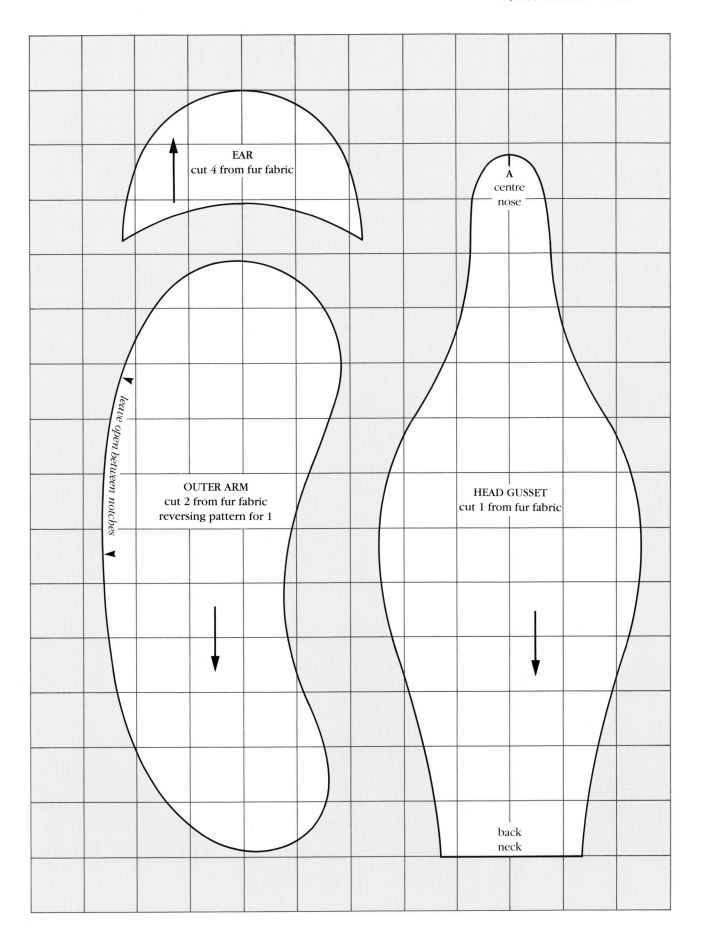

EAR
cut 4 from fur fabric

A
centre
nose

OUTER ARM
cut 2 from fur fabric
reversing pattern for 1

leave open between notches

HEAD GUSSET
cut 1 from fur fabric

back
neck

MINIATURE BEAR

Once teddy bears had established themselves firmly in the toy trade, so various manifestations appeared. One of the most endearing and popular types was the tiny or miniature bear.

What defines a real miniature is often subject to conjecture. One of the early Steiff lines was a small bear of 9in (23cm) in height, but it is generally agreed that bears must be no taller than 7in (18cm) to be classed as miniature.

One of the principal manufacturers of tiny bears was Schreyer, a German company, often known more commonly as Schuco. Established in 1912, the company produced an unusual range of bears over the years. Its tiny stuffed bears were often made in various colours; the smallest one measured just over 2in (5cm) tall. Schuco also manufactured bears which could nod or shake their heads. These 'Yes/No' teddy bears were also produced in miniature versions.

During the 1920s scent bottles and lipstick cases came in the guise of little bears to put into a handbag or evening purse.

Miniature bears have the advantage that they can be popped into a pocket and carried around with their owner. Many people profess to having a miniature bear mascot which accompanies them everywhere. Small bears require a great deal of skill and patience to produce. Seams must be very accurately sewn and care must be taken when turning tiny sections, such as arms and legs. However, there is great satisfaction and pleasure in the final results, which have a distinctive charm. The obvious choice of fabric would be a short-piled mohair, but camel hair, cashmere or mohair cloth would be equally acceptable.

The bear featured here is jointed with the smallest commercially produced hardboard joints, but the joints for smaller bears can be made from two buttons, which can be pulled together using heavy duty thread. However, these joints will not be so readily moveable as a crown joint. Do take care when bending the split pin on some small joints, as they can be particularly unyielding. In some cases it may be best to substitute a longer pin, which can be curved over several times.

Some classic miniature bears were filled with sawdust, as wood wool would prove almost impossible to use.

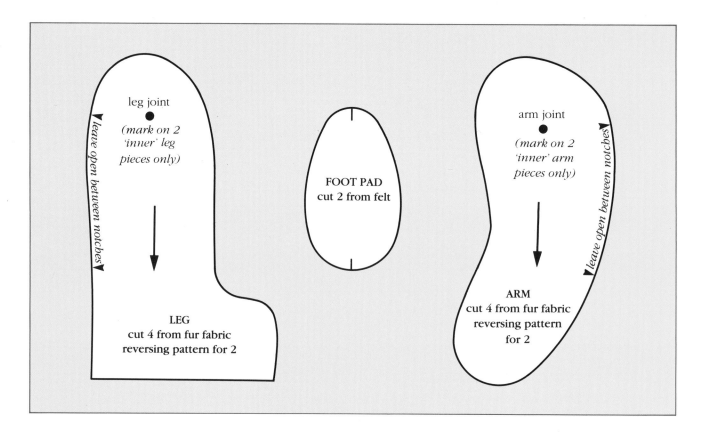

leg joint

*(mark on 2
'inner' leg
pieces only)*

leave open between notches

LEG
cut 4 from fur fabric
reversing pattern for 2

FOOT PAD
cut 2 from felt

arm joint

*(mark on 2
'inner' arm
pieces only)*

leave open between notches

ARM
cut 4 from fur fabric
reversing pattern
for 2

Materials

*¼yd (25cm) of 54in (137cm)
wide honeysuckle mohair
with ⅜in (9mm) pile (this
will be enough for several
bears)*

*3in (7.5cm) square of cream-
coloured felt*

Tacking (basting) thread

Matching sewing thread

Matching heavy-duty thread

Black heavy-duty thread

*One 1in (25mm) hardboard
crown joint*

*Four ¾in (18mm) hardboard
crown joints*

*4oz (110 g) 'firm-fill'
polyester filling (stuffing)*

*Two small round black glass
beads*

*One skein black 'stranded
cotton' embroidery thread*

MAKING THE MINIATURE BEAR

Before starting to make the bear, carefully read the chapter on Classic Bear-making. Following the step-by-step instructions there, make the 7 templates, cut out the fabric pieces and assemble the bear, taking into consideration the special points below.

Great care must be taken when machine stitching such a small bear. Seam allowances should be kept to a minimum – about ³⁄₁₆in (5mm). Areas which need special attention such as the pads and the muzzle are best stitched by hand, using a doubled thread and a firm backstitch. Any points which are likely to be strained during stuffing should be hand stitched with a double row of stitches.

The position of the eyes will depend on the size and shape of the beads chosen. This bear has eyes placed just outside the head gusset about ¾in (18mm) from the tip of the nose. Bead eyes are applied using a similar technique to glass, except that they sit on the fur fabric and are not inserted through it. Heavy-duty black thread should be used. This should be taken from the position of the ear, through the head, to the point where the bead is to sit. Thread on the bead and settle it against the head, checking that the position is correct. Take a small stitch the width of the bead back into the head and take the needle across to the position of the second eye. Fasten this with another straight stitch and take the needle to the second ear position before finishing off.

The nose is worked in horizontal satin stitches using six strands of black stranded cotton and forming a small rectangle. From the centre of the nose a ¼in (7mm) straight stitch is taken down the seamline and a smiling mouth is then made by taking a straight stitch to left and right upwards and outwards to each side.

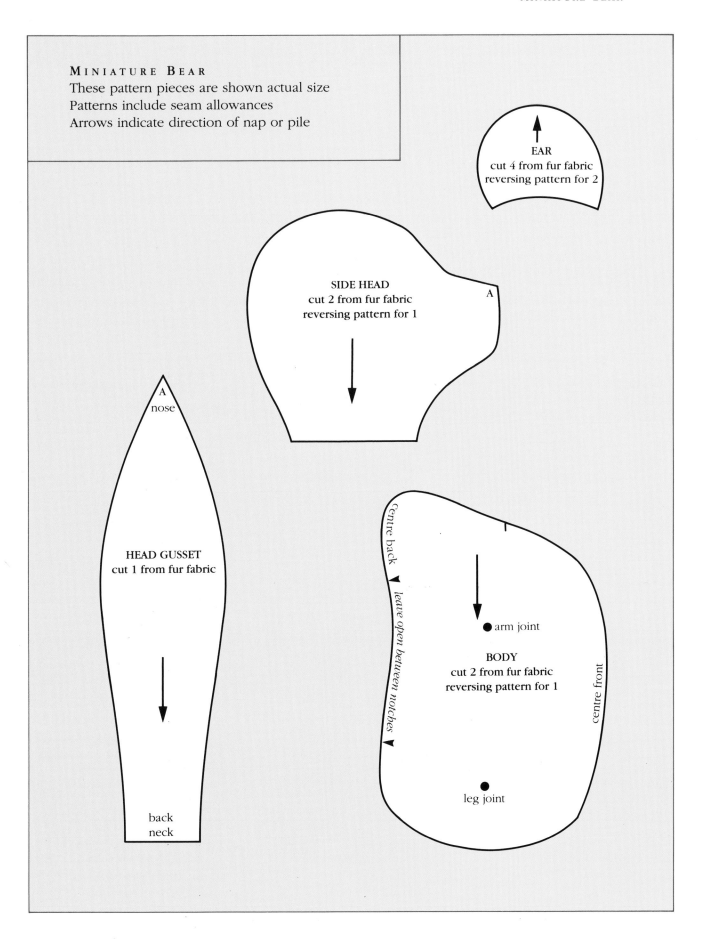

MINIATURE BEAR
These pattern pieces are shown actual size
Patterns include seam allowances
Arrows indicate direction of nap or pile

EAR
cut 4 from fur fabric
reversing pattern for 2

SIDE HEAD
cut 2 from fur fabric
reversing pattern for 1

A

A
nose

HEAD GUSSET
cut 1 from fur fabric

back
neck

centre back

leave open between notches

arm joint

BODY
cut 2 from fur fabric
reversing pattern for 1

centre front

leg joint

CLASSIC WHITE BEAR

The bear pictured here was inspired by a 1920s white bear. Made from ivory mohair pile fabric, it is 16in (40cm) tall and has ivory suedette pads.

The 1920s saw a great diversity in bear types; not least the colours and various kinds of fabrics used to make them. Shortages during the war years forced the manufacturers to experiment with a range of different materials and dyes, even though the most desirable and classic bears were still chosen from the range of mohair available.

White mohair bears are not perhaps as popular as their more usual honey-gold and brown cousins, but they do have a charm and appeal all their own.

One early white bear was produced by Steiff in 1921. This delightful bear was made from white plush and stood 15in (38cm) tall. It was of the classic shape although its legs were rather shorter than those of its predecessors. This white bear did not prove to be a huge success at the time and manufactured numbers were somewhat limited. This, of course, now makes white bears of this type extremely collectable and valuable.

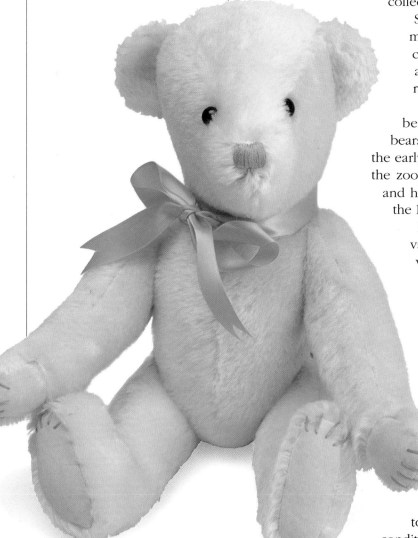

Some years later, in the year 1927, Steiff manufactured a small white teddy bear called Petz. This bear is being produced again by Steiff as one in their successful replica range.

Apart from teddy bears, there have also been a large number of lookalike polar bears. In Britain, toy polar bears dating from the early 1950s were based on real life animals in the zoo. Two well known examples include Ivy and her son Brumas, polar bears then living at the London Zoo.

Early Australian bears were made in a variety of colours, including white. These white bears often had blue glass eyes, giving them an almost human expression.

Over the years, many firms across the world have produced white teddy bears. In more recent years, white teddies seem to have grown in popularity with many bear ranges including more than one white-fur variety.

Keeping needlework clean is important whatever the task. However, when working with white mohair, it is absolutely essential. Following these simple guidelines will enable you to keep your fabric in the best possible condition throughout the sewing process.

This 15in (38in) bear is probably a 1930s Chiltern.

Materials

½yd (45cm) of 54in (137cm) wide ivory mohair with ⅜in (9mm) pile

Small square of ivory-coloured suedette

Tacking (basting) thread

Matching sewing thread

Matching heavy-duty thread

One 2in (50mm) hardboard crown joint

Four 1⅜in (35mm) hardboard crown joints

Small amount of 'firm-fill' polyester filling (stuffing)

1lb (450g) wood wool

Two ⁷⁄₁₆in (11mm) black glass boot button eyes

One skein light terracotta 'stranded cotton' embroidery thread

Before beginning to cut out the fabric, lay it face downwards on a clean pillow case. Cut it out using sharp-pointed scissors, picking up the fabric away from the pillow case as you work. When all the pieces have been cut, these can then be stored away in the pillow case, which can also be used as a table or lap cover when work is actually in progress.

No matter how carefully you work, fur fabric will shed some pile during handling. This is particularly noticeable with white and other pastel colours, so a lap cover serves the dual purpose of keeping the fabric clean and preventing loose pile from covering your clothes.

The ivory bear featured here is similar in style to the bear produced in the Steiff factory during the 1920s. However, it has small black boot button eyes, giving it a somewhat quizzical expression. In the traditional manner its nose has been embroidered in a rectangle of vertical satin stitches using a terracotta embroidery thread. The same thread has been used to embroider claws which are stitched across the fur fabric onto the pad itself.

MAKING THE CLASSIC WHITE BEAR

Before starting to make the bear, carefully read the chapter on Classic Bear-making. Following the step-by-step instructions there, make the 10 templates, cut out the fabric pieces and assemble the bear, taking into consideration the special points below. Take care to keep your working surfaces as clean as possible at all times.

When drawing around templates, it is absolutely essential to ensure that the inked markings will not transfer from the surface of the templates to the fabric and a sharp, soft lead pencil should be used to draw around each shape as lightly as possible.

Small black glass eyes have been used for the bear featured here, but you may like to try coloured eyes, blue in particular, for a different expression. Larger eyes will give your bear a more wide-awake and innocent look.

The teddy bear's eyes here are placed just below the head gusset seam, so that their lower edges are 1¼in (3cm) from the centre of the tip of the bear's muzzle.

The ears should be set so that they start at the gusset seam with the lower edges tilting backwards a little.

The nose is worked with six strands of stranded cotton in vertical satin stitches across the seam at the end of the muzzle, forming a rectangle about ¾in (2cm) wide and ½in (12mm) deep. Each side of the mouth is worked downwards from the centre of the nose in two short stitches to form a slight curve.

Four claws have been embroidered on each pad using six strands of stranded cotton embroidery thread. Insert the needle through the paw at the seamline and take it to the position for working the first claw about ½in (12mm) away from the seam into the fur fabric. Pull the thread through until the tail lies within the paw itself and make a straight stitch across the seamline to ½in (12mm) across the pad. Take the needle back through the paw to the stitching position for the second claw and repeat the process until four claws have been made. Take the needle back through the paw to the seamline, pull firmly and cut the thread. The tail should then disappear into the paw, leaving a neat and tidy finish.

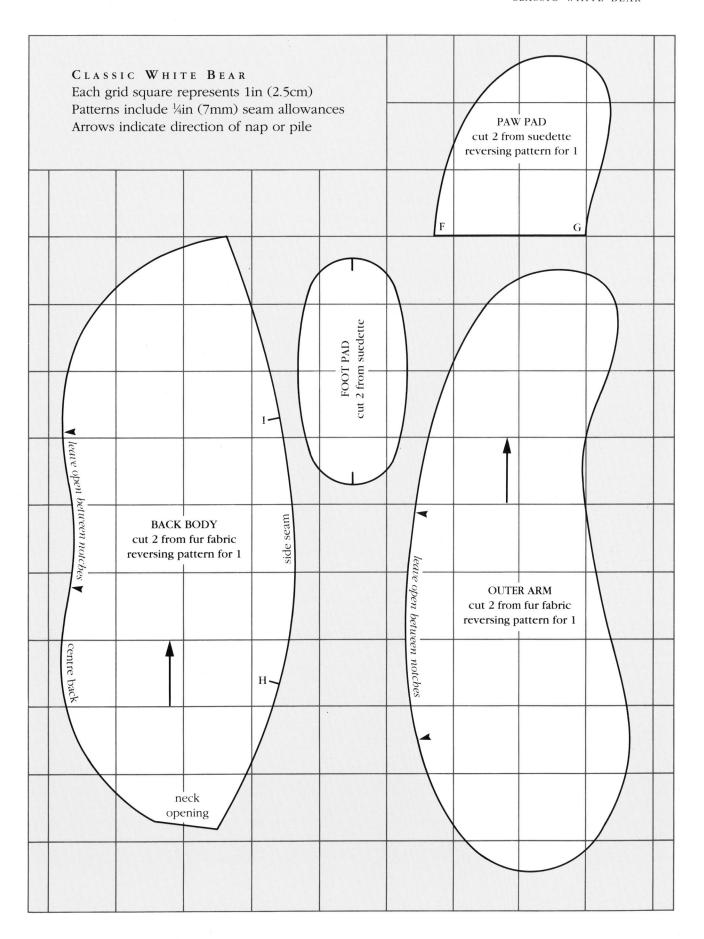

CLASSIC WHITE BEAR
Each grid square represents 1in (2.5cm)
Patterns include ¼in (7mm) seam allowances
Arrows indicate direction of nap or pile

PAW PAD
cut 2 from suedette
reversing pattern for 1

F   G

FOOT PAD
cut 2 from suedette

BACK BODY
cut 2 from fur fabric
reversing pattern for 1

leave open between notches

centre back

side seam

I

H

neck
opening

OUTER ARM
cut 2 from fur fabric
reversing pattern for 1

leave open between notches

SIDE HEAD
cut 2 from fur fabric
reversing pattern for 1

C

D

B

A

E

dart

F

G

INNER ARM
cut 2 from fur fabric
reversing pattern for 1

arm joint

leave open between notches

leg joint

(mark on 2 'inner' leg
pieces only)

LEG
cut 4 from fur fabric
reversing pattern for 2

leave open between notches

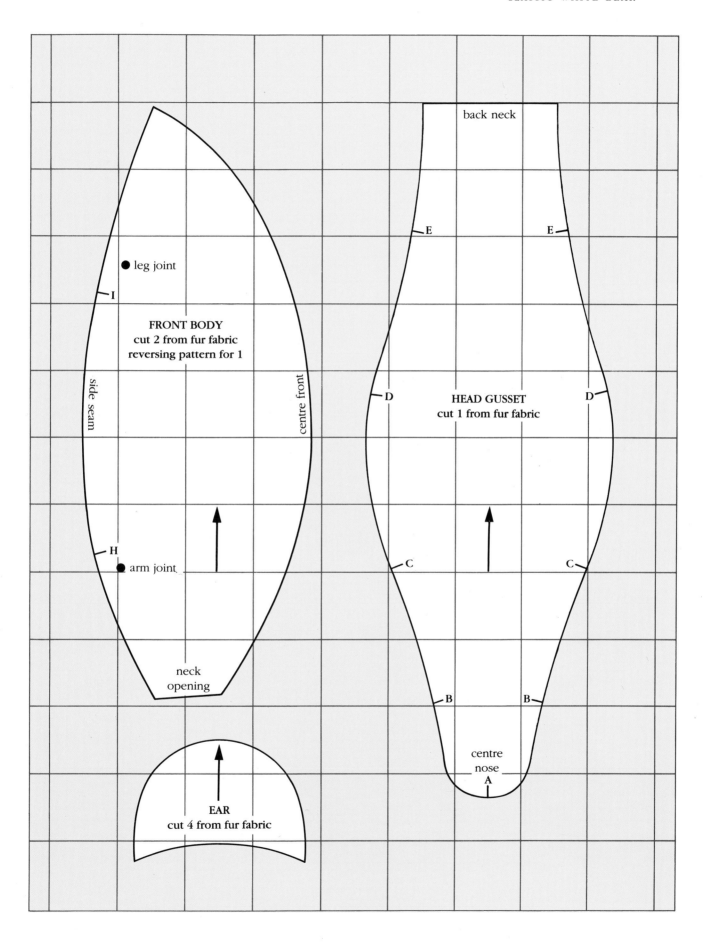

1930s BEAR

The bear pictured here was inspired by 1930s English bears. Made from fawn distressed pile mohair fabric, it is 28in (71cm) tall and has dark chocolate brown velvet paw and foot pads.

As 1930 dawned, the British teddy bear industry saw the genesis of a new company, Merrythought. Founded by C J Rendel of Chad Valley and A C Janisch of J K Farnell, Merrythought was established with the help of a mohair company – Holmes and Laxton – in Shropshire, central England. The shrewd mohair spinners were only too well aware of the growing threat from synthetic fibres to their industry; they saw teddy bear manufacture as a way to survival.

Merrythought's trademark is a wishbone (merrythought is an old English term meaning wishbone) which was imprinted on a celluloid button and sewn to the ear or the shoulder of the bear. Later the bears were labelled on the undersides of their feet.

Alongside Dean's and Chad Valley, the Merrythought Company flourished.

English bears had a generally softer outline and rounder form than their German counterparts. By the 1930s their pads were being made from Rexine, a simulated leather fabric.

Other popular teddy bears of the day were those made for the department stores and mail order catalogues. As these were produced en masse, they never had a lasting, formal identification mark label like the Merrythought or Steiff bears, so it is now difficult to trace their origins. However, the Chiltern Company, founded in the 1920s, almost certainly made a substantial number of these bears.

The department store and mail order bear came in a wide array of sizes and colours.

Merrythought produced a successful range of dressed bears called Bingie bears. These 1930s novelty bears often wore extravagant costumes. Their ears were lined with a new synthetic fabric called silk plush.

Although many of the teddy bear manufacturers thrived in the 1930s, J K Farnell sadly ceased production in 1934 owing to a big fire which devastated the factory.

By the close of the decade, World War II had begun and although many manufacturers were still in production, teddies were being replaced in the factories by more essential items. Then home-made bears made from all manner of fabrics and oddments began to appear.

The bear featured on the cover of this book is an early Merrythought teddy, purchased in the 1930s. It is 28in (70cm) tall and is fitted with a growler, which, sadly, no longer works. Over the years it has given and received much love and its fur in places has worn very thin! This bear is a delightful example of the pleasure to be gained from bears of all shapes and sizes.

MAKING THE 1930s BEAR

Before starting to make the bear, carefully read the chapter on Classic Bear-making. Following the step-by-step instructions there, make the 10 templates, cut out the fabric pieces and assemble the bear, taking into consideration the special points below. Take care to keep your working surfaces as clean as possible at all times.

As this bear is quite large, it is advisable to use heavy-duty thread for all machine stitched seams.

The centre head gusset of this bear is in two sections. Cut these out as a pair, turning over the template to produce a 'pair' of pattern pieces. Join the centre seam before attaching the gusset to the side-of-head pieces in the usual manner.

Before turning the head right side out, trim the side head and centre gusset seams around the muzzle. The head should then be stuffed and closed around the hardboard joint.

The leg templates are turned over along the back seamline to produce the pattern piece, so only two leg sections are cut. The stuffing opening in this case is on the front of the leg as there is no back seam.

As the distance from the ear position to the eye socket is too far to insert a bodkin, use a doubled, knotted length of heavy-duty thread, which should be inserted close to the final placing of the eye (about 2½in (6cm) from the nose tip along the side head gusset seam). Make a few very tiny oversewing (overcasting) stitches before bringing the bodkin out a little way from these. Enlarge the hole using a bodkin, thread on the eye loop and insert the eye. Take the bodkin across the muzzle to the approximate position of the second eye, pull the thread tightly and make a few more tiny oversewing (overcasting) stitches. Make a hole and insert the eye. Then take the bodkin to the tip of the nose, finishing off with oversewing (overcasting) stitches and snipping the tail thread closely. (These stitches will be covered by the embroidery stitches of the nose.)

The nose is a rectangle of vertical satin stitches measuring 1¼in (3cm) across and 1in (2.5cm) deep and is worked using six strands of stranded cotton. The edges are neatened with several horizontal straight stitches at the top and bottom.

The smiling mouth is formed from a few straight stitches, the horizontals of which are looped upwards slightly to form a smile.

An optional growler has been inserted in this bear. If you wish to include a voice, instructions can be found on page 27.

Materials

1yd (90cm) of 54in (137cm) wide fawn distressed pile mohair with ¾in (21mm) pile

Small square of dark chocolate brown velvet

Tacking (basting) thread

Matching heavy-duty sewing thread

One 3in (76mm) hardboard crown joint

Four 3½in (88mm) hardboard crown joints

1lb (450 g) kapok

2¼lb (1kg) wood wool

Two ⅝in (15mm) amber and black glass eyes

One large deep-voiced growler (optional)

Scrap of calico or muslin for growler (optional)

One skein black 'stranded cotton' embroidery thread

A 1930s Merrythought label.

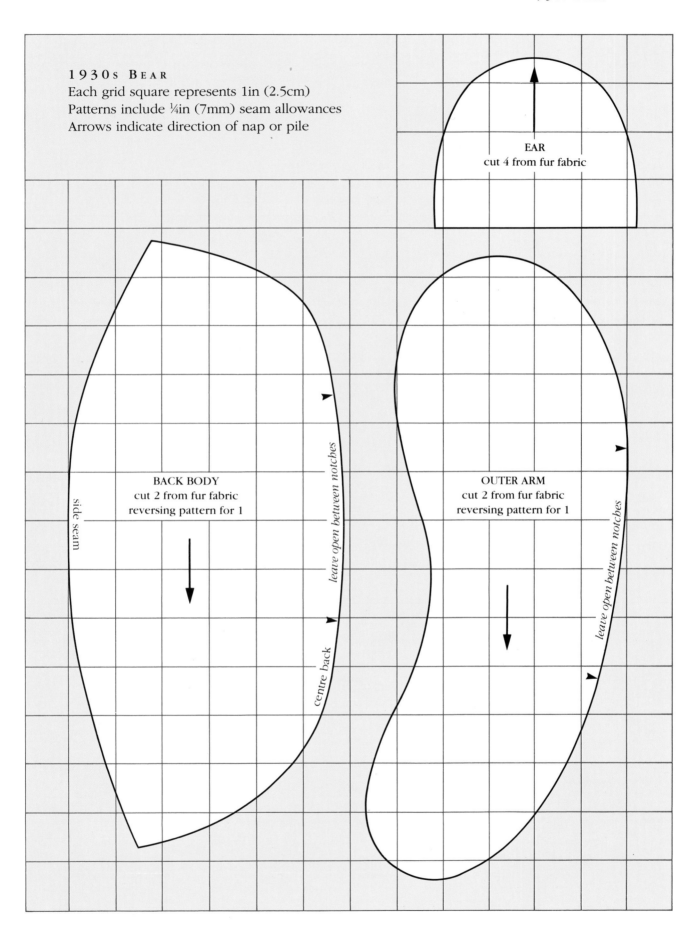

1930s BEAR
Each grid square represents 1in (2.5cm)
Patterns include ¼in (7mm) seam allowances
Arrows indicate direction of nap or pile

EAR
cut 4 from fur fabric

BACK BODY
cut 2 from fur fabric
reversing pattern for 1

side seam

leave open between notches

centre back

OUTER ARM
cut 2 from fur fabric
reversing pattern for 1

leave open between notches

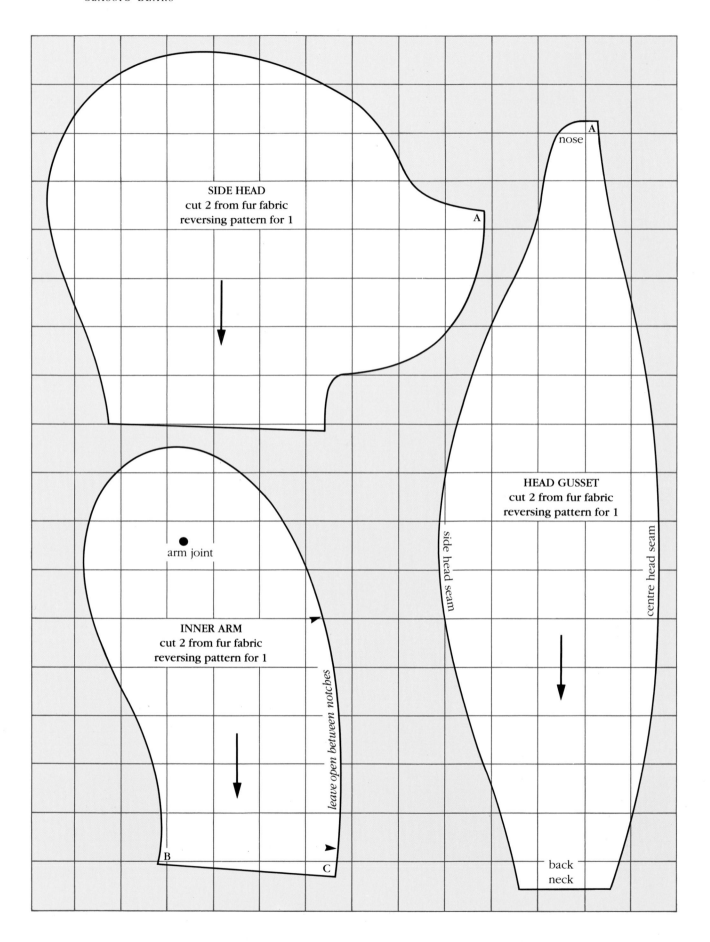

SIDE HEAD
cut 2 from fur fabric
reversing pattern for 1

A

nose

A

HEAD GUSSET
cut 2 from fur fabric
reversing pattern for 1

side head seam

centre head seam

● arm joint

INNER ARM
cut 2 from fur fabric
reversing pattern for 1

leave open between notches

B

C

back
neck

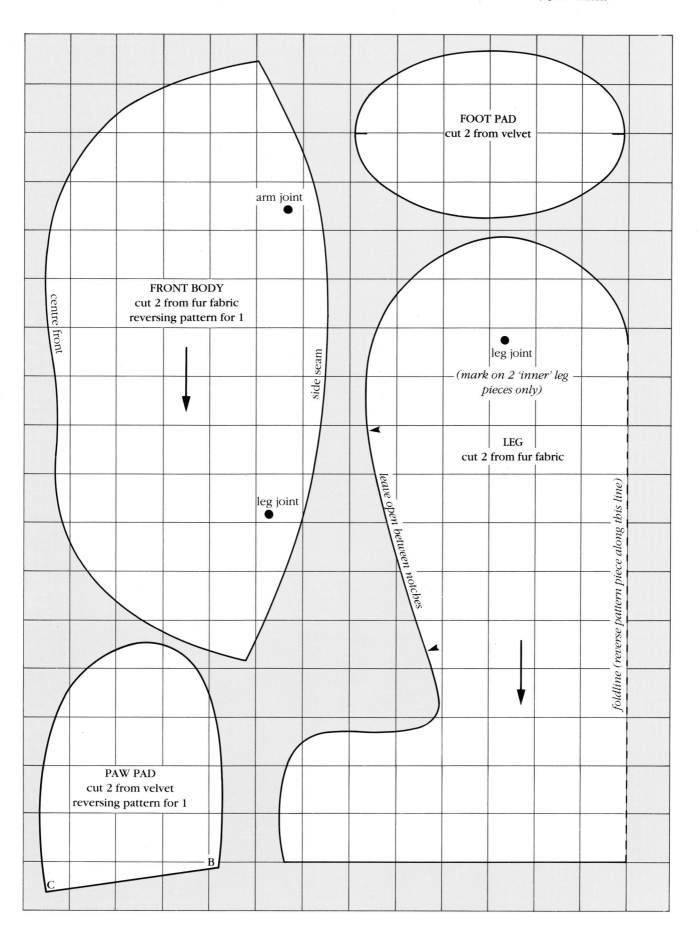

FOOT PAD
cut 2 from velvet

arm joint

FRONT BODY
cut 2 from fur fabric
reversing pattern for 1

centre front

side seam

leg joint

(mark on 2 'inner' leg pieces only)

LEG
cut 2 from fur fabric

leg joint

leave open between notches

PAW PAD
cut 2 from velvet
reversing pattern for 1

B

C

foldline (reverse pattern piece along this line)

FRENCH BEAR

Until World War I most bears sold in France, as in Britain, were imported from Germany. However, as the conflict continued, a small, but nevertheless significant domestic industry set about manufacturing teddy bears.

Generally, French bears were not of such high quality as German models; fur was usually a lower standard – being harsher and more bristly. It was also often a brasher, brighter gold. Later on, in the 1930s, many bears were made from an inferior artificial plush.

The most notable thing about the French teddy was its appearance. Being less substantial than its German counterpart, it tended to have much thinner arms and legs, as well as a shorter muzzle. Bodies were also often slimmer and straighter than other bears, especially if compared with quality Steiff or Hermann teddies.

Jointing on French teddies was also very different as a cruder exterior wire system was used which, when the fabric disintegrated, meant the bear really did fall to pieces. Eyes were usually clear glass, hand-painted on the back in black or brown. These were often held in place with glue or fastened singly by means of a wire loop.

As the French tended to favour dolls, teddy bear manufacture never took off like it did in Britain, the United States, Germany or even Eastern Europe.

As French bears were generally constructed in an inferior way, few good bear examples from the early part of the century exist.

One noted French producer was M Pintel Fils & Cie. Bears from this and similar factories can be identified by a trade button, rather like the famous Steiff mark, on the chest or ear.

The French are probably better known for their mechanical bears, some excellent examples of which still exist from around the 1920s.

Because of the French bears' rather slimmer shape, they make an interesting alternative to sew. This bear is made from a honey-gold mohair, although one of the bright new colours could be used as a substitute. The pads are dark beige suedette and the eyes are cheeky little boot buttons.

A little experience of making teddy bears will show that no two bears look exactly the same. The slightest variation in the positioning of the ears or eyes will produce a very different character from the

Materials

¼yd (25cm) of 54in (137cm)
wide honey-gold mohair
with ⅜in (9mm) pile
Small square of dark beige
suedette
Tacking (basting) thread
Matching sewing thread
Matching heavy-duty thread
One 2in (50mm) hardboard
crown joint
Four 1⅜in (36mm)
hardboard crown joints
Small amount of 'firm-fill'
polyester filling (stuffing)
1lb (450g) wood wool
Two ½in (12mm) black glass
boot button eyes
One skein black 'soft cotton'
embroidery thread

ones shown in the photographs in this book. One of the pleasures of making classic bears is that, as they are assembled, they take on their own particular personality. You will soon decide just how you like your bear to look.

Traditionally, bears have been given an inverted Y shaped mouth, but even within this guideline, there are endless variations of expression. Should the fur pile cause long stitches to shift position, hold them down with a few tiny straight anchoring stitches.

Most early bears have small eyes which are rather close-set. Placing eyes further apart will give a wide-eyed and innocent look. In general, teddy bears' eyes look best set low down on the head, not too far from the muzzle, but this again is a matter of preference. A rather vacant expression can be achieved by moving the eyes further towards the ears, spacing them widely apart.

MAKING THE FRENCH BEAR

Before starting to make the bear, carefully read the chapter on Classic Bear-making. Following the step-by-step instructions there, make the 10 templates, cut out the fabric pieces and assemble the bear, taking into consideration the special points below. Take care to keep your working surfaces as clean as possible at all times.

Stuff the muzzle firmly, using polyester filling (stuffing), to form a short, angular shape.

The eyes should be placed on the head seam, so that their lower edges are about 1¾ (4.5cm) from the tip of the muzzle.

The ears should be set vertically downwards from the head gusset seams on the sides of the head 1¾in (4.5cm) from the eye position. The top tip of each ear should just be touching the head gusset seam.

The nose is worked in horizontal satin stitches, following the tip of the head gusset seamlines and forming a blunt-ended triangle which finishes just below the point of the head gusset seam.

From the centre of the lower edge of the nose, make a ½in (12mm) straight stitch downwards, following the lower seamline and using two strands of soft cotton thread. The mouth is then formed by making a ¾in (18mm) straight stitch from the centre to the right, back to the centre and a ¾in (18mm) straight stitch from the centre to the left. The expression of your bear can be altered by varying the angle of these straight stitches. Upturned stitches will express a contented bear, while downturned stitches will portray a need to be cuddled!

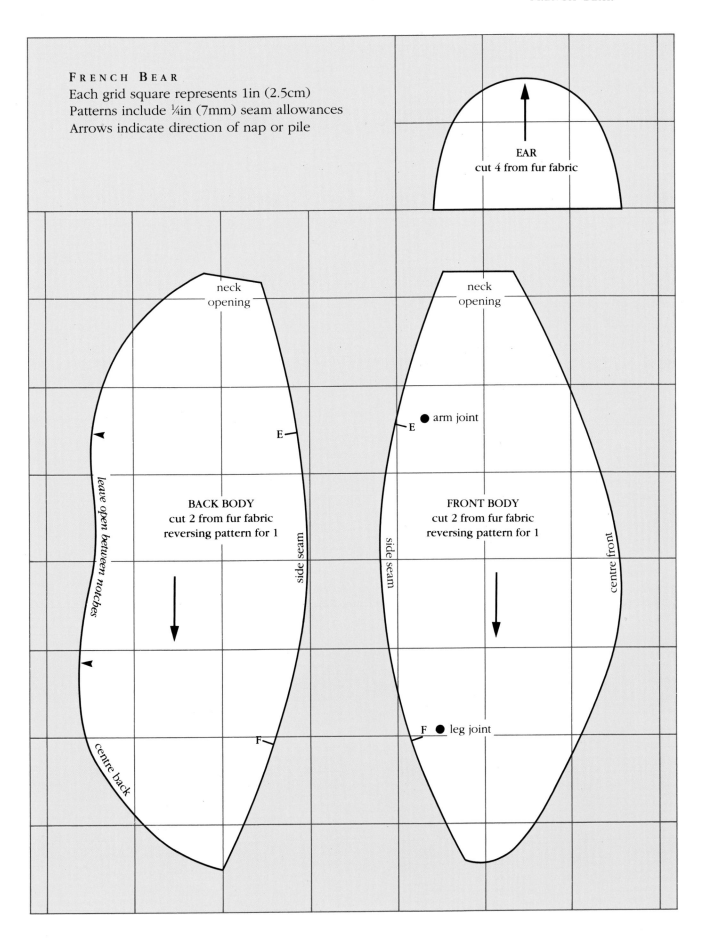

FRENCH BEAR
Each grid square represents 1in (2.5cm)
Patterns include ¼in (7mm) seam allowances
Arrows indicate direction of nap or pile

EAR
cut 4 from fur fabric

neck
opening

neck
opening

E

E ● arm joint

BACK BODY
cut 2 from fur fabric
reversing pattern for 1

FRONT BODY
cut 2 from fur fabric
reversing pattern for 1

leave open between notches

side seam

side seam

centre front

centre back

F

F ● leg joint

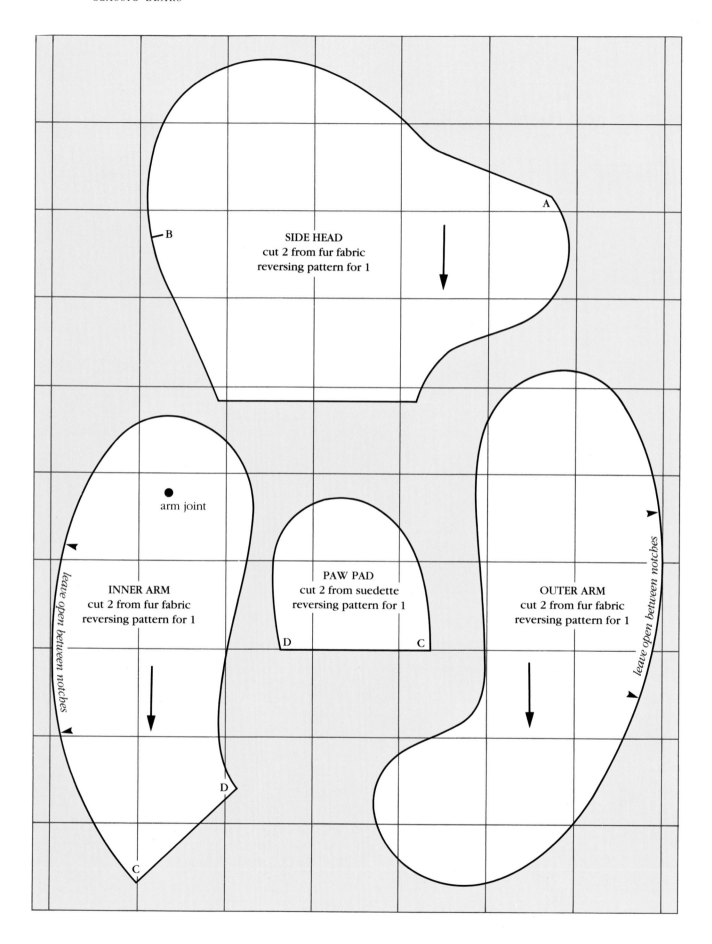

SIDE HEAD
cut 2 from fur fabric
reversing pattern for 1

A

B

arm joint

INNER ARM
cut 2 from fur fabric
reversing pattern for 1

leave open between notches

PAW PAD
cut 2 from suedette
reversing pattern for 1

D   C

OUTER ARM
cut 2 from fur fabric
reversing pattern for 1

leave open between notches

D

C

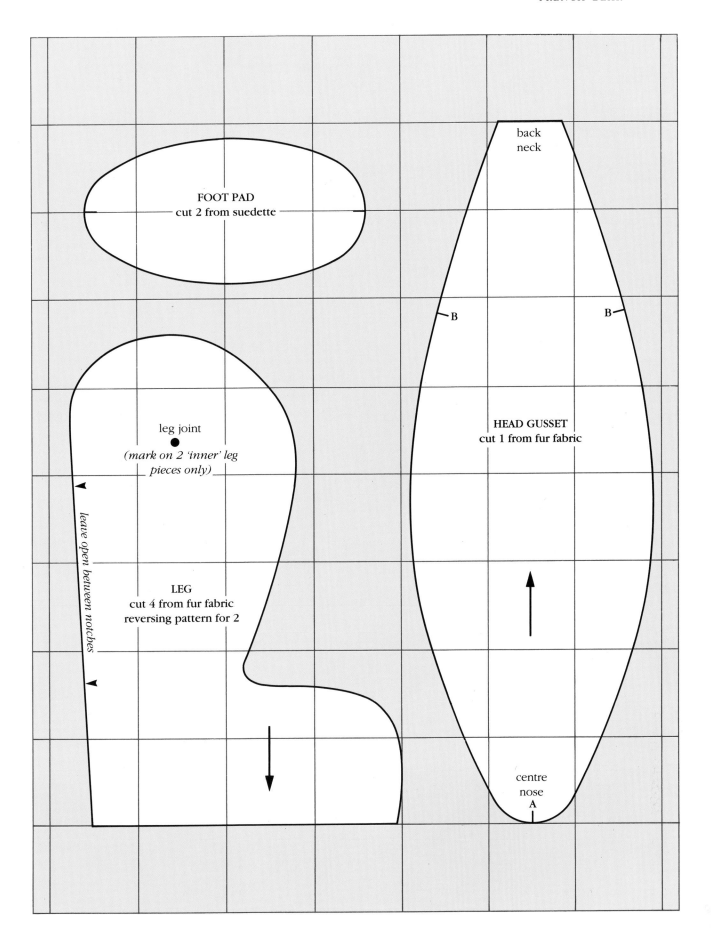

FOOT PAD
cut 2 from suedette

back
neck

B   B

HEAD GUSSET
cut 1 from fur fabric

leg joint
●
(mark on 2 'inner' leg
pieces only)

leave open between notches

LEG
cut 4 from fur fabric
reversing pattern for 2

centre
nose
A

WARTIME BEAR

The bear pictured here was inspired by a bear-style popular during World War II. Made from honey-gold mohair pile fabric, it is 14in (36cm) tall and has dark beige suedette pads.

During World War II, imports were once again restricted. In the early part of the war, the domestic markets boomed. In Britain, firms such as Chad Valley, Chiltern and Merrythought took advantage of the lack of competition from the mainly German factories. But as the conflict dragged on, supplies for toy manufacture diminished, even though the best mohair fabrics were produced in Yorkshire. Many smaller manufacturers which had been formed to meet the demand for teddy bears over the previous fifteen or so years, were forced to close down.

However, teddy bears continued to be made. As stocks on the shelves dwindled, publishers were quick to respond to the demands of needlewomen and produced instruction books for making a variety of soft toys. Patterns also appeared in women's magazines and newspapers. One publication stressed the therapeutic value of creative handiwork, recommending the satisfaction to be derived from producing a cuddly toy from the contents of a rag bag!

Some of the more unlikely materials suggested for recycling were moth-eaten swimming costumes, old vests and discarded hats. Old stockings and cotton fabrics were shredded to form the filling, while buttons and old leather gloves were recommended for creating the features.

Many much-loved bears exist from this time. Some were made from old blankets or coats. Others wore hand-knitted clothes. Because of the shortage of fur fabric, the bodies of some bears were made from clothing fabric while what little fur was available was saved for the head, paws and feet.

In other parts of the world, bears were being put together from equally unusual bits and pieces. Australia's small manufacturing industry turned out teddies made from sheepskin, a readily available material.

This bear is based on a style popular during World War II, but it has been made in a traditional short-pile mohair fabric. Its nose, however, has been cut from leather salvaged from a pair of soft leather gloves. The pattern could also be used to make a bear from an old cashmere or wool coat in line with the wartime 'make do and mend' spirit.

As with all the patterns in this book, the materials used have been listed for your convenience and guidance, but with a little experience, a variety of different fabrics can be used with any of the patterns to produce bears with very different characteristics and expressions. Try taking the ear shape from one bear and the eye

position from another to achieve a variety of permutations. Or change an arm or body shape to produce your own individual friend. Before cutting the precious fabric, however, fit together the templates to build the basic bear shape. You will soon be able to judge quite accurately the finished effect of your bear by assessing the cardboard cut-outs.

MAKING THE WARTIME BEAR

Before starting to make the bear, carefully read the chapter on Classic Bear-making. Following the step-by-step instructions there, make the 10 templates, cut out the fabric pieces and assemble the bear, taking into consideration the special points below. Take care to keep your working surfaces as clean as possible at all times.

The front and back leg sections on this particular bear are cut in one piece which is then folded over to form a single back seam. When cutting the legs out, cut two pieces, remembering to turn the pattern piece over and to reverse all the markings to form a 'pair' of legs.

The feet are formed from separate crescent-shaped sections which are attached before the back seam is stitched. Do take care to match the notches correctly. The half moon should sit centrally along the lower straight edge of the leg, and should be eased slightly to fit. There will be a small space on either side of the leg section. This is to accommodate the seam allowance. Tack (baste) and machine stitch the foot in place, before closing the back seam. The foot pad can then be positioned in the usual way.

The four arm pieces are cut from a single pattern piece. Again do remember to draw two sections, before turning over the template to draw the second pair. The suedette pads are slip stitched into position (turning a tiny hem) when the arms are completed, but before they are attached to the body.

Position the eyes just wide of the head gusset seam about 1¼in (3cm) from the nose tip. The inner edge of the eyes should sit just on the seamline on each side of the head.

Stitch the inner third of each ear along the head gusset seam, starting about 1¾in (4.5cm) from the top of the eye and working towards the back of the head. When the back seam of the ear has been secured, twist the remaining two-thirds downwards vertically and stitch in place. Complete the front seam of the ear in the normal way.

The nose on this bear has been cut from a small scrap of glove leather. If this is not available, felt can be used. Trim away a little of the fur pile at the tip of the muzzle before attaching the nose using a matching thread and small straight stitches. The mouth has been embroidered with straight stitches, using six strands of brown stranded cotton. The centre stitch following the muzzle seam and each of the two branches forming the mouth are all ¼in (7mm) long.

Materials

¼yd (25cm) of 54in (137cm) wide honey-gold mohair with ⅜in (9mm) pile

Small square of dark beige suedette

Tacking (basting) thread

Matching sewing thread

Matching heavy-duty thread

One 1⅜in (36mm) hardboard crown joint

Four 1in (25mm) hardboard crown joints

Small amount of 'firm-fill' polyester filling (stuffing)

1lb (450 g) wood wool

Two ½in (12mm) amber glass eyes

Small scrap of fine dark brown leather or felt

One skein dark brown 'stranded cotton' embroidery thread

A 12in (30cm) 1940s bear.

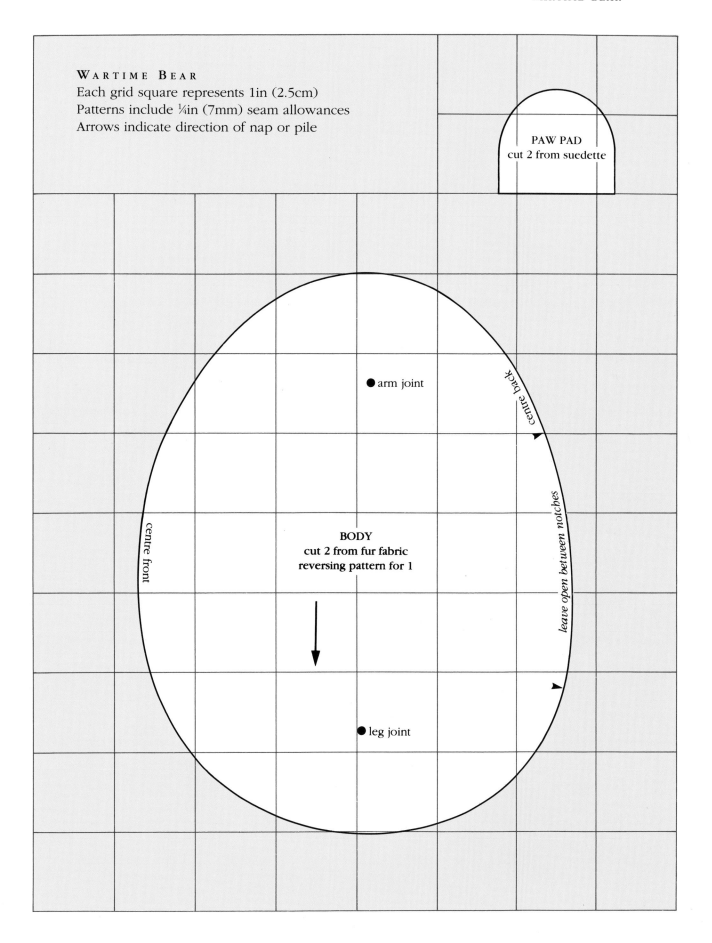

WARTIME BEAR
Each grid square represents 1in (2.5cm)
Patterns include ¼in (7mm) seam allowances
Arrows indicate direction of nap or pile

PAW PAD
cut 2 from suedette

● arm joint

centre back

centre front

leave open between notches

BODY
cut 2 from fur fabric
reversing pattern for 1

● leg joint

SIDE HEAD
cut 2 from fur fabric
reversing pattern for 1

A

FOOT PAD
cut 2 from suedette

leg joint ●

(mark on 2 'inner' leg pieces only)

NOSE
cut 1 from
leather

leave open between notches

LEG
cut 2 from fur fabric
reversing pattern for 1

leave open between notches

B

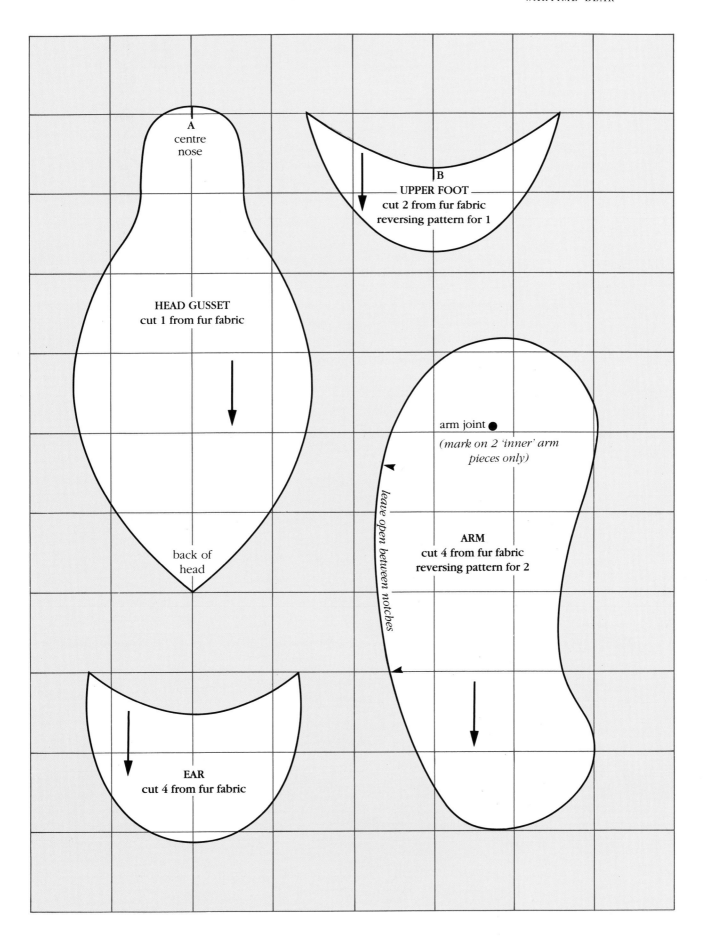

A
centre
nose

HEAD GUSSET
cut 1 from fur fabric

back of
head

B
UPPER FOOT
cut 2 from fur fabric
reversing pattern for 1

arm joint ●
*(mark on 2 'inner' arm
pieces only)*

leave open between notches

ARM
cut 4 from fur fabric
reversing pattern for 2

EAR
cut 4 from fur fabric

AMERICAN BEAR

The bear pictured here was inspired by 1940s American bears. Made from gold fur fabric, it is 14in (36cm) tall and has dark beige suedette paw and foot pads.

The years between the two world wars saw an unprecedented boom in the manufacture of teddy bears.

In America, production during this time thrived. One of the more successful companies was the Knickerbocker Toy Co Inc. Originally founded in the early 1900s in New York, some of the bears from this manufacturer still survive in excellent condition.

The bear featured here is similar to the Knickerbocker bear in production around 1940. It has a typically large round head with a relatively flat, snubbed muzzle.

Bear shapes and features were continually evolving. Around this time, the body shape was changing quite dramatically. Gone was the hump; legs and arms became shorter and thicker and claws were often omitted. Stuffing was almost entirely kapok, giving a softer shape to the bear's physique. Although most bears' arms still displayed the distinctive curve of the earlier models, these new varieties were much more familiar to the teddy bears we know today.

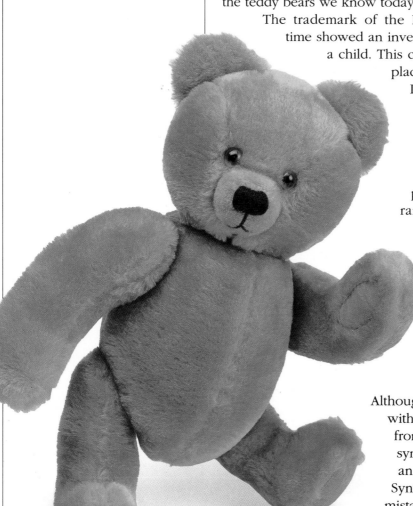

The trademark of the Knickerbocker Toy Company at this time showed an inverted horseshoe containing the figure of a child. This could be seen on sew-in labels, usually placed in the front body seam or in the ear. Later labels were to proclaim the slogan 'Animals of Distinction'.

The Knickerbocker toy factory is still famous for its Smokey bear characters, manufactured during the 1960s and 1970s Smokey was used to promote the work of the Junior Forest rangers and the young owners were encouraged to enrol in this organization which aimed to prevent the outbreak of forest fires. Several toy companies, including The Ideal Toy Co, were also licensed to produce this popular bear, which was named after Smokey Joe Martin, an employee of the New York Fire Department in the 1920s.

Although the Knickerbocker bears, in common with most others of that time, were made from mohair fabric, this bear is made from synthetic knitted fabric and is, therefore, an ideal bear for a beginner to attempt. Synthetic fabric is relatively cheap, and so mistakes in cutting out are not so crucial, as with expensive mohair. Fabric with a knitted

backing does, however, need careful handling during the stuffing process as it may pull out of shape or distort. For this reason a light polyester filling has been used, and, as in the original bear, the arms and legs have been less firmly stuffed than is usual. Polyester filling is non-allergenic and conforms to toy safety standards. If this bear is to be made as a child's toy, plastic lock-in safety eyes must be used.

Materials

½yd (45cm) of 54in (137cm) wide gold acrylic fur fabric
Small square of dark beige suedette
Tacking (basting) thread
Matching sewing thread
Matching heavy-duty thread
One 1⅜in (36mm) hardboard crown joint
Four 1in (25mm) hardboard crown joints
1lb (450 g) washable 'firm-fill' polyester filling (stuffing)
Two ½in (12mm) amber and black glass eyes
One skein black 'soft cotton' embroidery thread

MAKING THE AMERICAN BEAR

Before starting to make the bear, carefully read the chapter on Classic Bear-making. Following the step-by-step instructions there, make the 8 templates, cut out the fabric pieces and assemble the bear, taking into consideration the special points below. Take care to keep your working surfaces as clean as possible at all times.

On this bear four complete arm sections are cut out, making two pairs. These are then machine sewn together, leaving an opening between the notches for stuffing in the usual way.

The paw pads are formed from narrow ovals of dark beige suedette which are sewn in place after the side seams have been sewn, but before the arms are stuffed. The pads on the feet are large ovals, which are inserted in the usual manner.

The ears should be set at the centre of the top of the head across the gusset seams and at a slight angle with the lower edges tilting backwards a little. They are slightly padded out with a small amount of polyester filling (stuffing).

The bear's muzzle should be clipped to a neat oval, finishing just below the eyes.

Amber glass eyes with black pupils have been used and the securing thread has been pulled firmly to cause a depression for each eye socket. The eyes are placed on the head gusset seam, so that their lower edges are 1⅜in (3.5cm) from the centre of the tip of the nose.

The nose is worked in vertical satin stitches across the seam at the end of the muzzle, forming a horizontal oval about ⅞in (22mm) wide and ⅝in (16mm) deep.

The mouth is formed from three straight stitches in an inverted 'Y' shape, using soft cotton embroidery thread.

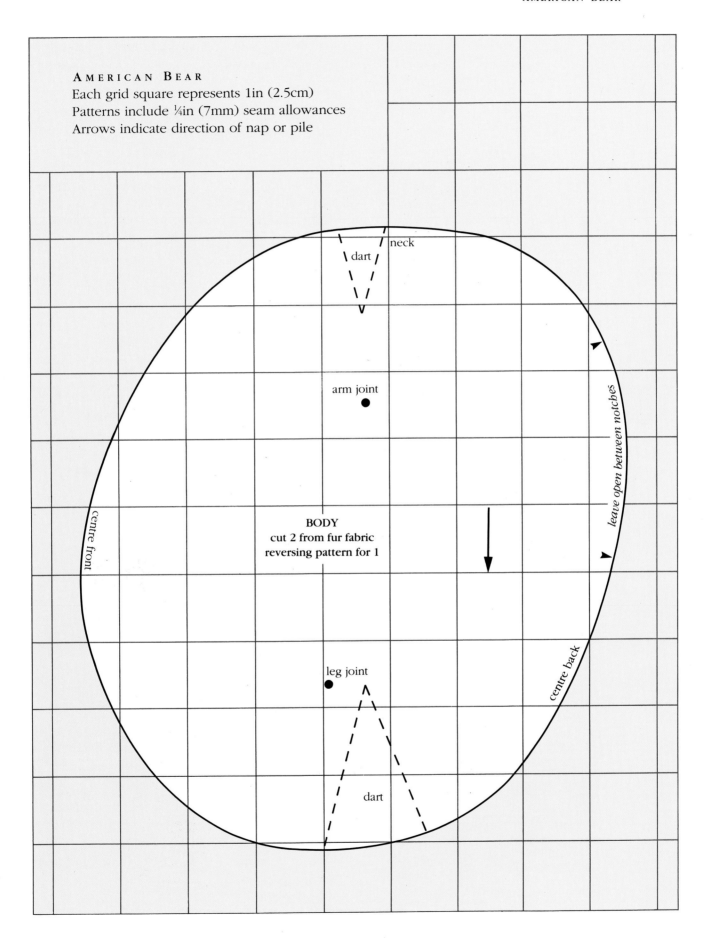

AMERICAN BEAR
Each grid square represents 1in (2.5cm)
Patterns include ¼in (7mm) seam allowances
Arrows indicate direction of nap or pile

neck

dart

arm joint

leave open between notches

centre front

BODY
cut 2 from fur fabric
reversing pattern for 1

centre back

leg joint

dart

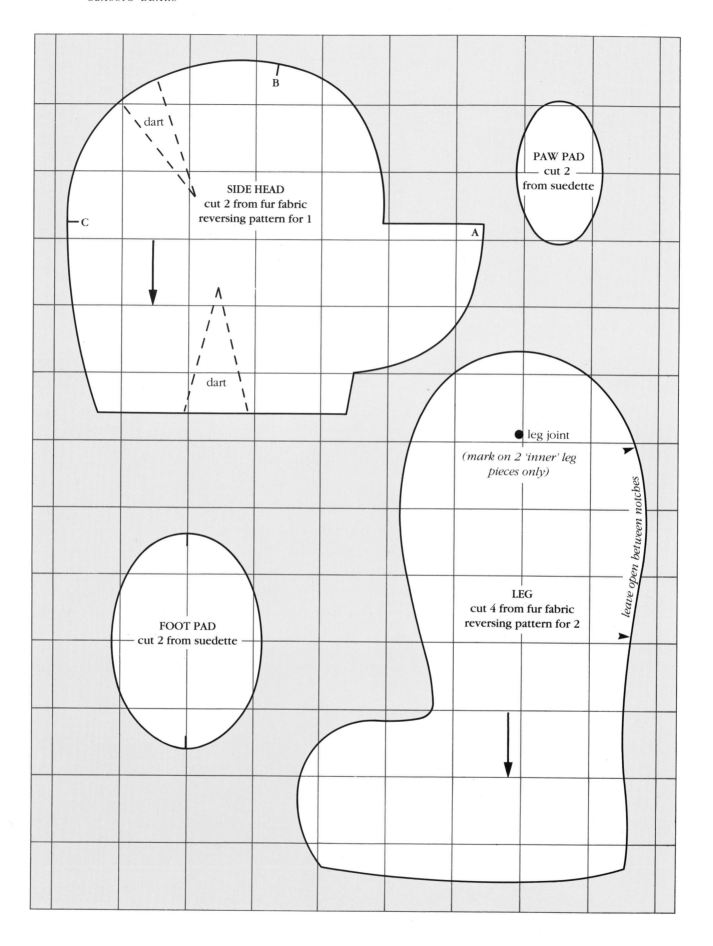

SIDE HEAD
cut 2 from fur fabric
reversing pattern for 1

dart

dart

B

C

A

PAW PAD
cut 2
from suedette

leg joint
*(mark on 2 'inner' leg
pieces only)*

LEG
cut 4 from fur fabric
reversing pattern for 2

leave open between notches

FOOT PAD
cut 2 from suedette

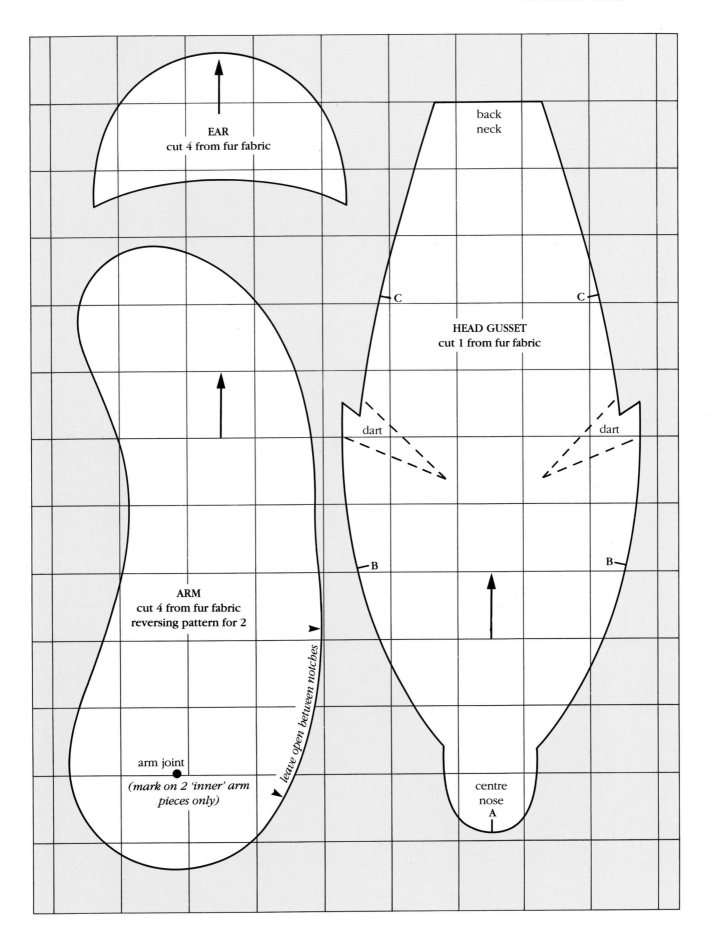

EAR
cut 4 from fur fabric

back
neck

C   C

HEAD GUSSET
cut 1 from fur fabric

dart   dart

B   B

ARM
cut 4 from fur fabric
reversing pattern for 2

leave open between notches

arm joint ●

*(mark on 2 'inner' arm
pieces only)*

centre
nose
A

CHARACTER BEAR

The bear pictured here was inspired by character bears. Made from honeysuckle mohair pile fabric, it is 14in (36cm) tall and has light beige pads.

Over the years, since the first teddy bears were developed, some of them have been characterized and thus immortalized in literature for everyone to enjoy.

As the teddy bear craze gained momentum at the beginning of the century, so teddy bears began to appear in print. The Tale of Teddy Bright-Eyes was published in Britain in 1909, teddies also appear in stories by Mrs Craddock in 1917. But it was not until the 1920s that two of the most famous bears of literature were born: Rupert and Winnie-the-Pooh.

Rupert Bear made his first appearance in Britain's *Daily Express* newspaper as a comic strip character. He was created by Mary Tourtel, a talented illustrator who was married to the paper's night editor. Rupert became an instant success and Mary Tourtel's stories set in the fictional world of Nutwood with a host of animal friends still delight children today, the world over.

When Mary retired in 1935, Rupert's adventures were taken over by Alfred Bestall who continued to submit a daily comic strip for another 30 years. As Rupert's fame continued, his adventures could be followed in annuals, cartoons, jigsaw puzzles and even in a television series.

Four years after the arrival of Rupert, Winnie-the-Pooh was to enter the arena with the publication of *When We Were Very Young*. A A Milne based his Pooh stories on his son Christopher's teddy, bought at Harrods in London one birthday. The bear – probably of Farnell manufacture – was named Edward.

It is the E H Shepard illustrations of Pooh (inspired incidentally by a different teddy – a Steiff called Growler) that will be familiar to Pooh devotees all over the world.

The original Winnie-the-Pooh now lives in the New York Public Library on Fifth Avenue.

More recently, other teddy bears have found fame in newspapers, books and television. In France, Gros Nounours began his career in newspapers during the 1960s before finding real fame on the television in a series which ran for over 1,000 episodes.

Nounours' career runs parallel with the British glove puppet Sooty and the American cartoon bear, Yogi. And there are so many others: Paddington Bear, SuperTed and Carebears are known across the world.

The character bear to make here could sport a scarf in the Rupert Bear tradition. He wears tiny bells in his ears. It is made from honeysuckle-coloured short-pile mohair and has paw and foot pads of light beige.

This 11in (28cm) tall Winnie-the-Pooh bear was produced in a limited edition in 1993.

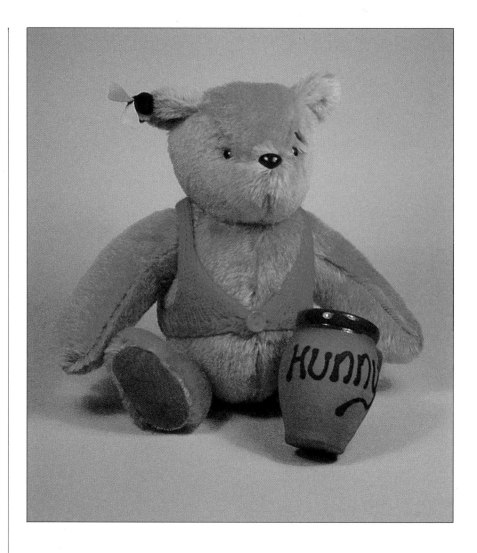

Materials

½yd (45cm) of 54in (137cm) wide honeysuckle mohair with ⅜in (9mm) pile
Small square of light beige felt
Tacking (basting) thread
Matching sewing thread
Matching heavy-duty thread
One 1⅜in (36mm) hardboard crown joint
Four 1in (25mm) hardboard joints
Two ⁹⁄₁₆in (15mm) amber glass eyes
Small amount of 'firm-fill' polyester filling (stuffing)
1lb (450 g) wood wool
One skein black 'soft cotton' embroidery thread
Two small bells (for ears)

MAKING THE CHARACTER BEAR

Before starting to make the bear, carefully read the chapter on Classic Bear-making. Following the step-by-step instructions there, make the 10 templates, cut out the fabric pieces and assemble the bear, taking into consideration the special points below. Take care to keep your working surfaces as clean as possible at all times.

A small bell has been placed in each ear before it is sewn in position. These will make the bear 'tinkle' gently when it is shaken. The ears have been placed slightly to the back of the head, slightly overlapping the centre head gusset on each side. The distance from the nose tip to the ear is about 4in (10cm).

The eyes are positioned just across the head gusset 2in (5cm) from the nose tip. They have been pulled in slightly to create an eye 'socket' and the fur has been trimmed away to give a wide-eyed expression.

The heart-shaped nose is worked in vertical satin stitches using black soft cotton embroidery thread.

The mouth is formed as a large inverted 'Y' following the muzzle seam. The first downwards stitch should measure about ½in (12mm) and each branch of the mouth ⅜in (1cm).

By following the pattern markings for placing the leg joints, the bear will have an endearing pigeon-toed appearance.

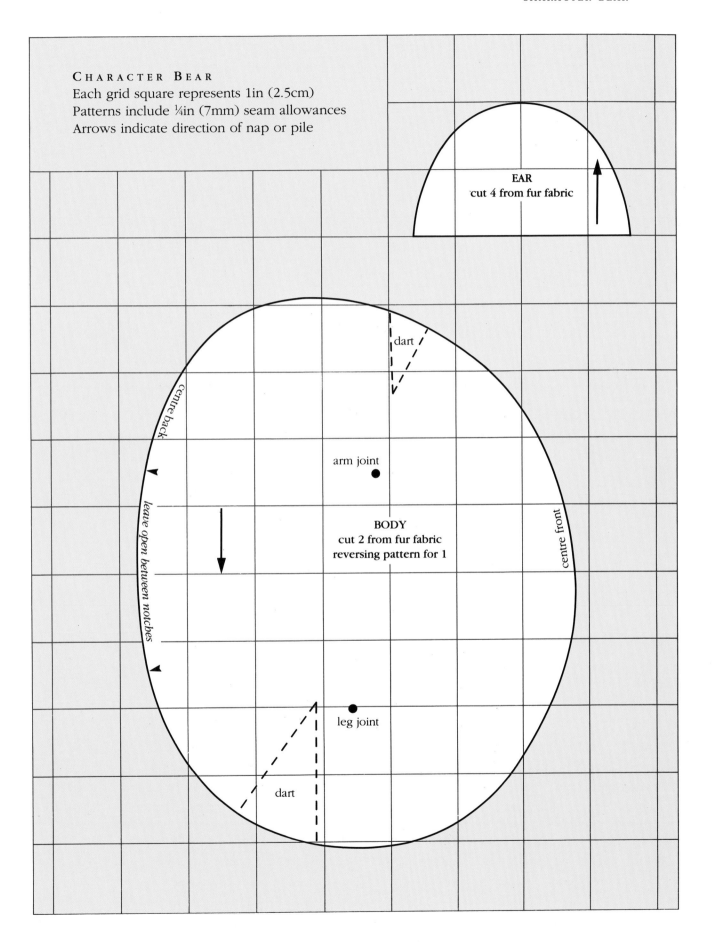

CHARACTER BEAR
Each grid square represents 1in (2.5cm)
Patterns include ¼in (7mm) seam allowances
Arrows indicate direction of nap or pile

EAR
cut 4 from fur fabric

dart

centre back

arm joint

leave open between notches

BODY
cut 2 from fur fabric
reversing pattern for 1

centre front

leg joint

dart

PAW PAD
cut 2 from felt

C   B

arm joint

INNER ARM
cut 2 from fur fabric
reversing pattern for 1

leave open between notches

FOOT PAD
cut 2 from felt

B

C

leg joint

INNER LEG
cut 2 from fur fabric
reversing pattern for 1

leave open between notches

OUTER LEG
cut 2 from fur fabric
reversing pattern for 1

leave open between notches

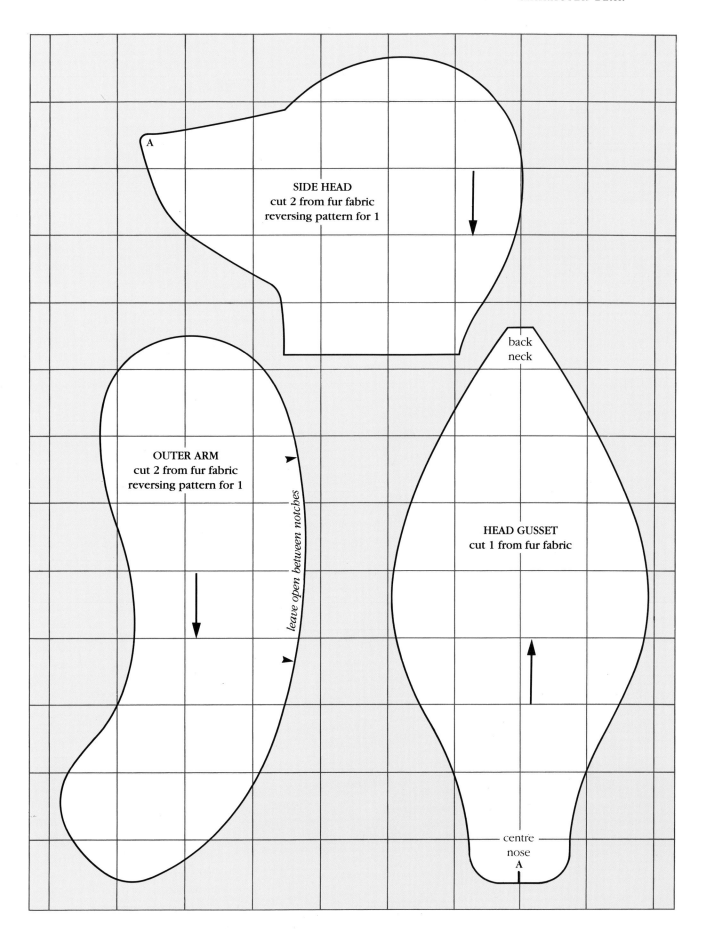

SIDE HEAD
cut 2 from fur fabric
reversing pattern for 1

A

back
neck

OUTER ARM
cut 2 from fur fabric
reversing pattern for 1

leave open between notches

HEAD GUSSET
cut 1 from fur fabric

centre
nose
A

1950s BRITISH BEAR

The bear pictured here was inspired by 1950s British bears. Made from gold fur fabric, it is 14in (36cm) tall and has dark chocolate brown pads.

Some of the most famous and early British bears came from the Chad Valley toy factory which began trading in that name in 1919. The company's origins are even earlier and date back to well before the turn of the century. However, Chad Valley teddy bears were not in full-time production until 1920.

Over the years, many soft toys were manufactured under the Chad Valley name but the most impressive must have been a range of large teddy bears which measured up to 28in (71cm). Chad Valley's advertisements proudly proclaimed that these bears were produced exclusively of British materials and were available in fabrics such as brown long beaver and best golden fur – the cheapest teddy in the range was described as an upright golden.

By the time World War II had ended and rationing across many countries had begun to subside, the 1950s had been ushered in along with a newer, brighter teddy. To begin with, its fur was probably of synthetic cotton-rayon rather than the more expensive mohair. Joints were cruder and several bear types had immovable limbs. The most important change in bears of this period was the introduction of the lock-in safety eyes, first patented by Wendy Boston for her washable bears of 1948.

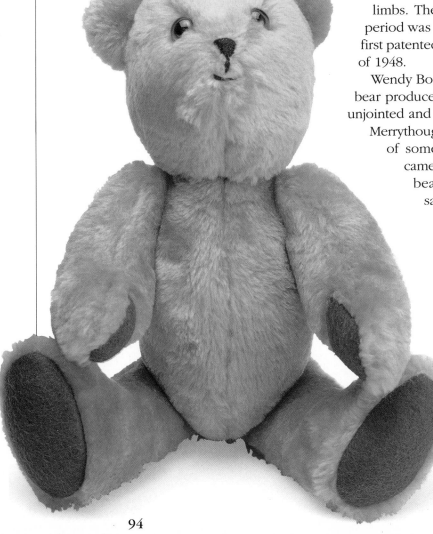

Wendy Boston was one of the most renowned teddy bear producers of the 1950s. Her designs were usually unjointed and stuffed with kapok for a soft teddy.

Merrythought, of course, was another manufacturer of some note. During the 1950s, the company came up with the Cheeky bears range. These bears have broad faces, velvet noses and safety eyes.

It is also worth mentioning the Irish company, Gaeltarra Eireann or Tara Toys. This state-sponsored company began manufacturing bears shortly after World War II for export to Britain and the US, as well as the domestic market.

In Northern Ireland, the Pedigree factory was producing teddy bears by the end of the 1940s. Pedigree's other factory in Merton, known as the Triang works, was the other source of 1950s bears. Pedigree bears are very much the teddies of child-hood – jointed limbs with brown velvet pads and glass eyes.

Lefray was the other British manufacturer of the day, producing traditional jointed gold and cinnamon bears with velvet pads.

Many bears from the 1920s onwards were stuffed with washed fleece. This makes a wonderful filling material, as it is hygienic, soft and easily worked. It is ideally suited for use with bears made from knitted fabrics, as it is less likely to distort the sewn shapes. Fleece should be used in the same way as kapok or polyester filling and can be bought from shops specializing in spinning requirements or by mail order from the suppliers listed on page 112.

MAKING THE 1950S BRITISH BEAR

Before starting to make the bear, carefully read the chapter on Classic Bear-making. Following the step-by-step instructions there, make the 8 templates, cut out the fabric pieces and assemble the bear, taking into consideration the special points below. Take care to keep your working surfaces as clean as possible at all times.

As the fabric used for this bear has a woven backing, great care must be taken when stitching and stuffing that it is not allowed to stretch and become mis-shapen. Tack (baste) all the seams carefully before machine stitching and do not over-stuff.

The felt front paws for this bear are stitched in position after the arms have been stuffed and closed. Use heavy-duty thread and tiny oversewing (overcasting) stitches to attach each paw, taking care to tease out any strands of pile which have been caught under the felt as you work.

The eyes are off-set slightly from the head gusset seam, so that their lower edges are about ⅞in (22mm) from the centre of the tip of the teddy bear's nose.

The ears should be set across the head gusset seams on top of the head, about 2in (5cm) apart. Do experiment with alternative positions, using 'T' pins to anchor the bear's ears in place, until you are satisfied with the results.

Trim the fur around the nose tip slightly, before working a small triangular nose in horizontal satin stitches, following the seamline at the tip of the muzzle for guidance. The mouth is then formed as an inverted 'T' from the tip of the triangle, using two strands of pearl cotton embroidery thread.

Materials

½yd (45cm) of 54in (137cm) wide gold acrylic fur fabric
Small square of dark chocolate brown felt
Tacking (basting) thread
Matching sewing thread
Matching heavy-duty thread
One 1⅜in (36mm) hardboard crown joint
Four 1in (25mm) hardboard crown joints
1lb (450g) natural fleece or polyester filling (stuffing)
Two ½in (12mm) amber glass eyes
One skein black 'pearl cotton' embroidery thread

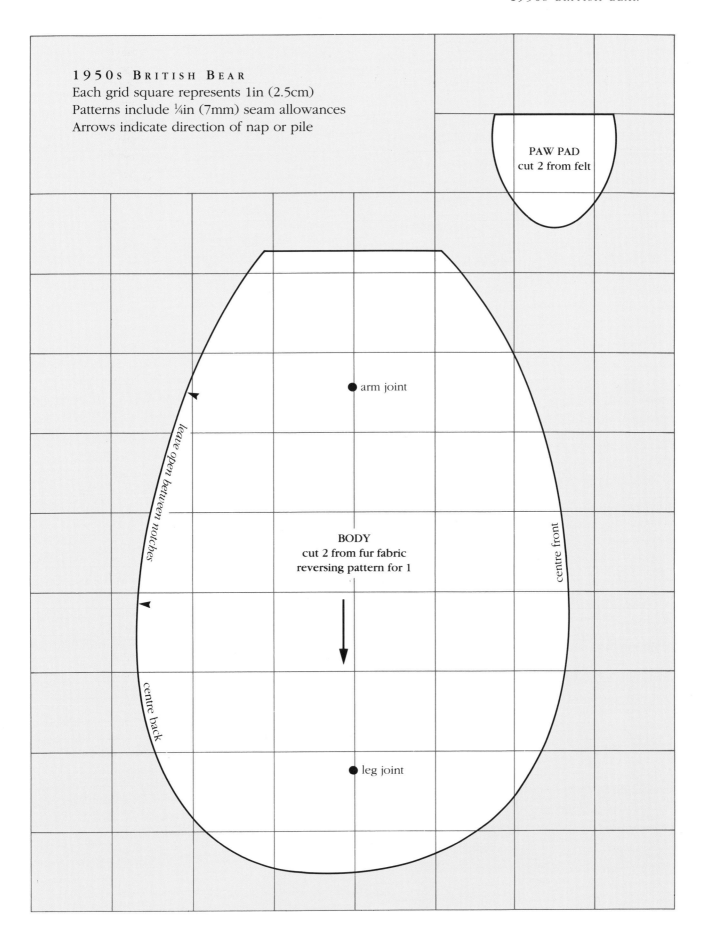

1950S BRITISH BEAR
Each grid square represents 1in (2.5cm)
Patterns include ¼in (7mm) seam allowances
Arrows indicate direction of nap or pile

PAW PAD
cut 2 from felt

arm joint

leave open between notches

centre front

BODY
cut 2 from fur fabric
reversing pattern for 1

centre back

leg joint

● arm joint

(mark on 2 'inner' arm pieces only)

ARM
cut 4 from fur fabric
reversing pattern for 2

leave open between notches

EAR
cut 4 from fur fabric

leg joint

(mark on 2 'inner' leg pieces only)

leave open between notches

LEG
cut 4 from fur fabric
reversing pattern for 2

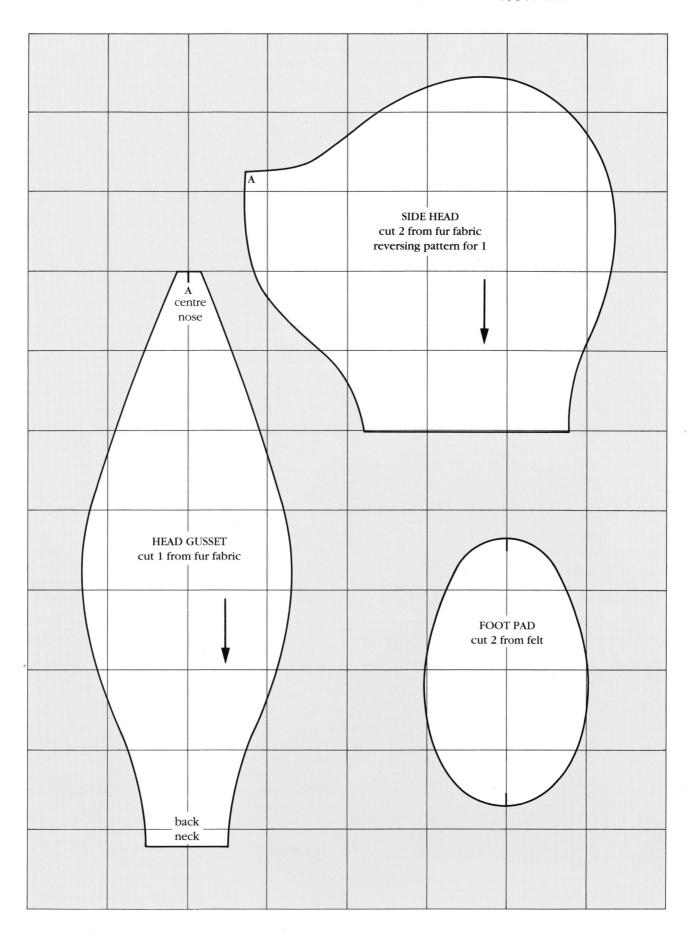

SIDE HEAD
cut 2 from fur fabric
reversing pattern for 1

A
centre
nose

HEAD GUSSET
cut 1 from fur fabric

FOOT PAD
cut 2 from felt

back
neck

A

1980s BEAR

In all his ninety years of life, the teddy bear has never been more popular than he is now in the 1990s. Despite the coming of high technology and electronic gadgetry the traditional teddy bear still wins everyone's heart.

Teddy bears themselves have not escaped this new age though. Teddy bears are now often equipped with hidden tape cassettes so that they can speak or play music.

Television has had a large influence on new characters: Rupert Bear and Winnie-the-Pooh have been around since the 1920s, but are still much watched. Toys of these characters are also produced in abundance. More recently, characters like Paddington Bear, the creation of author Michael Bond, SuperTed and Teddy Ruxpin have been viewed by millions.

However, many modern bears were not living up to the success of their ancestors. Cheaper exports from the Far East caused many toy manufacturers to close because they simply could not keep up with the competition. The Australian teddy bear industry, for example, died in the 1970s because of this economic pressure.

It was the traditional bear that many people sought and companies like the Knickerbocker Toy Company and Steiff discovered that now was the time to bring the classic bears back. Since the early 1980s, Steiff have begun to produce replicas of the antique bears. The new bears still carry a Steiff button, but this is larger than the original one, as well as a Steiff label.

Firms like Dean's Co Ltd (Dean's Rag Book Co Ltd) began to market a range of reproduction jointed bears. The House of Nisbet introduced their Childhood Classics range of bears, Bully Bear being modelled on a bear from Peter Bull's collection (Peter Bull was an English actor, renowned for his love of bears).

Many other companies produced replica bears, often made with new materials which give a softer feel. Because classic bears are now so sought after and therefore very expensive, many teddy bear collectors are looking to replica bears as one way of assembling a range of classics without spending an absolute fortune.

Modern bears based on classic designs have certainly found a place in

the market. Unlike replica bears, these teddies have all the hallmarks of a well-designed, jointed bear, but are not strictly based on any previous model. These bears are often made from the finest materials and may even possess a range of accessories like scarves, hats or boots.

This 1980s bear is sporting a pair of tiny round spectacles, giving it a studious academic look. Equipped with a little knitted muffler in college or university colours, it would be an ideal gift for a student or graduate.

This small, rotund bear has dark brown velvet paws, which contrast nicely with its honeysuckle-coloured fur. Alternatively, a light beige or mushroom fabric could be used.

Materials

¼yd (25cm) of 54in (137cm) wide honeysuckle mohair with ⅜in (9mm) pile
Small square of dark brown velvet
Tacking (basting) thread
Matching sewing thread
Matching heavy-duty thread
One 1⅜in (36mm) hardboard crown joint
Four 1in (25mm) hardboard crown joints
8oz (230g) 'firm-fill' polyester filling (stuffing)
Two ⅜in (9mm) black boot button eyes
One skein black 'stranded cotton' embroidery thread
Small pair of gold-rimmed glasses (optional)

MAKING THE 1980S BEAR

Before starting to make up the bear, carefully read the chapter on Classic Bear-making. Following the step-by-step instructions there, make the 10 templates, cut out the fabric pieces and assemble the bear, taking into consideration the special points below. Seam allowances should be kept to a minimum – about ³⁄₁₆in (5mm).

The paw and foot pads for this bear have been cut from velvet. Use very small, even tacking (basting) stitches and pull out any trapped pile before machine stitching the paw pad to the inner arm section. Use the same technique to sew inner and outer arm sections together, leaving the tacking (basting) stitches in place if possible.

The foot pads are quite tricky to machine accurately, so it may be best to backstitch by hand over the tacking (basting) stitches using heavy-duty thread. The tacking (basting) stitches can then be left in, giving extra strength to the seam.

The eyes are placed on the head gusset seam, so that their lower edges are ¾in (2cm) from the nose tip.

The extra large ears should be set vertically on the head, the upper edge just touching the head gusset seam about 3in (8cm) from the tip of the nose.

Clip the fur back lightly around the muzzle before embroidering the nose, using short horizontal satin stitches to form a small rectangle. An inverted 'T' then forms the mouth which is worked using six strands of the stranded embroidery thread.

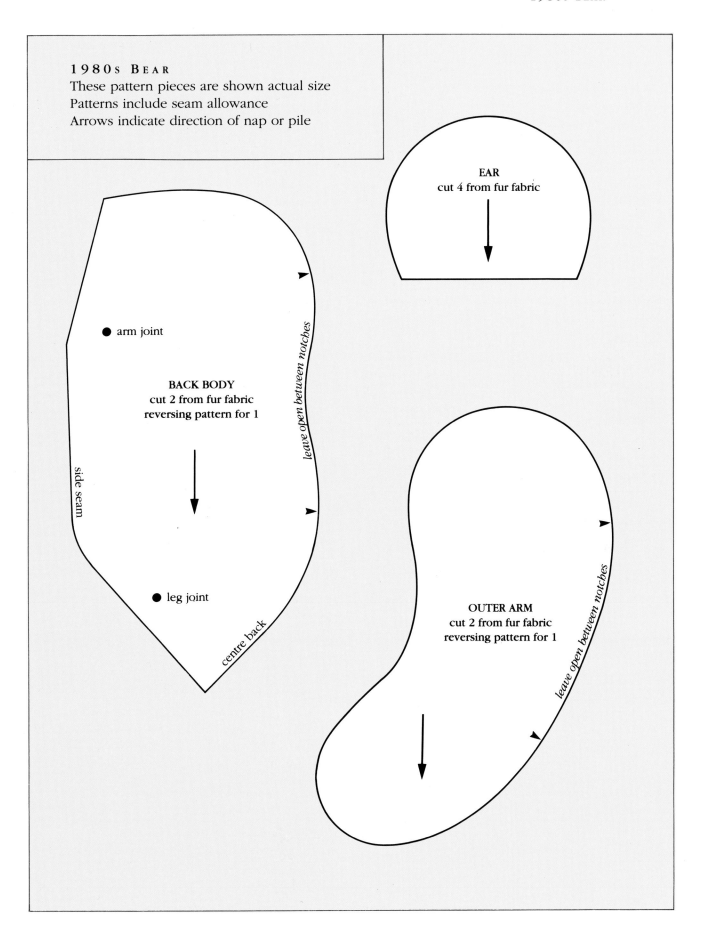

1980s BEAR
These pattern pieces are shown actual size
Patterns include seam allowance
Arrows indicate direction of nap or pile

EAR
cut 4 from fur fabric

● arm joint

BACK BODY
cut 2 from fur fabric
reversing pattern for 1

leave open between notches

side seam

● leg joint

centre back

OUTER ARM
cut 2 from fur fabric
reversing pattern for 1

leave open between notches

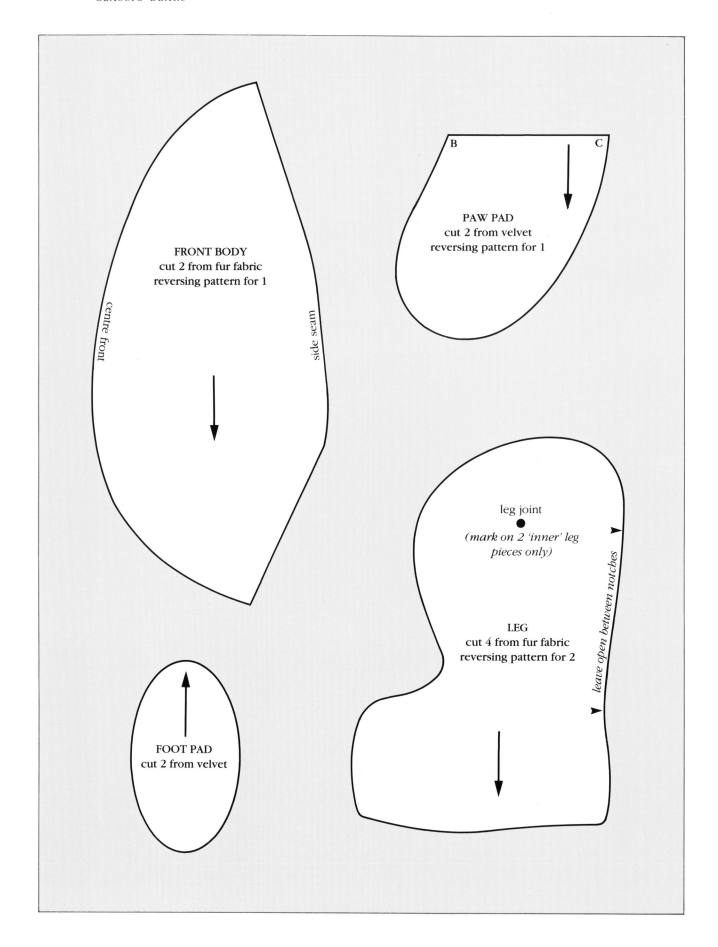

FRONT BODY
cut 2 from fur fabric
reversing pattern for 1

centre front

side seam

B   C

PAW PAD
cut 2 from velvet
reversing pattern for 1

leg joint
*(mark on 2 'inner' leg
pieces only)*

LEG
cut 4 from fur fabric
reversing pattern for 2

leave open between notches

FOOT PAD
cut 2 from velvet

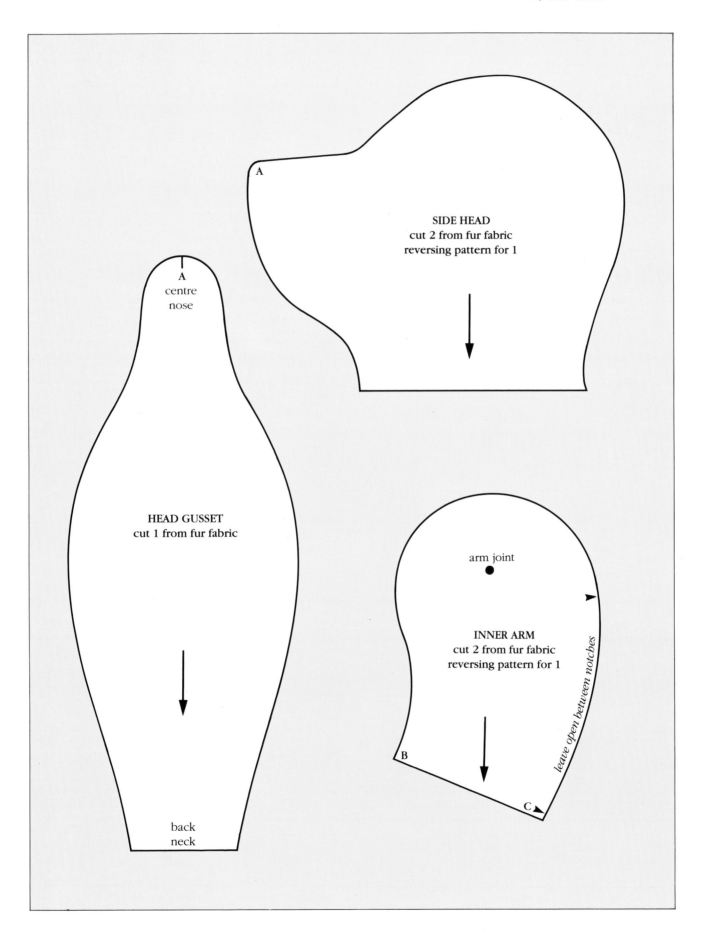

SIDE HEAD
cut 2 from fur fabric
reversing pattern for 1

A

centre
nose

HEAD GUSSET
cut 1 from fur fabric

back
neck

arm joint

INNER ARM
cut 2 from fur fabric
reversing pattern for 1

leave open between notches

B

C

MODERN BEAR

The bear pictured here is a version of a modern bear. Made from honey-beige distressed pile mohair fabric, it is 14in (36cm) tall and has pale beige suedette pads.

Is there a typical modern bear? With so many varieties of teddy on the market, it is almost impossible to define.

In the 1970s, cheap toys from the Far East put many Western manufacturers out of business. Certainly, the Australian industry, which had experienced a notable resurgence in the 1950s, could not compete, and teddy bear manufacturers in the country were just about wiped out.

However, with the craving for nostalgia, the classic bear has – since the 1980s – made something of a revival. Today, many companies in various countries produce traditional style bears from the highest quality materials with 'boot button' eyes and mohair fabric.

Traditional producers like Steiff and Merrythought quickly saw how this demand could be exploited and both companies now manufacture a successful line in replica bears – faithful reproductions of popular early teddy bears. These teddy bears are usually produced in a limited number and are made principally for the growing teddy bear collectors' market.

Teddy bear collecting in the United States and in Great Britain is experiencing something of a boom and interest is also strong in Germany and Japan. The widening availability of a large range of traditional mohair, cashmere and silk fabrics through mail order outlets and interest in teddy bear memorabilia has ensured that this interest should continue.

So great has been the revival of interest in classic teddy bears that many artists and craftsworkers have ventured into the field, producing distinctive bears, both classic and modern.

Generally, modern manufactured teddies display the most appealing characteristics from bears over a number of periods. However, the short, plump arms and legs give the modern bear a chubbier appearance. The modern bear's ears are also slightly padded to give the face an eager and inquiring look.

If you wish to experiment with your own style of bear, it is possible to adapt pieces from the various patterns in this book to create your own designs. By drawing the pattern shapes onto plain paper, it is possible to get an idea of how a finished bear might look by

A 1990s Big Softies bear called Marmaduke.

Materials

½yd (45cm) of 54in (137cm) wide honey-beige distressed pile mohair with ½in (12mm) pile

Small square of pale beige suedette

Tacking (basting) thread

Matching sewing thread

Matching heavy-duty thread

One 2in (50mm) hardboard crown joint

Four 1⅜in (36mm) hardboard crown joints

Small amount of firm-fill polyester filling (stuffing)

1lb (500g) wood wool

Two ½in (12mm) black glass boot button eyes

One skein black 'pearl cotton' embroidery thread

assembling these paper templates. With a little practice it becomes quite easy to gauge accurately the effect achieved by substituting a different ear shape or a thinner or longer arm.

It is a good idea, until you are confident in your abilities, to cut your experimental bear from a cheaper fabric. An inexpensive acrylic fabric is useful for testing on, even though it is slightly stretchier. Any adaptations and alterations can be made on the prototype bear at little cost until you achieve the type of bear that appeals most. This can be great fun and the result is a unique and totally individual creation.

The modern bear here has a cuddly, round body and an unusual but endearing expression. It has been made from a honey-beige, long-pile mohair and just longs to be hugged! Mohair can be obtained in a range of dramatic colours, including royal blue, purple and red, and this modern bear could be made in any of these shades – the choice is yours.

MAKING THE MODERN BEAR

Before starting to make the bear, carefully read the chapter on Classic Bear-making. Following the step-by-step instructions there, make the 10 templates, cut out the fabric pieces and assemble the bear, taking into consideration the special points below. Take care to keep your working surfaces as clean as possible at all times.

Fill the muzzle firmly with polyester filling (stuffing) before continuing to stuff the head with wood wool. Stuff the body very firmly using wood wool with some polyester stuffing, if necessary, taking care to pack out the upper back to form a definite hump on the bear.

The eyes are placed just below the head gusset seam, so that their lower edges are 1⅜in (3.5cm) from the tip of the muzzle.

Before attaching the ears, pad them out slightly using a tiny amount of polyester filling. Taking care when sewing them in position, that strand of the filling do not become entangled with the stitching. The ears should be set towards the back of the head across the gusset seams and about 2½in (6cm) apart.

The triangular nose is worked in horizontal satin stitches over the tip of the head gusset.

From the tip of the nose triangle, the thread is doubled and two vertical straight stitches about 1in (2.5cm) in length are made following the centre seam of the lower muzzle. From the lower point of the straight stitches, still keeping the thread doubled, a smiling mouth is formed by stitching two straight stitches at an angle to left and right.

The fur pile around the nose and mouth can be trimmed away slightly, just to tidy up the muzzle if necessary.

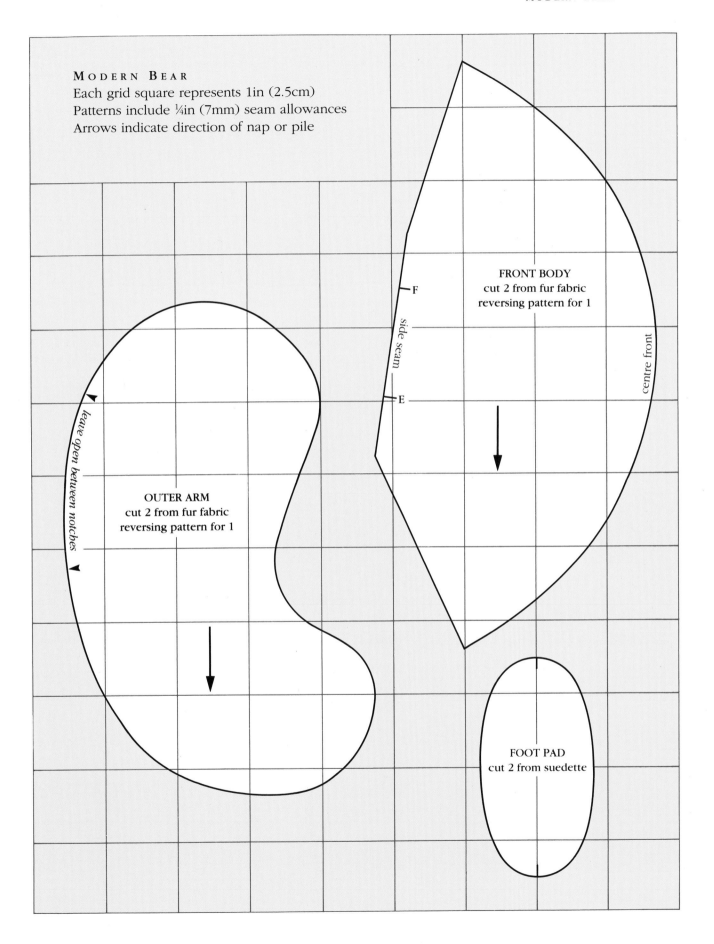

MODERN BEAR
Each grid square represents 1in (2.5cm)
Patterns include ¼in (7mm) seam allowances
Arrows indicate direction of nap or pile

FRONT BODY
cut 2 from fur fabric
reversing pattern for 1

F

side seam

E

centre front

leave open between notches

OUTER ARM
cut 2 from fur fabric
reversing pattern for 1

FOOT PAD
cut 2 from suedette

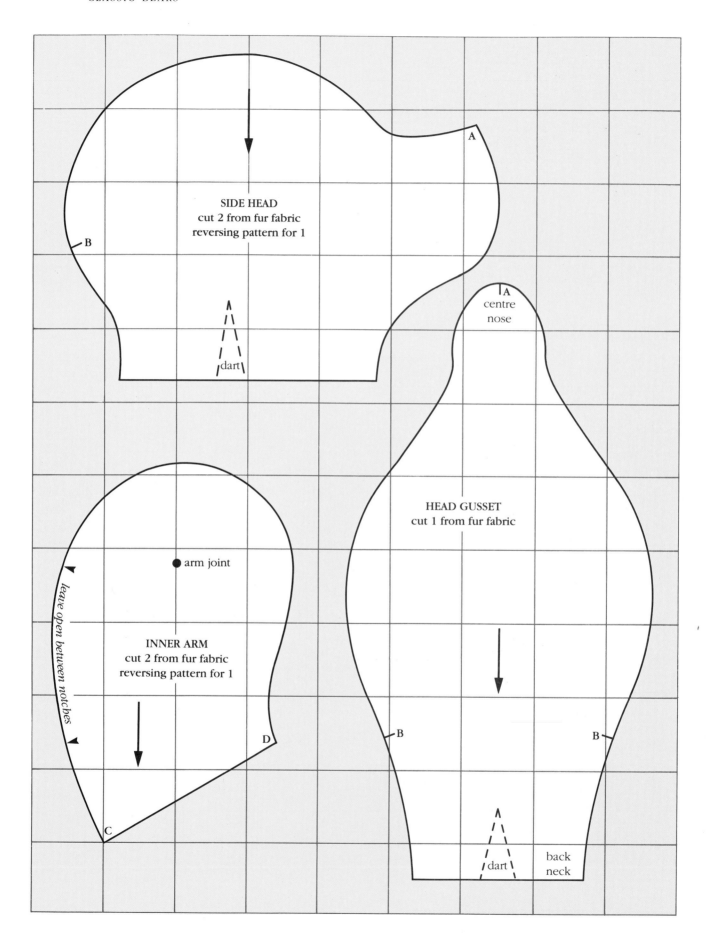

SIDE HEAD
cut 2 from fur fabric
reversing pattern for 1

A

B

dart

A
centre
nose

HEAD GUSSET
cut 1 from fur fabric

arm joint

leave open between notches

INNER ARM
cut 2 from fur fabric
reversing pattern for 1

C

D

B

B

dart

back
neck

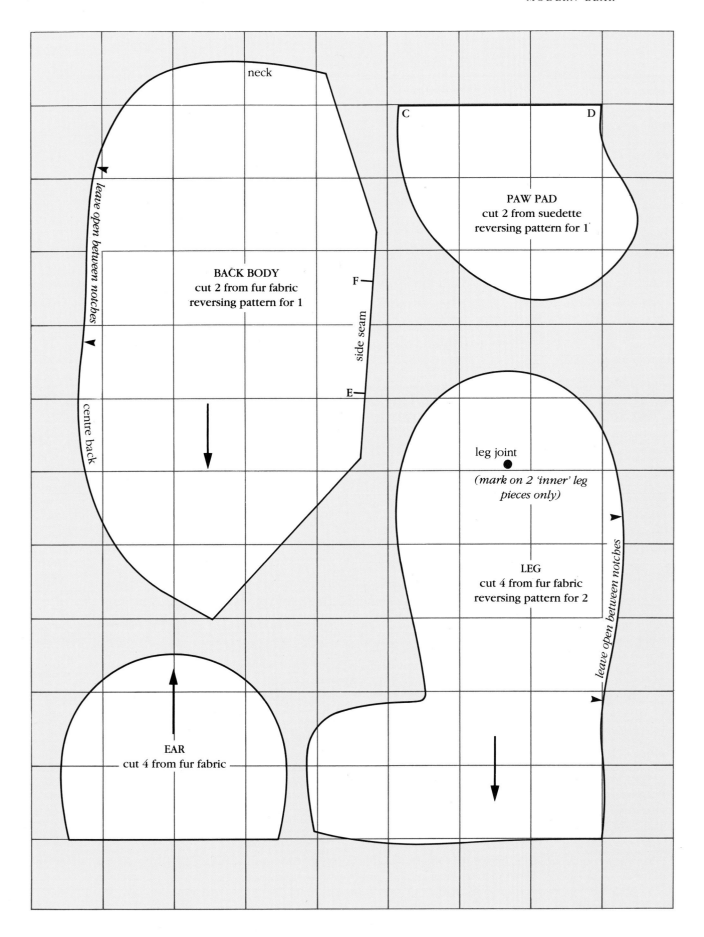

neck

C   D

PAW PAD
cut 2 from suedette
reversing pattern for 1

leave open between notches

BACK BODY
cut 2 from fur fabric
reversing pattern for 1

F

side seam

E

centre back

leg joint
●
(mark on 2 'inner' leg pieces only)

LEG
cut 4 from fur fabric
reversing pattern for 2

leave open between notches

EAR
cut 4 from fur fabric

USEFUL ADDRESSES

Author
Julia Jones' Collectors' Bears,
PO Box 16, Swadlincote,
Derbyshire DE12 8ZZ, Great Britain.
For specially commissioned bears. Also after-dinner speaking engagements and illustrated lectures.

Bear supplies
For fabrics and/or bear components and stuffings contact the following:

Oakley Fabrics Ltd, 8 May Street,
Luton, Beds LU1 3QY, Great Britain.
Tel: 0582 424828. Fax: 0582 29362.
(Mail order supplies worldwide)

Nonsuch Soft Toys, 51 Dudley Close,
Tilehurst, Reading, Berkshire RG3 6JJ,
Great Britain. Tel: 0734 413006.
(Mail order available)

Bridon Bears of Cheltenham,
2 St Margaret's Terrace, Cheltenham,
Glos GL50 4DT, Great Britain.
Tel: 0242 513102.
(Mail order available)

Animal Crackers, 5824 Isleta,
Albuquerque, NM 87105-6628, USA.
Tel: (505) 873 2806.

Golden Fun, Box 10697-TBF, Golden,
CO 80401-0600, USA.

Carver's Eye Company, Dept 60,
PO Box 16692, Portland, OR 97216,
USA. Tel: (503) 666 5680.

Spare Bear Parts, PO Box 56F,
Interlochen, MI 49643, USA.
Tel: (616) 275 6993.
Fax: (616) 275 6230.

Bear Clawset, 27 Palermo Walk,
Long Beach, CA 90803, USA.
Tel: (310) 434 8077.

Bear charity
Good Bears of the World (UK)
Tel: 081 891 5746.

Toy safety information
British Standards Institute,
Linford Wood, Milton Keynes,
MK14 6LE, Great Britain.
Tel: 0908 220022. Fax: 320 856.

Publications
The Teddy Bear Times, Heritage Press,
Shelley House, 104 High Street,
Steyning, West Sussex BN4 3RD,
Great Britain.

The UK Teddy Bear Guide and Teddy
Bear Magazine, Hugglets, PO Box 290,
Brighton, West Sussex BN2 1DR,
Great Britain.

Teddy Bear and Friends Magazines,
Cumberland Publishing, Inc.,
900 Frederick Street, Cumberland,
Maryland 21502, USA.
Tel: (301) 759-5853.
Fax: (301) 759-9108.

Teddy bear clubs
British Teddy Bear Association,
PO Box 290, Brighton, West Sussex
BN2 1DR, Great Britain.
Tel: 0273 697974.
Fax: 0273 62655.

Teddy Ecosse, The Wynd, Melrose,
Roxburghshire, Scotland TD6 9PA.

International League of Teddy Bear
Collectors Club, c/o 1023 Don Diablo,
Arcadia, California 91006, USA.
Tel: (818) 447 3809.

Teddy's Patch, Le Club des Amis de
l'Ours, 34 Rue Lieu de Santé, 76000
Rouen, France.
Tel: 35 88 96 00.

Associations and guilds
British Toymakers Guild,
124 Walcot Street, Bath, Avon
BA1 5BG, Great Britain.
Tel: 0225 442440.

Teddy Bear Traders Association,
c/o Gerry Grey, The Old Bakery
Teddy Bear Shop, 38 Cambridge Street,
Wellingborough, Northants NN8 1DW,
Great Britain.
Tel: 0933 229191.
Fax: 0933 272466.

Museums with bear collections
Bethnal Green Museum of Childhood,
Cambridge Heath Road, London
E2 9PA, Great Britain.
Tel: 081 981 1711.

The Bear Museum, 38 Dragon Street,
Petersfield, Hants GU31 4JJ, Great
Britain. Tel: 0730 265108.

Pollock's Toy Museum, 1 Scala Street,
London W1P 1LT, Great Britain.
Tel: 071 636 3452.

The Teddy Bear Museum, 19 Greenhill
Street, Stratford-upon-Avon CV37 6LF,
Great Britain. Tel: 0789 293160.

The Margaret Woodbury Strong
Museum, Rochester, New York, USA.

Margarete Steiff Museum, Giengen,
Germany.

Romy's Bazaar, 2 Badgery's Crescent,
Lawson 2783, Australia.

Auctions
Classic Bears are sometimes featured in sales held by auctioneers Christies and Sotheby's. For information contact main offices in London or New York.

ACKNOWLEDGEMENTS
The Author would like to thank the following for their immense help, both practical and material, in the researching and writing of this book: Roy Pilkington of Oakley Fabrics; Alastair McMinn and Donald McMillan of Coats Patons Crafts; David Fish of Tootal; Kath Mason of Mason Bears; Bridon Bears of Cheltenham; David and Susan Rixon of Nonsuch Bears and Mr and Mrs Wharnsby of Good Bears of the World.

Special thanks to Jon Stewart for the photography and Kate Yeates of Anaya Publishers, Alison Leach and Clare Clements for their editorial and design skills and finally to my brother and sister-in-law, Roger and Pam Smith, for their continuing encouragement and support.